ORTHO'S COMPLETE GUIDE TO

Successful Houseplants

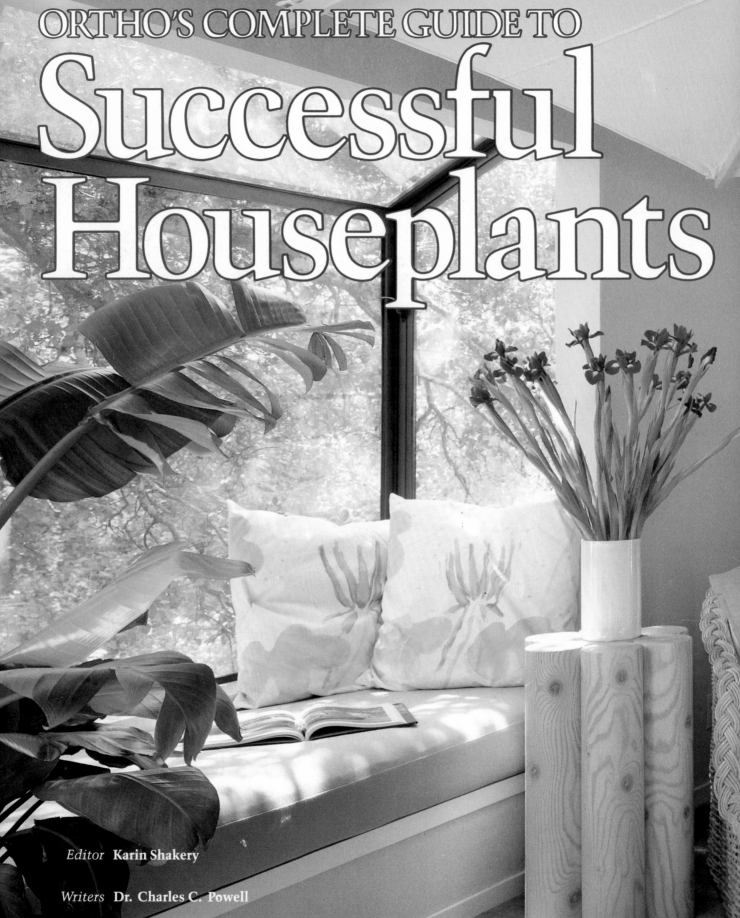

ORTHO'S COMPLETE GUIDE TO
Successful Houseplants

Editor **Karin Shakery**

Writers **Dr. Charles C. Powell**

Donald M. Vining

Ortho Books

Publisher
Robert L. Iacopi

Editorial Director
Min S. Yee

Managing Editors
Anne Coolman
Michael D. Smith

Production Manager
Ernie S. Tasaki

Senior Editor
Sally W. Smith

Editors
Jim Beley
Susan Lammers
Deni Stein

Design Coordinator
Darcie S. Furlan

System Managers
Mark Zielinski
Christopher Banks

Photographic Director
Alan Copeland

Photographers
Laurie A. Black
Richard A. Christman
Michael D. McKinley

Production Editors
Linda Bouchard
Alice Mace
Kate O'Keeffe

Asst. System Manager
William F. Yusavage

Photo Editors
Anne Dickson-Pederson
Pam Peirce

Production Assistant
Don Mosley

National Sales Manager
Garry P. Wellman

Sales Assistant
Susan B. Boyle

Operations/Distribution
William T. Pletcher

Operations Assistant
Gail L. Davis

Administrative Assistant
Georgiann Wright

Copyright © 1984
Chevron Chemical Company
All rights reserved under
international and Pan-American
copyright conventions.

First Printing in August, 1984

1 2 3 4 5 6 7 8 9

84 85 86 87 88 89

ISBN 0-89721-028-X

Library of Congress Catalog Card
Number 84-061502

Chevron Chemical Company
575 Market Street, San Francisco, CA 94105

Acknowledgments

Contributing Editors:
Tom Bass
Barbara Helfman

Writing Stylist:
Naomi Wise

Photographers: Front Cover: Fred Lyon; Page 1: Josephine Coatsworth. *Pages 2-59:* Laurie Black; Additional Photography: Alan Copeland: 29; Stephen Marley: 37; Photographic Plant Stylist: Milana Hames; Photographic Scout: Stefan Hames. *Pages 61-193:* Bill Apton: 164; Martha Baker: 185; Laurie Black: 67, 86B 97, 98 (above), 102, 114-115, 117, 141, 150 (right), 153 (below), 157 (below), 182, 184, 191; John Blaustein: 89 (above), 91, 136; Clyde Childress: 155; Richard Christman: 98 (bottom), 99; Josephine Coatsworth: 148 (above); Alan Copeland: 66, 110, 111; Douglas C. Evans: 165, 167 (below), 179; Bob Footorap: 103, 127; T. Goldmintz: 85 (above); Tony Howarth: 85 (below), 174 (left), 176 (two above), 177 (above right), 180; Michael LaMotte: 96 (left); Michael Landis: 80, 85 (center), 88, 89, 95, 118, 121, 122, 123,140 (right), 174 (right), 175 (left), 177 (above left), 177 (below), 183, 188, 189, 193; Stephen Marley: 149; Michael McKinley: 81, 137, 144 (below), 145, 148 (below), 150 (left), 151, 158, 159 (two below); James McNair: 153 (above); Ortho Photo Library: 65, 69, 70, 71, 76 (below), 77, 78, 83, 86A, 87, 94, 96 (right), 98 (center), 101, 105, 108, 109, 114, 116, 128, 130, 133, 134, 135, 140 (left), 146, 147, 152, 154, 157 (above), 159 (above), 167 (above), 170, 172, 173, 175 (right), 176 (below), 178, 181, 190, 192; William Reasons: 156; Tom Tracy: 100, 144 (above). *Pages 195-290:* Michael McKinley; Additional Photography: Ivan Massar: 220, 222, 223 (left), 224 (right), 224 (right); Jack Napton: 228 (above left), 233 (left), 241 (center & right), 243 (right), 288 (below); J. Parker: 228 (below left). *Pages 296-315:* Max E. Badgley: 297B; R. Byther: 310B; Kristie K. Callan: 301A, 302C, 306A, 309B, 312A; James S. Coartney: 299A; Alan Copeland: 303A; D. Cross: 311A; J. A. Crozier: 300C; Spencer H. Davis: 299C; C. M. Fitch: 296A, 298C, 309C, 312B; W. E. Fletcher: 307B; Raymond F. Hasek: 302B, 309A, 315B; R. W. Henley: 308A, 312C; R. K. Jones: 308B; M. Keith Kennedy: 296B, 310C; Michael McKinley: 304C; Jean R. Natter: 297C; L. Nichols: 307A; S. Perry: 306B; C. C. Powell: 301B; R. Raabe: 299B, 300A, 300B, 301C, 302A, 303, 304A, 305A, 305C, 306C, 307B&C, 308C, 310A, 311B, 311C, 313 A,B,C, 314A, 315C; M. Shurtlett: 314B; Michael D. Smith: 297A; Lauren B. Swezey: 296C, 298A, 298B, 304B, 315A

Illustrators: Kirk Caldwell: 74; Ron Hildebrand: 62-63, 64, 73, 80, 84, 92-93, 112, 113, 119, 162, 163, 164, 168, 169, 171, 172, 186, 187

Designers: *Pages 2-59:* Ruth Livingston, Tiburon, CA: 2-3, 11, 22-23, 32-33,49, 51; Molly McGowan Interiors, Oakland, CA: 12; Trudi Copland, Alamo, CA: 13; Michael Taylor/Bob Bell, San Francisco, CA: 17; Helen Craddick, Cole-Wheatman Interior Designers, San Francisco, CA: 21, 24-25, 30, 58-59; John Wheatman, Cole-Wheatman Interior Designers, San Francisco, CA: 30; Angel Tardy/Interior Plant Systems, San Francisco, CA: 35, 43, 44-45; Suzanne Brangham, San Francisco, CA: 37; Myra Posert, Laura Ashley Interior Design Service, San Francisco, CA: 41; Nan C. Rosenblatt/Gabrielle Whitney, San Francisco, CA: 47; Sandy & Babcock Architects Planners, San Francisco, CA: 53; CoClico & Co. Inc., Interior & Exterior Landscape Design, San Francisco, CA: 54, 57. *Page 61-193:* John Wheatman, Cole-Wheatman Interior Designers, San Francisco, CA: 81; CoClico & Co. Inc., Interior & Exterior Landscape Design, San Francisco, CA: 97; Angel Tardy/Interior Plant Systems, San Francisco, CA: 102; Chula and Warren Camp, San Francisco, CA: 191

Engravings: Biology Library at the University of California, Berkeley; Helen Crocker Russell Library, Strybing Aboretum Soc., San Francisco, CA; Natural Resources Library at the University of California, Berkeley Page 8: Dendrobium Macranthium var. marginata from Illustrations d'Orchidees des Indes Orientales Neerlandaises; Page 60: Billbergia moreliana from Paxton's Flower Garden, Vol III; Page 124: Tillandsia ionantha from Flores Des Serres et Jardins de Europe; Page 142: Passiflora aerulea, P. alato caerulea, P. tacsonia pinnatistipula from Ladies Flower Garden (Ornamental Greenhouse Plants); Page 160: Phyllocactus speciossimo crenatus from Paxton's Flower Garden, Vol II; Page 194: Hoya ovalifolia, H. pallida from Paxton's Flower Garden, Vol I; Page 294: Capiscum annuum from Das Kleine Buch der Tropenwunder

Special thanks to: Pamela Bain, William D. Ewing, Geoffrey A. Gratz, Jay Kilbourn, Alan Krosnick, Tralelia Twitty, Bruce Alan Van Natta, Charlotte Vrooman, Jacqueline Young, Adachi Florist and Nursery, El Cerrito, CA; Benefit Guild of the East Bay, Piedmont, CA; Berkeley Horticultural Nursery, Berkeley, CA; Cactus Gems, Cuppertino, CA; Conservatory of Flowers, Golden Gate Park, San Francisco, CA; East Bay Nursery, Berkeley, CA; Floorcraft, San Francisco, CA; Living Green, Plantscape Design, San Francisco, CA; Magic Gardens, Berkeley, CA; Phyllis Sutton, San Francisco Decorator's Showcase; Shelldance, Pacifica, CA; Tommy's Plants, San Francisco, CA

Manufacturers of self-watering planters: Aerie Nature Series, P.O. Box 303, Louisville, CO 80027; J & J Swift, (for African violets), P.O. Box 28012, Dallas, TX 75228; Jackson & Perkins, Luwasa Hydrocultrue, Medford, OR 97501; Natural Spring, Planter Technology, 999 Independence Ave., F-11, Mountain View, CA 94043; Plant Minder, 22582 Shannon Circle, Lake Forest, CA 92630; Plexi Mats, 1423 West 134th St., Gardena, CA 90249; Riviera System USA, 2103 East Magnolia, Phoenix, AZ 85034; Windowsill Gardens, US 4, Grafton, NH 03240

Contents

*Beautiful leaves that are
  striped with gold
Spangled with silver, or
  mottled with white,
Welcome as flowers, for when
  ye unfold,
Ye shine forth in day, as stars
  shine at night.*

**Beautiful Leaved Plants,
E.J. Lowe, 1864**

Why do we have a fondness for plants in our homes? If all we're looking for is a particular shape, texture, or color, wouldn't something else—a piece of furniture, an urn, or a basket—do as well? The answer is a resounding no. In this technological age, there is a need to stay in touch with nature—a desire to have living, growing things around us. A happy, healthy plant fulfills these needs and supplies a sense of meaningful accomplishment.

The successful indoor gardener is someone who does more than merely garden indoors. Obviously, indoor and outdoor conditions are very different and what you grow is also different. But beyond the practical limitations, there is a different philosophy attached to indoor gardening. A houseplant on display has to look good at all times of the year. It must enhance and coordinate with other furnishings in your home—inanimate objects—whereas the outdoor plant is surrounded by its own kind.

Designing with Houseplants deals with relating plants to the architecture, to the furniture, to art and accessories. Scale, shape, texture, color, and pattern all come into play in a well-designed room; and although most people recognize the importance of these basic principles, they overlook the fact that the same principles are just as applicable to plant choices as they are to furniture selection. If you feel the solution is to omit any living, growing elements in your decorating scheme, just remove the plants from a well-designed room that you find warm and exciting. Don't the resulting voids prove the point?

Having established the importance of the role that indoor plants play, your next decisions revolve around your attitude toward them. Are you a person who loves plants because they are "warm puppies"—creatures to be nurtured, nourished, and coddled? Or do you consider a plant an attractive accessory you are prepared to sustain but not pamper if it causes problems or gets sick? Throughout this book you will find references to "growers" and "maintainers"—our way of differentiating between the two types of plant owners. It is not a matter of the right attitude and the wrong one. It is a matter of recognizing which group you belong to and selecting appropriate plants.

To help with this decision, read the chapter on plant care and look through the gallery that lists the maintenance requirements of individual plants. For the growers, there is a chapter on propagation techniques. Maintainers shouldn't feel excluded, but the time, effort, and patience required to grow a plant from a cutting may outweigh the appeal.

On the other hand, flowers appeal to everyone; so there is a special chapter on flowering houseplants. It includes methods for prolonging the blooming period of outdoor annuals and perennials by bringing them inside, as well as forcing bulbs and flowering branches into bloom.

Greenhouses, solariums, and window greenhouses have become such popular architectural features that they are included in this book. In many houses these additions serve partly as increased living space, partly as solar heat storage components, and partly as a growing environment.

A sick plant is an ugly plant, and the easiest solution is to throw it away. But for some people, that is like suggesting they discard a child. So for them and those not-too-terribly-sick plants, the final chapter deals with the recognition and cure of common diseases and infestations.

In summation, this book aims to impart the joy of indoor gardening. It contains ideas and practical information, but the primary intent is to encourage you to bring life—houseplants—into your home.

What is a weed? A plant whose virtues have not yet been discovered.

Fortune of the Republic, Emerson, 1878

Designing with Houseplants

With every passing year, our world becomes simultaneously more complex and more oppressively uniform. Highrises, subdivisions, superhighways, shopping malls, and fast-food chains engulf our once-rural landscape. And video games and home computers make astonishingly casual use of a technology that a short time ago was confined to government and business offices. Little wonder so many people feel a need to renew their contact with nature and are creating home environments where plants are at least as visible as technology.

Most people recognize that you cannot fill a room with furniture and hope that scale, texture, and color principles will be magically incorporated. By the same token, you cannot merely fill a room with plants and expect it to look like anything other than a greenhouse. The same design principles apply.

Plants are three-dimensional balanced shapes, each one a complete original. Large leaves make bold patterns and cast strong geometric shadows, just as a Calder mobile does. Delicate, lacy leaves evoke images of impressionist paintings. Variegated leaves make as strong a statement as a striped cushion. Feathery fronds drape as romantically as ruffled bedspreads. And flowering houseplants offer as many blooms as chintz upholstery.

Comparing houseplants to inanimate furnishings is intentional. It is a way to emphasize the role plants play and the drama they bring to the design of a room. This is the reason that you rarely see a photograph in a home magazine without at least one plant in it. This is the reason that lobbies in most offices are furnished with plants. The intent is to make you feel comfortable and to recognize that this is a space to live in. How to achieve this designed look, rather than living with plants merely scattered about, is the subject of this chapter.

Dear friend, theory is all gray
And the golden tree of life
* is green.*

Apprentice Scene,
Johann Wolfgang von
** Goethe,**
1749-1832

The Plant as a Fashion Statement

The way we use houseplants in interiors is subject to fashion, just as the shifting trends in decoration are. Old photographs reveal that Victorian interiors were plant-ridden, with palms, ferns, and aspidistras looming out of elaborate cachepots. In fashionable interiors of the Twenties and Thirties, live plants were conspicuously absent, having been replaced, under the influence of English designers, by bouquets of fresh flowers from the garden. A Fifties interior can be easily identified almost entirely by the rubber tree plant or the split-leaf philodenron growing on a slab of bark. In a late Sixties or early Seventies home, the renewed profusion of plants was reminiscent of Victorian excesses, although the ubiquitous hanging Swedish ivy stands in for the earlier potted palm. The increased numbers of plants were a sign of concern for the web of life, the environment, and living things in general—especially green ones. However, integrating them into a design scheme was not a particular concern.

Today, we still like to see plants in our rooms, but we've moved away from the fussy, care-intensive look. Instead, the aim is to make some sense out of our plant collections. In place of "every room a jungle" it's "every room a garden," an effect that requires planning, forethought, and selection.

In current architecture or home magazines, the trend is toward quality rather than quantity. Commonly, there is one big plant per room, but one with the space-filling ability and the structural force of a steel girder. There may be flowering plants too, but they tend to be treated as bouquets and arranged on tables. The "statement plant," or the "architectural plant," as it is occasionally called, usually has equal status with the other elements of the design. In the contemporary use of plants in design, the overall shape of the plant (fan, columnar, graphic, for example), the texture (fine or coarse), and the color are as important as the fact that it's a plant.

Right: This mammilaria cactus is no shrinking violet. It proclaims its presence and asserts itself as a vital element in the decorating scheme of this bedroom. The irregular form and complex texture serves as a contrast to the clean, smooth surfaces of the walls and floor. The soft color of the cactus harmonizes with the muted shades of the walls and carpeting and the large, strong shape is in keeping with the scale of the other furnishings.

Right: Weeping fig (Ficus benjamina) turns a tiled tub area into an indoor garden. Bromeliads, placed within the boundaries established by the spread of the ficus branch, add a touch of pink. Note how the staggered heights of the plants and their containers repeat the stepped surfaces of the bathroom and how the towel has been chosen to repeat the pink of the bromeliads. These plants appreciate bright, indirect light and the higher humidity levels usually found in a bathroom.

Left: Plants and baskets are natural companions. Textures, shapes, and hues are complementary and although either the plant or the basket can make a statement of its own (especially when the baskets are as exotic as these), together the statement is far more dramatic.
 Note how the basket acting as a cachepot for this large palm is an inverse version of the shape of the plant.

Why Plants?

Why do we want plants in our homes? If we're looking for a particular shape, texture, and color, wouldn't something else—a piece of furniture, an urn, or a basket—do as well? The answer is a resounding no. Although most objects could probably be replaced by other objects of similar size, shape, and color, the only substitute that comes close to plants is sculpture.

Plants create a dynamic three-dimensional shape, and within that shape, the parts of the plant (its leaves and stems) form a balanced though not overly precise pattern.

In a pattern-on-pattern interior, plants add their own inimitable patterns. In a spare interior with primary colors and hard-edge furniture, plants add softness and detail. The "country look" is dependent on plants, and a solarium without a profusion of plants is like an empty greenhouse.

Part of the rationale for including plants in a design scheme is the shock value. When you consider it, bringing the great outdoors inside is a bold notion in today's high-tech society. It would be quite understandable if someone unfamiliar with our traditions wondered why there was a fir tree in the living room. In our casual acceptance of the Christmas tree, we forget how remarkable it is.

Another aspect of the shock value is the contrast between natural and slick furnishings. Art Deco designers of the Twenties included primitive carvings in sumptuously furnished interiors to make lacquer and ivory accessories seem even more refined. Plants can serve the same purpose.

Finally, there is the issue of life itself. Plants add life and warmth to interiors, and the fact that they are living things enhances their contribution to our spaces. If shape alone were the primary consideration, sculpture would suffice. If pattern were the only requirement, plastic plants or dried flowers would do. If contrast were the major design intent, decorative accessories would suffice. Plants remind us of the wilderness and of the beauty and diversity of this incredible planet.

Right: This room is an example of how plants add life and warmth to interiors. The occupants obviously love plants and have arranged them with care to flank the chairs, fill the etagere, and frame the windows. The shapes harmonize with the patterned rug and the baskets (acting as cachepots) are in agreement with the wicker and rattan furniture.

Establishing a Focus

Few people make a distinction between growing plants and using them in interior design, but decorating with plants is not the same as growing plants. Often, the spot that a plant occupies is chosen for pragmatic rather than aesthetic reasons, so by default the plant is displayed where it will grow well with no thought as to where it will look the best.

The placement of plants in a room should be a matter of taste and design rather than a question of available light, but are the two compatible? It's possible. Sometimes the place where a plant would look best in a room happens to be near a window. Sometimes the furnishings in a room can be rearranged to accommodate a plant near a window, or special lighting can be installed to keep plants thriving in a dark corner. Nonetheless, decorating with plants does impose some restrictions and pose some problems that have to be solved. To decorate with plants, you must first establish purpose and intent. Begin by asking yourself where you would put the plant and how you would display it if it were some other decorative object—a large jar or a piece of sculpture. This is the most effective way to make the distinction between growing and decorating.

A delightful example of decorating with houseplants is described in a word picture taken from the biography of Victoria, Lady Sackville, the mother of one of England's most famous gardeners, Vita Sackville-West: "Two Bacchanalian little vines, dwarfed but bearing bunches of grapes of natural size, stood in gold winecoolers on either side of the door." Aside from the undeniable charm of the idea, the little potted grapevines were treated like pieces of furniture, like elements of the decorative scheme. Their stations by the doors were fixed, their mode of display constant, and the plants themselves were kept picture perfect by rotation and renewal from a stock of similar fruiting vines in Lady Sackville's greenhouses. This example points out the difference between a view of plants that is strictly horticultural and one that includes the possibility of plants as decoration, as well as the possibilities of blending a skillful appreciation of both outlooks.

Right: A red Bougainvillea (left rear), rhododendrons, and a bright cinereria have been brought in at their prime to create a splendid solarium garden. Japanese maples can live indoors from the time they begin to leaf out to the time their leaves begin to fall. In areas with mild climates, they can spend the winter outdoors.

Using Ideas from Magazines

Home magazines do the finest job of presenting ideas for decorating with plants. *Architectural Digest,* for instance, once showed a fireplace (with a roaring fire) flanked by a pair of juniper trees pruned into spiral shapes. The photograph may have led the uninformed to assume that junipers will grow indoors (which they won't) or that they would survive next to a blazing fire (which they wouldn't), but the scene exemplified the use of plants as pure decoration. The designer decided that the mantlepiece needed two tall shapes on either side and that spiral topiaries would be perfect. There was no question about growing them there—they were simply put there for the photograph.

There's nothing wrong with this approach to decorating with plants as long as you know that such plants can stay by the fireside for only a short period without dehydrating, wilting, or burning. Then they must be placed somewhere else to grow—in a greenhouse or on a patio with full sunlight and good air circulation.

Magazines can afford to decorate perfectly because they can rent or buy greenery just for the photography session. The editors and photographers don't have to worry about the future of the plants; they can arrange them how and where they will look best. But can the home decorator or plant grower be equally cavalier with houseplants? Well, yes and no. You can decorate with plants the way magazines do, but you will still have to make arrangements to provide appropriate plant care. This may mean having two locations: one where the plant looks best and another, possibly in a different part of the house, where it grows best.

Right: The blossoms of this cymbidium orchid repeat and accent the glowing tones of the wood staircase and textured wall covering. But, this healthy specimen would not thrive permanently in such a dark location. Cymbidiums handle and even prefer lower light levels while buds form and open, but they should be returned to a location that gives them ample light and air circulation after they have flowered.

Establishing Plant Stations

To design effectively with houseplants, start by deciding where you'd like to locate plants without regard for light or other practical considerations. Would you like to see a plant arching out from behind a favorite table and chair combination, or at the end of the sofa to soften a hard edge? Would you like to flank a doorway with a matched pair of plants to create a sense of formality? Perhaps you've always wanted to put a small plant on a desk or a bookshelf or in the middle of the dining table. The places that seem to call for a plant, places where a plant is a perfect decorative statement, are called "plant stations."

A plant doesn't have to be at its station all the time, and the station doesn't have to be occupied by the same plant all the time. The ficus tree by the window can be moved into a dark corner on special occasions and lit from below for drama. Two specimens of the same kind of plant can be alternated weekly between a dark station and a brighter one. For instance, you might rotate two philodendrons between a bright bedroom window where a large plant is needed and a spot in the curve of the grand piano where there is no light at all. This means that if you have a sunny window, a light garden, or a greenhouse, plants can be prepared for display and returned when their moment on the stage is over; then understudies (another set of plants) fill their roles.

How welcoming to walk into a windowless entrance hall and be greeted with a display of bulbs in bloom. Your guests won't know that if they had visited last week the bulbs would have been in hiding and their station manned by aspidistras. Establishing plant stations in this fashion means there will always be something at the station. The coffee table in the living room can be graced by a small plant that's been on a bright windowsill or under fluorescent lights elsewhere in the house and changed from week to week according to what is blooming and looks fresh. Essentially, you can be your own florist.

What would be the plant stations for the corner of a room furnished with a wingback chair and a round pedestal table? One, obviously, is on the table, but it's not the *(continued on page 24)*

Right: Bonsai plants are not houseplants, but if you have a small terrace or patio, you can grow them outside and bring them in as temporary decorative accents. The pine, on the coffee table in this living room, is an occasional centerpiece. The same holds true for the Japanese maple temporarily stationed by the window.

Establishing Plant Stations *(continued)*

best architectural solution. The voids, the spaces that need filling, are around the grouping of furniture, behind and above the table and chair, or on each side. There are at least three good architectural solutions: a low fan-shaped plant on the floor beside the table; a tall plant in the corner behind the table and chair; or a combination, with a third plant on the floor on the other side of the chair for balance. There are no rules for plant placement, only ways of thinking about how plants can fill space and relate to other shapes in the room.

Obviously, the more elaborate your facilities for growing and rejuvenating plants, the more display stations you can have and the more frequently the plants in them can be changed. Few people remember that potted plants are not fastened in place; it's easy to move them around. Usually, the plant that starts on the windowsill stays on the windowsill and never graces the dining table. Similarly, the African violet that's relegated to the coffee table never gets moved to the windowsill, even if it doesn't bloom.

Another common situation is a long buffet against the dining room wall, with a chair at either end and a large bowl in the middle. Where are the plant stations? The voids are on either side of the bowl. The chairs fill the voids at the ends of the buffet, and the bowl fills the middle. A pair of candlesticks or two vases of flowers could fill the empty areas between, but using a pair of plants could lend formality to the setting. A plant could replace the bowl, or the bowl could be moved to one side and balanced with a plant on the other. If there is space beyond the chairs, plants could be added there at floor level.

Previous Page: Several blooming Amaryllis plants arranged in a basket with some cut sprigs of Cytisus scoparius (Scotch broom) make a colorful arrangement. Tillandsia (a bromeliad often called Spanish moss) obscures the growing containers. This sleek-lined and unadorned kitchen calls for for a bold, out-of-the-ordinary plant choice.

Right: The two plant stations chosen in this room, the mantelpiece and the table, can be filled by different plants to change the mood. The iris now displayed on the mantel could be replaced with a trailing plant, or a row of matching, low plants. At the moment, the table is a stage for an off-centered bonsai birch tree. Although this is too large a plant to act as a centerpiece while dining, it is an extremely effective sculptural shape set off against the bare wood top.

Cornering a Plant

A recent trend in interior design is the placement of seating pieces away from the walls. The sofa can occupy the middle of the room facing the fireplace; it can be set on the diagonal of the room; or, if perpendicular to a side wall, it can face another sofa or a pair of chairs. The conversational grouping is a return to the Victorian fashion of having a central table with chairs distributed around it at varying distances. In both the contemporary and the Victorian arrangements, walls are used to display pictures and artwork and are a background for secretaries, breakfronts, armoires, and bookcases. This arrangement leaves the spaces between the wall and the seating areas, especially the corners, open for plants. The architectural plant is best stationed in a corner rather than elsewhere in the room.

If one of the corner walls includes a sliding glass door or large window, the plant, in addition to acting as part of the decor, will be able to meet its light requirements and not need a separate growing location. If, however, the corner is a dark one, what can be done? One solution is to turn the corner into a plant station and to grow the plant in a lighter part of the room. Another solution is to use artificial plant lighting, such as grow lights in track lighting.

You can also try the mirror trick. A mirrored, freestanding screen or long mirror panels mounted directly onto the wall can brighten a dim corner. When the mirrors are positioned opposite windows, light is reflected into the foliage of the plant, which may be just the boost that a permanent plant needs (although it will have to be a shade-loving species). The decorative bonus is that the mirror image doubles or triples the plant, amplifying and magnifying even small plants and making them appear much more important.

Left: A bed set on the diagonal creates a corner plant station in this luxuriant bedroom. It is a corner that gets a lot of light and is therefore suitable for the chosen plants—a Kentia palm, Cymbidium orchids, and a bird's nest fern. The cachepots and the colors of the flowers tie in with the colors in the screen, accenting the flow between the painted flowers and the living ones. This flow adds interest and the humor generally associated with trompe l'oeil.

Displaying a Plant

The presentation of plants can make the difference between decor and mere clutter. Decorating with African violets, for instance, is no easy job. The plants are small, and avid growers often have dozens of them covering every available surface or crowding into fluorescent light gardens. Individually the plants are quite beautiful, but to be decorative they must be properly presented. For example, put a single small plant, pot and all, into a small yellow cachepot (French term for "a hiding pot"). Set the cachepot on a round black stand just slightly larger in diameter than the cachepot. Immediately, the African violet becomes a star.

Two important display principles are illustrated here. First, the mechanics must not show. The green plastic pot with the rolled edge that violet growers prefer is part of the mechanics. It is serviceable but not attractive. The decorative cachepot makes the presentation work, and since it has no hole in the bottom, it doesn't drip water on the table. Second, whatever you want to display must look important. Isolate a single plant from its fellows, spotlight it, put it in a showy pot, and set in on a stand. Any accessory looks more important when it is placed on a base.

The stand and the cachepot can be placed wherever they look best, thus creating a new plant station. Blooming violets can be rotated between their growing areas and the display station. Plants that are dressed up and viewed one at a time can be more enjoyable than those remaining in customary group arrangements in which some are flowering and some aren't. And a special pot will look more attractive than a group of plastic pots set on top of margarine containers, the complete antithesis of display.

Right: The jewel-like beauty of African violets glows in an appropriate setting. If you raise many similar plants as a hobby, make a star out of the one that is looking its best by displaying it separately. The easiest way to spotlight a plant is to put it in a cachepot that adds to its beauty, set it on a stand , and center stage the arrangement on a suitably sized table that does your star justice.

Containers

Pots can be as fascinating as the plants they contain. They can be bonsai pots, antique American redware pots, handmade clay flowerpots from Italy, dimestore-variety clay flowerpots, colorful glazed pots with built-in saucers, or a large assortment of decorative cachepots that serve as covers for utility pots.

In the Japanese philosophy of plant display, the pot must not call attention to itself, unless that's specifically what you have in mind. Among bonsai enthusiasts, to comment on the pot before you say anthing about the tree is a polite way of saying that the tree isn't worthy of comment. Although we may enjoy compliments on our unusual pot choices, strong-colored and garishly decorated ones should be avoided so that the beauty of the plant is always shown to its best advantage.

Be aware that there may be a difference between the best pot size for horticultural reasons and the best size for an aesthetic balance. From a horticultural standpoint, it's generally better to use pots that are on the small side. People often repot their plants into larger pots, motivated by the generous but anthropomorphic notion that the roots need a big, comfortable pot with room to grow. In fact, what roots need is air, and a giant pot full of wet soil frustrates that need.

If you need a larger pot for aesthetic reasons but not for horticultural ones, consider placing the growing container inside a cachepot. The ideal cachepot is only large enough to create a balance between pot and plant. Those great bulbous pottery caches with their own stands are period furnishings and can be interesting when used in Mission or Victorian settings, but they tend to be overwhelming for general use unless you have an immense plant. A slender dracaena emerging from a vast base simply won't work.

When deciding on the size of a cachepot, bear in mind that plants tend to look better when the pot is fairly small. The plant should always be larger than its pot. Jade plants, which have notoriously small root systems, are too often potted in immense containers that give the impression they are ingesting the plant. The Japanese bonsai aesthetic may be more appropriate; a small pot contributes to the illusion that the tree is large.

Always remember that a special plant should have a special pot. A large, mature, and exquisitely groomed specimen deserves the loveliest pot you can afford. While the primitive, folksy beauty of redware pots might best set off small ivies, a green antique Oriental pot is more suitable for a full-grown sago palm. Similarly, although a patterned pot might enhance greenery, it can clash with a flowering plant. The basic principle is to make sure that the container enhances what it contains.

Left: The importance of the pairing of a plant and its container and the appropriateness of both to their surroundings is illustrated in this living room. The ming araulia (Polyscias fruticosa) and the hand-thrown pot are both in keeping with the highly textural emphasis in the design scheme.

The floors are smooth and gleaming, and so is the pot. The wicker furniture and the artwork are strong, but simple, shapes, and so is the plant.

Elevating Plants

The indoor gardener who wants to decorate with plants would be wise to accumulate a collection of plant stands and pedestals, along with plant pots and cachepots, and to collect them in pairs for elegant two-of-a-kind displays. Among the most striking low stands are the Oriental footed stands used under Imari bowls or Japanese flower arrangements. These black or brown wooden stands may have elaborate carving. Using stands like these is instant decorating magic.

The use of tall stands and pedestals can also add impact. A photograph of an English Victorian interior reveals plants that seem at first glance to be tall rubber trees (*Ficus elastica*). However, they are not trees at all but short rubber plants on five-foot stands, each one in a cachepot and the trunk draped or tied with a shawl, hiding the soil and the utility pot. The shawls seem a bit excessive by modern standards, but the overall idea is ingenious.

A tall plant stand or pedestal can elevate a mass of foliage to the size of a small tree and serve visually as a "trunk." Instead of trying to grow a ficus where a ficus can't grow, use a spathiphyllum or some other low-light plant on a pedestal to give the height and grace of a tree, as well as ease of maintenance.

Tall stands can also be topped with seasonal displays of forced blooms. In spring, use tulips (10 bulbs per 10-inch pot); in summer, fill the stands with white flowering angel wing begonias ('May Queen'); and at Christmastime, display pink poinsettias. Tulips and poinsettias are generally bought or grown for the occasion and then discarded, but begonias can be kept for a number of seasons.

Left: Mirrored walls add to the importance of a plant station by doubling, and sometimes tripling, the effect. Tall stands and pedestals of different heights also add to the impact of this indoor garden and act as "trunks," elevating pots of pothos (Epipremnum aureum) to small tree status.

Pothos thrives in low light, but if the levels are too low, you can, like here, supplement them with artificial light placed within the translucent pedestals.

The white azalea is a temporary visitor to this plant station. It prefers bright, indirect light while blooming, but can be used to add beauty to any room on special occasions.

Hanging Plants

One of the reasons hanging plants are so popular is that this method of display gets them up high. They are special favorites of the greenhouse grower because they use all the wasted space near the roof of the greenhouse. They hang from the struts and rafters and leave the benches free for other plants. If light comes from directly overhead, the plants thrive and the grower is happy. Hanging plants flourish best under a skylight. In fact, some exceptionally beautiful gardens have been created around skylights, using hanging plants in combination with plants on the floor or in planter boxes.

Despite their popularity, hanging plants should be used indoors only with discretion. When a plant is hung at a window, light comes in from the side, leaving half the plant in darkness. The top, which needs the most light, receives the least light; and the tips are bathed in sunlight. Soon it can turn leggy, stringy and unattractive, especially when silhouetted against the window. One solution is swiveling ceiling hooks; these make it easy to rotate the plant so that it receives optimal light.

Any plant that can be hung can also sit on a stand, often to greater advantage, if there is room for the stand. If height is the goal, and if there is no skylight, pedestals and tall plant stands are an effective alternative, freeing the windows of obstructions.

In some situations, however, a permanent window obstruction may be just what the grower desires. Many urban gardeners use hanging plants instead of window treatments to obstruct an objectionable view without completely blocking the light. Others hang plants because there is insufficient space for them in the room or, in the case of herbs, to have them readily available in the kitchen window. In these situations, no matter what the species, the hanging plant must be rigorously groomed and turned to prevent spindly, unbalanced growth.

Hanging plants really work wonders in conservatories, greenhouses, and the new solar additions, which are essentially greenhouses without plants. There, hanging plants can be thought of as trees without trunks and can be placed accordingly, not hanging above other things but tucked behind them. A group of several plants, preferably the same variety, hanging together at different levels is a wonderful way to fill and soften a corner in a glassed-in space. They are less attractive hung high overhead, when it's mostly the base of the pot that shows, or when they are suspended from a rod like a line of clothes hung out to dry.

Right: A solarium provides optimum conditions for hanging plants such as these matching pothos specimens.

Setting a Stage

Staging, a common practice in flower shows, is another way to elevate plants. Usually it consists of placing a plant on an empty, upturned flowerpot to give it a little extra height and raise it above its companions. A second, smaller plant is then set in front of the staged plant to hide its base. Staging can, of course, be quite elaborate, with lush, tall banks of potted plants.

At home, proper staging can turn a motley group of undistinguished houseplants into a showy display. For example, at least one common problem can be solved with staging. Many house plants lose their bottom leaves, either as a part of their normal growth pattern or because they have dried out once too often. To hide this problem, stage a companion plant (or two plants at different levels) to cover the naked stem and then disguise the staging with a third plant (or more, if necessary) at windowsill or floor level. In this pyramid structure, the new grouping will be more attractive than any of the three plants alone and will amplify the visual impact.

People who are credited with having an eye for designing with plants often have simply learned to stage well and to fill in the front of the plant display so there are no visible gaps. If the display is raised, a trailing plant should be added in front, such as an ivy or any cascading plant whose leaves hang over the edge of the container. This will break and soften the hard lines of the arrangement, as well as cover up pots and spaces.

Left: The "stage" for the white-leaved caladiums, bird's nest ferns, and ornamental grass is an arched alcove, and the way the plants are grouped reflects this. Simple cachepots, made from sections of PVC pipe, are used to raise the individual plants so that they, too, form an arch.

Right: A mass of plants around a Victorian bathtub are in keeping with the romance of this bedroom. Shapely dracaenas flank the ends of the bath and cissus fill in the front, yet do not obscure the decorative claw feet. A forced hyacinth adds color and aroma.

Plant Profiles

It is important that both design considerations and plant growing requirements are in sync when the architectural plant is relegated to one location. You must decide on both the shape of the plant, which is paramount in decoration, and the plant's needs, which usually center on light requirements.

Tall Fan Shapes

These large lovely plants are the designer's workhorses, often pictured in home magazines. These plants fill the corners, bracket the sofas, back the wing chairs, and hide the radiators. (In real life, of course, hot radiators are anathema to any plant.) Their virtue is that they spread out at the top but take up little floor space. They can be so integral to the scheme that if they are removed the room looks bare and lifeless.

Palms are the queens of the tall vase-shaped plants. The fronds rise from a small base and fan out at the top. The best known are the areca palm (*Chrysalidocarpus lutescens*), the date palm (*Phoenix roebelenii*), the Kentia palms (*Howeia fosteriana* and *Howeia belmoreana,* which were the original potted palms of Victorian salons), the Chinese fan palm (*Livistona chinensis*), the palmetto palm (*Chamaerops*), and the parlor palm (*Chamaedorea elegans,* also called *Neanthe bella*).

The problems with these houseplants are primarily horticultural. They can be attacked by mites, which multiply rapidly in hot rooms and finally overwhelm their hosts, and they will deteriorate when low light levels are combined with too much water in the soil. Since palms will tolerate abuse for a long time before they slowly start to expire, one leaf at a time, you should watch them closely. The ideal location is a cool room, near a large east or west window. The dark corner behind the couch, no matter how nice it looks in a magazine, is no place for a palm to live permanently.

The weeping fig (*Ficus benjamina*) is a fashionable replacement for or complement to the palm. It is a tall, delicate, well-shaped tree, suitable for filling high empty spaces above and between furnishings. Unfortunately, it is particular about where it grows well. In most rooms (even ones with several windows), the upper walls and ceiling are too dark. The ideal spot for a tall ficus is an atrium, light well, or projecting greenhouse window. You can achieve some success with overhead spotlights supplementing the natural light, but if you don't have an appropriate spot, choose a different plant for your home and enjoy the *Ficus benjamina* in the glass atrium at your office.

That office institution, the corn plant (*Dracaena fragrans*), also fits well in the home. Three to five individual plants of this trunk-forming species can be placed in a pot to make one full, fan shape.

Previous Page: When choosing a plant to fulfill a design function, you must select a specimen that will survive in the place that it is needed and grow to the shape and size required.

Two lady palms (Rhapis excelsa) meet the design specifications and are obviously flourishing in this living room. Because of their size, the palms are not overpowered by the panoramic vista but, because of careful placement, they also do not obscure it.

Although palms will not survive behind a sofa, a corn plant usually will as long as there's a window nearby. In dark locations, growth is extremely slow and overwatering becomes a danger.

An additional possibility is the variegated screw pine (*Pandanas vietchii*). A mature specimen is striking and the same size as a large indoor palm. It resembles a spider plant. The whorl of long tapering blades, which spring from the stem in a perfect spiral, are bordered with yellow and striped longitudinally with paler green bands. It can be killed by prolonged exposure to temperatures below 60°F but can survive nearly every other condition. Give it a sunny location and watch it grow.

In southern California and other sunny climates, dwarf banana trees (*Musa* species) in tubs can be brought inside occasionally to provide a tall fan shape. Patio-grown citrus or loquat (*Eriobotrya japonica*) can also be brought inside for a while.

Below: This Kentia palm (Howea forsterana) fills and decorates an empty corner. Palms are classic and popular tall fan shapes, but be sure to place them where they will get bright indirect light and inspect them regularly for possible spider mite infestation.

Other choices include the spiky spineless yucca (*Yucca elephantipes*), especially if you use several mature canes fashioned into a clump; the spreading umbrella tree (*Brassaia actinophylla*) and other variants (these are prone to spider mites); and the rare and beautiful silk oak (*Grevillia robusta*).

Low Bushy Shapes

These plants look handsome sitting alone on the floor next to a low piece of furniture and softening the lines of the furniture by their roundness, or by filling any other ground-level design void. They also look very good on stands. In fact, if you place one of these plants on a tall stand (at least 4 feet high), it can substitute for one of the tall plants mentioned above. These are best used alone rather than in combination with other plants, since they are still too large to be considered as tabletop plants. Rather, they are part of the architecture.

A full pot of spathe plant (*Spathiphyllum* 'Mauna Loa') is an excellent choice. Its shape and size are ideal, and like the corn plant, it grows well in low light. When it is thriving, it sends up white flags (the showy spathe cradling its real flowers) signaling contentment, not surrender.

Philodendrons are also highly suitable. The saddle-leaf philodendron (*Philadendron selloum*) is very popular, although its leaves tend to flop with age and poor light.

Another dependable low bushy shape is the cast iron plant (*Aspidistra elatior*). The common name carries a genuine recommendation. Unlike most of the tropicals, which grow all through the year, aspidistra has a lengthy dormant period during which it is surprisingly undemanding. During dormancy, it can be used anywhere, window or no, and the cooler the room the better. When growth resumes in the late winter, it requires good light, water, and fertilizer. Aspidistra benefits from a summer outdoors, in deep shade, or in a moderately bright, well-ventilated room.

A mature pot of Chinese evergreen (*Aglaonema*), especially of a type such as 'Silverking', is a showy plant. This philodendron relative looks like a small dieffenbachia with its gray-green, cream, and emerald leaf patterns, but it is not as coarse as the latter. Because *Aglaonema* sends up new shoots from the base of mature plants, it soon fills the pot, with many leaves overlapping each other. It, too, is very tolerant of low light.

The kaffir lily (*Clivia miniata*), whether in flower or not, is a good decorative choice even though it can't remain in dim light. Design a pot using several individual plants so that there will be several bloom spikes (one per plant). The plant spends most of the year in a bloomless state, but its black-green, straplike leaves are very decorative. When the plant is in bloom, it is resplendent with clusters of yellow-throated, orange trumpets, 10 to 15 on each spike. *Clivia* requires a cool, bright, dry dormancy in late fall and early winter; then it needs warmth, light, water, and fertilizer in late February or early March, when flower spikes appear. During the summer, kaffir lily can be grown outdoors in deep shade or in bright, indirect light inside.

Surprisingly, orchids (*Cymbidium* species) also grow as low, bushy-shaped plants. In some varieties, both the straplike leaves and the flower stalks arch. The plant does best in a cool greenhouse, but once in bloom it can be displayed in a plant station. The uncut blooms last for 6 to 8 weeks.

Below: A row of peace lilies (Spathiphyllum), low fan-shaped plants, create an indoor "hedge." In this case, the lilies provide an effective foil, covering the back of the settee. In other situations, a grouping of this kind is a particularly successful way to separate or define a particular area. The plants can serve as a "wall" between a living and dining area or they can screen a home office.

Column Shapes

Sometimes space restrictions dictate a column—an exclamation point of a plant that stands like a sentinel. A column makes a more formal architectural impression than do the spreading vase shapes. Generally speaking, the sparer and harder-edged the decor, such as a minimal or high-tech interior, the more appropriate a columnar plant becomes.

Giant cacti and succulents, barely distinguishable from contemporary sculpture, are the obvious examples. *Cereus peruvianus,* a treelike cactus, looks like a branching baseball bat.

Many plants that would not normally grow into columns can be trained into upright forms through the use of cedar slabs, stakes, or osmunda fiber. Among them is the large-leaved philodendron 'Red Emerald'. Algerian ivy (*Hedera canariensis* 'Variegata'), kangaroo vine (*Cissus antarctica*), grape ivy (*Cissus rhombifolia* 'Ellen Danica'), and many nephthytis (*Syngonium* species) can also be bought trained into columns.

Other naturally columnar plants include the coarse-leaved ficus plants, including the familiar rubber tree plant (*Ficus elastica*). It should be renamed the supermarket ficus, since it's so often sold there. Although it is all green, several of its relatives have greater color interest. *F. elastica* 'Schrijveriana' is mostly yellow, with variegations of green and gray-green. *F. elastica* 'Abidjan' has a distinctly reddish cast, with new leaves a true shade of burgundy before they mature to their distinguishing reddish green color. Both of them will grow in an upright column unless forced to branch by pruning. This is also true of the fiddle-leaf fig (*Ficus lyrata*), which deserves more attention than it usually gets.

Right: The columnar forms of these cacti make dramatic statements against a white wall. In the daytime, they stand out in stark relief, and at night they cast intriguing shadows. A large skylight permits the sunloving cacti to thrive without large windows nearby.
If you are considering the purchase of a specimen-size plant, you would be wise to buy a smaller, less expensive version of the same species first. Place this in the chosen location and make sure it is happy before buying the larger plant.

Soft, Feathery Shapes

Airiness can be a very desirable characteristic in decorative plants, making them appear soft, refined, and gentle—a green cloud rather than a thunderbolt. Airiness can soften a hard-edged interior or complement a busy, heavily patterned, ultradecorated room.

The weeping fig (*Ficus benjamina*) is the ultimate airy tree, which accounts for much of its success. However, the silk oak (*Grevellia robusta*) is also a feathery tree and is perhaps even more interesting because its fernlike foliage is silver-green. The only problem with the silk oak is its scarcity in most nurseries.

A most popular feathery tree is the ming aralia (*Polyseias fruticosa*). It is also the most fickle of trees, full of leaves one moment, denuded the next. It requires absolute consistency in care and location. Sudden changes in temperature, light, and availability of moisture (both at the root and in the atmosphere) trigger its strip-tease act. Tree-sized ming aralias, newly available to home gardeners, are not cheap, but they're worth the investment if you have the money, the conditions, and the expertise.

The Japanese yew (*Podocarpus macrophyllus*) is also worth investigating. This "weeping" plant has a long needlelike leaf and an arching habit. It makes an elegant columnar plant, although it may require permanent staking to keep it upright. A south window and life on the dry side improve its growth.

Among the smaller feathery plants, *Asparagus densiflorus* 'Sprengeri' is a popular choice. This common asparagus fern drapes itself over anything in its path, turning hard objects into soft, shapely forms. An upright plant with feathery leaves is the false aralia (*Dizygotheca elegantissima*). If overwatered, however, it will rapidly lose its leaves.

Right: Softly draped curtains, a light floral-patterned slipcover and a spring bouquet are complemented by the feathery plumes of a fern pine (Podocarpus gracilior). This plant, like Podocarpus macrophyllus, benefits from the bright, filtered light that shines through filmy fabric. Likewise, the room benefits from the soft play of light through the needles.

Strong Graphic Shapes

Sometimes you're not as interested in a specific plant as you are in a bold pattern or form suggested by a plant. This is especially true when the background is a solid wall of color and the plant will serve as the focal point against it. Line—not mass—is desired. The first choice is the dragon tree (*Dracaena marginata*), especially a mature specimen with many trunks. The spiky umbrella of foliage cascades from the ends of the branches, and the interplay of the beige trunks below makes a beautiful display. Many growers deliberately train the trunks into contorted angular shapes when the plants are young, in order to achieve that striking graphic effect. The ponytail plant (*Beaucarnea recurvata*), with its furrowed bark and elephantine swollen base, also has a strong sculptural presence, as do mature, multiple-trunk specimens of *Yucca elephantipes*. In addition, many succulents have good lines, but they require sunny locations as permanent stations.

Right: Graphic shapes are generally large, strong ones and this Strelitzia (bird of paradise) is certainly an example. These plants take a long time to mature—seven to eight years—and will not bloom until they do so. Then, they will burst forth every year, in spring and summer. The blooms are worth waiting for and, like the leaves, are also very graphic. The large flowers form in clusters on a long stalk and the individual flowers are reminiscent of a bird in flight, hence the common name.

A plant of this size and scale needs a lot of room and a simple background to show it off to full advantage. Here, a simple clay container, the smooth floor, and the simple lines of the settee fill these design requisites.

Flowering Plants

Except for an occasional mature gardenia or greenhouse-grown yesterday, today, and tomorrow (*Brunfelsia pauciflora* 'Floribunda'), flowering houseplants seldom achieve the size needed to make a significant design statement; they can rarely stand alone in an interior. Flowering plants are more useful as centerpieces, tabletop decorations, or part of an indoor garden.

View blooming houseplants as long-lived bouquets. For the price of cut flowers, you can buy a great deal of living color, which will last a lot longer. Instead of a bunch of daisies, for instance, you can buy a pot of cineraria (*Senecio cruentus* hybrids). Instead of cut gerberas, buy growing ones. The list of flowering houseplants is rich in variety: kalanchoe, begonia, azalea, guzmania, gloxinia (*Sinningia*), African violet (*Saintpaulia*), cape primrose (*Streptocarpus*), primrose (*Primula*), cyclamen, star-of-Bethlehem (*Campanula*), ornamental pepper (*Capsicum*), hydrangea, amaryllis (*Hippeastrum*), heather (*Erica*), pocketbook plant (*Calceolaria*), sapphire flower tree (*Browallia*), and flamingo flower (*Anthurium*). You may have other favorites. Some of these are available only seasonally, and some can be bought all year round.

Although flowering plants are an easy way to add a dash of color, you can't expect them to keep on performing. Cut flowers don't last forever, and neither do flowering plants. You should set them in their plant stations, enjoy them, and if you want, discard them when their blossoms fade.

To tie the plant into your decor, place it in a pretty cachepot or basket. You may want to hide the edges of the utility pot and cover the soil with green sheet moss or dried Spanish moss, but that is not essential. Remember that flowering plants last longer in cooler temperatures rather than warm ones and they have to be watered to stay alive. (Just removing a flowering plant to a cooler room overnight can extend its life by a week.)

If you need a more dramatic effect than one or two small plants can give, buy several (alike or different) and combine them in a bowl, tray, or basket. You can also add some of your homegrown plants to the store-bought ones for a more lavish display. (In horticultural circles, this is known as refreshing your garden.)

Right: Although some people insist that flowering plants should fill a room with blossom, there are subtler ways to introduce color. Bromeliads, such as this Achmea fasciata, have bright blooms and long-lasting colored bracts. The plant dies after blooming, but produces "pups" before doing so.

Indoor Gardens

Large architectural plants and the changeable beauties that temporarily fill plant stations operate as loners for the most part. Yet that's not the way indoor gardening is normally done. If you have more than four potted plants, you probably have a great many, and if they are bumping against one another and competing for light and attention, they probably look more like a hodgepodge than a well-ordered potted garden. Yet, interesting indoor gardens can be made from collections of potted plants, small and large.

The Skylight Garden

Many people who have skylights don't realize that they have a superb opportunity for a garden. This is the best situation for hanging plants, since all the light is coming from overhead.

Plants can be hung around the sides of the skylight, some high and some low. If there is nothing directly under the skylight, such as a table or passageway, this striking cascade of plants could reach to the floor. You might even want to build a large pebble tray of the same size as the skylight and create a floor-level tray garden to mirror the one hanging above. A flexible arrangement for hanging plants can be achieved by attaching a metal grid below the skylight.

Using only one plant variety in a hanging garden can create a spectacular effect. Unattractive arrangements are most likely to result from an attempt to combine plants. A striking display of six perfect spider plants will draw more praise than a random assortment of plants in baskets. Plants that renew themselves from the center will maintain their beauty longer and have a more luxurious appearance than vining plants, with their ever-lengthening stems. The spider plant is especially useful. The all-green variety, *Chlorophytum comosum* (originally called the airplane plant because of its flying offsets) is a stronger grower than the variegated variety. Its entire leaf produces food, but the white areas in the leaves of variegated plants do not. Ferns of all kinds, especially the Boston types (which are varieties of *Nephrolepis exaltata*), renew themselves from the center, as do the asparagus fern *Asparagus densiflorus* 'Sprengeri' and all the *Hoya* species.

Pots of trailing plants can be kept full, high, and bushy in the center by reintroducing small rooted cuttings of the parent plant into the main pot. That pot, by the way, should be plastic. Hanging plants dry out too quickly to bear the added porosity of clay pots, not to mention inherent weight problems.

Right: The weeping fig (Ficus benjamina) is always much happier when it gets bright, overhead light. This atrium, with a large skylight, fulfills this need perfectly and should prevent the common problem of leaf drop that affects these plants when they are in less-than-ideal locations. The variegated leaves of the chinese evergreen (Aglaeonema modestum), the shiny ones of the peace lily (Spathiphyllum), and the heart-shaped ones of the Philodendron oxycardium add variety and interest to this indoor garden.

The Windowsill Garden

An unplanned assortment of plants sitting on a windowsill does not make a garden. More often than not, it makes a mess. However, plants can be successfully arranged around a window.

In the early 1970s, sills overflowed with plants that cascaded to the floor, and the glazing was covered with plants hanging from ingeniously knotted cords. Currently, many exciting window treatments are back in fashion and the window garden has become a less overwhelming affair.

The first rule for a genuine sill garden is that all the pots should match. They don't have to be exact clones, but they should, for example, all be clay or all be green. By doing this, you focus attention away from the pots and onto the plants.

Think of the plants as a frame for the window rather than a screen. Tall plants, such as a swordlike snake plant (*Sansevieria trifasciata* 'Laurentii') or an airy false aralia (*Dizygotheca elegantissima*) go at the edges or on one side. Medium-sized plants come next so that the arrangement slopes down to the sill. Especially suitable are flowering plants and plants with variegated leaves, such as begonia, cyclamen, kalanchoe, gloxinia, a column-shaped bromeliad (*Vriesea spendens*), the beautifully marked Moses in the bullrushes, or the oyster plant (*Rhoeo spathacea* 'Vittata'). Finally, something should cascade below the sill level—a creeping fig (*Ficus pumila*) or a wandering Jew (*Zebrina* or *Tradescantia* species), for example. If you want a hanging plant, don't suspend it in the middle of the window; substitute it for one of the tall side plants.

Windowsills can be considered as plant stations to be filled from a collection of houseplants growing elsewhere. If the plants are permanent residents, however, choose only those that will flourish in that setting. Remember that window-grown plants must be turned regularly to prevent them from slanting toward the light.

Deep bay windows can accommodate a lot of plants without appearing overcrowded. To emphasize the feeling of a garden rather than a collection of individual plants, consider a pebble tray with sides that are high enough to conceal the containers. The overall effect will be enhanced if the tray matches the shape of the sill. If the bay extends from floor to ceiling, shape the pebble tray to match the floor area defined by the bay. For the healthiest plants, artificially light the sides facing away from the window.

Left: A windowbox does not necessarily have to be on the outside. This indoor one groups Philodendron oxycardium, bromeliads, and asparagus ferns.

The Tray Garden

A group of plants placed together in a container form a tray garden. The container can be a tin tray with a layer of pebbles at the bottom, or it can be a deep planter that hides the pots.

In small trays that will hold three to five potted plants, repetition is desirable. Three ferns, three syngoniums, three chrysanthemums, or three Reiger begonias make a much better group than a mixture of three different plants. If you do want a mixture, center a tall plant at the back of the stand as the focal point, flank it with shorter plants on both sides (still in the rear of the tray), fill in the front with two matching plants, and complete the ends with a pair of plants that cascade and conceal pots, edges, and foliage. This makes a total of seven plants. If a plant is not tall enough to fill its niche, stage it on an upturned pot or saucer. The final shape will be a plant pyramid.

A variegated plant with a lot of white can be a "spotlight" in a tray garden. Use only one, placed low in front so that it draws attention to the tallest plant.

In a larger tray garden, such as an indoor raised bed or planter box, many of the same principles apply. There must be tall plants for focus, but you could also add sculpture or fountains. An effective arrangement would be a tall, airy umbrella plant (*Cyperus alternifolius*), a weeping fig (*Ficus benjamina*), a silk oak (*Grevillea robusta*), or a dragon tree (*Dracaena marginata*) supplemented with shorter blooming plants, such as kalanchoe, begonia, azalea, chrysanthemum, hydrangea, geranium, or forced bulbs. This is a good way to use seasonal or occasional plants, which you can buy in bloom and then discard. Alternatively, since variegation can substitute for bloom, in the second tier of plants you might use colorful crotons (*Codiaeum species*), dieffenbachia, peacock plant (*Calathea*), or peperomia. Fill in the edges with spider plants, grape ivy, English ivy (*Hedera helix* and its cultivars), or any fern. When you've finished, no pots should show and there should be no gaps in the foliage.

The ultimate in tray gardens is a raised bed on casters in which the leakproof tray is deep enough to hide the largest pot and the casters are concealed. The exterior finish can be painted or laminated to coordinate with the room's color scheme.

Right: Bromeliads, sansevieria, and philodendrons form the permanent basis of a tray garden supplemented with cut flowers. Glass vials hidden in the moss are the secret to putting bloom where you want it.

The Centerpiece

The center of a dining or occasional table can be one of the most important places to make a design statement. You can emphasize a look that your furniture or color scheme already suggests, or you can create a mood with an appropriate and individual display. If you think of a centerpiece as a plant station rather than a plant, you will realize that any object can be placed on a table.

An arrangement of jade plants forms an unusual centerpiece that is hard to equal for beauty and durability. Plant approximately a hundred jade cuttings in a perlite and sand mixture in a shallow bonsai pot. When the cuttings have rooted, set the pot outdoors or in an airy, bright room. The little forest can be brought in and placed on the table at any time. Another lovely centerpiece can be made from any beautiful blooming plant, such as the Cape primrose (*Streptocarpus* 'Constant Nymph'), set in a deep bowl. Isolate and elevate the bowl on a pedestal and the centerpiece will look especially rich and elegant on the dining table.

The same bowl, this time containing an assortment of apples, oranges, tangerines, avocados, and bananas, is the basis for yet another centerpiece. Make pockets among the fruit and tuck in African violets or any other small blooming plant. Hide the pots among the fruit and spread the leaves to cover the pockets.

Give your plants as much thought as you would a menu. For a formal dinner, do an arrangement of plants in colors that match the china or linen. For a special party, consider individual plants at each setting. Disguise the containers by wrapping them in napkins that match or coordinate with the ones intended for your guests. With imagination, your plants will become a complementary part of any table setting.

Conclusion

It is not enough to purchase a plant and set it beside a window. In order to make a plant feel at home, and make a home feel as if the plant belongs, you need to deal with all the design principles that have been described in this chapter. To ensure that plants are happy and healthy at the stations you have chosen (and that you've chosen the right plants), read the following chapters.

Right: A centerpiece is an obvious place to display your ingenuity and sense of style. Here, strawberries grow in a plastic-lined basket.

The Basics of Plant Care

Many people think of interior living greenery as a relatively recent phenomenon, but indoor plant cultivation is actually thousands of years old. The Egyptians, Assyrians, Babylonians, Chinese, Greeks, Romans, and Incas all grew plants in containers indoors. By the early eighteenth century, more than 5,000 species of tropical and semitropical plants were cultivated for use indoors.

Houseplants are domesticated wild plants and differ from outdoor plants only in their location. Many were bred from natives of shady tropical forests and are naturally accustomed to seasonal temperature changes, heavy rainfall, extremely high humidity, and a soil rich in nutrients from decayed vegetation. The plants that were selected for indoor gardening have one essential feature in common with their wild cousins—adaptability. They can endure filtered light, widely varying temperatures, and the low humidity found in most homes, stores, and offices.

Today, the selection of indoor plants includes countless new hybrids specifically adapted to the modern interior, but they should be chosen wisely. They should be selected for their shape and appeal, but also with an eye to where they will be placed. But before committing yourself to a plant, you must decide how much effort you are prepared to put into maintaining it. If you want a plant that can take care of itself, be sure to choose one that can.

In order to make your choice easier, the following pages deal with the basic growing requirements. You will find discussions on watering and watering methods; pots, soil, and planting methods; preferred lighting conditions for specific plants, and lots more. All the information contained here is designed to make sure you choose a suitable plant and that it stays healthy and good looking.

Plant: any member of the group of living organisms exhibiting irritability in response to stimuli, though generally without voluntary or true sense perception; a vegetable in the broad sense as distinguished from an animal.

Webster's New International Directory, 1919

Houseplant Basics

To the beginning indoor gardener, whether grower or maintainer, caring for houseplants can be difficult at first. Watering, lighting, fertilizing, grooming, propagating, and seasonal care might be initially bewildering; but they will become easy and natural once you understand the basic processes of plant survival.

Photosynthesis: Storing Energy

Like all other living things, plants need food for energy. The basic food element for all living things is sugar or other carbohydrates. Unlike animals, however, plants harness the energy of the sun to manufacture their own sugar, through the process of photosynthesis.

In photosynthesis, light energy, carbon dioxide, and water interact with the green plant pigment, chlorophyll, to produce plant sugars and oxygen, which is released into the atmosphere. The carbon dioxide is drawn in from the atmosphere by plant leaves, and the water is supplied by plant roots. Plant photosynthesis supplies most of the oxygen on our planet.

Photosynthesis requires an environment with adequate light, warmth, and humidity. No amount of fertilizer can compensate for an unfavorable environment, since fertilizer provides only nutritional building materials, not the plant's real food—the sugar it manufactures by photosynthesis.

Respiration: Supplying Energy

In plant respiration, the sugar created by photosynthesis is combined with oxygen to release energy. This energy is used for growth and survival and enables the plant to convert the building materials provided by nutrients in the soil into plant tissues. materials provided by nutrients in the soil into plant tissues. Respiration produces carbon dioxide, water, and a small amount of heat as by-products that are released into the atmosphere.

Transpiration

Sunlight falling on a leaf can heat it well above the temperature of the surrounding air. Transpiration, the movement of water vapor from a leaf into the atmosphere, is important in stabilizing leaf temperatures (keeping them cool), in much the same way that human perspiration has a cooling effect.

As water vapor leaves the plant through leaf pores (stomata), the leaf cools. The higher the temperature and the lower the humidity, the faster plants transpire. If they lose more water than they can absorb through the roots, they wilt; that is why correct watering is so essential to the survival of a houseplant.

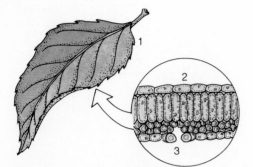

1. Leaves produce food for the plant and release water and oxygen into the atmosphere.
2. Chloroplasts are the chlorophyll bodies within cells in which photosynthesis takes place in order to manufacture carbohydrates (starches and sugars). They give the leaf its green color.
3. Stomata are specialized "breathing pores" through which carbon dioxide enters and water and oxygen are released. They close when water is limited.

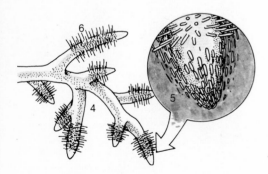

4. Feeder roots grow from the lateral roots and serve to transport water and nutrients absorbed by root hairs.
5. Root caps produce a continuous supply of new cells that are sloughed off and serve to lubricate the advance of the growing root tip through the soil.
6. The root hairs are microscopic appendages to the feeder roots. They absorb water and nutrients.

The Parts of the Plant

There are four parts to most plants: roots, stems, leaves, and flowers. All are crucial.

Roots anchor the plant and absorb the water and minerals that nourish it. Most absorption occurs through the root tips and the tiny hairs on young roots. These tender tissues are easily injured. Transplanting often destroys them, causing the top of the plant to wilt; but under the proper conditions, new root tips will grow within a few days. Roots send water and nutrients to the stem, to start their journey to other parts of the plant. Roots of some plants also store food, sometimes in special structures.

The stem transports water, minerals, and sugar to the leaves, buds, and flowers. It also physically supports the plant. Stems can store food during a plant's dormant period. In many houseplants, stems are herbaceous, or soft, rather than woody. Whatever their form, all stems function in a similar manner.

The leaf manufactures the plant's food through photosynthesis, absorbing light over its thin surface area. Its pores absorb and diffuse gases and water vapor during respiration, photosynthesis, and transpiration.

The flower is the plant's sexual reproductive organ. Most plants can flower in their natural environment, but only certain plants will bloom indoors.

Most Houseplants Are Tropical

Florida, California, and Texas (to a lesser degree) are the major producers of foliage plants in the United States. Plants of all types and in all stages of development, from cuttings to 20-foot specimens, are available from multiacre greenhouses and vast growing fields. Depending on the size and type of the foliage and the buyers' specifications, some are shipped directly from the field and others are placed in "shade houses" to prepare them for the lower light levels they will soon encounter. In either case, they are boxed and carefully loaded into trucks for shipment to florists, nurseries, and garden centers across North America.

Once delivered, the plants will be readied for immediate sale, repotted into larger containers for further growth, or placed under still lower light for further conditioning (acclimatization). The sizes and types of plants and their intended use dictate how they are handled by wholesalers and retailers.

Compare Plant Needs and Personal Schedules

Some plants require little care. Others require a lot. Some plants can withstand erratic treatment, such as over-watering one week and neglect the next. Others demand regularly-scheduled care.

Plant Costs

Several factors, besides the obvious ones such as rarity or availability, affect the price of a plant. Obviously, if a plant is rare, it will cost more than a variety that is easy to obtain.

Another factor that affects price is the cost that must be put into developing the plant prior to purchase. Species vary enormously in how long it takes or how easy it is to grow them. A Kentia palm, for instance, takes twice as long as a parlor palm to reach 5 feet; and because it needs twice the labor and energy to grow to 5 feet, the Kentia palm costs more.

Some plants are hardier than others and may be grown in open fields rather than under more expensive greenhouse conditions, so they cost less than greenhouse plants.

Two seemingly identical plants of the same species may vary in cost because one was shipped directly from the field for immediate sale while the other was shade-grown or held for a period of acclimatization to lower light level.

Above: Delicate fuchsias, with flowers in a variety of stunning colors, will grow indoors, but only if you place them in a cool room.

Opposite: It is always wise to buy plants from a reputable florist or plant dealer who will be able to offer advice and suggestions.

Below: Before buying a plant, inspect it closely. Large gaps between new leaves suggest that the plant has been overfertilized. Leaves should be free from dust and grime but should not look unnaturally shiny.

How to Select a Plant

Shopping for plants from a truck parked at the gas station or supermarket is risky business. Such plants have most likely not been acclimatized, and their growing and shipping conditions have probably been far from ideal. They are much less likely to survive than plants purchased from a reputable nursery or florist. But often, if plants don't survive, the owners feel responsible. Their guilt feelings about not being able to keep the plant alive may cause them to give up plant growing instead of just shopping more carefully for replacements.

Starting with the healthiest plants possible is one key to success. Wise beginners will ask for help in choosing plants that suit their homes and their life-styles. Beginners are well advised to avoid starting out with such difficult plants as orchids or *Ficus benjamina.* It is far better to begin with something less touchy and to progress, as skills improve, to more demanding species. Wherever you shop, be prepared to answer questions that may be posed by a conscientious florist or plant dealer. The following checklists should enable you to either answer or ask the questions and help you to buy a suitable plant.

Study light levels before choosing plants   The most important variable in plant care is light. Will the plant be living in a garden room with skylights? Or, as is more often the case, will it fill a corner far from any light source? The light level (low, moderate, or high) should dictate the plant choice.

Compare plant needs and personal schedules   Some plants require little care; others require a lot. Some can withstand erratic treatment, such as overwatering one week and neglect the next. Others demand systematic, regularly scheduled care.

Consider room size and furniture scale   Buying a tree for outdoor planting is simple; purchase the largest specimen that will fit in the station wagon, plant it, and watch it grow to the desired size. But, indoors, there are constraints other than the ceiling height and the available light level. The corner of a room is not a greenhouse, and greenhouse growing conditions can't be simulated in most living spaces. A 2-foot plant is not likely to grow into the 6- or 7-foot tree that the scale of the room demands. And, even if it does, will it grow into a graceful or symmetrical plant that suits its setting?

Look closely at the plants on display   Start out with the healthiest plants you can find, and examine them carefully. Plants should have few brown-edged leaves and few leaves that have been trimmed, particularly on new growth. They should be full and bushy, with small spaces between leaves. Large gaps between new

How to Select a Plant (continued)

leaves suggest that the plant has been overfertilized and crowded to induce rapid growth, or that it has spent a long period under inadequate light.

Inspect the leaves and junctures of stem and leaves for any sign of insects or disease. Anything on a new plant brough into a home may soon infect an entire collection. Leaves should be free from dust and grime but should not look unnaturally shiny.

Flowering plants should have many buds that are just beginning to open. Plants in full bloom may have exhausted much of their beauty. This is particularly important with those plants that will never bloom again under less that ideal conditions or plants that will be discarded after the blooms fall. If you wish to get the plant to bloom again, refer to the Gallery of Houseplants.

Flowering plants should be properly wrapped or sleeved at the nursery or florist to protect them during transportation from the store to their new home.

Plants received as birthday or anniversary gifts usually arrive decked out in foil, bows, and ribbons. These decorations may be suitable for the occasion but rarely do they look like an integral part of the decorating scheme of a room. Once the celebration is over, and the plant is permanently stationed, the bows and ribbons should be removed and the foil should be replaced by a decorative cachepot or a basket of a shape and size that is appropriate for both the plant and the room.

Acclimatizing New Plants

Plants need to adjust to new surroundings, and they may even go through a mild case of shock when first brought home. Over a short period of time the plant has traveled from the meticulously controlled environment of the commercial greenhouse, to a different environment at the retailer's, and finally to a home with yet another set of light, humidity, and temperature conditions.

Acclimatization takes several weeks. At first, leaves may yellow and blossoms drop. Pay special attention to the plant's needs. A plant that normally tolerates dim lighting may have been grown under strong light and will need time to adjust to the change. Ease the transition by placing it in interim locations with decreasing light intensity, leaving the plant in each spot for several weeks or more before placing it in its chosen site. Keep plants moderately moist during this adjustment period and do not allow them to dry out. Water thoroughly each time and discard excess water from the drainage saucer. Once a plant is acclimatized to a particular set of surroundings, try not to move it.

The Right Tools

Most garden centers stock inexpensive light meters. They read light levels in the areas where plants will be placed and indicate whether the light is low, moderate, or high. The readings are not scientifically exact, but they are accurate enough to enable you to choose a suitable plant.

Moisture meters are similarly helpful. They don't actually measure moisture; instead, they measure the presence of electrolytes or fertilizer salts in the soil. Since water carries the electrolytes, a high reading ordinarily indicates the presence of moisture. After a while, however, as salts build up in the soil, the meter will not give you accurate readings.

Misters are used to increase humidity around the plant. More important, misting washes grime from the leaves and helps to control pests as well as make plants look healthy and cared for.

A long-spouted water can, good pruning shears, sharp knives, a small trowel, clean cloths, soft sponges, and (for small-leaved plants) a soft ostrich feather duster or soft hair or paint brushes, are all tools needed by the indoor gardener.

You may find you need several sizes of pots, bags of potting soil, plastic flats for rooting cuttings, and powdered rooting hormone. A spray bottle for applying pesticide is also a handy piece of equipment. Make sure such spray bottles are well labeled, and don't store them until they have been emptied and washed out.

Above: Having the right tools will make plant maintenance easier.

Watering Your Plants

Houseplants are container plants; their roots are confined to the container and cannot reach farther for sustenance. Although watering sounds like an easy part of plant care, it is responsible for killing more houseplants than anything else. Overwatering is more often the culprit than underwatering. As roots cannot absorb more water than the plant needs, too much water, combined with poor drainage, displaces oxygen from the soil. This suffocates the roots and leads to rot. To avoid this, don't assume that a plant needs more water when it doesn't grow as expected; there may be some other reason. Also, do not allow a pot to stand in drained water. After watering, check the saucer and pour off excess or remove it with a turkey baster.

Don't water by the calendar. A plant that needs water every day during a hot spell may need it only every other day in cool, cloudy weather. The amount of water a plant needs varies with the species and its native habitat, the soil in which it is growing, and the light, temperature, and humidity it is exposed to in your home. Water needs are also determined by the plant's growth cycle. A plant absorbs more water during active growth periods than during rest periods. The size and type of container are other important factors; in a small pot, moisture is absorbed quickly. If you can't keep a plant moist, even if you water every day, it needs a larger pot. A plant in a porous clay pot will need water more frequently than one in a plastic or glazed pot.

Some gardeners solve the evaporation problem by placing one pot inside another and insulating the space between them with peat moss, perlite, charcoal, or gravel. If you do this, be careful not to overwater, or the insulation will become soaked. Another way to solve the evaporation problem with small pots is to group them in a wooden box, with ground bark or peat moss placed around the pots for insulation and as a temperature-moderating mulch.

To learn exactly when your plant needs water, the simplest

Right: A severely dried-out plant, such as this coleus, should be immersed in a pail of water. Leave it in water until the soil is well moistened or until the bubbles stop. Drain and return the plant to its growing station. After a short time, it will return to its original healthy-looking state.

method is to test by touch. Insert your finger into the soil to feel the degree of moisture. To double-check, rub a bit of soil between your thumb and index finger. With a little experience, you'll be able to tell when the plant needs water by how dry the soil feels.

Every plant needs a thorough soaking; it's the frequency that varies. Check the listings in the Gallery of Houseplants to determine your plant's watering needs.

Water Temperature

Water temperature is crucial. Cold water can harm roots or foliage, and excessively hot water can kill a plant instantly. Always use tepid water. It is better to take cold tap water and allow it to warm to room temperature than to use warm water from the hot water tap. Hot water contains dissolved solids that could harm potted plants.

Water Quality

In parts of the country where the water is very hard and the soil is alkaline, it is difficult to grow acid-loving plants such as camellias and azaleas. Adding acid soil amendments such as peat moss and using acidic fertilizers will help. Alkaline conditions make it difficult for plants to absorb trace minerals and iron. Regular applications of iron chelate, available at most nurseries, will help to keep the foliage green. When the new foliage on these plants is yellow, water every 2 weeks with a solution of 1 ounce of iron sulfate in 2 gallons of water until the growth regains its normal color.

Softened water contains sodium that may accumulate in the soil and harm plants. If your home has a water softener, use an outdoor tap for your plant water, or install a tap in the water line before it enters the softener, so you'll have a source of unsoftened water for plants. If this is not possible, draw water just before the softener cycle, when the sodium is at the lowest level.

How to Water

Always water thoroughly, until the soil is saturated. If your plant receives only superficial waterings, its roots will grow toward the surface of the soil. The water should take only a minute or so to drain. If it takes more than 10 or 15 minutes, the drainage hole may be blocked. If it is, poke a stick into the hole to loosen compacted soil. Don't let plants sit in water; if the plant is in a saucer, pour off any drained water within an hour. If the plant is too heavy to lift, use a turkey baster to remove the water.

If water drains through very rapidly, it may be running down between the rootball and the pot and not soaking in. This may happen after a plant has been allowed to dry out; it can be remedied by submerging the plant, as described on the next page.

Above: Plants can be watered either from above or from below. In either case, make sure you water thoroughly and that you pour off the excess drainage water.

Special Watering Techniques

There are times when your plants need more than a shower from a watering can.

Submerging   Submerging a pot in water to its rim is excellent for plants that have dried out completely and for plants in full bloom. This is also the best way to water hanging plants. Place the plant in a sink or tub and leave it submerged for several minutes, until the air bubbles have stopped.

Showering   An occasional trip to the shower is an excellent way to water plants thoroughly and to rinse dust and dirt from the leaves. Use tepid water, with a gentle flow to keep from washing the soil out of the container.

Leaching   Thorough watering will help wash out accumulated salts, which can build up from high salt levels in tap water or from overfertilizing and can harm the plant. A whitish deposit on the outside of a clay pot or on the inside of the pot at the soil surface indicates salt buildup. Plant symptoms of salt damage include brown and brittle leaf tips and margins. Place the affected plant in a sink, tub, or pail and water it several times, letting the water drain each time. You may need to repeat the process weekly for several weeks. Pots with salt deposits need not be replaced, since the salts on the outside usually won't harm the plants.

Watering Terrariums   Once established, terrariums need water only once every month or two. Excess water is difficult to get rid of because there is so little evaporation. Watch the container to decide when water is needed. When there is no condensation on the glass, and the plants are beginning to droop, add a little water. If this results in extreme fogging (a sign of overwatering), remove the top until the excess moisture evaporates.

Vacations   If you're going to be away for a few days and can't find someone to take care of your plants, you can easily set up a self-watering system for your indoor plants. Simply pad a sink or bathtub with matting or any thick, absorbent material. Set pots with drainage holes directly on the matting and leave a faucet dripping on it. Plants will draw up the moisture.

Another temporary self-watering method is to make a wick of stocking or nylon clothesline and put it into two small holes in the lid of a plastic refrigerator bowl. Run the wick from one of the holes in the lid to the drainage hole in the plant container. Fill the bowl with water and cover with the lid. Make sure that the wick is stuffed well inside the drainage hole and is in contact with the soil. Water will soak slowly from bowl to plant. Commercial wick waterers are also available at many garden centers.

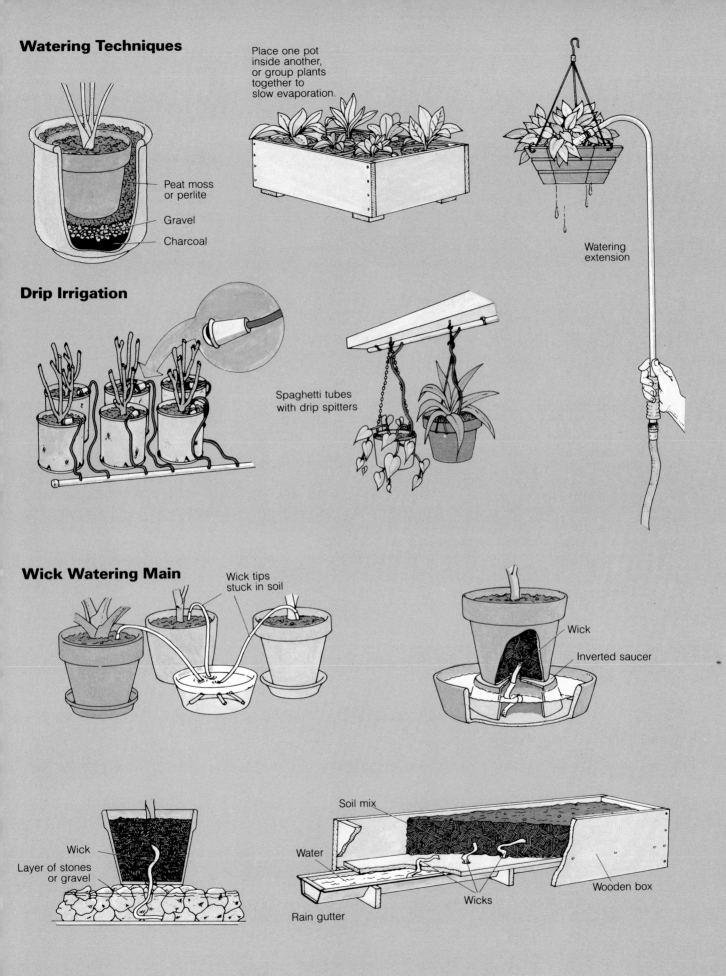

Watering Techniques

Place one pot inside another, or group plants together to slow evaporation.

Peat moss or perlite

Gravel

Charcoal

Watering extension

Drip Irrigation

Spaghetti tubes with drip spitters

Wick Watering Main

Wick tips stuck in soil

Wick

Inverted saucer

Wick

Layer of stones or gravel

Soil mix

Water

Wicks

Wooden box

Rain gutter

Light Requirements

Light means life for a plant. It regulates three major plant processes: photosynthesis, phototropism, and photoperiodism.

Photosynthesis is the plant's method of transforming light energy into food energy, as discussed earlier.

Phototropism refers to the natural tendency of plants to grow toward their light source. The process is controlled by auxins (growth hormones) in the stem tips and youngest leaves. Highly reactive to light, these auxins cause the plant to adjust itself to the light source. Indoors, where the natural light source is usually a window, plants will bend toward the window. Rotate plants to avoid excessive growth on the side nearest the light and weak growth on the other side. If artificial light is used, it should come evenly from directly above the plant.

Photoperiodism is the plant's innate programming to its environment. Plants perform best in a rhythmic cycle of light and darkness which most closely resembles that of their original habitats. For many plants, the length of the days and nights determines the time required to reach maturity. Some plants will

Below: The amount and intensity of sunlight varies according to the window exposure. A south-facing window receives the most intense sun for the longest period while a north-facing exposure receives only indirect light. Afternoon sun from the west is warmer than morning sun from the east.

Sunlight at Various Window Exposures

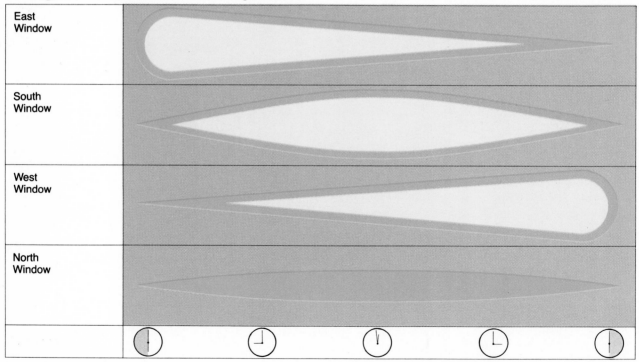

flower when the days are long (14 hours or more). Other plants produce blooms when days are short and they receive at least 14 hours of darkness while their flower buds are setting. Most plants, however, bloom without regard to the length of the day, provided there is a cycle of day and night.

The intensity and duration of light vary considerably inside the home, even within one room. Whether or not the windows are shaded or draped, the window's exposure and angle to the light, and obstructions (trees or nearby buildings) that block the sun's rays at certain seasons or times of day are determining factors. Furniture and reflective surfaces, such as mirrors and glass-framed paintings, can also alter light intensity. Most plants benefit from as much indirect light as possible. It is often preferable to direct sun and the potentially harmful intense heat that accompanies it.

Seasonal Light

With each season, the angle and intensity of sunlight change. Summer sun shines almost perpendicular to the earth, striking it with maximum intensity. In contrast, the winter sun hovers low in the sky, even at noon, sending light on a slanted path so that it becomes diffuse and scattered as it passes through more dust and moisture in the air. At noon on a clear day in midsummer, the level of illumination is as much as 20 times greater than that of a rainy day in December. As a result, many plants grow very slowly during the darker months and will welcome locations in which they receive full winter sun.

All plant care must harmonize with the seasonal changes in light intensity. During summer, all plant life processes speed up and plants absorb more water, minerals, and carbon dioxide; therefore, they require more moisture and fertilizer. In winter, when the light is dimmer and photosynthesis slows down, cutting back on water and fertilizer is desirable.

Where you live also affects how much light you receive. At higher elevations, less light diffusion through the atmosphere due to thinner air means stronger light. In winter, the sun rises and sets farther to the south, so southern states receive much brighter light than northern ones. Even within a specific area, the light intensity may vary. Smoke from local industry may turn sunny days into hazy ones. Trees and shrubs outside windows, as well as screened windows, doors, and porches, reduce light sharply. On the other hand, a white house next door or a white cement driveway will reflect sunlight and increase light intensity in your rooms. Snow, too, can reflect a great deal of light on a sunny day. Too little light diminishes photosynthesis, causing plants to elongate and lose leaves that they can no longer support. As the plants attempt to gather more light, the spaces on the stems between the leaves (internodes) lengthen and the leaves grow broad and thin.

There are several ways to remedy low light. You can increase the duration of light by simply moving the plant to a window that admits light for a longer time, or you can supplement daylight with artificial light. The added light, however, must be intense enough to stimulate photosynthesis. It is preferable to move the plant to a sunnier window, or to place it near reflective surfaces such as white or light-colored walls. You can even place mirrors, foil, or white backdrops around the plant.

Too much light causes plants to wilt and lose their color. Young, thin leaves are affected first because they cannot hold much water. Inexperienced indoor gardeners often mistake these symptoms as a need for nutrients. Before you fertilize a drooping plant, check its light requirements, keeping in mind that excessive light is most likely to occur at noon. Some plants may wilt slightly at midday and recover in the afternoon.

Light Categories

There are five basic light exposure categories for indoor plants. Before buying a plant, read through the descriptions of these categories and study the light levels in your home. If you have a particular plant in mind, check the list on page 79 and make sure that its requirements will be met. If you have a spot in mind but don't know what plant to put there, you can check the light level with a light meter that measures footcandles. (Most photographers own light meters of this kind.) Armed with this information, any consciencious plant dealer will be able to help you choose an appropriate plant.

Low Light   Only a few plants can tolerate extremely low light in dim areas far from windows. These are areas where the light is barely enough to read by. Plants kept at very low light levels are healthiest when they're moved regularly to locations with more light. Generally, the less light a plant gets, the lower its watering and fertilizing needs. If you use artificial light to supplement natural light, turn it on for a few hours at the end of the day to provide a more natural cycle of light and dark hours.

Moderate Light   Locations get indirect light of varying intensity. They are between 5 and 8 feet from a window that receives direct sun for part of the day, and include areas near sunless windows. Many foliage plants will adapt to this lighting.

Bright Indirect Light   These locations should receive a great deal of light but no direct sunlight. They could be situated within 5 feet of a window that receives direct sun during part of the day. Most foliage plants prefer this setting.

Opposite: A solarium should be treated as an indoor garden. Here, the plants are grouped carefully. Scale, balance, and individual light requirements have all been considered.

Below: This syngonium is a victim of phototropism. Note how it is reaching out for more light.

Above: Be sure that you choose appropriate plants to place in a room that gets a lot of light.

Some Direct Sun These brightly lit locations receive less than 5 hours of direct sun daily. This might include windowsills facing east or west and areas a little more than 2 feet away from a south window. Protection from intense summer sun is usually needed in west windows. These areas are ideal for many flowering house-plants, herbs and vegetables, and some leafy houseplants.

Full Sun Locations with full sun receive at least 4 or 5 hours of direct sun daily. These locations are usually within 2 feet of a south window or in a greenhouse or solarium. Very few plants other than cacti and some succulents can survive the heat of this setting in summer; but with some shade and plenty of water, many indoor plants will flourish there, including flowering plants, seedlings, cuttings, herbs, and vegetables.

Light Requirements of Various Houseplants

Botanical name	Common name
Plants for Low Light (dim reading level light)	
Aglaonema modestum	Chinese evergreen
Aspidistra elatior	Cast-iron plant
Asplenium nidus	Bird's-nest fern
Dieffenbachia species	Dieffenbachia (dumb cane)
Plants for Moderate Light (no direct sun)	
Adiantum species	Maidenhair fern
Araucaria heterophylla	Norfolk Island pine
Asplenium nidus	Bird's-nest fern
Cissus species	Grape ivy, kangaroo ivy
Davallia species	Deer's-foot fern
Dracaena fragrans 'Massangeana'	Corn plant
Epipremnum aureum	Pothos, Devil's ivy
Howea forsterana	Kentia palm
Nephrolepis exaltata 'Bostoniensis'	Boston fern, Sword fern
Philodendron	
P. bipinnatifidum	Twice-cut philodendron
P. gloriosum	
P. hastatum	Spade-leaf philodendron
P. oxycardium	Heart-leaf philodendron
P. 'Red Emerald'	
P. selloum	Lacy tree philodendron
Phoenix roebelenii	Pygmy date palm
Ptseriscretica	Ribbon fern
Rhapis excelsa	Large lady palm
Spathiphyllum species	Peace lily, Spathe flower
Plants for Bright Indirect Light (away from direct sun, or in a north window)	
Brassaia actinophylla	Schefflera
Ceropegia species	Rosary vine
Coleus x *hybridus*	Coleus
Dizygotheca elegantissima	False aralia
Episcia species	Episcias, Flame violets
Fatsia japonica	Japanese aralia
Ficus species	Ficus (fig)
Hippeastrum species	Amaryllis
Pilaea rotundifolia	Button fern
Saintpaulia species	African violet
Schlumbergera species	Christmas cactus
Plants for Some Direct Sun (curtain-filtered sunlight from a south, east, or west window)	
Aeschynanthus species	Lipstick plant, basket vine
Asparagus species	Asparagus fern
Beaucarnea species	Bottle palm
Begonia species	Begonia
Caladium species	Caladium
Camellia species	Camellia
Clivia miniata	Kaffir lily

Botanical name	Common name
Columnea species	Columnea
Crassula argentea	Jade plant
Cryptanthus species	Earth stars
Cyclamen species*	Cyclamen
Impatiens species	Impatiens
Platycerium bifurcatum	Staghorn fern
Polypodium aureum	Polypody fern
Primula species	Primrose
Rhododendron species*	Azalea, Rhododendron
Sedum morganianum	Donkey's tail
Senecio rowleyanus	String-of-beads
Streptocarpus species	Cape primrose
Plants for Full Sun (4 or more hours of direct sunlight)	
Abutilon species	Flowering maple, Bellflower
Aechmea species	Living vase plant
Agave species	Century plant
Allium schoenoprasum	Chives
Aloe species	Aloe
Ananas species	Pineapple
*Aphelandra squarrosa***	Zebra plant
Billbergia species	Vase plant
Cephalocereus senilis	Old man cactus
*Chrysanthemum morifolium**	Florist's mum
Codiaeum variegatum	Croton
Echeveria species	Echeveria, Hen and chicks
Echinopsis species	Urchin cactus
Euphorbia pulcherrima	Poinsettia
*Fatshedera lizei***	Tree ivy, Aralia ivy
Gymnocalycium denudatum	Spider cactus
Hydrangea macrophylla	Hydrangea
Kalanchoe species*	Kalanchoe
Lithops species	Living stones
Mammillaria species	Pincushion cactus
Opuntia species	Opuntia, Rabbit ears
Orchids**	
Cattleya	
Dendrobiums	
Oncydium	Dancing lady
Paphiopedilum	Lady slipper
Phalaenopsis	Moth orchid
Pelargonium species	Geranium
Rhipsalis species	Chain cactus
Rosa hybrids*	Miniature roses
Vriesia species	Vriesia

Needs full sun for production of a flowering plant. While flowering, the plant can be placed in bright indirect light.
**Needs full sun in winter but curtain-filtered sunlight during summer.*

Artificial Lighting

Artificial light can make a tropical garden bloom in an area devoid of natural light. It can supplement natural sunlight or be the sole light source. It can allow you to make a garden in a room where foliage plants would not ordinarily survive, and enables flowering plants to blossom in places that would normally support only foliage plants.

Artificial light cannot exactly duplicate sunlight, since its colors are present in different proportions. Light can be broken down into different wavelengths that are perceived as colors. You can see this when sunlight passes through a prism and breaks into bands of red, orange, yellow, green, blue, and violet—the range of colors called the light spectrum. The colors most necessary to plant life are those at the ends of the spectrum, red, blue, and violet. Red rays stimulate flowering, stem length, and leaf size. Blue and violet rays promote foliage growth. Both red and blue light waves play important roles in photosynthesis.

It's important to know the differences between the two types of artificial lighting—incandescent and fluorescent. Incandescent lights are most commonly used in the home, but fluorescent lights are better for the indoor garden.

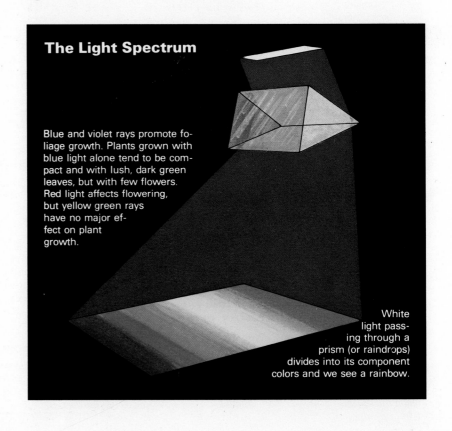

The Light Spectrum

Blue and violet rays promote foliage growth. Plants grown with blue light alone tend to be compact and with lush, dark green leaves, but with few flowers. Red light affects flowering, but yellow green rays have no major effect on plant growth.

White light passing through a prism (or raindrops) divides into its component colors and we see a rainbow.

Incandescent Light   Incandescent bulbs are cheaper and simpler to install than fluorescent lights; they are rich in the red and far-red light rays necessary for flowering and other plant processes. However, incandescent light spreads unevenly and emits few of the blue and violet rays needed for complete plant growth. Incandescent light can supplement daylight if the light deficiency is minimal; it can also be combined with fluorescent lamps to give plants a full spectrum of light.

Incandescents give off considerable heat, which can scorch plants placed less than 12 inches from the light source. Light decreases very rapidly with distance; a plant 2 feet away from a light source will receive only one-fourth as much light as it would if it were 1 foot away. Heat problems can be reduced by using several lower-wattage bulbs instead of one large one. This distributes heat evenly over a larger area so plants can be placed closer to the light source. A shield of glass or transparent plastic can also be placed several inches away from the lamp to absorb a large amount of heat while allowing nearly all the light to pass through.

Another method of avoiding excess heat is to use incandescent lamps that contain a silverized reflecting surface that sends light downward but conducts heat upward. Use these bulbs only in ceramic sockets, since they may burn out metal sockets.

Below: Light is food for a plant. If it doesn't get enough natural light, it may be necessary to use supplemental artificial light. However, rather than being a problem, it will add nighttime drama to a room.

Fluorescent Light   Fluorescent lamps, commonly used in offices and industrial settings, are popular because of their low cost, long life, and evenness of light distribution. They emit 2½ to 3 times more light per watt than incandescent lamps and generate only a small amount of heat. Although initially more expensive than incandescent bulbs, fluorescent tubes last about 15 to 20 times longer and are less costly to run all day. Their economy and efficiency make them the mainstay of light gardening.

The fluorescent lamp's long glass tube is coated on the inside with a phosphor, a mixture of phosphorescent chemicals that determine the color wavelengths the tube gives off (visible color doesn't indicate the proportion of red and blue waves emitted). Electricity stimulates a current between the electrodes at the ends of the tube, which activates the phosphor and lights up the tube. The light is stronger in the center of the tube than at the ends.

Electricity is regulated by ballasts, the small transformers that reduce the tube's current to the voltage required by a particular lamp. The ballast is usually contained in the fixture and emits a small amount of heat. If a fluorescent fixture seems to be radiating too much heat downward, the ballast can be removed from the metal tray that houses it and a piece of asbestos placed between ballast and tray.

Generally, fluorescents throw off so little heat that they can be placed as close as 1 inch from many blooming plants, although 6 to 9 inches is more common. For best results, leave fluorescents on for 12 to 16 hours per day if they are the sole light source, or for a few hours every evening if they are supplementing sunlight. Automatic timers can help to maintain the light schedule.

Because fluorescents grow dim with age, replace the bulbs when they reach 70 percent of their stated life expectancy (usually listed on the bulb package). With a grease pencil, note the installation date on the end of the tube to ensure timely replacement. A flickering lamp signals imminent burnout and should be replaced immediately. Indoor gardeners who use light banks often stagger lamp replacement to prevent light shock to plants that have grown accustomed to dimming light.

Fluorescent bulbs are available in various colors, according to the quality of the light given off (not the bulb's temperature): white, cool white, warm white, daylight, soft white, deluxe warm white, and deluxe cool white are the colors most often encountered in housewares stores.

The cool white tube is the traditional lamp of the light gardener. Because most fluorescent lights are rather harsh, many people leave them on during the daytime so that natural daylight can offset the glare. This adds only a few cents per day to the electric bill. The deluxe warm white is the most flattering fluorescent light for complexions and furniture. Many indoor gardeners combine both the warm white and cool white bulbs in equal proportions in order to provide a wider light spectrum which is beneficial for the plants and which additionally provides a softer room lighting.

Ordinary fluorescent light in the right intensities can promote lush foliage growth, even without a ray of sunlight. However, it's short on certain parts of the light spectrum needed for balanced plant life, specifically, the red and far-red waves, which promote flowering.

In locations where no natural sunlight is available, you can either combine fluorescent and incandescent light (reflecting or cool-beam incandescent lights mentioned earlier are most suitable, although like all incandescents, they produce high electric bills), or you can use wide-spectrum plant-growth lamps.

Below: Even if there is not sufficient natural light, you can grow herbs on a kitchen counter. Here, fluorescent tubes mounted on the underside of the wall cabinets provide enough light to keep the plants healthy.

Fluorescent Lighting Ideas

Here are three simple light gardens to alter "daylength" or start seedlings. The fluorescent fixture on the adjustable shelf brackets can be moved up or down to give your plants more or less light.

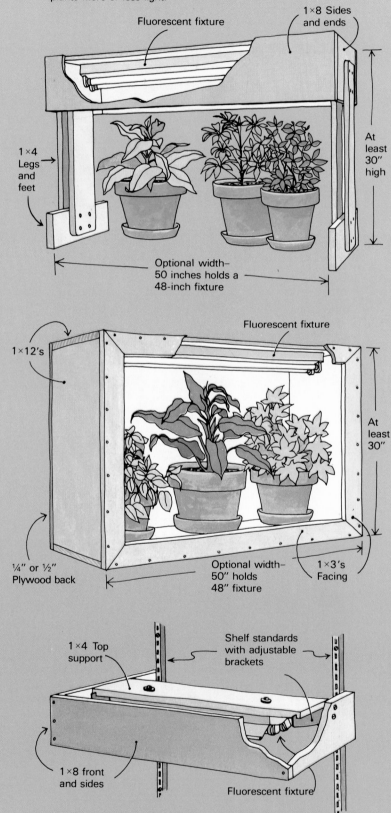

Fluorescent fixture

1×8 Sides and ends

1×4 Legs and feet

At least 30″ high

Optional width–50 inches holds a 48-inch fixture

Fluorescent fixture

1×12's

At least 30″

¼″ or ½″ Plywood back

Optional width–50″ holds 48″ fixture

1×3's Facing

1×4 Top support

Shelf standards with adjustable brackets

1×8 front and sides

Fluorescent fixture

Opposite: The advantage of a light garden is that large numbers of plants can be reared in a basement or attic and, when they are looking their best, they can be moved to display stations throughout the house. When the flowers fade, the plant is returned to the light garden to be groomed for its next appearance.
You can buy a light garden complete with shelves and lights, but making one is an easy project for a competent do-it-yourselfer.

Plant-Growth and Wide-Spectrum Lamps   These modified fluorescent lamps are sold under such trademark names as Gro-Lux, Plant-Gro, and Plant-Light. They minimize the parts of the light spectrum that have no known influence on plants and concentrate on emitting the blue and red rays that plants need. Because of these missing colors, their light appears purplish or pinkish, which has the effect of making flower colors glow and foliage look lusher.

The wide-spectrum growth tubes include the visible blue and far-red rays, and sometimes ultraviolet rays as well. They provide a more natural-looking color than the pinker growth lamps described above, and the light appears less glaring than that emitted by cool white tubes.

Light Gardens: Fixtures and Equipment   If you are lighting your garden with incandescent bulbs, make sure that bulbs stronger than 75 watts have porcelain sockets.

Fluorescent tubes require their own special fixtures. The most common types are industrial, which have a built-in reflector, and strip or channel, which do not. The industrial type is hung in the open and is very often used in banks by light gardeners with large setups. Often the setup consists of a standard industrial fluorescent with a reflector; the unit can be adjusted to stand or hang 12 to 24 inches above the plants. The height of the fixture should be made adjustable, to meet varied light intensity requirements. Plants with varying light requirements, when grouped together under one fixture, can be placed closer to the light source by raising the containers. Use the channel type in constricted places, such as within a bookcase or cabinet, and paint its background white to provide reflection.

Both strip and channel fluorescents are available in units that accommodate from one to four tubes, and the fixtures can be installed so that the light source is concealed. However, this means that the distance from lamp to plant is fixed. Temporary clamp-on lights with reflectors, or a photographer's lamp on a tripod, allow you to position and move the light source easily.

There are also many attractive plant stands, grow-light furniture pieces, and plant carts on the market containing two or three plant trays with built-in fixtures, reflectors, and timers. These can be an instant way to install a light garden, but they must be incorporated into the design of the room. If necessary, the shelves may be waterproofed with a lining of heavy-duty polyethylene or by putting a galvanized or plastic tray under the plants. When gardening under lights, it is important to maintain the proper humidity for your plants.

Top: A bathroom is generally humid enough for moisture-loving plants.

Above: By keeping the bed of vermiculite well watered, this marantha gets lots of moisture.

Temperature, Humidity, and Air Circulation

All the elements of a plant's environment must be kept in balance to ensure healthy and sustained growth.

Temperature

Temperature interacts with light, humidity, and air circulation to affect plant metabolism. Most indoor plants adapt to normal indoor temperatures (55°F to 75°F). At night, almost all plants benefit from at least a 5° drop in temperature. This gives them a breather from any rapid water loss that may have taken place during the day. Overnight, water deficits in the leaf cells are corrected as roots take in water from the soil or growing medium.

Few houses have uniform temperatures in each room. Use a thermometer to check temperatures in different locations of your house, and even in various parts of the same room.

Also, temperatures can change with the seasons, even indoors. In winter, temperatures can vary widely due to home heating and cold drafts from windows and doors. Seasonal changes can be severe enough to warrant moving plants to a different location, especially plants growing on windowsills.

Tropical plants native to areas with high temperatures and humidity (episcias, prayer plants, and bougainvilleas, for example) may grow best in a south window in a room that contains an appliance that vents wet heat, such as a dishwasher, clothes dryer, or humidifier. In addition, tropical plants can thrive in cool rooms if the soil is heated by electric heating cables or propagation mats. Cold-loving plants (55°F to 60°F days, 50°F nights) such as cyclamen, camellias, azaleas, and some orchids do well in rooms where indirect sun keeps temperatures low.

Humidity

Humidity is the moisture content of the air; it is expressed as a percentage of the maximum amount of water vapor the air can hold at a given temperature (the relative humidity).

Nearly all houseplants grow best in a relative humidity level of 50 percent or higher; but this level is rare in drier climates and indoors in winter. In winter, home heating robs the air of moisture; humidities of only 4 to 10 percent are common.

A cool-vapor humidifier can increase the humidity by 25 or 30 percent, even on the coldest days, making the air more comfortable for both people and plants. Portable units can be placed where needed, or a humidifier can be installed as part of the central heating system. The simplest method for humidifying the air around plants is to use trays or saucers filled with pebbles, perlite, or vermiculite. Put water in these trays and place the plants on top.

This method is strongly recommended for gardens grown under artificial lights. Fill the saucers or trays with water to just below the surface of the rocks. Check that the bottom of the pot is not touching the water; if it is, you are risking root rot. As the water evaporates, it fills the surrounding air with moisture. Add water as necessary. You may also group the plants so that the leaves will catch and hold transpired moisture. Leave enough room between plants to encourage air circulation, which helps prevent disease.

Misting, unless done several times a day, raises the humidity only temporarily. In dry rooms, moisture evaporates quickly. Humidifying the air and adequate watering are the only ways to ensure that plants have sufficient moisture.

Air Circulation

Plants enjoy fresh air as much as people do. Soft breezes of warm humid air supply oxygen and moisture, keeping the plant healthy. Dry air movement over leaves can cause moisture stress and leaf burn, especially in direct sun. Sudden changes in air movement and temperature can send plants into shock. Be especially careful with plants kept near a window, particularly during winter.

You also need to consider air pollution. Fumes from burning propane or butane gas may cause flowering plants to drop their buds, and leaves to yellow and drop. Fumes from burning natural gas are not harmful to plants.

Dust and dirt can accumulate on plant leaves, clogging the stomata and slowing growth. This can be remedied by giving your plants a shower once a month for a good rinse (see "Watering Your Plants," page 70). Between showers, you can gently wipe off dust with a soft rag or feather duster.

Humidify the air around a plant by placing the container in a cachepot and adding a layer of moss. The moss will obscure the growing pot and, if kept wet, will add moisture to the air.

How and When to Fertilize

Photosynthesis provides plants with the sugar and other carbohydrates they need for energy. Fertilizers provide the nutritive minerals they require for healthy growth; nitrogen, phosphorus, and potassium are the three major nutrients that plants need.

Fertilizers come in many different formulations, reflecting differences in the balance of these nutrients according to the preferences of various types of plants. Containers of houseplant fertilizers usually list three numbers on their labels. These are, in order, percentages of nitrogen, phosphorus, and potassium that make up the fertilizer. A fertilizer labelled 12-6-6, for instance, is 12 percent nitrogen, 6 percent phosphate, and 6 percent potash.

Nitrogen primarily enriches the deep green color of plants and promotes stem growth. Fertilizers designed for flowering plants usually contain less nitrogen and more phosphorous and potassium. Phosphorus encourages bloom and root growth, and potassium contributes to stem strength and disease resistance.

In addition, plants need three secondary nutrients (sulfur, calcium, and magnesium) and minute quantities of iron, zinc, manganese, copper, chlorine, boron, and molybdenum. These latter are called micronutrients, or trace minerals or elements.

Fertilizers are available in many forms: water-soluble pellets, powders, liquids, dry tablets, time-release pellets, and sticks to

Right: Yellowing of mature leaves is often an indication of nitrogen deficiency and a general slowing in the growth rate. Because nitrogen stimulates growth, it should not be applied when plants are dormant.

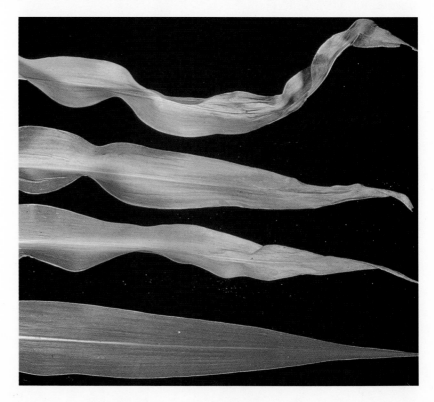

insert in the soil. Their value and strength vary widely. Always read the label before you apply the fertilizer, and follow directions carefully. If necessary, consult with the person who sold you the plant. Remember that more is not better, since excess fertilizer can burn roots or leaves.

Overfertilization is a common error, particularly with plants on maintenance rather than growth programs. These plants do not require the same amounts of fertilizer as plants in active growth. Too much fertilizer will cause leaf burn; too frequent fertilization may cause odd-looking, unwanted growth.

Most fertilizers on the market have been formulated for use every 2 weeks; this is safer than large monthly doses. If monthly doses are recommended, reduce the suggested amount by one-half and feed biweekly instead. For most foliage plants, fertilizer should be applied at half strength and only during March through October. Fertilizing should be reduced or stopped during the winter months.

The worst time to fertilize is when a plant is ailing. Sickly, pallid plants will decline even more rapidly under heavy fertilization, and may even die.

Before deciding that the plant needs fertilizer, review its requirements to determine whether they are being met. If a regularly fertilized plant isn't growing, it's likely that the plant is dormant or sick.

If you mistakenly overfertilize a plant, thorough watering should solve the problem. Thorough watering will also help wash out accumulated fertilizer salts, which can build up and harm the plant. This buildup can be recognized by a whitish deposit on the outside of clay pots or by salt burn on the edges of leaves. The condition is a serious one but can be remedied by watering through— leaching—the soil. Place the plant in a sink, tub, or pail and water it several times, letting the water drain each time. If salts have become a problem they will not leach out in one day; the process may have to be repeated weekly for several weeks. As a last resort, you can gently wash the old soil from the roots and repot the plant in fresh soil.

Foliar Feeding

In their native habitats, plants can absorb nutrients from rain and bird droppings falling onto their leaves. Fertilizers recommended for foliar application (directly onto leaves) are available at garden stores. Apply these with a sprayer or mister, following label directions.

Foliar feeding acts quickly but lasts a relatively short time. It is best used as a supplement applied directly to the soil. Trace elements are often applied to plants through foliar sprays.

Top: Fertilizer burn is often the reason for brown leaf tips.
Above: Leach out excess salts if a plant has been overfertilized.

Grooming Techniques

People like plants because they symbolize life and vitality, but yellow leaves and brown tips destroy that look. Container plants demand regular grooming, trimming, and pruning to keep them attractive and free from disease and infestation.

Cleaning Plants

Dust and dirt on leaves keep light from reaching the leaf pores, harming the plant as well as making it unsightly. Cleaning the plant allows the leaves to breathe, and also helps rid it of insect eggs and mites. A cloth or soft sponge dampened in mild soapy water will remove grime from smooth-leaved plants. Support the leaf in one hand while gently wiping away from the stem. Avoid cleaning very new young leaves.

Use a dry, soft hair brush or paint brush to clean the fuzzy leaves of plants such as African violets and velvet leaf that do not react well to water on their leaves. For large plants with many tiny leaves, such as ficus, a soft feather duster—especially one made with ostrich feathers—is ideal.

Exercise caution with all cleaning materials, especially dusters, to avoid transferring pests from an infested plant to a clean one. To avoid contamination, clean the cloths, sponges, and dusters in warm, soapy water and allow them to dry before using again. You can also spray them with a disinfectant after use. Let them air out for a day or so after spraying to avoid any plant damage.

Shining Plant Leaves

The leaves of certain plants look good with a bit of extra sheen. There are commercial "leaf shine" products on the market, but they should be used with care and only in moderation. Mix liquid shiners in a clean mister bottle, then spray a soft cloth or sponge applicator. Use the cloth or sponge to apply the solution; don't spray the leaves directly. Monthly application is sufficient. Shiners in aerosol cans should be avoided, since many plants are harmed by the propellant. Oils and shiner products with heavy oil bases are not advisable; they produce a glow, but also attract harmful dust and grime.

Trimming

Once a leaf has turned yellow, it will never become green again. It should be removed to improve both the look of the plant and its general health. When the tip of a leaf turns yellow or brown, trim away the discolored area for the same reasons. When cutting, use sharp shears and follow the original shape of the leaf, taking as little green, vital material as possible. Small leaves and those that have completely changed color should be pinched off at the base of their stems.

Yellow and brown leaves are not always signs that the plant is ailing. Some attrition is part of most plants' natural life cycle, and is necessary to the growth process of many species.

Pinching

By using thumb and forefinger to pinch off a young stem tip, you force the plant to branch out below the pinch and become bushier and healthier. A young coleus plant, started from a seed or cutting, must be pinched during its active growth period or one stem will grow straight up and become gangly and weak. To avoid this, nip off the growing tip as soon as the plant has four to six leaves. This causes dormant buds to spring into active growth, producing additional stems. After 2 or 3 weeks, pinch the tips of these new stems and the plant will soon become bushy. Pinching works well for most plants, but is especially recommended for soft-stemmed plants such as certain begonia species, and young geraniums.

Pruning

Pruning requires care and some basic knowledge, but it is not difficult and, with careful shaping, you can get a compact, cared-for, topiary look instead of shapeless random growth.

If a stem is removed at its point of origin, new growth will take place in the remaining stems or at the base of the plant. If the stem is cut off above a leaf, one or more new growth tips may appear near the cut and make the plant denser. With a good pair of small hand-pruners, make cuts on branching plants just above a node or just above a leaf to avoid unsightly bare sticks all over the plant. Make the cuts at a slight angle so that the bare white stem faces inward toward the center of the plant.

Vining plants, such as pothos, grape ivy, and wandering Jew, require different pruning methods. To achieve both length and fullness at the top, allow just a few vines to grow to full length and keep all the others pinched well back. Pinching induces branching and will help to keep the plant looking lush. Periodically, vining plants should be cut back extensively. Make cuts just above leaf buds or branches, and save the cuttings for rooting. These trimmings may be replanted back into the original pot to add even further to the plant's full, healthy look.

Sometimes an older plant, while still healthy, loses the design characteristics desired for the space. To salvage the plant, yet hide the loss of bottom foliage, place it into a larger container and add several smaller plants of the same species (or a ground-cover type of foliage, such as pothos) to fill in the empty space.

Above: Pinching out new growth on soft-stemmed plants (top and center) and pruning woody growth (above), encourages plants to branch out and become fuller.

Potting and Transplanting Houseplants

During months or years of good care, many plants grow until they're too large for their original containers and need repotting to maintain their health and growth. There are several reasons why you should repot your plants as part of regular maintenance.

If a plant seems to need enormous amounts of water, it has probably grown too many roots for its container and needs a larger pot. Long strands of roots coming out of the drainage hole or a rootball that fills the pot completely are signs of this problem. Another reason to repot is that tall plants (such as ficus, avocado, and certain dracaenas) eventually look overgrown or even fall over when they become top heavy.

The plants most urgently in need of repotting are seedlings and "starts" packaged by the plant nursery in temporary containers such as plastic cell packs, metal cans, fiber balls, or biodegradable peat pots. Many indoor gardeners buy these starter plants because they're available in a wider choice of species and at less expense than mature plants in elegant containers, but such plants must promptly be transplanted to more permanent pots. Professional growers often use ultralight potting soils, composed mainly of perlite or vermiculite, to decrease shipping costs to retailers. This soil is not intended for long-term use. The nutrients are quickly exhausted, and the porous texture causes it to dry out quickly. If, after a week of adjustment to its new home, a new plant still needs constant watering, it should be repotted.

The final but no less important reason for repotting is that plants in handsome new containers can change the look of a room almost as dramatically as new furniture.

When to Repot

Repotting is essential when a plant outgrows its container. To see whether the roots are compacted, turn the plant on its side and knock the rim of the pot gently against a solid surface to loosen the rootball. If it doesn't come out, the soil may be too wet. Let it dry a bit, then try again. If the roots are massed along the sides of the pot and at the base of the rootball, repot the plant.

As a rule, the new pot should be no more than 2 inches larger than the old one. A repotted plant will not grow well until its roots begin to fill the container. Also, the greatly enlarged mass of soil with few roots may hold too much water, leading to root rot. This rule, however, does not apply to seedlings of fast-growing species (annual flowers, herbs, and vegetables) that are packaged in tiny plastic pots or cell packs. These seedlings can be transferred into considerably larger containers to avoid multiple transplantings during growth spurts that may follow a move to a roomier pot.

A basic guideline to pot size is that the diameter of the rim should equal one-third to one-half the plant's height. Tall, slender plants will grow in smaller pots, as long as the pot is wide enough to provide a stable base. Vining or trailing plants can also be grown in smaller pots.

How to Repot

Wet the potting soil before using it, preferably a day in advance. If the soil comes in plastic bags, add tepid water and tie the top of the bag tightly to keep the soil moist. If you are using homemade soil mix, scoop some into a plastic bag and moisten it in the same way. Or place the soil in a large bowl, knead in water by hand, and cover overnight with plastic wrap or foil.

To remove a large plant from a metal can, pot, or tub with sloping sides, hold the container sideways and tap it against a hard surface. Hold the rootball with the plant stem between your fingers, and gently ease it out of the pot. If the plant is sold in a straight-sided metal can, ask the seller to cut the can for you.

The easiest way to remove small plants and seedlings from cell packs is to squeeze the bottom, forcing the rootball above the lip. When removing plants that have grown side by side in flats or market trays, don't pull the plants out: cut the soil in blocks. Biodegradable containers, such as peat pots, paper pots, or (for much larger plants) burlap balls, should be handled carefully, with transplanting done as quickly as possible. Snip off burlap and peel it away, taking care not to injure the plant's roots. Plant peat pots below the soil line in their new containers. Punch holes in the bottom of the peat pots, and cut off exposed edges after planting. The rootball will dry out quickly if any part of a peat pot remains above the surface of the soil.

To transplant, prune the roots of the plant if necessary (see below), then partly fill the new container with soil. Place the plant at the height it grew in its previous pot. Firm the soil around the rootball, then fill the container with soil. Tamp the planting mix with your fingers, especially near the edges of the container. Water thoroughly, and keep the roots moist until they have spread into the surrounding soil.

Root Pruning

When transferring a pot-bound plant from a round container, you will notice that the roots have circled around the inside of the container. If necessary, prune them by making three or four ½-inch-deep cuts from the top of the rootball to the bottom with a sharp knife. The pruning will stimulate new root growth and aid the penetration of roots into the soil surrounding the rootball.

Top: Holding the plant securely, tap the plant out of the container.

Above: Position plant in new pot, firm the soil, and water well.

Basic soilless mixes are available prepackaged from your local garden center. Shown left to right: a humus—content mix for such plants as African violets, an all-purpose mix for most houseplants, a formula suited to terrariums, and a gritty, lean-growing medium for cacti and other succulents.

Soil

The water, air, and minerals that plants need are held in the minute spaces among soil particles. Good soil provides an environment that drains well, leaving plenty of air yet retaining enough moisture and nutrients for healthy growth.

Soil is made up of minerals, organic matter, and microorganisms that convert organic matter into plant nutrients. The mineral portion may be classified as sand, silt, or clay, depending on the size of its particles. The larger the particles (sand is considered large), the more swiftly the soil drains and the fewer nutrients it holds. Loam soils are ideal for growing plants. Loam combines the moisture and nutrient-holding capacity of silt and clay with the good drainage and aeration of sand.

When the organic matter in soil is broken down by microorganisms it forms humus, the dark, crumbly material that colors the soil and allows it to hold air, water, and nutrients. Adding organic amendments such as peat moss, sterilized manure, ground bark, leaf mold, or compost will improve any soil.

In fact, most indoor plants are especially adapted for use in such organic soils. There are many brands of ready-to-use soil available, with different types designed for specific plants. Most are primarily organic soils, and some have no mineral soil components at all. Choose soils that are appropriate for your plants and are light enough to provide adequate drainage and root aeration. If the packaged soil does not drain well, it can be lightened with organic amendments such as perlite, pumice, or vermiculite.

Acidity and Alkalinity

The acidity or alkalinity of soil is also important. It is expressed as the soil's pH value. The pH scale ranges from 0 to 14, with 7 being neutral. A pH reading higher than 7 is alkaline, and one less than 7 is acid.

Different plants have different acidity preferences, but most indoor plants flourish in a slightly acid soil. Commercial potting soils and homemade soil mixes must be moderately acidic. An alkaline soil generally causes loss of leaf color and stunted growth. Highly acid soil produces wilting and dropping of leaves.

Mixing Your Own Soil

Mixing your own soil is not highly recommended since so many good soil mixes are available at reasonable prices. Remember that even the best garden soil requires some processing before it is suitable for houseplants.

Soil from the garden must be sterilized, to eliminate weed seeds, pests, and soilborne plant pathogens. Place the soil in an ovenproof

Peat moss

Redwood soil conditioner

Fir bark

Vermiculite

container with a cover, insert a thermometer, bake at 200°F, and hold your nose (many soils smell decidedly unpleasant while baking). The soil should reach a temperature between 150°F and 180°F and remain there for 30 minutes. Garden soil may need organic amendments to enrich and aerate it before it can be used for houseplants. Soil from vacant lots will almost certainly need heavy enrichment and very thorough sterilization. It should be pushed through a strainer to remove glass shards, plastic shreds, and other bits of nonbiodegradable garbage. Soil from lots near heavily trafficked streets and highways carries such a concentration of poisonous lead that it should not be used as a potting medium for houseplants.

Instead of using garden soil, you can make your own mixes from purchased ingredients. Each of the following types is also available premixed.

All-Purpose Mix   An all-purpose potting mix can be made by combining 1 part sterilized garden soil, 1 part peat moss, and 1 part clean builder's (horticultural) sand. Never use beach sand, because the salt content and fineness of the particles will kill your plants. This mix is suitable for most houseplants; soilless mixes (see below) are also excellent for most purposes. Unless your garden soil is naturally alkaline, add 1 tablespoon of ground limestone per 2 quarts, to adjust the pH into the moderately acid range.

African Violet Mix   African violets, begonias, philodendrons, and azaleas require a mixture that has a high humus content and a higher acidity than that of the all-purpose mix. Combine equal parts of sterilized garden soil, builder's sand, peat moss, and leaf mold or composted bark pieces (¼ inch or less). Add 1 tablespoon of bone meal per quart to enhance calcium content.

Cactus Mix   Desert plants need a growing medium that is gritty, neutral in pH, and low in organic matter. Most cacti and succulents thrive in a mixture that is 1 part garden soil, 1 part sand, ½ part decayed leaf mold, and ½ part crushed clay pieces from flowerpots or bricks. To each ½ bushel (16 quarts) of this mixture, add 1 cup of ground horticultural limestone, to neutralize the soil's pH, and 1 cup of bone meal.

Soilless Mixes   Epiphytes, or air plants, including most orchids and bromeliads, derive much of their moisture and nutrients from the air and rain. They do not need soil and are grown in such media as osmunda fiber, unshredded sphagnum moss (not sphagnum peat), and chipped redwood bark.

Substitutes   Commercial soil amendments can replace many of the ingredients in these mixes. Horticultural perlite makes a good substitute for sand. Vermiculite can take the place of leaf mold, to lighten and condition heavy soils.

Perlite

Sand

Pots and Containers

Pots directly influence the growth, appearance, and needs of the plants they contain. They can be as casual as a coconut shell or a repainted coffee can or as formal as a glazed bonsai planter. Plastic and cloth bags, old whiskey and wine barrels, stoneware bowls, and pieces of driftwood can all be converted into unusual plant containers.

Whether or not a plant needs repotting depends on whether it will be actively growing or just maintaining its present state. You may want to repot the plant into a larger container just to allow it to continue growing. The new container should have the same drainage provisions as the old pot, such as a drain hole and saucer combination or a layer of pebbles in the bottom of a closed container. Extra room for soil, nutrients, and root growth will encourage the plant to flourish. The most common kinds of containers are described below.

Clay Pots

The standard clay pot is both functional and attractive. It comes in many shapes and sizes (generally ranging from 2 to 18 inches in diameter) and has a drainage hole in the bottom. Clay saucers may be sold with the pots or separately.

The unglazed porous clay allows air and water to move through the pot wall, so clay pots should be soaked in a basin of water for several hours before being planted. Otherwise, the dry clay will absorb too much water from the soil, robbing the new plantings of moisture.

Because they are porous, clay saucers eventually create water stains on surfaces where they're placed. To protect your furniture and floors, cut a round of cork ½ inch thick to fit beneath the

Opposite: As well as being decorative, this brass cachepot prevents water stains on the wood floor.

Below right: Davallia mariesii, squirrel's foot fern or ball fern, looks elegant in a glazed ceramic pot.

Below: Handsome pottery planter holds deep maroon Aeonium arboreum 'Zwartkopf', Haworthia cuspidata, and Crassula.

saucer, or use a thick cork coaster. A more practical solution is simply not to use clay saucers; instead, choose moisture-proof plastic or glazed ceramic. Clay pots should be scrubbed clean with a stiff brush and warm water before they are reused. To sterilize them, run the pots through the dishwasher or put them into the oven for 1 hour at 180°F. They can also be soaked in a freshly prepared solution of 1 part chlorine bleach to 10 parts water.

Plastic Pots

Plastic pots are lighter and less expensive than clay and come in the same range of sizes. Since they are not porous, they retain moisture much longer, so plants in plastic pots need watering less often. Because air does not move through the plastic, these pots require soils with excellent drainage.

Jardinieres

Plants on a growth program eventually require larger pots than the ones they came in. If, however, the 5-foot plant purchased from the nursery exactly fills the space, maintenance rather than growth may be prescribed. In this case the original pot should simply be set inside a decorative container, or jardiniere. Make certain that the container is at least 2 inches higher than the grow pot. Since the grow pot provides drainage, the outside container may either be watertight or have a saucer. Put a 1-inch layer of some open material that will not decompose in the bottom of the decorative container; styrofoam chips and crushed chicken wire are good materials to use. Set the grow pot in the decorative pot and pack more of the bottom fill material around the sides. To hide the grow pot, spread a top dressing mulch of sphagnum moss, Spanish moss, or bark chips over the surface. When using such pots, water thoroughly each time. The water that drains through should evaporate. If it doesn't, loosen the top mulch to get more air into the fill material.

Glazed Pottery

Glazed pottery containers can be very decorative, lending a distinctive touch to almost any decor. They are available in a wide array of sizes and designs, including bonsai pots and trays that can be used for miniature landscapes or bulbs.

Some glazed containers have no drainage holes and are best used as cachepots for slightly smaller clay or plastic pots. When using the jardiniere technique described above, you can camouflage the edges of the smaller pot inside the cachepot with a mulch of florist's sheet moss, sphagnum moss, bark chips, water-polished stones, small shells, or some other decorative top dressing.

Opposite: Pots directly influence the growth, appearance, and needs of the plant they contain. Wood, ceramic, clay, glass, and plastic containers in a wide variety of shapes and sizes are readily available in plant stores.

Opposite: Light is reflected onto this indoor window box by angling the movable mirror screens.

Below right: A simple wood planter is handsome enough to use as a centerpiece. This allows guests to add fresh herbs of their choice to soups or salads.

Window Boxes and Wood Planters

Planters made of rot-resistant redwood or cypress are exceptionally handsome and long-lasting. Unfortunately, not all of them are well constructed. The metal bands holding them together can rust quickly, and the spaces between the slats are frequently so large that water seeps out, ruining floors, carpets, or windowsills while the plants go thirsty. When buying these containers, look for ones that combine adequate insulation with good drainage. A good solution is to build (or have someone else build) your boxes and to place them on trays or stands with a lip around the edge to hold drained water. Wood planters are probably best used as cachepots, concealing the growing pots and drainage trays placed inside.

Plastic- and enamel-coated metal window boxes are also available. The best of these have drainage holes. Those placed on the inside of a windowsill should have matching trays to catch drained water.

Woven Baskets

Woven baskets look attractive but they rot quickly from contact with moisture. They, too, are best used as cachepots, covering a more utilitarian pot. Even with an interior saucer to catch moisture, wet baskets can cause extensive moisture damage to flooring. To avoid this, place baskets on plexiglass mats or masonite-backed cork pads.

Opposite: Plants and baskets are natural partners and, in this aqua and pink bedroom, add an appropriately romantic touch. The growing pots of the palm and cymbidium are carefully hidden within the wicker cachepot.

Left: A Chinese steamer conceals the container in which these freesias are growing.

Below: A small, masonite-backed cork pad is placed underneath this woven basket to protect the table from possible water damage.

Hanging Planters

Hanging planters add an interesting dimension to a home, high-lighting fine architectural details and disguising unattractive ones. They make efficient use of space and avoid the monotony of having all plants at one level. A trailing plant with its vines cascading over the edges of a planter hung high in the air provides a very graceful effect. But bear in mind that the vines will cascade only if there is sufficient top light. Hanging plants should always be located under skylights, or in light wells or solariums.

Hanging Pots

The simplest hanging planter is a clay or plastic pot suspended by a wire hanger or attached through holes in the pot or clamped on. Most of these have saucers built into the container or attached underneath; if not, they must be watered in the sink and then drained, or they will drip onto the floor. Use hangers that have built-in swivels so that every side of the planter can be rotated toward the sun. Regular pots can be transformed into hanging planters with a simple string or rope macrame cradle, supporting and surrounding both the pot and its saucer. These can be purchased in many plant centers, but they are simple to make using heavy twine or strong waterproof nylon cord.

Wood Planters

Many hanging planters are made of wood. These are attractive but they dry out very quickly.

Wire Baskets

Line wire baskets with coarse, unmilled sphagnum moss and then fill with soil. As drained water will be a problem, only use this kind of hanging planter where there is a masonry floor.

Care Requirements

Whichever type of hanging planter you use, it's important to leave enough watering space at the top. Fill the planter with soil to within ½ inch from the top, not up to the rim. In a moss basket, pack sphagnum moss thick and tight around the top inch of the basket to create a watering basin.

A hanging container needs more frequent watering than one on the ground or in a windowsill, since exposure to air on all sides causes the water to evaporate faster. Give the soil a good soaking whenever you water it or water sparingly several times a day. Plants also require vigilant grooming. Remove all spent blooms, and prune off straying shoots. Pin shoots or vines to the moss with old-fashioned hairpins or with paper clips broken apart. Rotate the planter frequently so that all sides get evenly exposed to the sun.

Above: Hanging plants thrive when they get sufficient top light. Here, they trail happily when hung beneath a skylight.

Left: Strong light filters through a window display of spider plants and Boston ferns.

Above and opposite: Almost any jar or bottle with a wide mouth can be used as a terrarium.

Terrariums

When you place several different plants in one container, you create a miniature landscape. This can be done in a shallow cast-iron or glazed ceramic bonsai tray or in a terrarium made from a fish tank, bubble bowl, brandy snifter, or bottle. Depending on personal preferences, the plants used, the location, and the type of container, you can create the effect of a woodland dell, a desert, a rocky coastline, or a tiny jungle.

Terrariums can be used as tabletop decorations, but they can also be suspended from ceiling hooks or wall brackets. If there is space in your terrarium, you can even add a shallow container of water to serve as a pond in the midst of your landscape.

Care Requirements

The most common misconception about terrarium plantings is that they require no care and will thrive just about anywhere indoors. In fact, they need occasional watering and regular grooming to remove spent growth and to prune fast-growing plants. Buying a preplanted terrarium stuffed with plants is not a good investment, as it will soon be overgrown.

Planting

Before you add any plant to a bottle garden or terrarium, inspect it carefully for insects, disease, and rotted roots, since these conditions are especially contagious under glass.

Most containers used for terrarium gardening have no drainage holes. To keep the growing medium sweet-smelling and healthy, line the bottom of the container with a ½-inch of charcoal chips (available where indoor plants are sold). Then add at least 1½ inches of potting soil; the best soils for terrariums are the soilless mixtures or commercially prepared potting soils with a little extra sand or perlite added for drainage.

Tools

Plants do best under clear glass, not tinted. Bowls, dishes, brandy snifters and fish tanks are easy to plant and maintain because you can reach inside them with your hands.

Small-necked bottles are quite a challenge, requiring delicate, long-handled tools. To place the growing medium in such a bottle, fashion a funnel from a rolled-up piece of newspaper. To move the soil around and shape the terrain, use a slender wooden stake (a thin chopstick or bamboo skewer) with a half-teaspoon measuring spoon taped to its end. When ready to "bottle" your plants, gently remove most of the soil from their roots, drop each plant through

How to Plant a Bottle

1. Clean and polish bottle with moist paper towel held in wooden tongs. Dampen towel with window-cleaning spray to remove stains. Let dry before planting.

2. Add 1 inch layers of sand and charcoal chips — then a few inches of potting soil using a funnel and paper tube extension to help keep dust down and off sides of bottle.

3. Roll larger, leafy plants in paper cylinder to slip them through the neck without damage.

4. Use wooden tongs to lower small plants through the neck and to maneuver all plants into position.

5. A spoon taped to a stick is great for digging planting holes, positioning plants, covering roots, and shaping the terrain.

6. A spool on a stick can be used to tamp and firm soil.

7. Shaping and pruning can be done with a razor blade taped to a stick. Pick up prunings with tongs.

8. Use a bulb syringe to wash sides of glass, water roots into place and settle soil. Use it dry to blow dust and soil particles off glass or leaves.

the neck of the bottle, coax it into the right position with your "spade" and cover the roots with soil.

After the plants are in place, a final mulch or ground carpet of moss will complete the scene. Mist with clear water to settle the roots and remove soil particles from the leaves as well as from the sides of the bottle.

Light and Water Requirements

Bottle gardens and terrariums do best in bright indirect light. Sun shining directly through the glass for more than an hour or two is liable to cook the plants. They also do well under two fluorescent tubes—one cool white, one warm white, either 20 or 40 watts—for 12 to 14 hours a day.

If the soil appears dry, no moisture droplets appear on the container, or the plants appear droopy, add a little water. To remove yellowing leaves, spent flowers, or excess growth from a narrow-necked bottle garden, tape a single-edge razor blade to a thin wooden stick and use it as a cutting tool. You can remove clippings with slender pieces of wood manipulated like chopsticks (slender, pointed Japanese-style chopsticks will serve very well). You can also use a mechanic's pick-up tool (sold at auto supply stores). Remove dying leaves and flowers before they rot, since rot may quickly infect healthy leaves and shoots.

Below: Planting and caring for a terrarium is an ideal hobby for people who enjoy miniatures. Here, palms and ferns are kept small in a bubble jar.

Self-Watering Containers

Do you consider watering and caring for plants part of the enjoyment of indoor gardening, or is it a chore? If you belong to the latter group and prefer to spend your time enjoying your plants rather than remembering to water them, then self-watering containers are for you.

Self-watering containers have a water reservoir that is refilled when it gets low, usually every couple of weeks. Since fertilizer is often added to the water, feeding and watering become tasks to be done every couple of weeks instead of daily. Meanwhile, the pot automatically delivers water at the rate the plant uses it, adjusting to changes in light, humidity, or temperature. This means that plants in self-watering pots are usually more evenly watered than plants in conventional pots.

Most self-watering units have been developed for the plant rental industry and are not widely available in retail outlets. You may find it difficult to locate a supply, but most nurseries can order them for you from the manufacturer—or you can contact the manufacturer yourself. (For a list of manufacturers, see page 4)

There are several different types of self-watering containers available. Both the wick-watering and reservoir units provide water to plants that are growing in soil. The plants can be fed with liquid or soluble plant food dissolved in the water, or with fertilizer placed within (but not on top of) the soil. In the hydroponic units, plants grow in a soilless medium and a nutrient solution. In the hybrid hydroponic system, a plant in a conventional growing medium is poised over the solution.

Wick-Watering Units

Many self-watering pots work by capillary action. The water reservoir is in the bottom of the pot, and water is carried into the soil by a wick. When purchasing this type of pot, be sure that the reservoir can't be overfilled. If the water comes in contact with the soil, the soil will become saturated and the plants will probably be killed. On most pots, there is a float that shows the water level and lets you see at a glance when it is time to refill the reservoir.

If you are transferring a plant from a conventional pot, it is usually necessary to acclimatize it. This will take a few weeks, during which time you should top-water in the usual way.

Reservoir Units

This type of pot has an airtight reservoir built into the walls and bottom of the pot. Water is released into the soil through a small hole in the bottom until a vacuum develops in the reservoir, which stops the flow of water into the soil. No more water will be

Below: This peace lily is being grown in a self-watering container. Water is released into the soil when the plant needs it.

Bottom: Plants grow in clay pebbles and a nutrient solution in this hydroponic unit.

Above: Self-watering containers come in a variety of shapes and sizes. This selection shows examples of the types discussed in this section.

Left: An African violet blooms in a reservoir-type unit that is easy to fill.

released until the soil dries enough to let some air into the small hole and break the vacuum.

A larger version of this vacuum pot breaks the vacuum through a plastic tube. The tube has a porous clay tip that is buried in the soil. As the soil around the clay tip dries, air seeps through the clay and breaks the vacuum in the reservoir, allowing more water to pass into the soil through the hole in the bottom of the pot. The moisture level can be controlled by the depth at which you bury the clay tip. The more deeply it is buried, the drier the soil is kept.

Vacuum pots have no float to show the water level; you have to shake the pot to see how much water is left. This is difficult with large plants, so you should top them off regularly.

Hydroponic Units

In a hydroponic pot, the plant grows in a soilless medium— usually clay pebbles. A nutrient solution in the bottom of the pot is drawn by capillary action from one clay pebble to the next. Although the medium sits directly in the solution, the size and texture of the pebbles controls the rate at which the solution is carried to the plant, and ensures that there is enough air at the roots. Like capillary pots, this type can be overfilled, drowning the roots. Be sure there is some mechanism to prevent overfilling.

Since plants do not transfer easily from soil to a hydroponic medium, some manufacturers supply the pots with the plants already adapted and growing. The plant draws all its nutrients from the water, so special fertilizers must be purchased and the manufacturer's directions followed carefully.

Wick-watering Unit

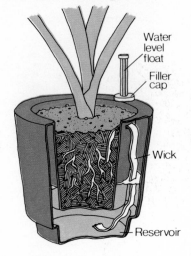

Water level float

Filler cap

Wick

Reservoir

Reservoir Unit

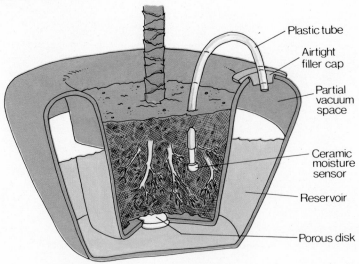

Plastic tube

Airtight filler cap

Partial vacuum space

Ceramic moisture sensor

Reservoir

Porous disk

Hybrid Hydroponic Units

A hybrid hydroponic unit poises a plant growing in a conventional potting mix over a reservoir of nutrient solution. The roots grow through a porous bottom into the solution. Because the roots are allowed to become established in this solution, they adapt to it, and get oxygen from the layer of air between the potting mix and the solution reservoir. This innovation makes it easier to adapt plants to hydroponic growing and makes it possible to transplant them to a larger pot.

Selecting a Self-Watering Container

When choosing a self-watering container, it is important to get the answers to the following questions before deciding on a model.

Planting Requirements   Can plants be easily moved from one container to another as they grow? In some designs, the plant roots grow through a screen or tray in the container and transplanting is not advised. Does the manufacturer advise growing plants from seed or seedlings.

Filling Requirements   Can the water level be easily determined? If there is a gauge, is it easy to read? Do you have to lift and shake the pot to tell whether it needs water? If so, it is not suitable for a large, heavy plant. How is the reservoir filled? Is the filler cap easy to remove and to secure? How often do you have to add water?

Special Requirements   Do you have to use special supplies (distilled water, nutrient solutions, planting media, bactericides) that will add to your expense? Does the container have special maintenance requirements that make it less than carefree?

Hybrid Hydroponic Unit

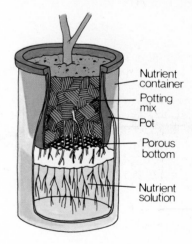

Nutrient container
Potting mix
Pot
Porous bottom
Nutrient solution

Hydroponic Unit

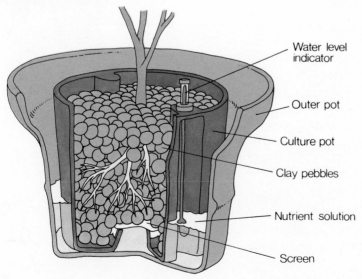

Water level indicator
Outer pot
Culture pot
Clay pebbles
Nutrient solution
Screen

*Above: Geraniums, very
hardy plants, enjoy a summer
vacation outside.*

*Right: Even though many plants
enjoy a dose of fresh air, too
sudden a move can damage them.
A screened courtyard provides
an ideal transitional location
for this palm.*

Moving Indoor Plants Outdoors

After a long, dark winter, many houseplants enjoy a dose of fresh
air and rainwater. This rejuvenates them and adds a fresh touch of
greenery to porch, patio, or yard. It is not highly recommended,
however, for plants on maintenance schedules, and it does require
care and planning.

Take only the hardiest plants outdoors, those that can stand
unexpected wind and cold. Wait until all threat of frost has passed
and temperatures remain above 45°F at night. Make the transition
gradually, starting with at least a week in a protected, well-shaded
spot. Never place the plant in full sun. After a few weeks, most
plants can be moved to a location that provides a few hours each
day of filtered sunlight and protection from the wind. During

these first few weeks, keep a close watch for evidence of excessive dryness, pest infestation, or shock.

As temperatures begin to dip in autumn, prepare to bring your plants indoors again. Set the container on a bench or table where you can examine it carefully, and clip off every yellowed leaf, spent flower, and seed pod. If the plant has grown too large for its indoor location, reshape it with some careful pruning.

Before bringing the plant inside, clean both the plant and the outside of the pot. Examine the foliage carefully for pests and disease, since these can infect your other plants. Treat pest-infested plants with the appropriate pesticide, following label directions. After bringing the plants back inside, expect them to go through acclimatization just as they did when you first bought them.

Cacti and Succulents

Cacti and succulents exhibit a wide variety of colors, shapes, textures, and sizes. Succulents are the camels of the plant kingdom; their well-developed water conservation techniques can carry them through periods of drought. Unlike desert cacti, however, not all succulents are native to arid areas. Some come from the tropics, where long dry seasons are followed by a short season of heavy rain. As a group, succulents are easy to grow if their general preferences are followed.

A clay pot just large enough to accommodate the plant without overcrowding its roots is best. If a small plant is placed in too large a pot, its roots may rot in unabsorbed water. Bonsai containers are splendid for displaying succulents, and the drainage holes are ideal.

Most succulents need to dry out between waterings. Clay and other porous materials make it easier to control the moisture level, although plastic pots can be used if the plant is watered less frequently. Water quality is especially important for succulents, which are sensitive to mineral salts.

During their growing season, cacti and succulents should be watered whenever the soil begins to dry out. During dormancy, however, water sparingly (just enough to keep the roots alive). Don't let them get dehydrated; water before foliage and stems go limp and shrivel. In springtime, when plants show signs of fresh growth, begin thorough watering again. Set the pots in a pan of water and allow them to "drink" until the soil is just moist on top.

Fertilize succulents only during the growing period, and never with more than a quarter to a third of the recommended dilution for the fertilizer. Feed in small amounts about every third watering, but stop as soon as plants cease their seasonal growth.

Good air circulation is crucial, since stagnant air encourages mealybugs. Keep the plants cool at night but not cold, and place them where they will get strong light during the day unless, like the tropical cacti, they prefer filtered light.

Right: The harvest from this hydroponic greenhouse includes corn, broccoli, cucumber, beets, and chard.

Hydroponics—Soilless Plant Care

For many people, hydroponics conjures up images of alchemy, convoluted systems of tanks and pipes, and complicated chemical baths that make plants grow without soil. In fact, hydroponics is an exciting way to produce vegetables for your table and flowers for your house. And a hydroponic unit works equally well if you put it on the patio in summer, in the basement under a bank of lights, or in the greenhouse for year-round production. Many people claim that vegetables grow faster hydroponically than in regular gardens, and they even taste better.

Hydroponics is becoming so easy that more and more people are using it. A system is not complex, and a hydroponic setup can be bought or made at home. Nutrient mixes are available in nurseries and garden supply stores. Using them does not require a degree in chemistry, merely the knowledge that you are growing plants in a solution of nutrients rather than in soil.

This solution is washed or pumped through a mix of light gravel that anchors the plants and retains the liquid. Hydroponics allows plants and vegetables to grow in a minimum of space, whether in a greenhouse or a small apartment. The system works best, however, in a greenhouse with ample light and humidity.

Hydroponic systems often take less work and cause fewer problems than ordinary outdoor gardens. Usually, about 20

Basic Home-built Hydroponic Garden

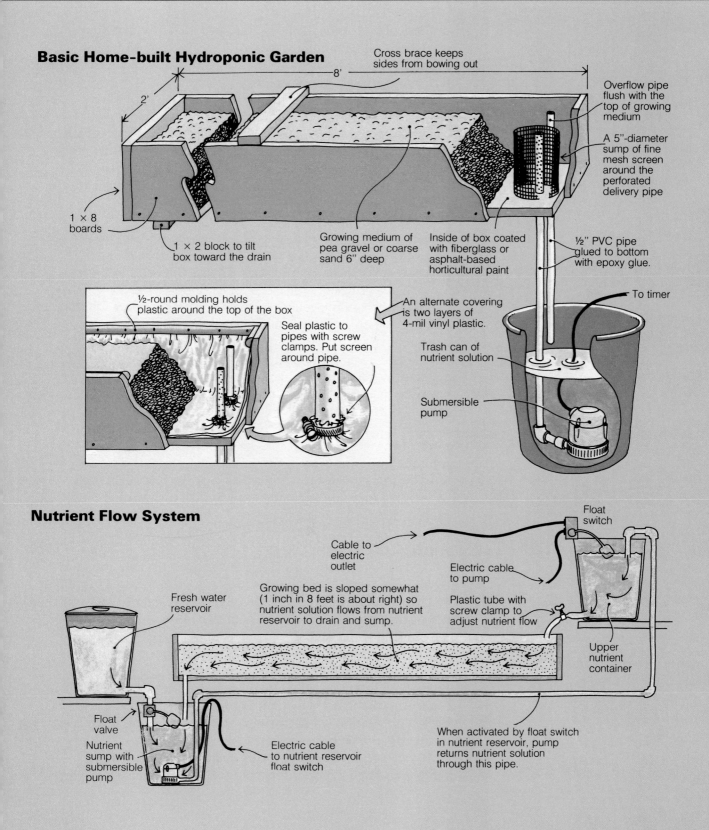

Cross brace keeps sides from bowing out

8'

2'

Overflow pipe flush with the top of growing medium

A 5"-diameter sump of fine mesh screen around the perforated delivery pipe

1 × 8 boards

1 × 2 block to tilt box toward the drain

Growing medium of pea gravel or coarse sand 6" deep

Inside of box coated with fiberglass or asphalt-based horticultural paint

½" PVC pipe glued to bottom with epoxy glue.

½-round molding holds plastic around the top of the box

Seal plastic to pipes with screw clamps. Put screen around pipe.

An alternate covering is two layers of 4-mil vinyl plastic.

To timer

Trash can of nutrient solution

Submersible pump

Nutrient Flow System

Float switch

Cable to electric outlet

Electric cable to pump

Growing bed is sloped somewhat (1 inch in 8 feet is about right) so nutrient solution flows from nutrient reservoir to drain and sump.

Plastic tube with screw clamp to adjust nutrient flow

Fresh water reservoir

Upper nutrient container

Float valve

Nutrient sump with submersible pump

Electric cable to nutrient reservoir float switch

When activated by float switch in nutrient reservoir, pump returns nutrient solution through this pipe.

minutes of your time each day will keep such a garden flourishing—even less with automation. An extraordinary variety of plants can be grown this way, including a large selection that will not grow outdoors in many climates.

This growing method won't eliminate all work, however. Plants grown hydroponically respond rapidly to poor growing conditions and must be inspected closely and frequently. Setting up the system takes time, too. Boxes must be built or bought to hold the mix, pipes must be installed, and pumps hooked up. Once the system is installed, it must be carefully maintained.

A Basic System

A basic hydroponic system can be made from ordinary household items and set up within an hour. Although simple, it is as effective as the more sophisticated systems. You need nothing more than a dishpan, some clean gravel or coarse sand, a length of plastic or rubber hose, a bucket, and a bottle of nutrient solution.

Cut a hole in a dishpan and a bucket, near the bottom. Insert one end of a six-foot section of hose into the hole in the dishpan and the other end into hole in the bucket and seal both ends in place with epoxy glue. Move this hydroponic garden to a sunny protected spot. Fill the dishpan with 6 to 8 inches of pea gravel and plant it, with green peppers for example. Pour the nutrient solution into the bucket and raise the bucket until the pea gravel in the dishpan is submerged in solution. After no more than 30 minutes, lower the bucket, tilt the dishpan down, and let the solution from the dishpan drain back into the bucket. Do this once in the morning and once at night, and you will have more peppers than you can eat.

Automated System

The system described above is effective, but it requires attention twice a day. A more advanced system with a small electric pump and timer eliminates both the daily obligation and the danger of forgetting. The basic principle—saturation followed by drainage—remains the same.

This larger automated system requires a growing bed (comparable to the dishpan) and a nearby sump, such as a large plastic garbage can or bucket. A submersible electric pump plugged into a timer runs the nutrient solution into the growing tray at a set time. The solution drains from the tray back into the sump. Later in the day, the process is repeated.

A wide variety of containers are available for hydroponic gardening, ranging from this simple dishpan arrangement to vinyl-

Above: Clips hold tomato plants to string supports without cutting into the stems.

Above left: Electric controls automatically fill hydroponic bed with nutrient solution.

Left: In hydroponic gardening, a nutrient solution is pumped through a soilless growing medium such as pea gravel or clay pebbles.

lined wooden boxes to fiberglass growing beds. Most work through this pump-and-sump technique, in which the growing bed is drenched in nutrients and quickly drained. In other systems, the solution is fed to the roots from below (the subirrigation technique) or flows slowly but steadily in a much smaller quantity (nutrition film technique, or NFT).

Starting a Hydroponic System

Once the bed, pump, and sump are in place, the bed must be filled with a planting medium so that the plants can anchor themselves. In this case, the medium is aggregate. The most common form of aggregate, and by far the most trouble-free, is medium-coarse pea gravel, about ¼ to ⅜ inch in size, and free of calcium or limestone.

Nutrient solutions are also necessary. One of the advantages of hydroponics is that you know your plants are receiving all the nutrients they need, provided you have the right mix and are changing it as needed. Using a commercial nutrient formula is much easier than creating your own. To find the nutrient mix and the changing frequency that work best in your setup, try out different formulas for a week at a time and see if the plants show any signs of wilt. Once you have settled on a particular mix, gradually extend the time between changing the solution, watching the plants for signs of stress.

The formula must be checked for pH balance after it is poured over the aggregate, using any commercial pH test kit. An ideal growing level is slightly acid, with a pH of 6.5 to 7. If it is above 7 it is too alkaline and should have a little white vinegar added to increase the acidity. If it is too acid, adding baking soda will increase the alkalinity. Check the growing solution every 3 days while it is running through the aggregate.

Special sanitary precautions are necessary to avoid fungus and diseases that can spread rapidly among the roots. Serious gardeners often change shoes and slip on clean coveralls before entering a hydroponic greenhouse and, to prevent infection of the plants by tobacco mosaic virus, forbid smoking or chewing tobacco near the growing area. Use only chlorinated water, well water, or heat-sanitized pond or rainwater to mix up the nutrient solutions. Sanitize the nutrient solutions and lines occasionally with a disinfectant (see below).

Hydroponic Planting

Once the setup is complete, it's time to plant. Larger seeds that will not wash away can be sprouted directly in the growing box. Set them into the aggregate by making a small hole with your finger. For tiny seeds, remove the bottoms of small paper cups and place

Below: It is important to maintain the pH balance in a hydroponic garden.

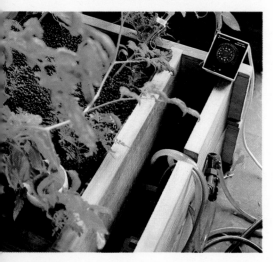

Left: Hydroponic beds can be placed inside, outside, or in a greenhouse. They are ideal for growing vegetables such as beans and tomatoes (shown here) because closely grouped plants will yield a large crop.

them in the growing bed. Fill them with a mixture of gravel and vermiculite, to hold more moisture, and set the seeds in them. Seeds can also be germinated between two damp paper towels and the sprouts transplanted later.

Soil-grown seedlings can be transplanted directly to the growing mix, but even if the roots are washed, these seedlings increase the risk of infecting other plants with fungi.

The planting bed should be filled and drained twice a day, but during dry, hot summer days you may have to increase this to three or four times a day. The growing medium should remain damp, like a wrung-out washcloth, at all times. Check periodically to see that the solution level remains 90 percent water, or the nutrient salts may become too concentrated and burn the roots.

Finally, flood the growing container with fresh water every 2 weeks. This washes away the buildup of residual nutrient salts that could eventually damage the roots.

Maintaining the System

Even if there are no signs of plant disease, a hydroponic bed should be sterilized at least once a year. If plants are attacked by disease in the interim, remove them and sterilize the bed completely.

Using a freshly prepared solution of 1 part liquid chlorine or household bleach to 10 parts water, plug the end drain hole and fill the box until the growing aggregate is completely submerged. Let soak for 24 hours, then drain and throw away the chlorine solution. Flood and drain the box with fresh water three times a day for the next 2 days, and plant again.

The plants in a hydroponic garden cannot survive on nutrients alone. They have the same needs as plants growing in pots. These include ample light and correct temperature (most plants do well at 65°F to 75°F). Follow the manufacturer's directions in changing the nutrient medium, and check the pH level frequently.

You can grow almost any plant you like in your hydroponic tank. Many will grow so luxuriantly, in fact, that you may find you've planted too closely. When you start your first crop of any plant, give each one lots of room and alternate slow-growing plants with fast-growing ones.

GF lith & pinx in Horto Van Houtteano

Propagation Techniques

Collecting plants is no different from collecting art, furniture or clothes—increased knowledge tends to lead to rarefied tastes and subsequently higher prices. So once you're hooked, indoor gardening can be an expensive hobby. Propagation is one way to hold down the costs and at the same time intimately involve you in the entire cycle of plant growth.

Starting new plants from old ones offers several benefits. You can multiply a few plants into a sizeable collection as well as increase the numbers of a favorite specimen. If a plant is difficult or expensive to buy, you can produce your own by taking cuttings from friends' collections. And you can repay those same friends with gifts reproduced from plants in your collection.

Most houseplants are easiest to propagate through cuttings, which are right there for the taking and don't cost a thing. All you need is the knowledge of the correct techniques, a minimal investment in propagating materials, a little time and effort, and the patience to wait for a cutting to reach maturity. As long as you give a plantlet some growing time before you expect it to stand in for its parent and play the same space-filling role, you will find that propagation adds an entirely new dimension to the enjoyment of growing plants.

On the following pages, you will find discussions on how to propagate from stem, leaf, and root cuttings as well as how to divide plants, separate plantlets, perform air layering, germinate seeds, and grow ferns from spores.

The correct propagation method to use depends on both the plant and your personal preference. If in doubt, check The Gallery of Houseplants. Under each individual plant listing in that chapter, you will find the recommended propagation method.

Where did you come from, baby dear?
Out of the everywhere into the here.

At the Back of the North Wind,
George MacDonald, 1824-1905

Cuttings

Inducing a cutting to form roots is the most popular method of vegetative propagation. It is an easy way to duplicate the attractive features of the original plant, as the new plant is genetically identical to the original. The new plant is called a clone; they can be grown from parts of stems, leaves, and roots. Cuttings can be placed in a rooting medium, in water, or in potting mix until the plantlets are large enough to move to individual pots. Prepare the rooting medium before you take the cutting from the plant, regardless of what technique you're using.

Rooting media

Work in an area out of direct sunlight. Before you make the cutting, have the container and the rooting medium at hand. Cuttings shouldn't be left out for more than a few minutes or they may wither. Various rooting media may be used. The medium should be light and porous, hold a lot of water, and be coarse enough to allow air to circulate through it and reach the plant's roots. One of the best rooting media is a mixture that is 1 part sand and 1 part sphagnum peat moss. You can also use straight vermiculite, perlite, milled sphagnum moss, or a mixture of 10 parts perlite to 1 part peat moss. Do not use potting soil as a rooting medium; it is not loose enough for immature roots. Wet the rooting medium and let it drain.

Plastic pots are preferable to clay pots because they retain moisture longer. A clear plastic box also makes an excellent propagator for multiple cuttings. Use a heated ice pick or awl to punch a few ventilation holes in the top, add 2 inches of rooting medium to the bottom, moisten, then insert the cuttings. Replace the lid and set the box in a bright, warm place out of direct sunlight. A similar propagating box can be made from a seed flat or fruit box, covered by a sheet of polyethylene film held up by wire coat hangers or by a sheet of glass. Be careful not to overwater, as these rooting boxes have no drainage holes.

Use your index finger or a pencil to make a hole in the rooting medium, insert the bare stem portion of the cutting, and put soil around it until it is firmly in place. Cover with glass or plastic (making sure that it doesn't touch the foliage) and set it in a warm, light place with no direct sun. Since the cuttings initially have no roots and can't supply the leaves with water, they must not dry out. Water once or twice a day, particularly if you don't use a plastic or glass cover. Be careful not to waterlog the growing medium, however, because this will lead to root rot.

Another popular method for rooting cuttings is to place them in a glass of water until roots have formed, then transplant into a soilless mix. Rooting occurs more quickly when individual cuttings are placed in separate glasses. Several plant species that root readily in water can remain there permanently if fed frequently with liquid plant food; tradescantia (wandering Jew), arrowhead, and philodendron can easily be grown this way (see the discussion of hydroponic culture that starts on page 118).

Many perennials and foliage plants, such as columneas and begonias, root so easily that cuttings can be placed directly in their final containers. Given reasonable humidity, a porous soil mix, and ample water at the start, they will root in weeks and produce a mature container plant in one season.

Left: This healthy spider plant, handsomely displayed on a pedestal, has several plantlets that are ready to start life on their own. Do this by rooting them either in water or a light, porous rooting medium. (For more on plantlets, see page 134.)

Stem cuttings

Using a sharp knife, shears, or a razor blade, remove a leafy stem that is 1 to 6 inches long. Cut it at an angle just below a node—the joint from which the leaf stalk arises—and trim the stem with a clean cut about ⅛ of an inch above the lowest leaf node. Make sure the cutting has at least one node.

Strip off all but the top two or three sets of leaves. If the leaves are small and bunched together, you may leave a few more; if the leaves are very large, retain only the last two and cut them in half with scissors. Try to leave about 2 square inches of leaf surface on each cutting—this may be several small leaves or only a part of one large one.

Although some gardeners routinely dip all cuttings in powdered rooting hormone, this step is not usually necessary and may actually inhibit fast-rooting plants such as coleus or Swedish ivy. Plants with slightly woody stems, such as fuchsia and miniature rose, are more likely to benefit from use of a rooting hormone.

Right: Take cuttings from a geranium using scissors or a sharp knife. Remove the lower leaves as well as any excessive top growth. With a pencil, make a hole in a moistened soilless medium, insert the trimmed cutting into the hole, and cover the cutting with a plastic cup or a staked plastic bag. Remove the plastic cover after a few days.

Herbaceous Plant Cuttings

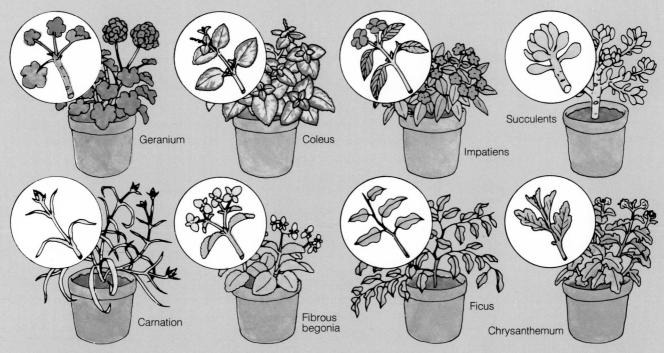

Geranium

Coleus

Impatiens

Succulents

Carnation

Fibrous begonia

Ficus

Chrysanthemum

Herbaceous plants are among the easiest plants to propagate; a selection of them is illustrated above. Cuttings from plants with fibrous or succulent stems should be air dried before planting. This helps prevent the transmission of disease from the soil.

Basic Techniques

Make cuttings 3 to 5 inches long; cut just below a node (where the leaf joins the stem).

Strip off the bottom leaves. The top leaves are necessary for root formation.

Dust the end with hormone powder. This is not absolutely necessary, but helps promote vigorous root growth.

Stick and firm the cutting in the soil mix with the leaves just above the soil.

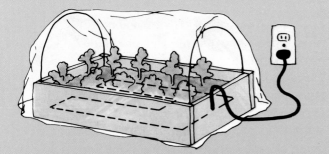

Herbaceous cuttings root readily if given bottom heat and constant high humidity. An electric heating cable (see page 113) in the bottom of a flat, plus a plastic cover, works well.

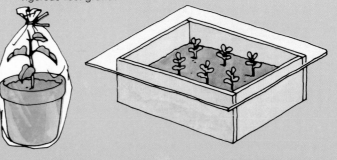

For propagating just a few cuttings, a pot in a plastic bag or a cutting box with a glass cover will provide the high humidity beneficial to the root development of the cuttings. Be sure to open the bag or remove the cover for a few hours every day to allow fresh air to circulate.

Above: Some plants can be propagated from a single leaf. To do this, use a broken leaf, or cut one off the parent plant. Make a diagonal cut at the base of the stem with a sharp knife. Place cutting in a moistened growing medium and cover it with plastic for a few days.

Leaf cuttings

Some plants have the amazing ability to propagate from a single leaf cutting. The African violet is well-known for this characteristic, but the same technique works equally well for rex begonias, gloxinias, sedums, kalanchoes, and even some philodendrons and peperomias.

Certain species will produce new plants from only a part of a leaf if the piece contains a part of the midrib. Cape primrose (*Streptocarpus* species) will do this when leaf pieces are simply laid on top of the rooting medium.

Root cuttings

Some plants can be propagated from latent buds in their roots. Relatively few houseplants are propagated this way; they include the edible fig and the popular ti plant (*Cordyline terminalis*).

Bouvardia longiflora is a showy plant that was popular in Victorian gardens but is now rare. It is very difficult to propagate from stem cuttings, but segments of its roots will quickly produce new plants in spring. Simply set the root pieces vertically in the rooting medium. The end that was closest to the crown should be at the top.

Tree and shrub cuttings

Most trees and shrubs can be propagated from softwood or hardwood cuttings. Softwood describes this year's growth which should be taken early or midseason. Hardwood describes the growth at the end of the season.

The condition of the stem tissue determines how easily a cutting will root. Softwood cuttings usually succeed when the plants are growing rapidly; after this first flush of growth, they are much more difficult to root. The best time to take a cutting is when the stem begins to harden, or when it snaps off easily instead of bending.

Plants that can be propagated well from softwood cuttings include flowering maple, gardenia, and rose. They should be kept in a cool, bright, and airy atmosphere, with no direct sun until roots have formed. It is also important to give the cuttings plenty of moisture. Some growers use a mist system with jets timed to mist the cuttings every few minutes.

Hardwood cuttings are usually made in autumn, some time after frost. Dip the base of each cutting in rooting hormone before planting. Cover with plastic or glass and keep moderately cool (60°F to 70°F).

One of the best places to root hardwood cuttings is in a cool basement equipped with a fluorescent light garden.

Bottom heat source

Nearly all cuttings benefit from the addition of bottom heat. They will grow best if you keep the top of the plant cool (55°F to 65°F) and the bottom warm (70°F to 75°F). Experiment with different locations to find the one that works best for cuttings. Many gardeners have had success with flats placed on top of the refrigerator or on a gas dryer in the laundry room (the pilot light provides bottom heat).

Electric heating mats and heating coils are also available at many garden supply stores. If you intend to root cuttings regularly, consider constructing a bottom-heated bench. If you install a heating source, adjustable ventilation, and automatic misting, you can leave cuttings unattended for a few days.

Problems

Rot is the most common problem for cuttings, so renew the rooting medium with fresh materials every 6 months, if it's in continuous use. Fallen leaves and rotted stems should be removed promptly. If the mix is constantly wet, try using pure perlite. If it dries out too quickly, add fine peat moss in the proportion of $\frac{1}{10}$ to $\frac{1}{5}$ of the total mix.

The season of the year also has an effect on the rooting of cuttings. Many species simply won't root in winter. As you will note from the instructions given in the Gallery of Houseplants, some plants root only from cuttings taken from new shoots (softwood cuttings). If a cutting fails to root, or if the new plant dies, try it again a few weeks later.

Transplanting Cuttings

The time needed for rooting varies from 1 to 6 weeks, depending on the plant. You can tell that roots have begun to grow when the foliage perks up and the plant puts out new growth. You can also test by tugging gently on the cutting; if it doesn't pull out of the soil readily, you know it has rooted.

Remove the plastic cover after the cutting has rooted, at first for an hour or two daily and then for several hours. Then discard the cover and move the plant to a permanent container.

The best way to determine when the plant is ready to be transplanted is by gently lifting it out of the rooting medium and observing the root length. The roots should not be more than an inch long when you transplant; otherwise, they may tear off.

Move new plants out of the sterile rooting medium and into soil as soon as possible, since the rooting medium holds no nutrients to feed the plants. Be sure the container is the right size and not too large for the cutting (see page 92).

Division

Some plants are easiest to propagate by division. These are plants whose stems (which in some cases are actually elongated leaf blades) grow in tight clumps. Examples are the cast iron plant, papyrus, ferns, many begonias, cluster-forming succulents (like certain sedums and crassulas), African violets, and many marantas. When multiple stems emerge from the base of a plant, you can use division to propagate them. Foliage plants should be divided in early spring, when the plants are just beginning to produce new growth. Flowering plants are best divided during their dormant periods. Division is not a delicate technique. Remove the plant from its container and divide the rootball with a sharp knife, a sharpened spade, or whatever works best. Some plants (such as cane palms) may have to be sawn apart, but others may be gently broken apart by hand. (Don't worry about damaging the plants or treating the cuts, just replant or repot the parent.) Each division should include some of the main root and stem system. Plant the divisions immediately in permanent containers with potting soil and water thoroughly. Keep them in bright light but out of direct sun; water frequently until they root. When they appear upright and healthy, place them in a permanent location.

Offsets

Offsets are new plants that form at the base of the old one and can be broken off and planted to form new plants. Many succulents and bromeliads produce secondary growths from dormant buds on the main stem, near ground level. These growths, or rosettes, can completely surround the central growth of the plant and are ready to take over when it dies. They can be cut off close to the main stem and placed in an appropriate rooting environment. For most succulents and bromeliads, this means setting the rosette in a slightly smaller pot amid pieces of fir bark. Provide the temperature and light conditions that the plant grows best in, and new roots will form quickly. The screw pine (*Pandanus veitchii*), a foolproof houseplant, can be propagated this way.

Bulbs

Many plants, such as tulips and narcissus, produce new bulbs that can also be divided. After flowering, the foliage of most bulbous plants continues to grow in order to produce food for storage in the bulbs and bulblets for the next season. The foliage begins to yellow as the plants enter their dormant period. When this happens, withhold water until all the foliage has died back. Then you can dig the plant out of the container and divide the bulb or remove the small bulblets that may have formed beside the parent bulb. It may take several years for a plant started from a bulblet to become large enough to produce a flower. Bulbs of the scaly type (Easter lilies, for example) can be increased by peeling off one or two layers of scales and laying them on the rooting medium. Dust the scales with fungicide and a rooting powder and seal them in a plastic bag filled with damp vermiculite. Keep the bag at room temperature until bulblets form—about 2 months—and then cool them in the refrigerator for another 2 months before planting.

Tubers

Many houseplants have a thickened stem or root, modified for food storage, from which leaves and flowers grow. Corms, rhizomes, and tubers are examples. Timing is very important in propagating these plants. If they have a dormant period, propagate when the plant is about to send up green shoots.

Tuber division works for large specimens of gloxinia, tuberous begonia, and caladium. After the eyes have begun to swell in the spring and are clearly visible, simply cut the tuber into pieces, being sure that every section has a bud. Dust the cut surface with a fungicide (such as thiram), and plant each piece just under the surface of a moist rooting medium. Provide air movement to reduce the chance of fungus or bacterial rot; if you see rot beginning, cut off the infected surface and start over.

The lovely gloriosa lily (*Gloriosa rothschildiana*) produces cigar-shaped tubers that can be broken into pieces and replanted. Transvaal daisies (*Gerbera jamesonii*) can be propagated by removing all the leaves in late winter and exposing the top half of the rhizome. As new growth begins, sever the rhizome into segments (each containing a leaf bud) and carefully separate them, including their roots, for repotting. Replant immediately just under the surface of the soil. Rhizomes of epiphytic plants and of rhizome-forming orchids can also be divided.

When growth begins in spring, propagate aroids (like the familiar philodendron) by removing both the leaves and the aerial roots from a stem or cane section containing several nodes. Partially plant this section in the rooting medium; it should root quickly. Ferns that make rhizomes (such as rabbit's foot fern and *Polypodium aureum*) can also be rooted this way, if given bottom heat and high humidity.

Theoretically, plants with corms, such as gladiolus and acidanthera, can be divided, but getting a bud in each division is tricky. It is easiest to use the many small new corms, called cormels, that form around the original plant. Separate them from the parent corm and plant separately, about 2 inches deep.

Above: Bromeliads can be propogated by the division of offsets from the parent plant. Slice through the soil with a sharp knife, making sure you take some of the basal growth and roots. Pot the division in its own container and provide it with the same growing conditions as the ones for the parent plant. Water the cup formed by the bromeliad leaves and, very infrequently, moisten the roots.

Plantlets

Several common houseplants reproduce by sending out miniature new plants on runners or shoots. These include spider plant, rosary vine, flame violet, and some species of African violet. These plantlets can be separated from the parent to form new plants.

Root by filling a small pot with moist rooting medium and placing it alongside the parent plant. Lay the plantlet on the soil in the new pot without severing the runner, and hold it in place with a hairpin or wire. Active new growth will signal that the young plant has rooted and can be severed from the parent. Alternatively, the runner can be clipped off and the base of the plantlet inserted into a moist propagating medium. Cover with glass or plastic film until new roots have formed.

Right: It is not always necessary to remove a plantlet to get it to root. Plantlets formed on the runners or shoots of the spider plant (above) and the piggyback plant (below) can be pinned into moist soil in a pot. Leave them growing alongside the parent plant until they are rooted.

Air Layering

Air layering makes it possible to root a stem without removing it from the plant. The great advantage of air layering is that the original plant supplies the cutting with water and nutrients while the roots are forming on the new growth. Daily maintenance is not necessary.

This technique allows the gardener to root cuttings without elaborate equipment or even exact knowledge of the normal propagation technique for the particular species. It also can provide an immediate and large specimen plant.

Air layering is especially useful for salvaging leggy plants that do not have lower leaves. However, the method does require patience, since it may take several months for the air-layered cut to form new roots.

With a sharp knife, make a cut about three-fourths of the way through a stem and insert a thin piece of wood (like a matchstick) to hold the cut open. Wrap the stem with a handful of coarse wet sphagnum moss, cover with polyethylene kitchen wrap, and secure with tape or rubber bands above and below the cut.

Eventually, new roots will form in the moss. If months go by before rooting occurs, you may have to wet the moss by poking a small hole in the wrap and squirting water inside. If the cutting fails to root, open up the wrapping, nick the stem, dust the cut with rooting hormone, and retie.

Above: To air layer a plant, cut into, but not through, the stem with a sharp knife and insert a wedge to keep the cut open. Cover the cut with damp moss and wrap it in plastic. When roots appear, cut off the stem and pot the rooted plant.

Above: Plastic bags are very useful propagation materials—they can be used as miniature greenhouses. When sealed firmly, drops of moisture form on the inside creating a humid atmosphere for seeds and cuttings. Prevent the bag from touching a plant by using stakes or a simple wire frame.

Opposite: Coleus is simple to grow from seed. It is also fun because the plants that result from a package of mixed seed can be any of a rainbow of possible color variations.

Seeds

A number of excellent houseplants can be propagated only from seed. Single-trunk palms, florist's cyclamen, and many annuals used in hanging baskets fall into this category, as do such herbs as parsley, chervil, sweet basil, marjoram, and summer savory. As an experiment, try starting citrus plants from seeds that have been washed and allowed to dry (lemon, lime, orange, and citron all make lovely houseplants). If you have children, you can delight them by planting a few dry peas or beans, or unroasted peanuts, all of which are seeds. Under the right conditions, they will burst into growth.

A seed is a tiny plant waiting for the right conditions to propel it into its life cycle. For germination, it needs a pathogen-free growing medium, proper warmth and moisture, and adequate light. A few standard houseplants are easily raised from seed, such as asparagus fern and primroses, but most tropical plants require time, skill, and heated conditions for success.

Houseplant seeds are available from garden centers and through a selection of quality mail-order nurseries. They may be sown by the same methods used for outdoor plants, with bottom heat (70°F to 75°F) added to expedite germination. An easy way to start seeds is to sow them in moistened vermiculite or milled sphagnum moss. Many growers sow them in a 1-inch layer of medium-grade sand. Place the seeds on the sand and cover them with a thin layer of coarser sand to hold them in place when they are watered. All these supplies are available at garden centers.

For containers, use flats, small pots, styrofoam fruit jugs, cut-off milk cartons, or plastic egg trays with small holes punched in the bottom with a needle. Small plastic or styrofoam greenhouses – trays with clear plastic covers – make excellent seed propagators. Large seeds with hard coats should be nicked with a file and soaked in water until the coat softens, and then planted. Slow-germinating seeds (all species of the carrot family, including parsley and chervil, for instance) also benefit from a day or two of soaking.

Sow seeds sparingly so that seedlings don't get crowded. Scatter tiny, dustlike seeds on top of a moist growing medium. Cover larger seeds to a depth twice their own diameter. Firm the growing medium around the seed by pressing gently. Label each type of seed with its name, date planted, and any other information. (It may also be useful to keep the seed packets so you can refer to them for information on transplanting and suggested growing conditions.) Water lightly and slip the seed tray into a plastic bag or cover it with paper or glass. The seed packet will indicate whether light or darkness is required for germination. Follow the

directions and check seeds daily, watering when necessary. If you are growing exotic tropical houseplants, be prepared to wait—some seeds take several years to germinate!

When seedlings emerge, move them to brighter light. The first two leaves to appear are generally not true leaves but cotyledons, which nourish the stem tip and the true leaves that follow. Wait for true leaves to appear before placing the seedlings in sunshine, then give them the same light you would give the mature plant. When seedlings are 3 to 4 weeks old, fertilize them every 2 weeks with a diluted liquid solution of fertilizer (one-third to one-fourth the regular strength.)

Transplant seedlings when they have at least four true leaves. Dig them out carefully and place them into individual small pots filled with an appropriate potting mix.

Plants that can be grown from seed

Avocado (*Persea*)
Calceolaria
Chives (*Allium shoenoprasum*)
Citrus (but not for fruit)
Coleus
Impatiens
Nasturtium (*Tropaeolum*)
Nicotiana
Mango (peel outer husk; half-bury seed upright)
Petunia
Salvia

Other houseplants may be grown from seed, but most are either easier to propagate vegetatively or the seed requires special treatment. If you do decide to try a more challenging seed, try to learn its needs first. Many specialty seed sources will tell you what they are, as will horticulture texts or local plant societies. Be sure you know whether the seed should be covered or sown on the surface, since some seeds need light to germinate. Learn how long you can expect to wait for germination. Some species can take months to show first growth.

Finally, see if the seeds must be treated before they will germinate. Some require stratification, which is cold treatment in the refrigerator for 6 weeks or longer at 35°F to 40°F. Other seeds have a coat so tough that it must be broken before the seed can germinate. This treatment, called scarification, is achieved by nicking the seed coat with a file or sandpaper.

Seed Starting Accessories

Peat pellets

expand when dampened

Peat pots

Plastic pots

Growing blocks

Electric warming cable (in flat) or propagating mat will keep soil at the proper temperature for germination.

Propagating mat

Warming cable

A stand with several tiers of fluorescent lights

One-step Method

Sow seeds, two at a time, directly into plastic pots, peat pots, growing blocks, or Jiffy-7 pellets. Water thoroughly and place on a tray in a plastic bag. They'll be ready to transplant when about 6 inches high.

Two-step Method

Step 1.

Sow seeds in tray of damp vermiculite. Set seeds about ¼" deep; cover; and water lightly. Slip tray into a plastic bag and keep at about 75°. No water is needed until after germination and then just keep it slightly damp.

PETUNIA

Step 2.

Press soil around roots and stem.

When the first true leaves are formed, transplant to peat pots.

Put pots on a tray and in a plastic bag until ready for hardening off.

Growing Ferns from Spores

Unlike most other plants, ferns produce dustlike spores, not seeds. and are challenging to germinate. Look on the undersides of the fronds for ripe spore cases and brush the spores into an envelope. Allow them to dry for a few weeks.

To germinate the spores, place a brick in a transparent plastic box and half-fill the box with water. Sprinkle ½ inch of milled peat moss on top of the brick. Wet the brick and moss, and dust the fern spores on top of the moss; cover the box with glass or plastic to retain moisture. Check the water level every few days while the spores are germinating and add water when necessary.

Place the box in a dimly lit spot that is not too warm and leave it there for several months. Eventually, a mossy mat will appear on top of the covered brick. When the mat looks strong, break off 1-inch pieces and plant them on the surface of a mixture of peat moss and vermiculite in a pot. Keep the pot moist and covered for several more months or until small ferns appear. When they are 2 to 3 inches high, transplant them to individual pots.

Opposite: Boston ferns make handsome houseplants whether they are displayed in hanging pots or placed on a window ledge. Here, two ferns grow happily beside shuttered windows. The well-designed grouping is an example of how plants can relate to each other without appearing overcrowded. The arrangement also shows how effective it is to relate plants to furnishings. Note how the size of the ferns matches the bowl of the tub chair and how the radiating spokes in the wickerwork repeat the pattern formed by the plant growth.

Below: Growing ferns from spores takes time and patience—read the directions above— but the results are worthwhile. The young staghorn fern (right) was recently transplanted into a nest of sphagnum moss.

1 Passiflora caerulea 2 Passiflora alato-caerulea 3 Tacsonia pinnatistipula

Flowering Houseplants

If you want to add color and pattern to your indoor garden, there are several foliage plants that fill the bill. But a flowering houseplant is something special that will bring a burst of joy to the most cheerless room. However, like most good things in life, joy doesn't come without some effort.

Flowering houseplants need more water than foliage plants, especially if they are positioned where the humidity is low and the temperature high. In fact, many plants bud only when they are stressed by decreased watering. Let plants dry out, but don't withhold water if they wilt severely and no buds appear. Once a plant has been induced to flower, it should be watered thoroughly and often.

Moisture stress also encourages a pot-bound houseplant to flower. Transplanting disrupts the growing routine and gives the roots more room, which inhibits flowering. Instead of transplanting just before flowering, replace the top third of the soil with new mix until the blooming period is over.

Pruning and shaping enhance flower production, but only if there is enough foliage left for buds to form. Don't remove flower buds when pruning— pinch back the flowers after they've bloomed.

Often, a plant that refuses to bloom isn't receiving enough light. And certain species (such as gloxinias, poinsettias, and chrysanthemums) flower only after constant exposure to daylight.

Soil acidity is another factor that affects blooming. If the pH level is below 5 or over 8, the plant is unlikely to bloom. Furthermore, plants that are very young or dormant can't be rushed into flowering.

Nurturing a flowering houseplant may sound like a lot of work. But don't let that deter you. There are few aspects of gardening that give more joy than watching a bud form, open, slowly take shape, and then burst into full bloom.

Clean as a lady,
cool as glass,
fresh without fragrance
the tulip was.

Tulip,
Humbert Wolfe, 1885-1940

Right: A sunny kitchen windowsill is a convenient spot for herbs to winter indoors. Colorful cans make appropriate containers. Many herbs are annuals, but the ones that survive can be replanted outside as soon as the weather allows.

Opposite: You have nothing to lose by bringing annuals indoors—you know that they are going to fade anyhow. When carefully transplanted, alyssum, ageratum, and petunias will all grow indoors.

Below: If you grow outdoor plants in containers, it is an easy job to move them inside for a special occasion. It is also possible to extend the flowering season by bringing plants inside when the outside temperatures start to drop. The geranium can be moved to or from the balcony to add a splash of color.

Bringing Plants in from the Garden

Many tender perennial flowers grown outdoors in warm weather as annuals can be brought inside before a frost for an extended flowering season. They will, however, require a sunny indoor location and moist air. On a sunny windowsill, under fluorescent lights, or in a home greenhouse, some plants will bloom indefinitely. Others merely yield a few more flowers before they die.

Plants can be dug out of the garden and potted, although they will suffer more shock than the potted plant that is simply transferred indoors. The best time to dig up and pot a plant is 2 to 3 weeks before frost is expected.

Water the plant a day or two before you plan to dig it up. This will make your work easier and will protect the plant from root damage. Using either a sturdy trowel or a spade, dig up the plant with a good chunk of earth surrounding the root system and follow the potting instructions given on page 92.

Leave the newly potted plants outdoors in a shady, moist spot for several days so they can become acclimatized to the container and the lower light. Scrutinize and groom these plants as carefully as your indoor plants that have vacationed outside.

What Flowers to Save

Annual or tender perennial flowers that send up sturdy new shoots whenever the tops are cut back are the best to save. These include wax and ever-flowering begonias, petunia, and nicotiana.

With careful transplanting and culture, you may be able to cultivate geranium, heliotrope, ageratum, lobelia, French marigold, lantana, impatiens, torenia, browalia, sage, sweet alyssum, and verbena as houseplants.

Once these plants are indoors, keep them moist. After they have adjusted and begun to grow again, feed monthly with a liquid fertilizer and clip off spent blooms.

You can bring in frost-sensitive bulbs such as caladium, achimenes, tuberous begonia, and amaryllis. Herbs such as borage, lemon verbena, sweet basil, marjoram, young parsley, and scented geraniums can also be potted and brought indoors.

Forcing Blooms Indoors

Day length, light intensity, and temperature all change naturally in a seasonal cycle; gardeners can imitate these changes to promote flower development. Adjusting temperature to control flowering is called forcing. Forcing is usually defined as an application of extra warmth to induce early flowering, but the full range of possibilities is far greater. Some plants are photoperiodic, which means that they will bloom only after they have been exposed to the correct ratio of light and dark periods during a day. Other species may require a cool period that imitates winter. Some may not develop flowers, even if the day length is correct, unless the temperature is also correct.

Photoperiodism

A poinsettia grown indoors will not ordinarily bloom. The controlling factor is the photoperiod, or length of time during each day that the plant is exposed to light. A poinsettia is called a short-day plant because it needs a series of short days and long nights to begin budding. The critical factor is actually the length of the night. Inside a house, plants receive light in the evening from electric bulbs, so a poinsettia grown indoors will never bloom unless you give it special treatment to mimic the long, dark nights of autumn outdoors.

To initiate flower buds that will mature by Christmastime, in late September or early October place the plant in a closet or other dark area for 12 to 16 hours a night for at least 2 weeks (preferably 6 weeks). Be careful not to open the closet door during treatment, and seal any cracks under the door. The dark periods must be total and continuous; even a small amount of light may cause sparse budding or deformed flowers.

The florist chrysanthemum industry is based on the fact that chrysanthemums are also short-day plants. Although they flower naturally only in the fall or early winter, black-cloth shading techniques make flower production possible all year. Commercial crops can thereby be made to coincide with any holiday and or seasonal needs.

Photoperiodism is a relatively recent discovery, and information for all species is not complete. Few flowers seem to be as extremely sensitive to it as chrysanthemums and poinsettias. It has been found that photoperiod adjustment can encourage flower development in many species that do not absolutely require specific photoperiods, begonias and many gesneriads for example. With long-day plants, the dark period is adjusted by providing light at night. Even short bursts of light in the middle of the night may be enough to stimulate flower formation.

Opposite: A handmade willow table serves as an appropriate plant station for a grouping of plants. A Fishtail palm and Swedish ivy, nestle around the legs of the table while a mother-in-law's tongue and cuttings from a piggyback plant form a green background for the flaming red amaryllis plants.

Below: Chrysanthumums require ten hours or less of light per day (at least 14 hours of total darkness) before they will flower.

Below: Even outdoor species of tuberous begonias will give lovely display blossoms if grown in abundant bright light. An ideal location is under a skylight.

Bottom: The episcia is a close relative of the African violet and makes a striking hanging plant. To be sure that the episcia receives enough moisture, pack damp peat moss around the base of the plant.

Vernalization

Some plants can be brought into bloom if they are placed in cool storage (45°F or lower) for several weeks. The process of using cool storage to create an artificial winter is known as vernalization. Plants that normally lose their leaves in winter, such as hydrangeas and many bulbous plants, can be kept in cool storage for several months. The cooler the area and the longer the storage, the more quickly flowers will develop when the plants are returned to normal growing temperatures. Refrigerators can be used for treatments if basements and garages are not cool enough, but a minimum of 35°F is advised to prevent frost damage. Plants in cool storage should be kept moist but not wet, and artificial light should be installed for some plant types to prevent excessive leaf drop caused by extended stays in dark areas. Even for those species that do not require cooling to produce flowers, a cool period may have an invigorating effect. This can result in healthier growth and increased flower production.

Blooming Needs of Popular Houseplants

African violets   Need long days to promote growth. Leggy stems and the absence of blooms indicate insufficient light. Older varieties bloom for 4 months and then rest for 4 months, but newer hybrids may not need a rest period. They are perfect for indoor culture because they thrive at night temperatures between 65°F and 70°F. They bloom best when their roots are crowded.

Anthuriums   Need high humidity and temperatures (80°F to 90°F). Long days encourage blooming. Low humidity or temperatures for even a few days may harm the developing flowers.

Aphelandras   Bloom best at high temperatures (75°F to 80°F) and when cut back to maintain bushiness. Long nights promote flower bud formation.

Azaleas   Belgian Indica types (florist's azaleas) like cool temperatures for growth, warmer temperatures for setting flower buds, and then cooler temperatures to mature the buds. Well-pruned plants will be bushier and produce more blooms. Plants grown outside can be moved indoors in October to bloom by December.

Begonias   *Hiemalia* and other everblooming types need lower temperatures and long nights to set buds. Tuberous and fibrous types grow best during long days. Tubers require long nights before going dormant to set new flower buds for the next year.

Bougainvilleas   Bloom best in strong light and high temperatures (70°F to 80°F). Flowers form when day and night are equal length. Plants do not like to be moved.

Bromeliads   Grow well in long days, but many, including pineapple, need long nights to set blooms. Keep warm and give plenty of light (60°F minimum at night, 75°F during the day).

Cacti   Need cool nights (45°F to 50°F) to set flower buds. Watering after a long dry period also induces blooming. They need strong light to flower properly.

Calceolarias   Like cool night temperatures (40°F to 45°F) and day temperatures 15° higher. Growing plants to a large size is difficult. Flower buds will set when given short-night treatments.

Carnations   Bloom best when given short nights. They need strong light to produce fragrant flowers.

Chrysanthemums   Need cool nights (45°F to 50°F) to set buds; warm temperatures help buds develop into blooms; 13- to 14-hour nights also help bud set. However, the combination of warm temperatures (above 68°F) and long nights prevents bud formation.

Cinerarias   Difficult plants to force into bloom indoors. They need cool nights, warm days, and good air circulation.

Citrus   Plants bloom best in strong light. Cool nights encourage compact growth.

Clerodendrums   Flower only on new growth, so prune and then fertilize to encourage new growth.

Columneas   Grow well in long days. Need cool nights (50°F to 60°F) to promote flowering.

Cyclamen   Like cool temperatures; 40°F to 50°F at night is best. Go dormant in summer and need this resting period in order to bloom well.

Cymbidiums   Give as much light as possible, but watch for burning. Dark green leaves indicate insufficient light. Cymbidiums are thermoinductive, meaning that they will not bloom if nights are too warm. Night temperatures of 50°F to 55°F are best.

Episcias   Similar to African violets, but will bloom in less light. Like long days, crowded roots, and plenty of fertilizer. Keep air around them humid.

Exacums   Need short nights to bloom well. Growing plants to attain good size indoors is difficult. Give strong light and fertilize heavily.

Felicias   Grow a large plant by pinching flowers off young plants until desired size is reached. Warm temperatures and decreased watering increase blooming. Warm temperatures and bottom heat encourage rapid growth.

Fuchsias   Need cool temperatures (50°F to 55°F at night, 68°F to 72°F during the day). Must have high humidity to perform well. Long days encourage bud set.

Gardenias   Need long, cool nights (under 65°F) to set flower buds. Buds often drop if the humidity is low, soil is too wet, or light is too low.

Geraniums   Zonals (round leaf edge) bloom in strong light and

Above: With their dark green, heart-shaped leaves and butterfly-like flowers, cyclamens are popular flowering houseplants. This plant prefers a cool room and will go dormant during the summer.

warmth. Pelargoniums (jagged leaf edge) need 12- to 13-hour nights to set flower buds, and then need long days to develop buds into flowers.

Hibiscus   Bloom best in long days and high humidity. Do not like to be moved around. Indoors, prune heavily to keep bushy.

Hoyas   Fragrant blooms form on stubby twigs that look like leafless stems. Bloom best in short nights. During winter, need rest period of decreased light, water, and fertilizer.

Hydrangeas   Need a long, cool storage period during dormancy. Strong light and warmth promote flower development. Fertilize heavily to grow plants to good size. Splitting flower stems indicate too short a cooling period.

Impatiens   Like intermediate day length. New Guinea types develop best leaf color with long days, but bloom best in intermediate days (12 hours light, 12 hours dark).

Kalanchoes   Require 6 weeks of long nights for flower bud formation. Plants bloom 3 months after long nights begin. Most

Below: Gardenia jasminodes or Cape jasmine has large, glossy, dark green leaves and produces an abundance of flowers. The heady aroma of these creamy, spiraling blossoms is sure to please everyone.

Below right: A bathroom supplies the humidity necessary to keep the orchids blooming and the bromeliad collection healthy.

succulents bloom best when given long nights to promote flower bud formation and then long days and strong light to bring buds into bloom.

Lantanas   Like high heat (75°F to 85°F) and strong light. Will bloom indoors in winter if given short nights after being kept cool and shaded the previous summer.

Marigolds   Grow best during periods with 16-hour days; they bloom best in 12- to 15-hour days. Give as much light as possible indoors.

Nasturtiums   Bloom best in long days. Need cool nights (40°F to 55°F) and day temperatures below 70°F.

Orchids   Most epiphytic (not grown in soil) orchids grow best in bright light. Should have short days and cool nights (65°F or less) to set flower buds. Usually bloom 4 months after growing conditions are right.

Petunias   Good performers indoors. Need strong light; bloom best with short nights. Need cool nights (55°F to 65°F) to promote flowering if grown indoors in winter.

Philodendrons   Will bloom if the plant is mature enough and large enough. Long nights and high humidity will encourage blooming.

Poinsettias   Require long nights for 6 weeks to form flower buds. Plants placed in dark closet for treatment in late September through October will bloom by Christmastime. Bushy plants produce more blooms. Strong light and warmth (75°F to 80°F) encourage larger plants and blooms.

Roses   Grow best with long days and warm temperatures (60°F to 65°F at night, 75°F to 80°F days). Miniature roses do very well indoors. Increased light gives flowers better color. Miniatures can be kept blooming for 8 to 9 months. Then they require a rest period of 1 to 2 months. Night temperatures during the rest period should be approximately 40°F, and plants should be shaded.

Snapdragons   Bloom best with short nights and cool temperatures. Dwarf varieties do well indoors any time of year. Seeds will germinate best if given a cooling treatment prior to planting.

Spathiphyllums   Mature healthy plants bloom best. Like crowded roots and low-nitrogen soil. Plants kept too wet may grow well but fail to bloom.

Tomatoes   Need to dry out before flowers form. Wet plants grow large but will not produce fruit. Long days promote flower formation. Like bottom heat when grown indoors out of season. Plants given excessive nitrogen may fail to bloom.

Zinnias   Need good air circulation and strong light to grow well indoors. Bloom best during long days. Dwarf varieties are easier to grow indoors.

Above: African violets—originally collected in Africa in the late 19th century—are one of the most popular flowering plants. With plenty of bright indirect light, evenly moist soil, warm temperatures, and high air humidity, African violets will bloom constantly.

Above: These bulbs have been cooled in a cold frame and are ready for forcing. However, a cold frame is not essential—bulbs can be forced in a variety of containers and mediums

Opposite above: Amaryllis is one of the most spectacular bulbs. Huge trumpet-shaped flowers make a strong statement in any room.

Opposite below: Nothing removes winter gloom like a house or courtyard full of flowers. Most of these bulbs have been forced so that they all bloom at the same time.

Forcing Bulbs

One rewarding aspect of indoor gardening is that you can persuade plants to bloom out of season. By duplicating—but shortening—the stages bulbs go through outdoors, you can have tulips, crocuses, daffodils, and hyacinths blooming indoors in the middle of winter.

Other plants that can be easily forced include Dutch iris (*Iris reticulata*), grape hyacinth, *Scilla tubergeniana, Hippeastrum, Ornithogalum,* and *Clivia.* Several hardy perennials can also be forced, along with annual flowers and branches of flowering shrubs.

Forcing Hardy Bulbs

Begin by buying the largest bulbs you can. Select only those varieties clearly marked "good for forcing." If you are buying by mail order, place your order as early as possible so that the bulbs will be delivered in early fall. If you can't plant the bulbs immediately after their arrival, store them in opened bags or boxes in a cool place (35°F to 55°F) or in the refrigerator, but for no more than a few weeks.

Plant bulbs around the beginning of October for flowers at Christmastime, in the middle of October for February flowers, and in November for March and April flowers. Use clean pots and a well-drained soil mix or synthetic soil. Pot size depends on the type and quantity of bulbs: one large daffodil or tulip bulb, or three small crocuses, can be planted in a 4- to 5-inch pot. Six tulips, daffodils, or hyacinths require an 8- to 10-inch pot. When planting several tulips in one pot, place the bulbs with the flat sides facing toward the outside of the pot so that the leaves will emerge facing outward.

Fill each pot loosely with soil mix. Place the bulbs in the pot so that their tops are even with the rim. Cover the tops of tulips, hyacinths, or smaller bulbs (like crocus) with an inch of soil, but do not cover the necks and tops of daffodils. Do not compress the soil or press the bulbs into it; the soil should remain loose so that roots can grow through it easily. After the bulbs are in, water the pots two or three times to moisten all the soil. Label each pot as you plant it, with the name of the flower and the planting date.

Most bulbs need a period of cool temperatures after potting so that they can form a vigorous root system to support healthy foliage and blooms. Some bulbs have been precooled by the producer and can be planted and forced immediately. To force bulbs that have not had this treatment, find a cool, frost-free place where they can be forced. This might be an unheated garage or basement, or an old refrigerator, where the temperature ranges from 35°F to 50°F. Keep the soil evenly moist while the plants are forming roots; check the pots weekly to see if water is needed.

At the forcing stage, the pots are brought out of the cool environment into warmth and light, triggering the formation of leaves and flowers in 3 to 4 weeks. You can start forcing the bulbs when sprouts begin to push up through the soil. Bring only a few pots indoors each week to provide blooms over a longer period, and place them in a sunny, cool (55°F to 70°F) spot. The cooler the area, the longer the flowers will last. Keep the soil moist and the bulbs away from radiators and gas heaters; flower buds will fail to open if the soil dries out severely. Bring all bulbs indoors by late February.

Problems in forcing bulbs are few. Sometimes they have basal rot. If foliage suddenly turns yellow and stops growing, give it a gentle tug. If the foliage is loose, there's a rootless rotted bulb in

Above: There may be snow and sleet outside, but a container full of daffodils brings sunshine inside. Daffodils are easy to force and, if kept in a cool room, will last a reasonable time.

Bulb Varieties for Forcing

Type	Color	Flowering Time
Crocus		
Remembrance	Purple	Winter and Spring
Purpureus grandiflorus	Purple	Winter and Spring
Flower Record	Purple	Late Winter, Spring
Victor Hugo	Purple	Winter and Spring
Peter Pan	White	Winter and Spring
Joan of Arc	White	Winter and Spring
Pickwick	Striped	Winter and Spring
Large Yellow	Yellow	Spring
Hyacinthus		
Jan Bos	Red	Winter
Pink Pearl	Pink	Winter and Spring
Lady Derby	Pink	Winter
Anne Marie	Pink	Winter
Amsterdam	Pink	Winter and Spring
Marconi	Pink	Spring
L'Innocence	White	Winter
Colosseum	White	Winter
Carnegie	White	Spring
Delft Blue	Blue	Winter
Ostara	Blue	Winter and Spring
Blue Jacket	Blue	Spring
Marle	Blue	Spring
Bismarck	Blue	Winter
Amethyst	Violet	Spring
Iris reticulata		
Harmony	Blue	Winter and Spring
Danfordiae	Yellow	Winter
Hercules	Purple	Winter and Spring
Muscari (Grape hyacinth)		
Early Giant	Blue	Winter and Spring
Narcissus		
Carlton	Yellow	Winter
Unsurpassable	Yellow	Winter and Spring
Joseph MacLeod	Yellow	Winter
Dutch Master	Yellow	Winter and Spring
Soleil d'Or	Yellow	Winter and Spring
Mt. Hood	White	Winter and Spring
Paper-white	White	Winter and Spring
Chinese Sacred Lily	White	Winter and Spring
Barrett Browning	Orange cup, white perianth	Winter and Spring
Fortune	Bicolor	Winter
Ice Follies	Cream cup, white perianth	Winter and spring
Magnet	Yellow trumpet, white perianth	Spring
Tulipa		
Bing Crosby	Red	Winter and Spring
Olaf	Red	Winter and Spring
Paul Richter	Red	Winter
Prominence	Red	Late Winter
Charles	Red	Winter
Stockholm	Red	Winter
Bellona	Yellow	Winter
Ornament	Yellow	Spring
Thule	Yellow with red	Winter
Hibernia	White	Winter and Spring
Christmas Marvel	Pink	Winter
Peerless Pink	Pink	Spring
Preludium	Pink	Winter
Kees Nelis	Red, var. with yellow or cream	Winter
Golden Eddy	Red, var. with yellow or cream	Spring
Karel Doorman	Red, var. with yellow or cream	Winter

the soil. Discard bulb and soil to prevent disease from spreading.

Bulbs will not stand forcing for a second year. Some of them, (especially tulips) are best discarded after forcing. Daffodils, however, can be transplanted into the garden in spring and will produce a full bloom again in 2 or 3 years.

Narcissus These can be forced without strenuous cooling in a semi-sunny or sunny location. Successive plantings made about 2 weeks apart, from mid-October on, provide indoor blooms from Thanksgiving to St. Patrick's Day. Plant the bulbs in a bowl with moist gravel, coarse sand, perlite, vermiculite, or moist pebbles, or pot them in a light potting mix. Plant so that only the bottom quarter is below the surface, and carefully maintain the moisture level throughout the forcing process. Keep in a cool (50°F to 60°F), dim place until roots form and shoots appear—about 2 to 3 weeks. Then gradually bring them into direct sunlight.

Hyacinths and Crocuses These bulbs will grow in water if placed in specially designed containers that hold the bulb in the top. Fill the container so that the base of the bulb is just above the water, and add water as needed to maintain this level. The water shouldn't touch the bulb, or it will rot. Change the water every 3 or 4 weeks. A small piece of charcoal in the water will deter harmful bacteria. Place the container in a dark, cool area until roots have formed (about 14 weeks) then move it into the light.

Above: Hyacinths are easy bulbs to force. The strong purple color is a handsome color accent and the aroma is heady. Growing several plants in matching containers allows you to create an impressive arrangement.

Forcing Flowering Branches

The delicate beauty of flowering apple, cherry, forsythia, pussy willow, and flowering quince branches can bring springtime indoors during those cold days of late winter. Branches, 2 to 3 feet long, should be cut during February or March when buds have formed and have begun to swell. (If cut too soon, the flowers will not open.) Smash the cut ends of the branches with a hammer to help the branches absorb more water. Place the branches in a large container of water in a moderately cool (60°F to 70°F) bright room. In about two weeks, blossoms will appear.

As with potted plants and cut flowers, heat and light promote the development of flowers while cool temperatures and darkness retard flower development and help to make the flowers last longer. To prolong the flowering period, some florists dip the stem ends into wax to seal the cut surface, and others cut a bit off the stem ends every day or so. Placing copper pennies in the vase water, dipping the stems in fruit preservative, and soaking stems in warm water and then refrigerating them are also popular practices.

Below: If you do a little shaping on a pear tree in late winter, you can have branches like these to enjoy indoors.

Above: The date when spring arrives changes from year to year, but you can insure the early arrival of spring blossoms by forcing flowering fruit branches.

Left: Flowering branches can be arranged in a vase or "planted" in a large container to simulate a living tree in your living room.

*Top: Marigolds are just one the
annuals that can be forced easily
in rooms with full sun.*

*Above: Matricaria also grows
indoors. Start it during the winter
to give as gifts or in order to get a
head's start on spring planting.*

*Above Right: Verbena is as
colorful indoors as it is outside.
Keep it in a cool, humid room
and make sure it gets a lot of
moisture.*

Forcing Annual Flowers

Some of summer's brightest annual flowers can be forced easily in
rooms with full sun and a moderately cool (60°F to 70°F), humid
atmosphere. Pot the flowers in a mixture of equal parts soil, sand,
and peat moss; keep evenly moist; and fertilize every 2 weeks.

Ageratum, sweet alyssum, dwarf balsam, browallia, and dwarf
cockscomb can be grown indoors for winter and early spring
bloom. Sow seeds in early August for these plants and for dwarf
marigolds, sweet peas, nasturtiums, and morning glories. As they
grow, transplant to individual pots, and keep moving the plants to
larger containers as they increase in size, stopping at 5- to 7-inch
containers. Provide a trellis for morning glory and sweet pea vines,
and try hanging baskets for the trailing plants.

Lobelia, nicotiana, petunia, snapdragon, torenia, and verbena
can be dug from outdoor plantings in autumn, before frost, and
carefully potted in 5- to 10-inch containers. Cut leaves and stems
back severely to encourage new growth, and keep plants in a cool,
shady place for a few days while they get accustomed to the pots.
Then place in sunlight and keep moist.

Forcing Hardy Perennials

If you have an outdoor perennial border that abounds with hosta, bleeding heart, astilbe, or lily of the valley, you may want to try forcing them in winter.

Dig vigorous clumps in early fall, trim them back, and pot in a moist mixture of soil, sand, and peat moss. Place them in an unheated garage or cool attic, where severe freezing will not occur. In midwinter, bring the pots indoors to a moderately cool (60°F to 65°F) sunny windowsill. Keep the soil evenly moist. When leaf growth becomes active, fertilize every 2 weeks with houseplant food. With luck, some of spring's loveliest flowers will appear weeks or months before their outdoor counterparts.

After forcing hardy perennials, replant them outdoors and do not force the same clumps again for at least 2 years.

Top: Gerbera grows happily beside a north window. This is one of the perennials that can be forced to bloom indoors.

Above: Hosta is another perennial that can be grown indoors by a careful and adventurous gardener.

Left: Astilbe is a plant that thrives in either shade or sun when outdoors. If you bring it inside, keep it in a cool, humid room.

Greenhouses & Solariums

Entering a greenhouse for the first time is like stepping into another world. It may be snowing outside, but inside a greenhouse you are transported to the steamy, languid tropics, surrounded by exotic arrays of orchids or lush displays of succulents.

Orchids amidst snow flurries—that is one of the advantages a greenhouse offers. In a controlled environment, you can fool Mother Nature, or at least play with her. You can dictate the length of the day with blinds or screens. With an automatic watering system, you can establish the greenhouse as either a desert or a rain forest. And with an efficient heating system, you can create a jungle. Whatever your choice, plants and flowers will thrive in an atmosphere designed for their specific needs. Here, the stubborn plant that refuses to bloom in the dining room bursts into flower. Here, you can harvest lettuce, radishes, and tomatoes in February while your neighbors bemoan the high cost and wretched quality of supermarket produce.

Today's greenhouses are simple, practical, and no longer the private domain of the wealthy. They can be added to a home or an office for a reasonable cost and, if used as solar heat collectors, can mean lower home heating bills. A greenhouse can be built wherever you have space: in a window, on a balcony, or on the roof. It can be small enough for a tiny backyard or large enough to cover several acres.

On the pages that follow, you will find some of your options, plus the steps and decisions involved in building a greenhouse. Some pages concentrate on installing effective heating, cooling, lighting, and watering systems. Others are devoted to designing and planning a greenhouse so you can produce plants, flowers, and vegetables that can be enjoyed inside your home and on your table all year round.

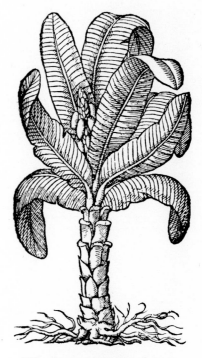

Who loves a garden loves a greenhouse too.
Unconscious of a less propitious clime,
There blooms exotic beauty, warm and snug,
While the winds whistle, and the snows descend.

William Cowper, 1731-1800

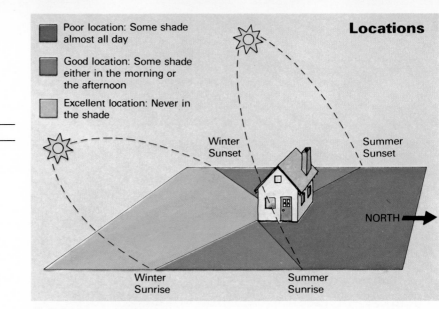

Locations

Poor location: Some shade almost all day

Good location: Some shade either in the morning or the afternoon

Excellent location: Never in the shade

Winter Sunset

Summer Sunset

NORTH

Winter Sunrise

Summer Sunrise

Basic Questions

Before you invest in a greenhouse, or in the materials to make your own, ask yourself some serious questions.

Function and Purpose   Do you see a greenhouse as display space, as growing space, or as both?

Size   How large a greenhouse do you want? Is there enough room for it on your property?

Build or Buy   Do you want a prefab or do you want to build your own? Include your time and money in this consideration. If you are a novice builder but want to construct your own, consider hiring an experienced carpenter to help you, or buy a prefabricated type that requires only assembly.

Building Permits   Do you need a building permit? Are there local design ordinances covering the buildings in which you live? Are there setback requirements on your property? In most residential areas, restrictions govern the distance of a building from property lines. The location of the greenhouse must meet all zoning and construction requirements. Your local government or building permit office can advise you and tell you what they need to grant a permit (a simple sketch is often sufficient).

Maintenance Costs   How much will it cost to maintain the greenhouse and supply water, heat, and electric light? Can you offset costs by selling the plants you grow?

Heating   The better the construction, the less the heat loss and the lower the heating bill. A layer of plastic sheeting inside creates a thermal barrier that can cut heat losses up to 40 percent. However, such sheeting greatly reduces light levels and may prevent you from growing the plants you wish. Simple solar systems can lower heating costs as well as reduce your residential heating bill.

Taxes and Rebates   Will a greenhouse increase your property tax? Ask the local building permit or tax office if the style of greenhouse you have chosen is classified as a temporary structure. If so, you may not have to pay additional taxes, and you may not even need a permit. Tax rebates can often be applied to the cost of installing solar heating devices, and it is worthwhile investigating different models and choosing among those that qualify.

Choosing the Site

Deciding where to locate your greenhouse is a critical first step. The primary consideration is sunshine. Look carefully at your property, noticing anything that will block sunlight (houses, walls, and trees). Keep in mind that in winter the sun will be considerably lower than it is in the summer. The orientation to the sun is an important factor in determining where to site your greenhouse.

The greenhouse should be placed at a distance from the light-blockingobstacles equivalent to 2½ times their height. For example, if a 10-foot-tall wall casts a shadow on your property, the greenhouse should be 25 feet away from it. However, if a nearby tree is a deciduous one, it can provide shade during hot summer days while allowing sunlight in the winter when it loses its leaves. The most important consideration is to get maximum value from winter sunlight.

Drainage is the next consideration. Try to avoid building in depressions that will catch rain and snow, or in boggy areas where the soil is constantly wet and unstable. If there is a slope behind the greenhouse, it may be necessary to put in tile or gravel ditches, or some other system to divert runoff.

Select a site that is relatively level, or that can be leveled easily. If you expect to plant directly in the soil, the ground where you build the greenhouse is an important factor. If the soil is full of rocks or clay, you may have to create raised growing beds or plan to do your gardening in containers.

The greenhouse will need water and electricity, so you must plan where to place the hookups. Locating the greenhouse close to these connections will make it easier, and cheaper, to install the utility lines.

Consider the distance you will have to walk to get from the house to the greenhouse. If you have to contend with freezing cold weather or blinding snow, a greenhouse should be close to or, better yet, attached to the house.

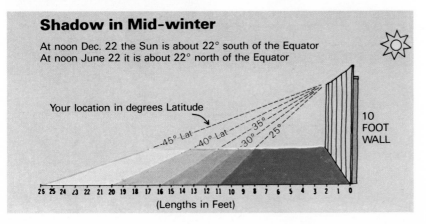

Shadow in Mid-winter

At noon Dec. 22 the Sun is about 22° south of the Equator
At noon June 22 it is about 22° north of the Equator

Your location in degrees Latitude

45° Lat   40° Lat   35°   30°   25°

10 FOOT WALL

25 25 24 23 22 21 20 19 18 17 16 15 14 13 12 11 10 9 8 7 6 5 4 3 2 1 0

(Lengths in Feet)

A-frame

Gothic

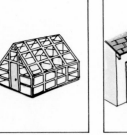
Free-standing

Attached

Above: These sketches indicate some of the more common shapes for greenhouses. Descriptions of the various types can be found on these two pages.

Above right: Two separate detached greenhouses allow the hobbyist to specialize in plants that require different atmospheric conditions.

Below Right: An attached greenhouse makes it easier to install plumbing and heating lines. It also makes it possible to enter the greenhouse directly from the house.

What Style of Greenhouse?

There are a wide variety of greenhouses you can build yourself. Here are some factors to consider before you start building. How permanent do you want it to be? Should it be attached to the house or freestanding? How much snow does your area get?

A-Frame   This type can be built on the ground, in sections, and raised into place and covered. It is quick and easy to construct, and is ideal in areas that get a lot of snow. However, there is limited head room, and proper ventilation is difficult to incorporate. Also, tall plants or vines on high supports may not fit inside.

Gothic   The laminated wood strips, make it easy to install

permanent coverings such as corrugated fiberglass.

Freestanding   This is the most common type of greenhouse. It can be built to any size and covered with anything from glass to polyethylene. The interior space layout is very practical, and there's easy access for a loaded wheelbarrow through doors at either end.

Attached   The attached greenhouse is becoming increasingly popular. It can be heated from the house, and its solar heat gains can in turn be transferred to the residence. Water and electricity are nearby, and the greenhouse is within easy reach. If open to the house, it becomes an attractive extension of the living area.

Left: As long as the sun is out, a greenhouse will trap an amazing amount of heat even on the coldest winter days. Thus, the occupants (both plants and people) are warm in this grenhouse/solarium that is designed to be an integral part of the house.

Below: When planning an addition, think in terms of a greenhouse. A unit of this type can be purchased in several sizes and erected on a simple foundation. A roll-down screen, mounted on the outside, prevents the interior from becoming too warm.

Greenhouse Coverings

Greenhouse coverings are chosen primarily on the basis of cost, ease of installation, the degree of permanence desired, and the owner's preference.

Glass

Glass remains popular because it provides an unobstructed view both into and out of the greenhouse, and because it can be very easily shaded from hot summer sun with screens, blinds, and awnings. It is highly resistant to scratching and can be cleaned repeatedly with no loss in light transition.

Glass is usually cheaper than rigid acrylic sheets. The disadvantage of glass is that it is breakable. If you live in an area with heavy hailstorms (or overactive children) this can be an important consideration. Double-strength glass should be used for roofs, but single-strength panes are adequate for the walls. (Check with your local building permit office; regulations may demand a certain glass strength.)

Acrylic

Clear, rigid acrylic makes a superb covering. It weighs half as much as glass and is 10 times more resistant to breakage. It is easily cut to fit, and can even be curved for special effects. It allows from 90 to 95 percent of the available light to penetrate and retains its clarity for at least 15 years.

Fiberglass

This type of covering is also popular. It comes in both corrugated panels and flat rolls, which are so easy to handle that simple greenhouses can go up in a day or over a weekend. Fiberglass designed for greenhouse use is specially treated to prevent it from expanding and then trapping dirt, which results in a sharp loss of transparency. Many greenhouse builders cover the roof with corrugated fiberglass panels and then cover the sides with flat fiberglass or glass.

Polyethylene

This film is the cheapest covering but the least durable. It can be used as a temporary covering over a simple greenhouse structure during the winter. It can also be applied rapidly and cheaply over large areas. However, it decays quickly under ultraviolet rays unless specially treated. When buying polyethylene for greenhouse use, choose only the type that is ultraviolet-resistant. One of the best uses for polyethylene film is as a lining for the inside of greenhouse walls, to reduce heat loss.

Above: Built on a foundation that also serves as an entry deck, this shed roof greenhouse is accessible from both indoors and the outside.

Left: One of the uses for a greenhouse is as a "hospital" for ailing plants. Plants that are suffering from low light and dryness will often respond dramatically to the warm, humid atmosphere in a greenhouse.

The Attached Greenhouse

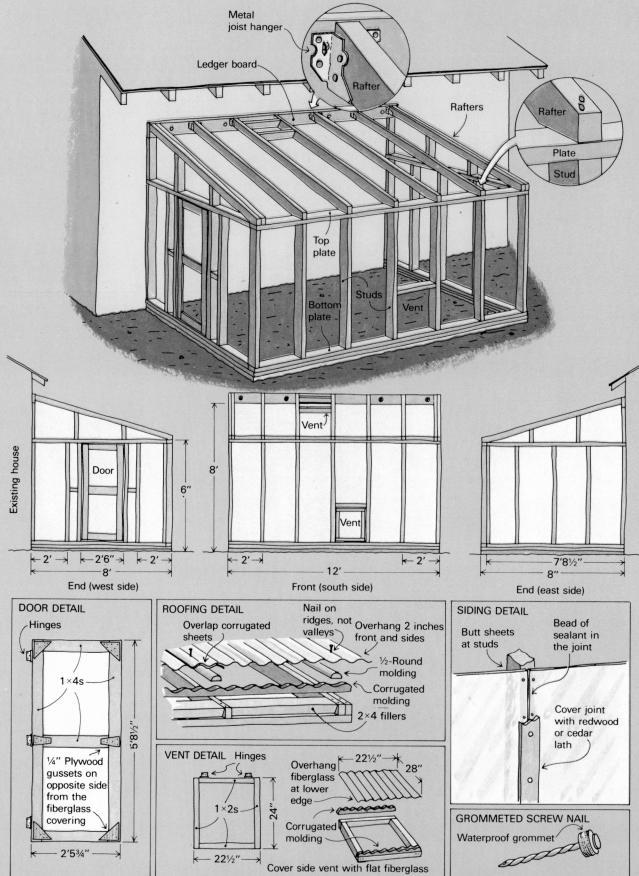

Metal joist hanger

Ledger board

Rafter

Rafters

Rafter

Plate

Stud

Top plate

Bottom plate

Studs

Vent

Existing house

Door

6"

8'

2' | 2'6" | 2'

8'

End (west side)

Vent

Vent

2' | 2'

12'

Front (south side)

7'8½"

8'

End (east side)

DOOR DETAIL

Hinges

1×4s

5'8½"

¼" Plywood gussets on opposite side from the fiberglass covering

2'5¾"

ROOFING DETAIL

Overlap corrugated sheets

Nail on ridges, not valleys

Overhang 2 inches front and sides

½-Round molding

Corrugated molding

2×4 fillers

VENT DETAIL   Hinges

1×2s

22½"

24"

22½"

Overhang fiberglass at lower edge

22½"

28"

Corrugated molding

Cover side vent with flat fiberglass

SIDING DETAIL

Butt sheets at studs

Bead of sealant in the joint

Cover joint with redwood or cedar lath

GROMMETED SCREW NAIL

Waterproof grommet

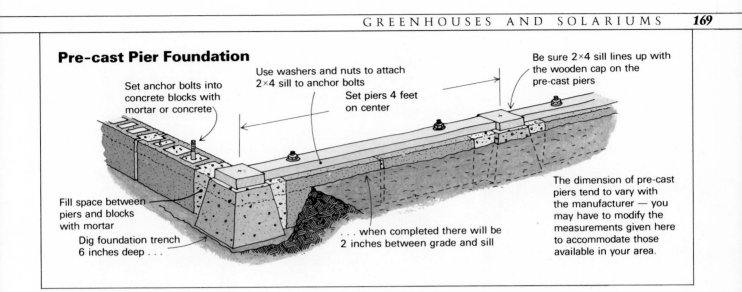

Pre-cast Pier Foundation

Set anchor bolts into concrete blocks with mortar or concrete

Use washers and nuts to attach 2×4 sill to anchor bolts

Set piers 4 feet on center

Be sure 2×4 sill lines up with the wooden cap on the pre-cast piers

Fill space between piers and blocks with mortar

Dig foundation trench 6 inches deep . . .

. . . when completed there will be 2 inches between grade and sill

The dimension of pre-cast piers tend to vary with the manufacturer — you may have to modify the measurements given here to accommodate those available in your area.

Building a Greenhouse

Whether you are building from the ground up or buying a prefabricated greenhouse, you need a foundation that is both level and square.

Site Layout and Foundation

The type of foundation you need depends on the type of greenhouse it will support. For a simple, lightly framed greenhouse with a plastic or fiberglass covering, an extensive foundation is unnecessary. A simple layout on painted railroad ties that are either sunk in ditches to just above ground level or staked with reinforcing rods (rebar) is adequate.

Another easy way to build a foundation in areas with mild climates is to dig a 6-inch-deep ditch to the dimensions of the greenhouse, line it with concrete building blocks, and fill the blocks with cement. You can insert anchor bolts for the frame, or set precast concrete piers around the perimeter of the foundation every 4 feet.

For heavier and more permanent greenhouses in areas where the ground freezes, you will need traditional concrete footings to form a foundation. Ortho's book *How to Build and Use Greenhouses* gives instructions on how to lay out and pour such a foundation and how to construct a greenhouse wall. It also provides detailed plans for several types of greenhouses you can build.

The Sill

The sill should be a 2-by-6-inch board—preferably redwood. It is used to top the footing or foundation wall and gives you something to nail to when you put up the walls. It is bolted to the foundation with anchor bolts that are spaced 4 to 6 feet apart.

Walls

The foundation or side wall can be both attractive and functional. This wall, usually 24 to 30 inches high, is not tall enough to cast a shadow but it keeps rain and snow from wetting the sill. The walls are usually made from concrete blocks (generally 16 inches by 8 inches by 8 inches) bonded together with mortar.

Above: Building a greenhouse need not be a complicated or expensive undertaking. This one is a simple wood framework with a corrugated fiberglass roof.

Above center: Measure the framework and work out how many full panels you can fit and how many you will have to cut.

Above right: Panels of plain plexiglass were used for the walls. These can be cut to size with tin snips.

Right: This greenhouse has no floor. Pots can be set directly on the pebble beds and water will seep into the ground. Bricks provide a level and dry working area. In order to prevent drafts, beads of sealant where laid along all joints.

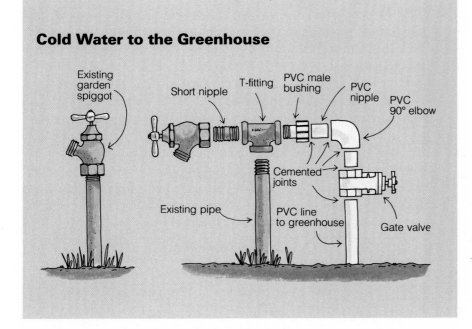

Cold Water to the Greenhouse

Existing garden spiggot

Short nipple

T-fitting

PVC male bushing

PVC nipple

PVC 90° elbow

Cemented joints

Existing pipe

PVC line to greenhouse

Gate valve

Water Lines

Consider laying the water lines for your greenhouse underground. This way, they won't freeze in winter and the pipes won't show. You can lay the water pipes in a trench dug under the footing before the concrete is poured.

If you plan to have a plumber install the connections for the watering system, just lay a section of plastic pipe under the footing as you install the foundation. The pipe can be connected later.

In areas with little or no danger of frost, a cold water tap can be installed in a greenhouse merely by hooking onto an outside water spigot. This is an easy way to get running water into the greenhouse, and it doesn't require complex connections or intricate plumbing.

If you want hot water in the greenhouse, you will have to tie into the hot water lines in your house. Unless you are an experienced do-it-yourselfer, it is advisable to have a plumber do this work for you.

Electric Connections

If your growing area will have ventilation fans, lights, and heating cables for propagation beds, you will have to install an electric system in the greenhouse.

Unless you are experienced in working with electricity, you should hire an electrician to do this work. In fact, local building codes may demand that all wiring, even in a greenhouse, be installed by a licensed electrician.

Brick Patterns

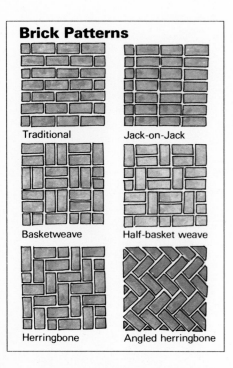

Traditional

Jack-on-Jack

Basketweave

Half-basket weave

Herringbone

Angled herringbone

Above: Brick, an attractive and utilitarian greenhouse floor, can be laid in several different patterns. These drawings show a few of the possible arrangements.

Right: Bricks can be laid in a sand bed as long as they are bordered by a solid frame. Once the main area is filled, it is necessary to cut bricks to fit. Mark and score each brick. Holding a cold chisel on the score line, give the handle a single sharp tap with the hammer. Nine times out of ten, the brick will break cleanly. Fit the pieces into position, then sweep fine sand into the gaps between the bricks. Repeat until the gaps are filled.

Opposite: A dramatic two story solarium has a brick floor, proving that brick is as decorative as it is practical.

The Floor

The easiest greenhouse floor is simply bare ground, which can be used for planting. However, the walkway can turn to mud when the plants are watered and when humidity builds up. Many gardeners lay large paving blocks, round concrete pads, or a flagstone floor to avoid this problem. Another alternative is to lay 3 to 4 inches of gravel. Inexpensive and easy to apply, it keeps your feet out of the mud. You can water freely and let the excess run into the gravel, where it will help increase humidity. If you plan to use the greenhouse as a solar heat trap, you may wish to build on a poured concrete slab. This will add to your installation costs, and the floor will require constant mopping and sweeping, since dirt cannot simply work itself back into the ground.

Brick laid in sand makes a most attractive and practical floor. The bricks catch and hold the heat of the sun during the day and release it back into the greenhouse at night for added warmth. They let water and fine grit disappear through the floor. Black bricks absorb the most heat. You can set them on a 3-inch layer of sand and floor the entire greenhouse, or you can lay them between 2 by 4s down the center of the greenhouse as a walkway and spread gravel on the rest of the floor. In houses and garden rooms, bricks are often waxed for a finished appearance, but in a greenhouse they are best left in their natural porous state.

Temperature Control

Being able to heat and cool the greenhouse requires careful attention and planning. The main heating considerations are providing enough heat and distributing it evenly. An automatic system lets you spend more time working with your plants.

Sunlight is free, so employ as many solar heating techniques as you can. Heat will be lost if it escapes through cracks, so ensure that the greenhouse is as airtight as possible. Put weather stripping around the door and vents, and use a flexible sealant to close all joints between the roof and walls. Check that the glazing is snug to the frame. Before you install any heat system, search for cracks around vents, doors, and glazing panes, and line them with 4-mil polyethylene film. The inner layer should be 1 to 6 inches away from the glazing. This film can also be stapled around the inside of the greenhouse. If it is stapled to a framework mounted at least an inch away from the wall, it can reduce heat loss by 30 to 40 percent. Greenhouses can also be lined with plastic bubble-pack, available in sheets from commercial suppliers.

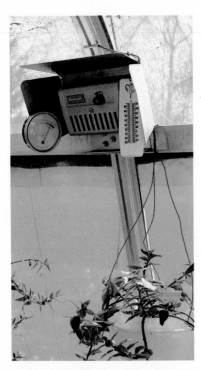

Above: A shielded thermometer, thermostat, and humidistat are basic needs to control the climate in a greenhouse.

Right: There are several different models of maximum/minimum thermometers available. These are some of them.

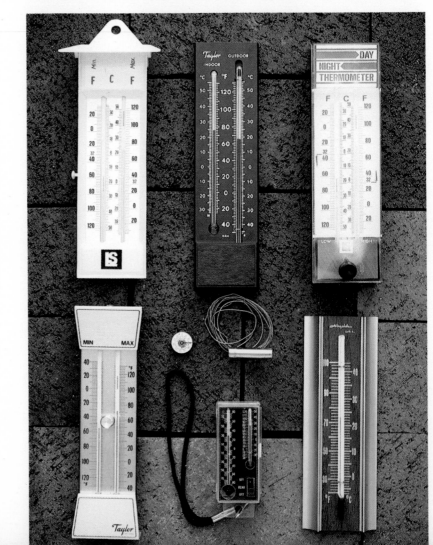

Heating the Greenhouse

The amount of heat your greenhouse needs depends on the total surface area and the difference between the outdoor temperature and the temperature you want to maintain in the greenhouse. The glazing is also part of this equation, as is the amount of wind in your area. Coal, wood, gas, electricity, or infrared radiant heaters may be used and heaters with fans and thermostats are most useful. The fan keeps the air moving, and prevents heat from collecting at the top. If you use a heater that cannot circulate air, install a small fan near the peak of the roof.

Infrared heaters have become increasingly popular. The units can hang close to plants without harming them, and the reflectors direct heat in uniform patterns so that it reaches into all corners.

Locate thermostats for all controls where they will not receive direct sunlight, such as under a shelf or in a small box. Thermostats should be at plant height, in the middle of the greenhouse. Battery-operated alarms can also be installed, in case the temperature falls suddenly or the heating system fails.

Above: A heater is necessary greenhouse equipment if you wish to keep the temperature constant.

Left: Before you install any type of heating system, double check for cracks around vents, doors, and glazing panels. Any small leaks will allow great amounts of heat to escape. Here, liquid foam is used for insulation. Still experimental, this method accounted for a 70% reduction in heat loss.

Above: A fan will draw in cooler outside air and blow out hot greenhouse air.

Top: A thermocouple type automatic vent

Top right: The electric vent in this greenhouse is coupled to a thermostat. A panel in the roof opens automatically when the temperature gets too high.

Cooling the Greenhouse

In much of the country, cooling the greenhouse in the summer is a greater problem than heating it in the winter. In the North, wall and roof vents may be sufficient; but in hotter climates, where temperatures are consistently above 80°F, some cooling device must be installed.

Heat buildup can be minimized by fans that will draw cooler outside air in while blowing hot greenhouse air out or by installing screens, awnings, or shades. Mount fans close to the roof to pull out the hottest air. The entire fan system will work more efficiently if it is hooked to thermostats and operates automatically. Translucent white plastic, bamboo, or aluminum screens can be mounted on the roof and rolled down when shade is needed. Vinyl shade cloth can be used inside the entire greenhouse or over individual benches. Sunflowers or pole beans planted on the south side of the greenhouse and trained over the roof will supply natural shade.

Humidity Control

If the humidity in the greenhouse is too low, plants will suffer and grow slowly. High humidity causes faster growth, but if it is over 90 percent for any length of time, there is a risk of leaf mold and stem rot.

Low humidity can be corrected by misting or watering the floor two or three times a day to build up water content in the air. An evaporative cooler fan ("swamp cooler") or rotary mister also increases humidity. A humidifier is needed only in extremely dry areas or in the winter.

Too much humidity is more common than too little. You'll recognize this problem when the roof and walls are so loaded with condensation that it feels like it's drizzling inside. This is not too

much of a problem if the leaves have a chance to dry out at night, However, damage can be done if they stay damp through the night. High humidity generally occurs during cold weather when hot greenhouse air, flowing along cold windows, cools so rapidly that the moisture in the air condenses into droplets. This problem can be reduced by putting a thermal layer of polyethylene film an inch or more away from the inside of the greenhouse windows, or by insulating the windows from the outside at night. A small fan to keep warm air circulating also reduces condensation.

Mist Systems

In areas with high temperatures and low humidity, a mist system may solve the problem of dryness. It is also excellent for propagation. It minimizes plant moisture loss, cuts greenhouse temperatures, and lowers leaf temperature so that photosynthesis can proceed efficiently.

Mist systems are normally set up with two timers: one to turn the system on during the day and off at night, and the other to run the spray nozzles. The spray nozzles turn on when the leaves are dry, staying on only long enough to wet the leaves. The required frequency varies with the heat and dryness of the day and the position of the sun. The newest misting systems do not have a clock control. Instead, they are fitted with a balance rod and a screen hooked to the on-off switch. When water builds up on the screen, as it would on a leaf, the misters shut off. When the water evaporates, the screen gets lighter and the misters switch back on.

For cuttings in flats, a special mist propagation bench can be set up. The growing medium should be warmed with electric cables, since misting tends to lower soil and plant temperatures. If only a small section of the greenhouse needs misting, hang curtains of clear plastic film around the misters to keep other areas dry.

Above: Mist spraying is a good way to keep the humidity high.

Top: Humidistat has both a dry bulb and a wet bulb to measure moisture in the air.

Top left: Although shading helps to keep temperatures down, a thermostatically controlled cooler is far more effective.

Interior Design

The design of a greenhouse should fulfill the needs of the kinds of plants that will be growing in it, as well as the needs of the grower. Plants can be grown either in beds or in planters placed on benches or tables.

The layout of the greenhouse is very important. It is preferable that benches run north and south so they get an even distribution of light as the sun moves across the sky. Bench layout usually follows either the aisle or the peninsula plan. In the former scheme, benches are placed end to end in long rows, usually running the length of the greenhouse, with an aisle between. In the peninsula plan, individual benches are set at right angles to the greenhouse walls with narrow aisles between them and a wider aisle down the center. In larger greenhouses, the peninsula plan allows for room in the center aisle for plants brought indoors for the winter.

Whichever system is used, it costs as much to heat aisle space as plant-growing space, so in the most efficient layouts no more than a quarter of the total floor space is devoted to aisles.

Ideally, benches and cabinets inside a greenhouse should be both functional and attractive. They should be designed for your own needs, taking your height and reach into consideration so that you can tend your plants comfortably. Many manufactured benches have casters so they will roll back and forth. These benches greatly increase the growing area in your greenhouse.

The benches should also provide a good display area for the plants and have maximum light exposure. They should allow air to circulate freely through them and among the plants. Use an open material for the surface area, such as expanded metal or snow fencing.

Right: Benches can be as simple or as elaborate as you wish. In this greenhouse, the bench on the right is a simple wood framework with a planked top. The bench on the left is merely planks laid ontop of two oil drums. The drums are filled with water that absorbs heat during the day and releases it at night.

Left: When building or buying benches and cabinets, it is important to consider your height and reach as well as the available space.

Types of Benches

Plan for benches 32 to 36 inches wide if they can be reached from only one side, and about 10 inches wider if they run down the center of the greenhouse. Place them on firm supports, such as leveled brick or concrete pads, never directly on the ground.

One variation on the straight, level bench is the stair-step bench. This gives the grower more display room. Steps should face south to catch the most sunlight, but plants must be rotated regularly unless they are placed against a white wall to give them reflected light. Shade-loving plants can go under the stair-step bench. There are other types of benches, including some filled with soil. (With these, be careful to prevent plants from becoming waterlogged and pathogens infesting the wet soil.) Some gardeners use planter benches to hold soaked vermiculite, so that potted plants placed on them remain wet for several days.

Remember that more room can be made by hanging plants in individual pots and by installing suspended shelves.

The Potting Area

A greenhouse and a potting area should go hand in hand. The potting area may be a sheltered area outside but near the greenhouse, or (for greater protection and warmth during the winter) it may be in the greenhouse itself. In the greenhouse, it is best placed in the northeast corner so you can leave sunnier areas for the plants and block the least amount of light with potting materials and miscellaneous equipment.

The potting area should be a flat, solid surface with sides 4 to 6 inches high to keep soil from spilling over. There should be space above the bench for tools, and room below for soil, fertilizers, and pesticide sprays. (Install locking cabinets if children have access to the greenhouse.) A small sink is convenient but not essential.

Greenhouse Lighting

The day length that plants are given is especially crucial for blooming plants. No matter how much you baby your plants, it is the short winter days that determine whether you have poinsettias at Christmas or crocuses on Valentine's Day. Some plants are very particular about when they bloom, responding totally to the amount of light they receive and to the day length. You can force flowers to bloom out of season with artificial lights, but you will have to shade other plants that aren't in the same cycle.

Sanitizing the Greenhouse

Once the greenhouse is constructed, an important final chore remains before it can be filled with plants—the interior must be completely sanitized.

The quickest, easiest, and safest way to sanitize it is to wash everything down with a sprayer and a freshly prepared solution of 1 part liquid household chlorine bleach to 10 parts water. Crevices, crannies, benches, walls, and floors should be scrubbed down; there should be no plants in the greenhouse when you do this.

Opposite: The plants in this solarium are arranged according to their individual light requirements. The Christmas cactus, in the window, enjoys full sun, while the African violets, which are too far away to get enough natural light, get their needs under fluorescent tubes.

Below: A center work table in a greenhouse is as convenient as a center island in a kitchen. It is accessible from all four sides.

Above: A greenhouse plus an attached lathe house offers three microclimates. Rows of cactus are placed on the top shelf to receive maximum sun while orchids sit on the cooler bottom shelves. Staghorn ferns hang in the lathe house where they enjoy the coolest air. When necessary, the two areas can be separated by closing a door.

Soil, Water, and Fertilizer

The needs of container greenhouse plants are much the same as those kept in the home. Most successful commercial plant nurseries use the same soil mixes (or soilless mixes) for greenhouse container plants as they do for other indoor plants. Watering requirements are also much the same as for houseplants. Water according to the needs of the plant rather than by the clock or calendar. Whenever the plant is watered, some nutrients are leached out of the soil and should be replaced with a fertilizer. The amount of fertilizer needed at any one time is very small, but the need is continuous. Mixing a timed-release fertilizer into the soil just before adding a plant is the easiest way to ensure continuous fertilization. Since a greenhouse is a controlled environment, there's no trick to growing pineapples or papayas in Montana or Maine. Just choose the exotic fruits you want for Thanksgiving dinner, or the flowers for your anniversary centerpiece, and follow the care requirements. The real fun is in working with nature. If you can recognize the natural cycle of a plant, you will learn to care for it according to its needs. In return, it will give you pleasure, nourishment, and beauty.

Plant Growth and Blooms from Heated Soil

Heating the soil rather than the surrounding air produces healthier, more vigorous plants. This method can produce dramatic results. It provides the indoor gardener with the opportunity to grow many interesting species in a greenhouse, an atrium, or even a simple indoor planter. In heated soil, most tropical and subtropical plants need cooler air temperatures than normal.

Heating the soil has several beneficial effects on the plants. Moisture-laden air that escapes from the soil raises the humidity around the plants, a condition favored by tropical and subtropical species. Heated soil also stimulates root growth, and increases a plant's resistance to disease. This stimulates more foliage growth. In addition, many tropical plants will bloom all year in heated soil. The merits of this approach are well known, but the cost of heating soil has prevented it from becoming common practice in commercial greenhouses. In smaller greenhouses or indoor planters, where energy requirements are much lower, it may barely increase the monthly utility bill. In fact, if waste heat is used, the overall energy consumption may be even less than normal, since the air space in the greenhouse can be kept almost 20° cooler if the soil is heated. This brings the temperature and humidity into a range closer to that of indoor living spaces. With bottom heat, plants usually grown in hot, humid greenhouses may thrive in cooler, drier areas of the home.

Methods

The soil can be heated by directly applying heat or indirectly by applying heat to the pot or bench that is in contact with the soil.

Electric cables can heat the soil directly. Small cables available at larger garden stores work well in containers, window boxes, and propagation benches. They are simple to install and operate. Use the highest quality cables you can afford, since cheaper ones may crack or deteriorate in damp soil and require frequent replacement.

Cables are available in a variety of forms, with and without built-in thermostats. Probably the most convenient is the propagation mat, which resembles an electric heating pad. Propagation mats heat an area equivalent to their dimensions. The length of cable you need if you are not buying a mat depends on the area you are heating and on the capacity of the particular brand of cable. As a general rule of thumb, use 2 to 4 linear feet of cable, or 10 to 15 watts per square foot. Obviously, propagation mats heat an area equivalent to their dimensions.

Lay the cable on the bottom of the plant container, being careful not to overlap the strands. (Clothespins are useful to hold the cable in place.) Cover the cable with about an inch of sand. Peat moss may dry it out and cause overheating. Place pieces of hardware

Above: Bottom heat can be most beneficial to plants and will speed rooting of most cuttings. Cables are laid ontop of a bed of gravel.

Above: Begonias, addiatum, and many different bromeliads are some of the plants that grow in this greenhouse.

cloth or screen on top of the sand, to avoid damaging the cable with tools. The rooting medium or soil lies on top of the screen. Electric soil cables are useful for starting seeds, growing plants from cuttings or seedlings, or for helping large specimen plants to become established during their first year or two after transplanting.

A newer method for heating the soil in which plants are grown is used by commercial growers in their large greenhouses. It relies on hot water from a gas or electric hot water heater or from a solar collector. In these systems, the hot water is circulated through plastic pipes and neoprene tubing. A network of tubing, spaced about 2 inches apart, is spread over the bench tops and pots are placed directly on top of it. The tubing is attached to hot water pipes on each side of the bench. Hot water flows through the pipe on one side, through the tubes to the opposite side, and returns to the heat source. A water heater, circulating pump, thermostat, pressure valve, gauges, and sometimes solar panels are part of this system.

For a hobby greenhouse, ½-inch plastic pipe and ⅛-inch neoprene tubing is adequate. Kits are available, complete with special fittings to attach the tubing to the pipe.

A gardener who grows many different plants in odd-sized containers may prefer a simpler system. For small greenhouses, you can easily make a soil-heating system by casting a concrete slab bench. Simply place plastic or copper tubing in the form, pour the concrete, hook up the connections, and place your potted plants or flats on the heated bench. This kind of bench is easy to clean. It radiates heat throughout the greenhouse as well as heating the pots directly on top.

Heating Recommendations

For optimum growth and flowering, heat the soil to around 70°F. Fluctuations below 70°F are acceptable, since this condition occurs in native habitats. Soil temperatures over 85°F are undesirable, as they can dry the soil and kill small roots.

Check the temperature with a thermometer. To prevent breaking the thermometer in the soil, don't simply push it into the soil. Instead, dig a hole and place the thermometer in it, then cover the bulb of the thermometer with soil.

Sources for Heating Systems

Many of the supplies needed for a soil-heating system are available at hardware and plumbing stores. Stores selling solar heating supplies are good sources for tubing and valves and small soil-heating cables can be bought at many garden stores.

Plants for Heated Soil

Many plants respond well to heated soil. Tropical palms, for instance, generally respond to heat with prodigious root growth. Avoid breaking the new fleshy roots, and repot the palm as soon as new roots come through the drainage hole. Many tropical species of the *Acanthus* family produce colorful flowers when grown in warm conditions. Among these are *Pachystachys leutea,* a medium shrub with bright yellow bracts and unusual white flowers, and *Justicia carnea,* a shrub with fist-sized clusters of pink flowers.

All the thunbergia vines do well in heated soil. So do the *Ruellias,* including *R. macrantha,* which has large pink flowers, and *R. colorata,* which has orange-red bracts and flowers. Many tropical bulbs and tuberous plants also thrive in heated soil. The spectacular *Gloriosa rothschildiana,* caladiums, achimenes, gloxinias, and sinningias are in this group.

Indoor vegetable gardeners may want to try bottom heating for tomatoes, peppers (both bell and hot varieties), eggplant, chayote, tropical vegetable varieties, and cultivated mushroom species.

Left: A greenhouse can contain a variety of plants or a specialized collection. Here, the owner has created a desert scene.

Attached Solar Greenhouse

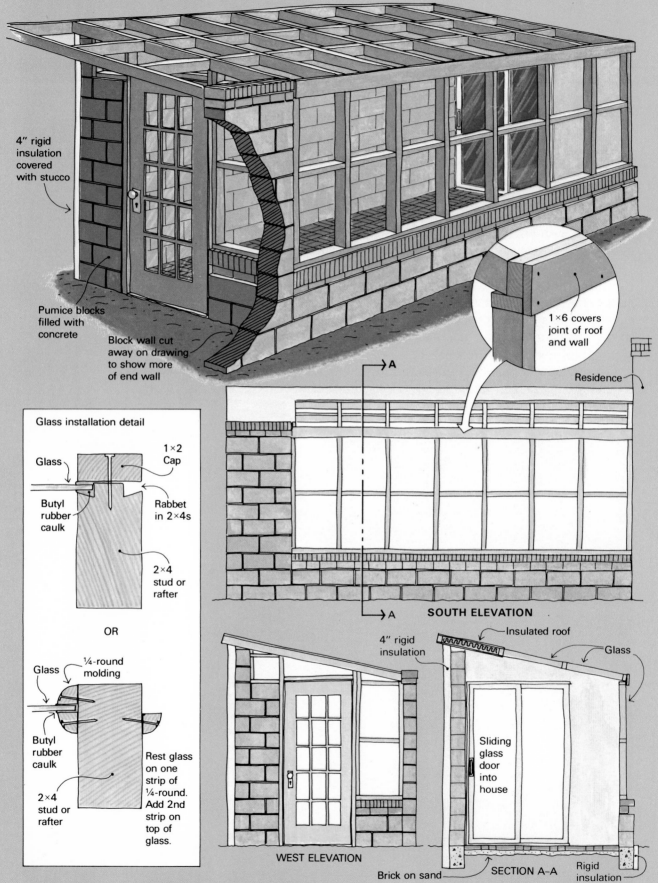

4" rigid insulation covered with stucco

Pumice blocks filled with concrete

Block wall cut away on drawing to show more of end wall

1×6 covers joint of roof and wall

Residence

Glass installation detail

Glass

Butyl rubber caulk

1×2 Cap

Rabbet in 2×4s

2×4 stud or rafter

OR

Glass

¼-round molding

Butyl rubber caulk

2×4 stud or rafter

Rest glass on one strip of ¼-round. Add 2nd strip on top of glass.

A

A

SOUTH ELEVATION

4" rigid insulation

Insulated roof

Glass

Sliding glass door into house

WEST ELEVATION

Brick on sand

SECTION A–A

Rigid insulation

Solar Heating

All greenhouses are solar-heated to some degree, but those we call truly solar-heated have some sort of solar heat collector. The greenhouse itself traps heat each day, but the heat is lost at night unless there is some means of absorbing and storing it. This is accomplished by a mass of heat-absorbing material, which can be barrels of water, piles of rock, or a concrete or concrete block wall. There are two types of solar energy systems: active and passive. Passive, most widely used in home greenhouses, relies on the thermal mass being heated during the day and naturally radiating the heat back at night. The active system involves installing a more sophisticated storage system. Distribution of the stored heat can then be controlled with thermostats. This method is more efficient but more costly and complex than the passive system.

The most widely used heat collector is water contained in a 55-gallon drum painted a dark color. Piles of rock are also used, but water is more efficient. The dark, heat-trapping color of the heat collector can cause phototropism problems (plants leaning toward

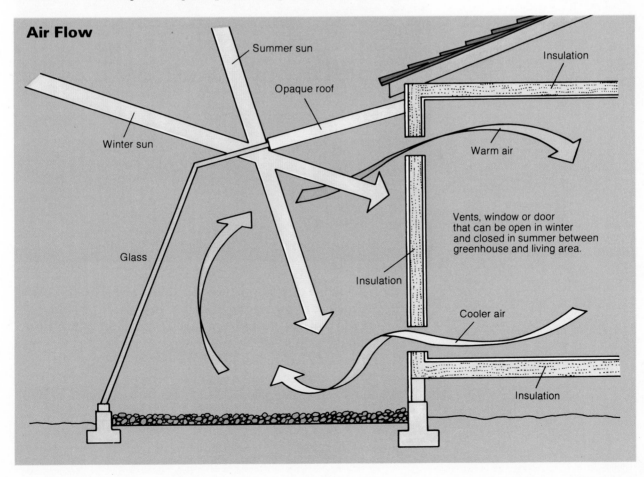

Air Flow

Summer sun

Opaque roof

Insulation

Winter sun

Warm air

Glass

Vents, window or door that can be open in winter and closed in summer between greenhouse and living area.

Insulation

Cooler air

Insulation

Right: A brick floor, especially if it is laid in a mortar bed, is an excellent heat-absorbing mass.

the windows), but these can be countered by strategic placement of reflective materials, such as white plaster or mirrors.

The north wall of a greenhouse is the great escape route for both heat and light, so this wall should be covered with a material that will both insulate and reflect light back into the interior. Rigid white styrofoam insulation, or batts of fiberglass insulation covered with plywood and painted white, can turn the north side of the greenhouse into a warm, bright area.

Whatever type of heat trap is used, it cannot be expected to completely eliminate the need for artificial heating. There should be a backup system, even if it is needed only occasionally.

Solariums

Solariums or sunrooms have become extremely popular architectural elements in many of today's homes. They are being installed by both builders and remodelers because of the unique appeal of an indoor-outdoor living space and because of the benefits of gathering solar heat. While these additions are not necessarily intended for indoor gardeners, they are as effective as a greenhouse for plants that enjoy a lot of direct light.

For a solarium to be an effective heat collector, the floors are generally masonry, often ceramic tile, brick, or slate. All of these materials retain heat, but just as important to the plant lover, they are impervious to water damage and require only a quick mopping to clean up excess drainage and spilled soil.

Although a solarium is an ideal spot for sun lovers—plants and people—both can be fried if there are no blinds or screens to control the amount of light. But even if the sun is shielded, a south-facing solarium will be a lot warmer than other rooms in your home. If you are in doubt as to whether a plant will be happy in a solarium, check the listing in A Gallery of Houseplants.

Opposite: A delicate moth orchid and an 18-foot high fiddle leaf fig both thrive in an atmosphere conducive to good plant growth and elegant living.

Below: Indoors and outdoors appear to meld into one enchanting space in this dramatic solarium.

Greenhouses You Can Buy

Many potential greenhouse owners don't have the time, tools, or desire to build their own greenhouses from scratch. Nowadays, however, this doesn't limit your choices of either size or quality, as there is a wide range of manufactured greenhouses available to the home gardener.

Some are prefabricated, requiring only assembly. These kits often include a fan, heater, and thermostat, in addition to wood, a covering, and hardware. You also have the option of buying more complicated models that are designed for installation by professional contractors.

Small temporary greenhouses are becoming increasingly available for gardeners who want to increase the outdoor growing season by intensifying the warmth and humidity of a section of their backyards (or balconies) without installing a foundation, plumbing, or lights.

Miniature indoor greenhouses can also be bought, for placement on a windowsill or on a shelf under lights. These are good for propagating new plants, curing ailing plants that have been suffering from dryness, isolating sick plants during treatment, or forcing bloom in flowering plants. They can also be permanent homes for humidity-loving tropical species. They are a useful addition for the indoor gardener.

Window Greenhouses

The permanent window greenhouse is smaller than the temporary garden greenhouse and more substantial than the miniature windowsill greenhouse. A window greenhouse can be an attractive addition to a house, appealing both to the indoor grower and to people passing by.

The window greenhouse is a true greenhouse on a small scale, not merely a bay window with plant shelves, and it closes on the inside to protect plants from the drying effects of the house. It is not difficult to install. Just remove the existing window and replace it with a projecting greenhouse window of a size chosen to fit into the window frame.

You can convert almost any window into a window greenhouse. South windows get the best sunlight, and east windows get the second best. With fluorescent lighting, however, a window greenhouse can be placed in any room of the house, even in an apartment bathroom that opens into a dim air shaft.

These greenhouses do have a minor drawback: they are small and heat up rapidly when hit with sunlight, and cool markedly at night. In order to keep the air temperature relatively constant, it is important to install a vent system.

Below: To install a prefabricated greenhouse into an existing window opening, just measure the frame and order the closest available size. Remove the window and install framing on which to mount the greenhouse. Run a bead of sealant around the frame and install the greenhouse.

Opposite: A window greenhouse can obscure an ugly view as well as add a plant station.

L. Constans. Pinx & Zinc.

Printed by C.F.Ch

A Gallery of Houseplants

As a result of scientific research and dedication by both amateur gardeners and botanists, there is a dazzling array of houseplants available to you. This Gallery of Houseplants is a catalog of possibilities to help you choose and care for plants that suit both your horticultural fancy and your design ideas.

In this chapter, the listings are divided into two categories—flowering and foliage—although many plants are not exclusively one or the other. For instance, cacti are included with foliage plants, although many gardeners grow them for their unusual and lovely blooms. The reason for placing plants in one category or the other is based on what was considered their most interesting feature.

Entries are in alphabetical order, by botanical name. Some plants are grouped by family and alphabetized under the family name. Bromeliads, citrus, gesneriads, and orchids are grouped in this way in the Flowering Houseplants section. In the Foliage Houseplants section, cacti, ferns, palms, and succulents are grouped as families.

Beneath the botanical name for each entry are the most familiar common names. These are followed by descriptions and general information about the plant and its growth pattern. For family groups and some of the larger and more varied genera—dracaenas and begonias, for example—introductory paragraphs cover an entire group. If you don't know a botanical name, use the index on page 291 at the end of this chapter, which lists plants by common names first.

Each listing contains plant care requirements in the following categories: light, water, humidity, temperatures, fertilization, propagation, grooming, repotting, and problems. The guides will help you select plants that fit your life-style and home, and are designed to give you a horticultural reference.

Variety is charming, therefore we should seek amongst many families for the furnishing of a plant-house, which is intended to afford delight to various minds at various seasons.

New and Rare Beautiful Leaved Plants, Shirley Hibberd, 1891

Flowering Houseplants

Plants that produce beautiful flowers of varying colors, forms, and fragrance are extremely popular for use indoors. Care requirements for these plants often vary, depending on whether they are cultured primarily for their flowers or for continued foliage production. The cultural information provided here promotes flowering.

Quite a few flowering houseplants are purchased as mature specimens already in bloom. Many of them are not well suited to continued culture indoors, except in a greenhouse or solarium setting with a great deal of light, space, and humidity. These might be classified as plants used indoors while flowering. Some of the most common indoor plants are in this category, such as poinsettias, Easter lilies, and chrysanthemums. The care guides generally refer to the conditions necessary to culture them continuously and to periodically bring them into bloom. In some cases, the care guides enable you to prolong the indoor life of the plants.

Many bulbous plants that can be forced or brought into flower indoors are included in this section of the Gallery. In many cases, blooming bulbous plants can be placed almost anywhere indoors as decorative items and then planted outdoors after flowering. Others need culture or tending after flowering, a care practice that usually involves initiating a dormancy period prior to reblooming. Because of these varying procedures, bulbous plants for flowering indoors are not grouped together in the Gallery. The individual care guides should make the correct cultural procedures clear.

Abutilon species
Flowering maple

This tropical viny shrub of the hollyhock family is extremely vigorous, growing several feet each year. Its rocket-shaped flowers are striking, and its leaves, sometimes dappled with yellow or white, are shaped like a maple's. Stems can be espaliered or trained onto a trellis.

Abutilon's popularity has spurred the development of hybrids producing larger blossoms in a wider range of colors. *A. hybridum* (Chinese lantern) produces white, yellow, salmon, or purple blooms. *A. megapotamicum* 'Variegata' (trailing abutilon) features red and yellow blossoms with large, dark brown, pollen-bearing anthers. *A. pictum* 'Thompsonii' has an orange-salmon flower.

With bright direct light and moist soil, this plant should grow rapidly and blossom most of the year. Fertilize monthly. Because the plant grows so rapidly, pruning is a must for retaining shape and size. Prune during the slow growth period in winter.

Light: Provide at least 4 hours of curtain-filtered sunlight from a bright south, east, or west window.

Water: Keep very moist, but do not allow to stand in water.

Humidity: Average indoor humidity levels.

Temperatures: 50°F to 55°F at night, 65°F to 70°F during the day.

Fertilization: Fertilize all year, but more heavily in summer.

Propagation: Take cuttings from stems or shoots before they have hardened or matured.

Grooming: Prune in early spring. Keep to desired height and shape with light pruning or clipping at any time.

Repotting: Repot in winter or early spring, as needed.

Problems: Dry soil or high soluble salts may damage roots, causing plant to die back. If light is too low, plant will get spindly and weak.

Abutilon hybridum

Above: *Acalypha hispida*
Below: *Agapanthus 'Peter Pan White'*

Acalypha species
Copper leaf, Beefsteak plant, Chenille plant

A. hispida is called the chenille plant because its long plumes (more than 20 inches) of tiny red flowers resemble chenille fringe. This fall- and winter-flowering plant needs light and warmth during blossoming. *A. wilkesiana* is usually grown for its distinctive leaves, which have red, copper, and pink tones that look like beefsteak. Winter flowers are tiny and not noteworthy. Acalyphas are bushy plants that will get too big for indoor culture unless they are pruned several times a year.

Light: In winter, keep in direct sun for about 4 hours. In summer, provide curtain-filtered sunlight from a south or west window.
Water: Keep evenly moist. Water thoroughly and discard drainage.
Humidity: Average indoor humidity levels.
Temperatures: 55°F to 60°F at night, 70°F to 75°F during the day.
Fertilization: Fertilize only during late spring and summer months.
Propagation: Take cuttings from stems or shoots that have recently matured.
Grooming: Prune in early spring. Keep plant to desired height (2 or 3 feet is best) and shape with light pruning or clipping at any time. Give these plants plenty of room.
Repotting: Infrequent repotting is best. Plants need a large container for blooming and attaining proper form.
Problems: Leaves will drop if soil is too wet or too dry. If plant is in a draft or dry air, leaves will scorch.

Agapanthus species
Agapanthus, Blue African lily, Lily of the Nile

Agapanthuses are large plants, bearing clusters of lilylike blue or white flowers in the summer. They bloom better when allowed to mature and get slightly pot-bound. They need room and should not get too dry between waterings. *A. praecox orientalis* is the largest species, reaching 5 feet with bloom clusters that contain a hundred flowers. Most of the other species are approximately 2 feet tall.

Light: In winter, keep in direct sun for about 4 hours. In summer, provide curtain-filtered sunlight from a south or west window.
Water: Keep evenly moist. Water thoroughly and discard drainage.
Humidity: Average indoor humidity levels.
Temperatures: 50°F to 55°F at night, 65°F to 70°F during the day.
Fertilization: Fertilize only when plant is growing actively or flowering.
Propagation: Start new plants by dividing an older specimen. Seeds are available but can be more difficult.

Allamanda neriifolia

Grooming: Pick off yellowed leaves.
Repotting: Infrequent repotting is best.
Problems: Low light or soil that is too wet or too dry will cause leaves to yellow.

Allamanda species
Allamanda

Allamanda is a woody vine with large, fragrant yellow blossoms in spring and summer. The plant needs warmth and lots of light. It will probably need staking or training onto a small trellis.
Light: Four hours or more of direct sunlight from a south window. Does best in a greenhouse setting.
Water: Keep evenly moist. Water thoroughly and discard drainage. In winter, keep plant dry with infrequent waterings.
Humidity: Requires moist air. Use a humidifier for best results.
Temperatures: 55°F to 60°F at night, 70°F to 75°F during the day.
Fertilization: Fertilize only during late spring and summer months.
Propagation: Take cuttings from stems or shoots before they have hardened or matured.

Allium schoenoprasum

Grooming: Pinch back new stem tips. Do not destroy flower buds.
Repotting: New plants have to grow in a medium to large pot until almost root-bound before they will bloom or set fruit. Transplant into larger pots as needed.
Problems: Plant will not bloom if light is too low. If left in a draft or dry air, leaves will scorch.

Allium species
Onion (flowering), Chives

Alliums are commonly seen in indoor gardens. All of the cultivars, even the ornamental flowering types, have at least some scent of onions. Chives will grow vigorously but remain small if their leaves are clipped continually for cooking. All alliums must be in a sunny window, free of cold drafts. Discard the larger flowering types after the bloom dies back. The aroma of onions becomes stronger as the bulb goes dormant. In winter, set chives in a cool (not freezing) spot for a few weeks to rest the bulbs and force new growth.
Light: Four hours or more of direct sunlight from a south window.
Water: Keep evenly moist. Water thoroughly and discard drainage.
Humidity: Average indoor humidity levels.
Temperatures: 50°F to 55°F at night, 60°F to 65°F during the day.
Fertilization: Fertilize only when plant is growing actively or flowering.
Propagation: Start from seeds. Begin in small pot and transplant as needed. Divisions or dried bulbs can be purchased for some of the alliums.

Above: *Anthurium scherzeranum*
Right: *Aphelandra squarrosa*

Grooming: Keep chives cut back to encourage new shoots.
Repotting: Not generally done.
Problems: If plant is in a draft or dry air, leaves will scorch. Poor drainage, too frequent watering, or standing in water will cause root rot.

Anthurium species
Flamingo flower, Tailflower

Anthuriums are among the best known tropical flowers. Blossoms are long-lasting and often used in weddings on Hawaii and other Pacific islands. They are popular in cut-flower arrangements around the world. The red or orange portion of the bloom is actually a bract (modified leaf), with tiny flowers appearing on a spike, or spadix. Most anthuriums are very large. *A. scherzeranum* is a much smaller species, more suited for indoor or greenhouse culture. Keep anthuriums in humid air, and fertilize well when plant is growing actively.
Light: At least 4 hours of curtain-filtered sunlight from a bright south, east, or west window.
Water: Keep evenly moist. Water thoroughly and discard drainage.
Humidity: Requires moist air. Use a humidifier for best results.
Temperatures: 55°F to 60°F at night, 70°F to 75°F during the day.
Fertilization: Fertilize 3 times a year: spring, midsummer, and early fall.
Propagation: Remove new plantlets or rooted side shoots as they form.
Grooming: Mound up soil as high crowns form. Remove aerial roots.
Repotting: Leave room at the top for mounding up soil as crown develops.

Infrequent repotting is best.
Problems: If left in a draft or dry air, leaves will scorch. Plant will not bloom if light is too low.

Aphelandra squarrosa
Zebra plant

For 6 weeks in the fall, this favorite of Victorian conservatories provides an impressive, orderly display of color. Large, conelike, deep yellow flowers emerge from golden bracts; this small evergreen shrub also has unusual foliage. Dark elliptical leaves striped with ivory veins create a zebra effect. The variety 'Louisae' is most popular. 'Apollo White', 'Dania', and 'Brockfeld' are more compact and produce leaves with striking vein patterns.

Aphelandras tend to become angly. To combat this, cut back after flowering, letting 1 or 2 pairs of leaves remain. Feed every 2 weeks, never allow the rootball to dry out, and keep the plant warm in winter.
Light: Place in a bright south, east, or west window with indirect sun.
Water: Keep very moist during growth and flowering. Allow to dry between waterings at other times.

Ardisia crispa

Above: *Begonia semperflorens*
Right: *Begonia tuberhybrida* 'Nonstop Orange'

Humidity: Requires moist air. Use a humidifier for best results.
Temperatures: 55°F to 60°F at night, 70°F to 75°F during the day.
Fertilization: Fertilize only when plant is growing actively or flowering.
Propagation: Take cuttings from stems or shoots that have recently matured.
Grooming: Prune in early spring.
Repotting: Repot in winter or early spring, as needed.
Problems: If plant is in a draft or dry air, leaves will scorch. Leaves will drop if soil is too wet or too dry.

Ardisia
Coralberry

Ardisias are woody ornamental shrubs that grow outdoors in warm climates. Their red berries at Christmastime are particularly popular. Foliage is shiny and waxy, with small, fragrant white or pink flowers. As indoor plants, they must have good light in winter. Cut them back severely in late winter, keeping them dry until they begin to grow. Keep only the strongest shoots, and train them to grow upward. Many gardeners place ardisias in shaded patio gardens during summer, to ensure better fruiting for the holidays.
Light: In winter, keep in direct sun for about 4 hours daily. In summer, provide curtain-filtered sunlight from a south or west window.
Water: Keep evenly moist. Water thoroughly and discard drainage.
Humidity: Requires moist air. Use a humidifier for best results.
Temperatures: 50°F to 55°F at night, 60°F to 65°F during the day.
Fertilization: Fertilize only during late spring and summer months.
Propagation: Take cuttings from stems or shoots before they have hardened or matured. Seeds are available, but can be more difficult to use.
Grooming: Prune just before the heavy blossoming period. Do not cut off flower buds when pruning.

Repotting: Infrequent repotting is best.
Problems: Watch for spider mites, especially if plant is dry. If plant is in a draft or dry air, leaves will scorch. Dry soil or high soluble salts may damage roots, causing plant to die back. It will not bloom if light is too low.

Azalea species
See *Rhododendron species.*

Begonia species

With more than 1,500 known species, this plant family offers a vast array of beauty, and is adaptable to almost any indoor environment. The varieties and foliage shapes and colors distinguish this group. Many begonias are grown primarily for their foliage (see page 250). Following are some flowering varieties. Florists and garden centers offer many of these plants already in bloom.

With a minimum of trouble you should be able to keep your begonias healthy and blooming. In general, plenty of bright light, a normal indoor temperature that drops slightly at night, and light applications of fertilizer ensure constant blooms. Begonias are very sensitive to overwatering, so take care to use soil that is rich in organic matter and drains well. Begonias differ in specific care requirements.

Begonia x cheimantha
Christmas begonia, Lorraine begonia

These hybrids are popular because they bloom profusely in winter. They are bushy dwarf plants, most frequently used in hanging baskets because of their stems' tendency to arch outward. Given enough light, Lorraine begonias will be covered with pink or white single flowers, on long stems or racemes. Since they bloom in winter, be sure they receive enough light and warmth and keep them evenly moist. After flowering, the plants become semidormant until late spring. Keep them drier then.
Light: Provide at least 4 hours of curtain-filtered sunlight from a bright south, east, or west window.

Begonia 'Mandarin Orange'

Water: Keep very moist during growth and flowering. Allow to dry between waterings at other times.
Humidity: Average indoor levels.
Temperatures: 65°F to 70°F at night, 75°F to 80°F during the day.
Fertilization: Fertilize only when plant is growing actively or flowering.
Propagation: Take stem cuttings at any time.
Grooming: Prune after flowering or fruiting.
Repotting: Cut back and repot when flowering stops.
Problems: Plant is subject to crown rot if planted deeply, watered over the crown, or watered late in the day. Its leaves will drop if soil is too wet or too dry. Some varieties may get powdery mildew.

Begonia semperflorens
Wax begonia, Fibrous-rooted begonias

These are the most popular of the fibrous-rooted members of the begonia family. Many cultivars and hybrids exist. They are bushy plants with shiny (waxy) heart-shaped leaves. Given ample light, they bloom profusely in a variety of colors. Wax begonias are most commonly used as outdoor bedding annuals or in hanging baskets for patio gardens. But they will flourish indoors with light fertilization, good light, and warmth.

Bougainvillea 'Raspberry Ice'

Light: Provide at least 4 hours of curtain-filtered sunlight from a bright south, east, or west window.
Water: Keep evenly moist. Water thoroughly and discard drainage.
Humidity: Requires moist air. Use a humidifier for best results.
Temperatures: 65°F to 70°F at night, 75°F to 80°F during the day.
Fertilization: Fertilize 3 times a year: spring, midsummer, and early fall.
Propagation: Take stem cuttings at any time. Seeds are available, but can be more difficult to use.
Grooming: Pinch back new stem tips to improve form. Do not destroy flower buds. Keep plant to desired height and shape with light pruning or clipping at any time.
Repotting: Cut back and repot when flowering stops.
Problems: Plant is subject to crown rot if planted deeply, watered over the crown, or watered late in the day. If plant is in a draft or dry air, its leaves will scorch. If light is too low, plant will get spindly and weak. Watch for mealybugs and powdery mildew disease.

Begonia x hiemalis
Rieger begonia, Hiemalis begonia

This begonia group originated through hybridization of a bulbous winter-flowering begonia with hardy and vigorous tuberous begonias. Many varieties are available in florists' shops. Hiemalis begonias are low-growing and very bushy. Many are pendulous and are used in hanging baskets. Some of the newer cultivars have bronze or red foliage. The flowers are usually large and double; they come in yellow, red, white, and orange. They prefer cooler locations

than most begonias, but do not like drafts. Give them plenty of light during flowering.
Light: Provide at least 4 hours of curtain-filtered sunlight from a bright south, east, or west window.
Water: Keep evenly moist. Water thoroughly and discard drainage.
Humidity: Average indoor levels.
Temperatures: 50°F to 55°F at night, 65°F to 70°F during the day.
Fertilization: Fertilize all year, but more heavily in summer.
Propagation: Take stem cuttings at any time.
Grooming: Pinch back new stem tips to improve form. Do not destroy flower buds. Keep to desired height and shape with light pruning or clipping at any time.
Repotting: Cut back and repot when flowering stops.
Problems: Plant is subject to crown rot if planted deeply, watered over the crown, or watered late in the day. Some cultivars susceptible to powdery mildew.

Begonia x tuberhybrida
Tuberous begonia

Cultivars of tuberous begonias produce the largest flowers of all begonias grown indoors. Most are large plants that need good light, cool temperatures, and moist soil and air. It is best to buy a mature tuber, plant it, enjoy a flowering period, and then discard it or place it in the garden. Older plants tend to get spindly and weak indoors.
Light: Keep in about 4 hours of direct sun in the winter. Provide curtain-filtered sunlight in the summer, from a south or west window.

Above: Bromeliad: Aechmea fasciata (see page 202)
Right: Bromeliad: Ananas comosus '*Variegatus*' (see page 202)

Water: Keep very moist at all times, but do not allow to stand in water.
Humidity: Requires moist air. Use a humidifier for best results.
Temperatures: 50°F to 55°F at night, 60°F to 65°F during the day.
Fertilization: Fertilize lightly. Do not fertilize when in flower.
Propagation: Start new plants from the small bulblets that develop beside the parent.
Grooming: Discard after flowering.
Repotting: Not usually done.
Problems: Leaves will scorch if plant is in a draft or dry air. Subject to crown rot if planted deeply, watered over the crown, or watered late in the day.

Bougainvillea glabra
Bougainvillea

Bougainvilleas are among the most popular and beautiful flowering shrubs in warm climates. Indoors, they must be pruned and trained to be manageable. They will probably not bloom in the winter unless they are in a warm greenhouse. These plants can sometimes be purchased from a florist.
Light: This plant does best in a greenhouse setting.
Water: Let plant approach dryness before watering, but water thoroughly and discard drainage.

Humidity: Requires moist air. Use a humidifier for best results.
Temperatures: 55°F to 60°F at night, 70°F to 75°F during the day.
Fertilization: Fertilize only during late spring and summmer months.
Propagation: Take cuttings from stems or shoots before they have hardened or matured. Seeds are available, but can be more difficult to use. Root cuttings are another option.
Grooming: Prune after flowering.
Repotting: Repot in winter or early spring, as needed.
Problems: Will not bloom if light is too low. Poor drainage, too frequent watering, or standing in water will cause root rot.

Bromeliads

Many people have discovered that bromeliads, with their exotic foliage and showy flowers, are not difficult to grow indoors. The most distinctive feature of the group is the rosette of leaves that mold into a cup to hold the water that nourishes the plant. In some varieties, flowers and large colorful bracts emerge from the center to create a spectacular display. These bracts are modified leaves that grow from the same axils as the flowers. Originating in the tropics, most bromeliads are epiphytes (air plants). They grow suspended in trees and on rocks in their native habitat, gathering moisture and nutrients from rainfall and particles in the air.

Bromeliad: Billbergia x calophylla (see page 202)

Bromeliads are available in flower in many florist shops and garden centers. Display them in pots or hanging baskets, or attach them to boards. If you decide to keep them in pots, use a light soil that drains easily. Overpotting and overwatering can be fatal to their small root system. When growing these plants in a pot, it is not necessary to water only by filling the rosette. Bromeliads

Bromeliad: Cryptanthus

Bromeliad: Dyckia fosterana

Bromeliad: Guzmania x 'Cherry'

need lots of sun and high temperatures to bloom. If you're having trouble inducing yours to bloom, place it in a plastic bag with a ripe apple for a few days. The ethylene gas from the apple will initiate buds. When the plant stops flowering, the rosette enters a slow dying process that can last as long as 3 years. Planting the offsets that form at the base of the plant will give you a collection that blooms year after year.

There are more than 2,000 different species. Some bromeliads are grown for their flowers, others for their foliage. The following are the best to include in your indoor garden.

Aechmea species
Living vase plant

An upright rosette of thick, silver-banded leaves distinguishes the striking *A. chantinii.* Its flowers last for several months. The most common of this group is *A. fasciata* (urn plant). Its broad thick leaves are mottled with gray and sea-green stripes. Its conical rosette of pink bracts and large blue flowers creates a splendid effect.

A. fulgens discolor, commonly known as the coralberry, has broad leaves that are green on top and purple underneath. The contrast in the foliage is heightened by the purple flower. Red berries form after the flower dies.

Ananas species
Pineapple

If you know what a pineapple is, then you know an ananas. Pineapples are the fruit of *A. comosus.* You can grow one by cutting off a bit of the fruit along with the fruit's tuft (the crown of leaves at the top of the plant), planting it in soil, and placing it in full sun. Narrow, gray-green leaves with prickly ribbing on the side form a striking rosette. The pineapple fruit will spring from the center for an unusual display, but this will happen only after several years. *A. comosus* 'Variegatus' (ivory pineapple) has the more attractive foliage.

Billbergia species
Vase plant

These are among the easiest bromeliads to grow, but they flower for only a short time. *B. nutans* (queen's tears) has grasslike gray-green leaves, and an arching spray of pink and green flowers. Another type, *B. windii,* sports long, green straplike leaves. Large bracts and pale green flowers tinged with blue cascade from this plant.

Bromelia species
Volcano plant

Bromelias are large plants with foliage rosettes that are 2 to 3 feet wide. The leaves are dark green and have sharp spines. When they bloom, the plants' centers turn brilliant red, giving rise to their common name. The flowers are borne on a stalk and are usually white.

Catopsis species

Catopsis are medium-sized bromeliads that can be easy to grow if given ample light. They are bottle-shaped and more upright and closed than many other bromeliads. The flowers are yellow. Keep the plants very moist when growing and flowering, and somewhat drier at other times.

Cryptanthus species
Earth stars

Called earth stars because of the shape of their rosettes, these plants' small size and great variation in leaf color makes them good for small spaces or dish gardens. *C. acaulis* (starfish plant) has small, wavy-edged leaves in varying shades of yellow and green. *C. bromelioides tricolor* (rainbow star) displays a colorful array of stripes down the length of its wavy leaves. *C. zonatus* (zebra plant) resembles zebra skin, banded in ivory and shades of brown.

Dyckia species

Dyckias are slow-growing medium-sized bromeliads with dark green variegated foliage. In bright light during the summer, the plants will produce orange flowers on spikes. Repot them infrequently and allow the soil to dry between waterings, especially in winter.

Above: *Bromeliad: Guzmania lingulata*
Above Right: *Bromeliad: Neoregelia*
Below Right: *Bromeliad: Nidularium*
   procerum var. Kermesianum

Guzmania species

Guzmanias can grow to a width of 20 inches. They bloom from late winter to summer, depending on the species. The true flowers are small but surrounded by large, showy bracts in reds, yellows, or oranges. Keep the plants moist, watering the vase-shaped rosette when the plants are growing and flowering.

Neoregelia species

These plants produce large rosettes composed of thick, shiny leaves. When mature, *N. carolinae tricolor* (blushing bromeliad) reaches a diameter of 30 inches. Large saw-toothed leaves, variegated in cream and green, jut out in an orderly pattern. Just before flowering, the young leaves at the base turn bright red. *N. spectabilis* features green leaves with pink-tipped ends, inspiring the name, painted fingernail plant.

Nidularium species
Bird's nest bromeliad

The center of the leaf rosette of nidulariums changes color many weeks prior to blooming. They are epiphytic and will tolerate moderate light, but may bloom only in bright light. Various species are available with foliage of different shades and patterns.

Portea species

Portea is a large bromeliad with foliar rosettes that can grow to 3 feet across. It

forms a large, showy flower head in the fall. The plant tolerates indirect light, but may bloom only in bright light.

Quesnelia species
Grecian vase

Quesnelias have narrow, upright foliage rosettes that can grow to 18 inches, depending on the species. Their small flowers are usually blue and surrounded by red bracts. With ample light, the plants may bloom in any season.

Tillandsia species
Blue torch, Spanish moss

Many species of tillandsias are available to indoor gardeners. Even the Spanish

moss commonly seen as an epiphyte in the South is occasionally grown indoors. Most tillandsias have narrow arching foliage, which can be grasslike or palm-like. Some of the smaller species are popular as hanging or dish-garden plants. Swordlike flower spikes appear in summer.

Vriesia species

This genus features many plants attractive for both their foliage and flowers. *V. splendens,* a popular variety, forms a rosette of wide purple-banded leaves. The common name, flaming sword, refers to its flower, a long spike of red bracts and yellow flowers. The bloom will last for several weeks.

Above: Bromeliad: Nidularium
'Robert Morobe'
Below: Bromeliad: Quesnelia
Above Right: Bromeliad: Tillandsia
Cyanea
Below Right: Bromeliad: Vriesia
splendens
(descriptions are on page 203)

Care of Bromeliads

Light: Abundant light. An east or west window is best. *Ananas* and *Cryptanthus* require full sun.

Water: Always keep the cup of epiphytic types filled with water (preferably rainwater) and change it occasionally. Allow plants growing in pots to dry, then keep barely moist. Overwatering and poor drainage will kill the plant.

Humidity: Dry air is generally not harmful.

Temperatures: Average constant temperatures of 65°F to 70°F are fine for foliage types and plants in flower.

Warmer temperatures (75°F to 80°F) are needed to initiate buds.

Fertilization: Fertilize lightly once a year, in early spring.

Propagation: Remove mature offsets and a good section of roots from larger plants and pot shallowly in light soil. Keep warm.

Grooming: Wash leaves occasionally.

Repotting: Rarely necessary.

Problems: Brown areas on the plant leaves usually indicate sunburn; move the plant out of direct sunlight. Brown tips on the leaves result from dry air. Watch for scale and mealybugs on the foliage and flowers.

Browallia species
Browallia

Browallia is a woody plant usually kept in a hanging basket, since its shoots tend to spread and trail. Potted plants can be pruned and staked. Given enough light, the plant will bear blue or white medium-sized flowers all year. In the winter, keep them watered with room-temperature water, and continue to fertilize them lightly if they are flowering.

Light: In winter, keep in about 4 hours of direct sun. In summer months, provide curtain-filtered sunlight in front of a south or west window.
Water: Keep very moist at all times, but do not allow to stand in water.
Humidity: Requires moist air. Use a humidifier for best results.
Temperatures: 55°F to 60°F at night, 70°F to 75°F during the day.
Fertilization: Fertilize all year, but more heavily in summer.
Propagation: Start from seeds. Begin in a small pot and transplant as needed. Take cuttings from stems or shoots that have recently matured.
Grooming: Prune after flowering or fruiting.
Repotting: Repotting should be done each year, in early summer.
Problems: If plant is in a draft or dry air, its leaves will scorch. It will not bloom if light is too low. Watch for whiteflies.

Brunfelsia pauciflora
Yesterday, today, and tomorrow

The common name of this brunfelsia comes from the fact that, as it ages, its flowers change from dark purple to almost white. The mildly fragrant, medium-sized flowers grow in clusters almost all year long, if they have plenty of light. They need a moderate rest period in late spring. Pinch back stems periodically to maintain adequate branching.
Light: In winter, keep in direct sun for about 4 hours. In summer, provide curtain-filtered sunlight in front of a south or west window.

Water: Keep very moist during growth and flowering. Allow to dry between waterings at other times.
Humidity: Average indoor humidity levels.
Temperatures: 50°F to 55°F at night, 65°F to 70°F during the day.
Fertilization: Fertilize only when plant is growing actively or flowering.
Propagation: Take cuttings from stems or shoots before they have hardened or matured.
Grooming: Prune well in early spring. Pinch back new stem tips to improve form. Do not destroy flower buds.
Repotting: Cut back and repot when flowering stops.
Problems: Will get spindly and weak if light is too low. Dry soil or high soluble salts may damage roots, causing plant to die back.

Calceolaria
Pocketbook flower, Slipperwort

Pocketbook flowers are popular in Europe, and are becoming increasingly available in the United States. The intricate flowers are shaped into a saclike form. Cultivars of calceolarias come in many colors, including red, pink, maroon, and yellow. Most have purple or brown markings on the petals. The plants are difficult to grow from seeds because they are sensitive to improper watering and fertilizing. They like cool nights and are suited to a small greenhouse or window box. Before they flower, pinch back stems and train them into a bushy plant.
Light: Blooming plants can be placed anywhere. Growing plants need curtain-filtered sunlight in summer and direct sun in winter.
Water: Keep evenly moist. Water thoroughly and discard drainage.
Humidity: Requires moist air. Use a humidifier for best results.
Temperatures: 40°F to 45°F at night, 60°F to 65°F during the day.
Fertilization: Fertilize 3 times a year: spring, midsummer, and early fall. Do not fertilize blooming plants.

Above: *Browallia speciosa 'Major'*
Below: *Brunfelsia pauciflora*

Propagation: Start from seeds. Begin in a small pot and transplant as needed.
Grooming: Pinch back new stem tips to improve form. Do not continue when the flowering period approaches. Discard after flowering.

Above: *Calceolaria herbeohybrida*
Below: *Calliandra haematocephala*

Repotting: Transplant seedlings several times, as the plants grow.
Problems: Whiteflies sometimes infest this plant. Subject to crown rot if planted deeply, watered over the crown, or watered late in the day. If plant is in a draft or dry air, its leaves will scorch.

Calliandra species.
Powder puff, Trinidad flame bush

If given lots of sunlight, calliandras will produce large red or pink flower heads with many stamens, resembling powder puffs. They are winter-flowering bushy shrubs. Their foliage of compound leaves is like the honey locust's. They will get quite large and should be pruned to a height of 3 feet. Because they need warmth and light, they are best suited for greenhouses or solariums.
Light: Four hours or more of direct sunlight from a south window. Does best in a greenhouse setting.

Water: Let plant approach dryness before watering, but water thoroughly and discard drainage.
Humidity: Requires moist air. Use a humidifier for best results.
Temperatures: 65°F to 70°F at night, 75°F to 80°F during the day.
Fertilization: Fertilize only during late spring and summer months.
Propagation: Take cuttings from stems or shoots that have recently matured.
Grooming: Prune in early spring. Keep to desired height and shape with light pruning or clipping at any time.
Repotting: Repot in winter or early spring, as needed.
Problems: Will get spindly and weak if light is too low.

Camellia species

These evergreen shrubs with dark green, glossy leaves produce large, fragrant flowers in shades of white, pink, or red in spring. *C. japonica,* a species commonly grown indoors, has more than 2,000 known cultivars in a variety of colors, sizes, and shapes.

Great care must be taken for this plant to grow well. A cool room with good circulation is a must. In the spring, a mass of buds will appear. At that point do not move the plant, and guard against temperature fluctuations and soil moisture or the buds will drop.
Light: Keep in about 4 hours of direct sun in winter. Provide curtain-filtered sunlight in summer, from a south or west window.
Water: Keep evenly moist. Water thoroughly and discard drainage.
Humidity: Average indoor levels.
Temperatures: 40°F to 45°F at night, 60°F to 65°F during the day.
Fertilization: Use an acid-balanced fertilizer and add trace elements once in spring.
Propagation: Take cuttings from stems or shoots that have recently matured.
Grooming: Prune after flowering. Pinch back new stem tips to improve form. Do not destroy flower buds.
Repotting: Infrequent repotting is best.
Problems: If plant is left in a draft or dry air, its leaves will scorch. They drop if soil is too wet or too dry.

Camellia japonica 'Dahurica Variegata'

Campanula
Star of Bethlehem, Bellflower

Campanulas are small, bushy plants that will bear an abundance of flowers from August through November. The flowers are purple, blue, or white, and often hang down in clusters on short stems. This is where the name "bellflower" comes from. Many indoor gardeners prefer to plant them in a small hanging basket. After cutting back, pinch back stem tips for 6 to 8 weeks to encourage branching.
Light: Keep in about 4 hours of direct sun in winter. Provide curtain-filtered sunlight in summer, from a south or west window.
Water: Keep very moist during growth and flowering. Allow to dry between waterings at other times.
Humidity: Average indoor levels.
Temperatures: 50°F to 55°F at night, 65°F to 70°F during the day.
Fertilization: Fertilize only during late spring and summer months.
Propagation: Take cuttings from stems or shoots before they have hardened or matured.
Grooming: Cut back in late fall or early winter, as needed. Pinch back new stem tips to improve form. Do not destroy flower buds.
Repotting: Repot in winter or early spring, as needed.
Problems: If plant is in a draft or dry air, its leaves will scorch. Poor drainage, too frequent watering, or standing in water will cause root rot.

Capsicum species
Ornamental pepper

These plants are not particularly note-worthy until they become loaded with fruit in late summer and fall. Since it takes very good light to accomplish heavy blossoming and fruit set, ornamental peppers are best suited for greenhouse culture. The fruit changes from green to yellow to bright red as it matures. Even small plants will set fruit. They make attractive tabletop or windowsill decorations. The fruit is edible but, being a chili pepper, it is extremely hot.

Light: Four hours or more of direct sunlight from a south window. Does best in a greenhouse setting.
Water: Keep evenly moist. Water thoroughly and discard drainage.
Humidity: Average indoor humidity levels.
Temperatures: 55°F to 60°F at night, 70°F to 75°F during the day.
Fertilization: Fertilize only when plant is growing actively or flowering.
Propagation: Start from seeds. Begin in a small pot and transplant as needed.
Grooming: Prune in spring. Pinch out new stem tips to improve form. Do not destroy flower buds.
Repotting: Repot in winter or early spring, as needed.
Problems: Will not bloom if light is too low. Its leaves will drop if soil is too wet or too dry. Aphids and spider mites may infest these plants.

Carissa macrocarpa
Natal plum

Dwarf cultivars of natal plum do well in greenhouses or solariums. They produce abundant foliage on woody stems. Their large white flowers are fragrant and are followed by red plumlike fruits. These are edible, but have a bitter, cranberry taste. Fruit and blossoms can appear together on the plant at certain times of the year. Keep natal plums pruned to between 2 and 3 feet to prevent legginess.

Light: Four hours or more of direct sunlight from a south window. Does best in a greenhouse setting.
Water: Keep evenly moist. Water thoroughly and discard drainage.

Campanula poscharskyana

Humidity: Average indoor humidity levels.
Temperatures: 55°F to 60°F at night, 70°F to 75°F during the day.
Fertilization: Fertilize 3 times a year: spring, midsummer, and early fall.
Propagation: Take stem cuttings at any time.
Grooming: Keep to desired height and shape with light pruning or clipping at any time.
Repotting: Repot in winter or early spring, as needed.
Problems: Will get spindly and weak if light is too low.

Cestrum, Jasminum
Jasmine

Jasmines are grown primarily for their extremely fragrant blossoms. The greenish white flowers may bloom all year; they are sometimes followed by black berries, which can stain and should be removed. The plants tend to get tall and leggy and may have to be staked. Frequent pruning by pinching stem tips will encourage branching. To promote winter flowering, keep warm and place in a greenhouse or solarium.

Light: Four hours or more of direct sunlight from a south window. Does best in a greenhouse setting.
Water: Keep evenly moist. Water thoroughly and discard drainage.
Humidity: Average indoor humidity levels.
Temperatures: 65°F to 70°F at night, 75°F to 80°F during the day.
Fertilization: Fertilize all year, but more heavily in summer.

Above: *Jasminum magnificum*
Below: *Jasminum magnificum*

Propagation: Take stem cuttings at any time.
Grooming: Prune after flowering or fruiting. Pinch back new stem tips to improve form. Do not destroy flower buds.
Repotting: Can be repotted at any time.
Problems: Will not bloom if light is too low. If the soil is either too wet or too dry, leaves will drop.

Chrysanthemum morifolium

Above: *Chrysanthemum morifolium*
Left: *Chrysanthemum frutescens*

Chrysanthemum frutescens

Marguerite, Boston daisy, Paris daisy

Marguerites are vigorous growers that produce yellow or white flowers intermittently throughout the year. Their lacy foliage has a distinctive aroma. The plants need lots of light to grow indoors. They tend to look rangy if not clipped. Keep them well branched and approximately 12 inches tall. Replace them when they get weak and spindly.
Light: Four hours or more of direct sunlight from a south window. Does best in a greenhouse setting.
Water: Keep evenly moist. Water thoroughly and discard drainage.
Humidity: Average indoor humidity levels.
Temperatures: 40°F to 45°F at night, 60°F to 65°F during the day.
Fertilization: Fertilize all year, but more heavily in summer.
Propagation: Take stem cuttings at any time.
Grooming: Pinch back new stem tips to improve form. Do not destroy flower buds. Start new plants and replace older specimens when they get weak.
Repotting: Can be repotted at any time.
Problems: Spider mites can be a problem, especially if plant is too dry. It will not bloom, and will get spindly and weak, if light is too low.

Chrysanthemum morifolium

Florists' mum

These greenhouse hybrids are often given as gifts. They are considered houseplants because they are usually purchased while blooming, for display indoors. They can be transplanted into the garden, but are difficult to grow outdoors. Think of florists' mums as cut flowers that last longer.

Commercial growers apply dwarfing chemicals to the plants and place them in the dark to induce flowering for certain dates. These small plants have large flowers of every color except blue, and are available throughout the year.

Avoid buying large, leafy plants that have no buds. Look for plants with a few open blossoms and lots of buds. Place the plant in a cool room on a windowsill where it will receive about 4 hours of direct sun daily. Morning or evening sun is best. It should bloom for 6 to 8 weeks.

If you want to save the plant, prune it back and reduce watering; then plant it in your garden. Without growth retardants, they can become quite leggy. Pinch back often to maintain a full, bushy plant.
Light: Place in a bright south, east, or west window.
Water: Keep evenly moist. Water thoroughly and discard drainage.
Humidity: Average indoor humidity levels.
Temperatures: 50°F to 55°F at night, 60°F to 65°F during the day.
Fertilization: Do not fertilize when in flower. Fertilize lightly at other times.
Propagation: Take cuttings from stems or shoots before they have hardened or matured.
Grooming: Discard after flowering.
Repotting: Not usually done.
Problems: Spider mites can be a problem, especially if plant is too dry.

Citrus

Plants in the citrus family are often used indoors as moderately sized shrubs. They include the familiar orange, lemon, lime, and grapefruit, as well as the limequat, tangelo, tangerine, and kumquat (*Fortunella* sp.). They are often chosen by indoor gardeners for their shiny green foliage. However, if given enough light, they will bloom intermittently throughout the year producing fragrant white blossoms. In addition, they may have fruit on them all year. The fruit may be of various hues of green, yellow, and orange because of variation in fruit maturity or ripeness. Most citrus plants used indoors produce rather sour fruit, but even these are good in cooking or making marmalade.

Since citrus may grow slowly indoors, they are often purchased as large plants. Be careful that they are free of scale and mealybugs before you bring them into the same room with other indoor plants. A few weeks in isolation would be a good idea. Keep the plants well pruned to maintain their shape and size. Prune mainly in the late summer, to avoid removing flower buds. Many indoor gardeners prefer to make bonsai specimens of citrus plants that have been in the same container for several years. This is done by cutting back both the roots and the tops each spring and replanting in the same container.

Most citrus can be started from seed. This can often be a good project for children. Place the seed in a small pot, moisten the growing medium, and cover the pot with plastic wrap. Keep the pot moist and warm, and a seedling will emerge in 2 or 3 weeks. It will take approximately 2 years to flower.

Citrus limon
Lemon

Lemons have been grown in greenhouses in the United States for many years. The Meyer lemon is one of the best of the citrus for indoor gardening. It requires lots of light and may not bloom unless light levels are quite high. It can be pruned and kept in bounds, however. Grow in a sandy potting soil and keep well fertilized all year, especially in the summer.

Light: Four hours or more of direct sunlight from a south window. Does best in a greenhouse setting.

Above: *Fortunella margarita* '**Nagami**'
Right: *Citrus limon* '**Lisbon**'

Water: Let plant approach dryness before watering, but water thoroughly and discard drainage.
Humidity: Average indoor levels.
Temperatures: 50°F to 55°F at night, 65°F to 70°F during the day.
Fertilization: Use an acid-balanced fertilizer throughout the year and add trace elements once in spring.
Propagation: Take stem cuttings at any time.
Grooming: Prune to control height; thin out foliage in late winter. Keep to desired height and shape with light pruning or clipping at any time.
Repotting: Repot infrequently.
Problems: Will not bloom if light is too low. If soil is too wet or too dry, leaves will drop. Watch for mealybugs, scale, and spider mites. High soluble salts, high pH, or lack of trace elements (particularly iron) may cause leaf yellowing.

Citrus x limonia
Rangpur lime, Mandarin lime, Otaheite orange

This hybrid citrus is a cross between a lemon and a mandarin orange or tangerine. The dwarf forms are becoming widely available as potted plants from florists or garden centers. They are medium-sized and have dull green leaves. Their flowers are white, tinged with purple. The small yellowish to reddish orange fruits are generally quite bitter but edible. The fruits of the Otaheite orange are sweeter, but they have a dull flavor.

Light: Provide 4 hours or more of direct sunlight from a south window. Does best in a greenhouse setting.

Water: Let plant approach dryness before watering, but water thoroughly and discard drainage each time.
Humidity: Average indoor levels.
Temperatures: 50°F to 55°F at night, 65°F to 70°F during the day.
Fertilization: Use an acid-balanced fertilizer. Add trace elements once a year, in the spring.
Propagation: Take stem cuttings at any time.
Grooming: Keep to desired height and shape with light pruning or clipping at any time.
Repotting: Infrequent repotting is best.
Problems: Will not bloom if light is too low. Leaves will drop if soil is too wet or too dry. Subject to infestations of mealybugs, scale, and spider mites.

Citrus reticulata
Tangerine, Satsuma orange, Temple orange

C. reticulata has many varieties known for fruit production in southern outdoor groves. They are large trees and are not usually grown indoors except in greenhouses. Small varieties make good foliage plants in a location with good light. They may even form an occasional flower, which will be extremely fragrant. Pot citrus in a sandy soil and fertilize often when it is growing, using an acid-based fertilizer. Prune it any time to maintain its shape and size.

Dwarf Citrus x limonia

Light: Does best in a greenhouse setting.
Water: Water thoroughly, but allow to dry between waterings.
Humidity: Average indoor humidity levels.
Temperatures: 50°F to 55°F at night, 65°F to 70°F during the day.
Fertilization: Use an acid-balanced fertilizer throughout the year and add trace elements once in spring.
Propagation: Take cuttings from stems or shoots that have recently matured.
Grooming: Prune just before the heavy blossoming period. Do not cut off flower buds. Keep to desired height and shape with light pruning or clipping at any time.
Repotting: New plants need to grow in a medium to large pot until almost root-bound before they will bloom or set fruit.
Problems: If soil is too wet or too dry, leaves will drop. Watch for scale, mealybugs, and spider mites. High soluble salts, high pH, or lack of trace elements (particularly iron) can cause leaf yellowing.

Citrus sinensis
Sweet orange, Common orange

Sweet oranges are full-sized oranges, so this plant is almost never grown indoors and is grown only occasionally in the greenhouse. As a small plant, it may

not set fruit. However, only a few blossoms are needed to fill a room with fragrance. The foliage, if well supplied with nitrogen and iron, is shiny green all year. Lightly prune at any time, and stake if necessary to keep ripening fruit from making the plant bend over. Do not be alarmed if the fruit fails to mature properly. This often happens indoors because of low light, improper nutrition, or poor pollination.
Light: Does best in a greenhouse setting.
Water: Water thoroughly, but allow to dry between waterings.
Humidity: Average indoor humidity levels.
Temperatures: 65°F to 70°F at night, 75°F to 80°F during the day.
Fertilization: Use an acid-balanced fertilizer throughout the year and add trace elements once in spring.
Propagation: Take cuttings from stems or shoots that have recently matured.
Grooming: Prune just before the heavy blossoming period. Do not cut off flower buds. Keep to desired height and shape with light pruning or clipping at any time.
Repotting: New plants need to grow in a medium to large pot until almost root-bound before they will bloom or set fruit.
Problems: If soil is too wet or too dry, leaves will drop. Scale, spider mites, and mealybugs can cause severe problems. Watch for leaf yellowing due to high salts, high pH, or lack of trace elements (particularly iron).

Fortunella species
Kumquat, Nagami kumquat

This member of the citrus family has a typical citrus fragrance in its white flowers. It blooms in the spring, if light is plentiful. It is best to grow this plant in a greenhouse, since so much light is needed for proper flowering and fruiting. The small but edible fruit will ripen in the fall. It is often made into marmalade. *F. margarita* is a large plant that can be pruned to approximately 3 feet. *F. lindsii* is a much smaller plant, more suited to a window planter. Keep kumquats warm at night and well fertilized with an acid-balanced fertilizer.
Light: Does best in a greenhouse.

Clerodendrum thomsonae 'Variegata'

Water: Keep evenly moist. Water thoroughly and discard drainage.
Humidity: Average indoor humidity levels.
Temperatures: 55°F to 60°F at night, 70°F to 75°F during the day.
Fertilization: Use an acid-balanced fertilizer and add trace elements in the spring.
Propagation: Take cuttings from stems or shoots before they have hardened or matured. Seeds are available, but can be more difficult to use. They take a long time to germinate, and seedlings will have to be carefully nurtured for a year or longer.
Grooming: Prune just before the heavy blossoming period. Do not cut off flower buds. Keep *F. margarita* at a height of 2 to 3 feet.
Repotting: Infrequent repotting is best.
Problems: Mealybugs and scale can be severe. Will not bloom if light is too low. Dry soil or high soluble salts may damage roots, causing plant to die back.

Clerodendrum species
Glory bower, Bleeding heart

Clerodendrums are actually woody shrubs that get quite large when growing outdoors. The most popular cultivar is *C. thomsonae,* which inspired the name "bleeding heart" because of its beautiful and intricate white and red flowers. It is often found in florist shops. The flowers cluster on trailing

stems, so the plant is commonly used in hanging baskets. Keep clerodendrums warm and give them plenty of room.
Light: Provide at least 4 hours of curtain-filtered sunlight from a bright south, east, or west window.
Water: Keep very moist during growth and flowering. Allow to dry between waterings at other times.
Humidity: Average indoor humidity levels.
Temperatures: 55°F to 60°F at night, 70°F to 75°F during the day.
Fertilization: Fertilize only during late spring and summer months.
Propagation: Take cuttings from stems or shoots before they have hardened or matured.
Grooming: Prune after flowering or fruiting. Pinch back new stem tips to improve form. Do not destroy flower buds.
Repotting: Infrequent repotting is best.
Problems: Spider mites can be a problem, especially if plant gets too dry. Poor drainage, too frequent watering, or standing in water will cause root rot.

Clivia miniata
Kaffir lily

This herbaceous plant is a member of the amaryllis family and is named after Charlotte Clive, Duchess of Northumberland, who developed it in 1866 as an indoor plant. Thick stems 12 to 15 inches long emerge from a crown of leathery straplike leaves and support large clusters of orange, trumpet-shaped flowers with yellow throats. French and Belgian hybrids bloom in yellow to deep red-orange. After flowers fade in late spring, ornamental red berries form and add a touch of lasting color.

This winter bloomer does well in a room that receives plenty of indirect sunlight and cools down during the night. Houses in cold climates are most suitable. Crowded roots that are left undisturbed for years produce the best blooms; repotting is rarely necessary. During the fall the plant rests; apply no fertilizer and reduce water. From January to August, fertilize monthly.
Light: Provide at least 4 hours of curtain-filtered sunlight from a bright south, east, or west window.
Water: Keep very moist during

*Above: **Clerodendrum thomsonae***
*Right: **Clivia miniata***

growth and flowering. Allow to dry between waterings at other times.
Humidity: Average indoor humidity levels.
Temperatures: 50°F to 55°F at night, 60°F to 65°F during the day.
Fertilization: Fertilize only when plant is growing actively or flowering.
Propagation: Start new plants from the small bulblets that develop beside the parent bulb.
Grooming: Pick off yellowed leaves. Cut flower stalks if you wish.
Repotting: Infrequent repotting is best.
Problems: Subject to crown rot if planted deeply, watered over the crown, or watered late in the day.

Costus species
Costus, Stepladder plant, Spiral ginger, Spiral flag

These summer-blooming, semiwoody plants need full sun and a lot of moisture. They are best suited for a greenhouse or solarium. Give them plenty of room. They are rhizomatous, with low creeping stems, although some cultivars may send up an occasional shoot that grows as high as 10 feet. *C. fappenbackianus* is a dwarf form more suitable for culture under glass. Costus flowers are large, wide blooms that appear like flags above the foliage. The stems often spiral upward, with leaves in a ladderlike pattern.
Light: Does best in a greenhouse setting.
Water: Keep very moist at all times, but do not allow to stand in water.
Humidity: Requires moist air. Use a humidifier for best results.
Temperatures: 65°F to 70°F at night, 75°F to 80°F during the day.
Fertilization: Fertilize only during late spring and summer months.
Propagation: Start new plants by dividing an older specimen.
Grooming: Prune after flowering or fruiting. Give plants plenty of room.

Repotting: Infrequent repotting is best.
Problems: If plant is in a draft or dry air, plant will scorch. Dry soil or high soluble salts can damage roots, causing plant to die back.

Crinodonna corsii
Crinodonna

This large bulb plant is reasonably easy to grow, once it has adapted to its environment. It needs ample light to produce its large fragrant pink flowers. The flowers form in late summer, in clusters on stalks that are 3 feet tall. The leaves can be 2 feet long, so give it plenty of room. As with most bulbs, this plant needs a dormancy period during the winter.
Light: Four hours or more of direct sunlight from a south window.
Water: Keep very moist during growth and flowering. Allow to dry between waterings at other times.
Humidity: Average indoor levels.

Crossandra infundibuliformis

Crocus

Temperatures: 50°F to 55°F at night, 60°F to 65°F during the day.
Fertilization: Fertilize only when plant is growing actively or flowering.
Propagation: Start new plants from the small bulblets that develop beside the parent bulb.
Grooming: Give these plants plenty of room. Remove old leaves when plant goes dormant.
Repotting: Infrequent repotting is best; once every 3 or 4 years is sufficient. Leave the top third of the bulb out of the soil when repotting.
Problems: Will not bloom if roots are disturbed.

Crinum species
Crinum, Bengal lily, Milk-and-wine lily

Crinums are one of the largest of the bulb plants used for indoor growing and flowering. The pink to red-and-white flowers are fragrant and sometimes 6 inches across. They are borne in clusters on top of a 3-foot-tall stalk. The leaves of the bulb are narrow and 4 feet long. It is a magnificent plant, but needs a lot of room. It flowers in the fall. Keep it well lit, moist, and fertilized from spring until October, and give it a moderately dry resting period during winter.
Light: Provide curtain-filtered sunlight in summer, from a south or west window.
Water: Keep very moist during growth and flowering. Allow to dry between waterings at other times.

Humidity: Average indoor humidity levels.
Temperatures: 50°F to 55°F at night, 65°F to 70°F during the day.
Fertilization: Fertilize only when plant is growing actively or flowering.
Propagation: Start new plants from the small bulblets that develop beside the parent bulb.
Grooming: Remove old leaves as plant goes dormant. Cut flower stalks if you wish. Give the plants plenty of room.
Repotting: Infrequent repotting is best.
Problems: No significant problems.

Crocus species
Crocus

Crocuses, because of their small size, make a good midwinter-flowering pot plant. Florists often sell them in late winter. The plants usually grow only a few inches; they look best in a broad shallow pot, planted in clumps. Varieties are available in many colors and shades. The corms must be given a cold (35°F) treatment in the pot, prior to forcing. Many indoor gardeners will pot newly purchased mature corms in October, place them in a cool (not freezing) place until January, and bring them inside for flowering. After foliage has died back, place the plants in the garden or discard.
Light: Place in a bright, indirectly lit south, east, or west window.
Water: Keep evenly moist. Water thoroughly and discard drainage.
Humidity: Average indoor humidity levels.
Temperatures: 40°F to 45°F at night, 60°F to 65°F during the day.
Fertilization: Do not fertilize when in flower. Fertilize lightly at other times.
Propagation: Start new plants from the small bulblets that develop beside

the parent bulb. It will take several years to get a new corm to blooming size.
Grooming: Cut flower stalks if you wish. Discard after flowering.
Repotting: None needed.
Problems: No significant problems.

Crossandra infundibuliformis
Firecracker flower

If given ample light and fertilizer, crossandras will bloom almost continuously. The flowers appear on short stalks at the ends of growing shoots, overlapping one another on the budded shoot. They are bright salmon-red. Keep these plants very moist with frequent waterings, but do not let them stand in water. Because they are constantly growing, fertilize all year. Cut them back as needed to maintain shape. Discard them when they get leggy or pot-bound.
Light: Four hours of direct sun in winter. Provide curtain-filtered sunlight in summer, from a south or west window.
Water: Keep evenly moist. Water thoroughly and discard drainage.
Humidity: Requires moist air. Use a humidifier for best results.
Temperatures: 55°F to 60°F at night, 70°F to 75°F during the day.
Fertilization: Fertilize all year, but more heavily in summer.
Propagation: Start from seeds. Begin in a small pot and transplant as needed. Take stem cuttings at any time.
Grooming: Keep to desired height and shape with light pruning or clipping at any time. Start new plants and replace older specimens when they get weak.
Repotting: Transplant seedlings several times as plants grow.
Problems: Poor drainage, too frequent watering, or standing in water will cause root rot.

Cuphea ignea

Cuphea ignea
Cigar plant

In good light, these plants will produce their unusual flowers for most of the year. Their red tubular flowers have a white tip that resembles ashes, giving this plant its common name. It is a bushy plant that must be pruned properly to maintain a good shape. Other species produce much smaller flowers and leaves. They all need good light to grow well and continue flowering.
Light: Four hours or more of direct sunlight from a south window. Does best in a greenhouse setting.
Water: Keep evenly moist. Water thoroughly and discard drainage.
Humidity: Requires moist air. Use a humidifier for best results.
Temperatures: 50°F to 55°F at night, 65°F to 70°F during the day.
Fertilization: Fertilize only during late spring and summer months.
Propagation: Take stem cuttings at any time. Seeds are available, but can be more difficult to use. Start in February for summer flowering, and again in July for winter blossoms.
Grooming: Discard after flowering.
Repotting: Transplant seedlings several times as plants grow.
Problems: No blooms in low light.

Cyclamen species
Cyclamen

Heart-shaped, dark green leaves surround upright stems, which are topped with butterflylike blossoms from mid-autumn until midspring. Of the 15 species in the genus, *C. persicum* is most commonly grown indoors and is readily available from florists. It's best to purchase your plants in early fall when the blooming season begins.

This plant does best in a cool room with good air circulation but no drafts. When blooming, it needs as much sun as possible. Fertilize every 2 weeks.

Many people automatically discard cyclamen after blooming, but the plants can be kept if they are given special care. When blooming ceases and foliage dies back, put the plant in a cool spot and let the soil dry. In midsummer repot the tuber with new soil in a small pot and place it in a warm spot to encourage good root growth. As the plant grows, gradually return it to a cool location (55°F) to induce blooming.
Light: Place in a bright, indirectly lit south, east, or west window.
Water: Keep evenly moist. Water thoroughly and discard drainage.
Humidity: Average indoor humidity levels.
Temperatures: 50°F to 55°F at night, 60°F to 65°F during the day.
Fertilization: Fertilize only when plant is growing actively or flowering.
Propagation: Start from seeds. Begin in a small pot and transplant as needed. It may take 2 years to get a blooming plant.
Grooming: Pick off yellowed leaves.
Repotting: Repot each year, in midsummer.
Problems: Subject to crown rot if planted deeply, watered over the crown, or watered late in the day.

Daphne odora
Winter daphne

This winter-flowering woody plant produces clusters of small pink or reddish flowers with a very sweet fragrance. Its leathery foliage is shiny green, with leaves about 3 inches long. There is a variegated form with creamy white leaf edges. The plants will get large, but are

Cyclamen persicum

most attractive if kept pruned to a foot high.
Light: Provide at least 4 hours of curtain-filtered sunlight from a bright south, east, or west window.
Water: Let plant approach dryness before watering, but water thoroughly and discard drainage.
Humidity: Average indoor humidity levels.
Temperatures: 40°F to 45°F at night, 60°F to 65°F during the day.
Fertilization: Fertilize lightly once a year in early spring. Use an acid-balanced fertilizer with trace elements.
Propagation: Take cuttings from stems or shoots that have recently matured.
Grooming: Prune in early spring. Keep to desired height and shape with light pruning or clipping at any time.
Repotting: Repot in winter or early spring, as needed.
Problems: Poor drainage, too frequent watering, or standing in water will cause root rot. Leaves may yellow from high soluble salts, high pH levels, or a lack of iron.

Erica

Eranthemum species
Blue sage

This plant produces clusters of medium-sized blue flowers on short stems. It is a winter-flowering plant so special care should be taken to keep it warm, give it plenty of light, and fertilize it lightly during winter. *E. nervosum* grows to 2 or 3 feet high. *E. wattii* is a smaller plant, with correspondingly smaller flowers. Give these plants a dormancy period in early summer.
Light: Keep in about 4 hours of direct sun in winter. Provide curtain-filtered sunlight in summer, from a south or west window.
Water: Keep very moist during growth and flowering. Allow to dry between waterings at other times.
Humidity: Average indoor humidity levels.
Temperatures: 55°F to 60°F at night, 70°F to 75°F during the day.
Fertilization: Fertilize only when plant is growing actively or flowering.
Propagation: Take cuttings from stems or shoots before they have hardened or matured.

Grooming: Pinch back stem tips of young or regrowing plant to improve form. Do not destroy flower buds. Cut back after dormancy period, just as new growth is starting.
Repotting: Repot infrequently.
Problems: Will not bloom if light is too low.

Erica species
Heath

The heaths are a large group of plants used in cool northern landscapes. A few cultivars are commercially grown for cut flowers. Many of the smaller types make fine indoor plants if given enough light. The blooms are of varying colors and are usually quite fragrant. The plants are bushy and produce dense branches and tiny narrow leaves that can be easily pruned or clipped. Heaths are very sensitive to soluble salts from excessive fertilizer or improper watering.
Light: Provide at least 4 hours of curtain-filtered sunlight from a bright south, east, or west window.
Water: Let plant approach dryness before watering, but water thoroughly and discard drainage.
Humidity: Requires moist air. Use a humidifer for best results.
Temperatures: 50°F to 55°F at night, 60°F to 65°F during the day.
Fertilization: Fertilize lightly once a year, in early spring.
Propagation: Take cuttings from stems or shoots that have recently matured.
Grooming: Keep to the desired height and shape with light pruning or clipping at any time.
Repotting: Repot in winter or early spring, as needed.
Problems: Will not bloom if light is too low. Dry soil or high soluble salts may damage roots, causing plant to die back.

Eriobotrya japonica
Japanese loquat

Japanese loquat is a small tree or shrub often used in southwestern landscapes as an informal hedge or an espaliered specimen plant. The 6- to 12-inch-long leaves are dark green on top and tan beneath. Clusters of small, fragrant white flowers are produced in the late

Eucharis grandiflora

fall or early winter. If given enough light, fertilizer, and warmth, small edible fruit will ripen in mid- to late spring. Loquats can get quite large, but will grow well in a solarium or greenhouse. Prune them well in the spring to maintain a proper size and shape.
Light: Four hours or more of direct sunlight from a south window. Does best in a greenhouse setting.
Water: Keep evenly moist. Water thoroughly and discard drainage.
Humidity: Average indoor levels.
Temperatures: 55°F to 60°F at night, 70°F to 75°F during the day.
Fertilization: Use an acid-balanced fertilizer and add trace elements once in spring.
Propagation: Take cuttings from stems or shoots before they have hardened or matured.
Grooming: Prune in early spring. Be careful not to cut off flower buds or young fruit.
Repotting: Infrequent repotting is best.
Problems: Will not bloom if light is too low. If soil is too wet or too dry, leaves will drop.

Eucharis grandiflora
Amazon lily

Amazon lilies are easy-to-grow bulbs that will flower even in indirect indoor light. They are very large plants. The flowers are white and borne in groups of 3 to 6 on a 2-foot-high stalk. The bulb

Eucharis grandiflora

Euphorbia milii

Euphorbia pulcherrima

may bloom as many as 3 times a year. The plant must be kept very moist and well fertilized while it is growing. Only a short resting period is needed. Never let it get excessively dry, and do not fertilize when it is not growing. Keep the plant warm, especially at night.
Light: Place in a bright, indirectly lit south, east, or west window.
Water: Keep very moist during growth and flowering. Allow to dry between waterings at other times.
Humidity: Requires moist air. Use a humidifier for best results.
Temperatures: 65°F to 70°F at night, 75°F to 80°F during the day.
Fertilization: Fertilize only when plant is growing actively or flowering.
Propagation: Start new plants from the small bulblets that develop beside the parent bulb.
Grooming: Give these plants plenty of room.
Repotting: Repot infrequently.
Problems: If plant is in a draft or in dry air, leaves will scorch. Poor drainage, too frequent watering, or standing in water will cause root rot.

Euphorbia milii
Crown of thorns

There are more than 1,500 species of euphorbias, including the popular poinsettia. Actually, crown of thorns is more typical of the genus. It is a shrub with spiny stems, and can grow to 3 feet. The small leaves are borne near the stem tips. Small red flowers appear on the plant in the summer. If given

ample light, blooming will persist for many months. After flowering ceases, keep the plant drier so that it can rest.
Light: Place in a bright, indirectly lit south, east, or west window.
Water: Keep very moist during growth and flowering. Allow to dry between waterings at other times.
Humidity: Average indoor levels.
Temperatures: 55°F to 60°F at night, 70°F to 75°F during the day.
Fertilization: Fertilize only when plant is growing actively or flowering.
Propagation: Take stem cuttings at any time. Seeds are available, but can be more difficult to use.
Grooming: Prune after flowering. Keep to desired height and shape with light pruning or clipping at any time.
Repotting: Cut back and repot when flowering stops. Infrequent repotting is best.
Problems: Will not bloom if light is too low.

Euphorbia pulcherrima
Poinsettia

The poinsettia was first found in Mexico in the 1800s, growing as a wild flower, and since has been cultivated in the United States to become the most popular living Christmas gift. The large white, pink, or red flowers are actually a group of bracts that surround a small, inconspicuous true flower. Ranging in height from 1 to 3 feet, some have blossoms that are 6 to 12 inches wide.

With proper care these plants will continue to bloom for several months, and some can be made to blossom the following season. While blooming, the plants simply need plenty of sun and protection from drafts and sudden changes in temperature. Reduce water during the rest period from spring to midsummer, then increase waterings and apply fertilizer every 2 weeks. These plants normally flower in the fall when the nights are long. Beginning

about October 1, they need 2 weeks of long (12-hour) nights, uninterrupted by any light source, before flowers are initiated. If your plant is indoors, be sure that household lights do not interrupt this darkness. You may have to place the plant in a dark closet at night or put it outdoors in a protected spot.
Light: Place in a bright, indirectly lit south, east, or west window.
Water: Keep evenly moist. Water thoroughly and discard drainage.
Humidity: Average indoor humidity levels.
Temperatures: 50°F to 55°F at night, 65°F to 70°F during the day.
Fertilization: Fertilize all year, but more heavily in summer.
Propagation: Take cuttings from stems or shoots before they have hardened or matured.
Grooming: Prune after flowering. Pinch back stem tips of young or regrowing plants to improve form. Do not destroy flower buds.
Repotting: Infrequent repotting is best. Repot in winter or early spring as needed.
Problems: If soil is too wet or too dry, or if plant is suddenly moved to a spot where light is low, its leaves will drop. Poor drainage, overwatering, or standing in water will cause root rot.

Above: *Exacum affine*
Below: *Felicia amelliodes 'San Luis'*

Exacum affine
Arabian violet

Arabian violets are popular because they will bloom in small pots. Plants are commonly covered with tiny blue flowers with yellow centers. Many florist shops carry them throughout the fall and winter. The seedlings must be handled carefully, because slight injuries may lead to stem rot and cankering. Keep the tiny seedlings in moist air and out of direct sun. As the plants get bigger, provide some direct sun in the fall to encourage blooming. Never place the plants in cool drafts, and don't water them with cold water.

Light: Keep in about 4 hours of direct sun in winter. Provide curtain-filtered sunlight in summer, from a south or west window.

Water: Keep evenly moist. Water thoroughly and discard drainage.

Humidity: Requires moist air. Use a humidifier for best results.

Temperatures: 55°F to 60°F at night, 70°F to 75°F during the day.

Fertilization: Fertilize only during late spring and summer months.

Propagation: Start from seeds in spring. Begin in a small pot and transplant as needed.

Grooming: Discard after flowering.

Repotting: Transplant seedlings several times as plants grow.

Problems: Dry soil or high soluble salts may damage roots, causing plant to die back. Subject to crown rot if planted deeply, watered over the crown, or watered late in the day. Susceptible to whiteflies.

Felicia amellioides
Blue marguerite, Blue daisy

If they get a great deal of light, felicias can produce their blue, yellow-centered blooms almost continually. The plant is normally a bit leggy and will need frequent clipping, but be careful not to clip off the flowering stalks. The leaves are a half-inch long, with a rough texture. Do not overfertilize this plant in the winter.

Light: Four hours or more of direct sunlight from a south window.

Water: Let plant approach dryness before watering, but water thoroughly and discard drainage.

Humidity: Average indoor humidity levels.

Temperatures: 50°F to 55°F at night, 65°F to 70°F during the day.

Fertilization: Fertilize all year, but more heavily in summer.

Propagation: Start from seeds in midsummer. Begin in a small pot and transplant as needed. Take cuttings in spring.

Grooming: Keep to desired height and shape with light pruning or clipping at any time.

Repotting: Repot in winter or early spring, as needed.

Problems: Dry soil or high soluble salts may damage roots, causing plant to die back. Will get spindly and weak if the light is too low.

Freesia

Fragaria species
Alpine strawberry

This strawberry is suitable for indoor gardens because it quickly multiplies to form dense growth in a pot, but it does not produce runners. It needs sun to flower and set fruit. The berries are small but very flavorful. Keep the plants cool and in moist air. Many gardeners take them outside into a patio garden during the summer. If you do this, make sure they are pest-free before bringing them back indoors.

Light: Keep in about 4 hours of direct sun in winter. Provide curtain-filtered sunlight in summer, from a south or west window.

Water: Let plant approach dryness before watering, but water thoroughly and discard drainage.

Humidity: Requires moist air. Use a humidifier for best results.

Temperatures: 50°F to 55°F at night, 65°F to 70°F during the day.

Fertilization: Fertilize only when plant is growing actively or flowering.

Propagation: Start new plants by dividing an older specimen. Seeds are also available, but can be more difficult to use.

Grooming: Start new plants and replace older specimens when they get weak.

Repotting: Repot in winter or early spring, as needed.

Problems: If plant is in a draft or dry air, leaves will scorch. Will not bloom if light is too low. Susceptible to spider mites, especially if plant is too dry.

Fuchsia x hybrida

Freesia species
Freesia

Freesias are bulbous plants grown widely in Europe and the United States for cut-flower arrangements. The flowers· are extremely fragrant and come in many colors and patterns. You can force them into bloom as you would tulips or daffodils. Purchase a mature bulb in the fall, pot it, and place it in a cool (not freezing) location until January. Then place the pot in a warm, brightly lit spot for forcing. Freesias can grow quite tall and may need staking. It is best to discard this plant after flowering. Freesias will not survive outdoors in climates where it freezes in the winter.
Light: Keep in about 4 hours of direct sun in winter.
Water: Keep evenly moist. Water thoroughly and discard drainage.
Humidity: Average indoor humidity levels.
Temperatures: 50°F to 55°F at night, 60°F to 65°F during the day.
Fertilization: Do not fertilize when forcing into bloom.
Propagation: Bulbs are generally discarded after blooming. In mild climates, they may be planted outdoors.
Grooming: Discard after flowering.
Repotting: Not needed.
Problems: No significant problems.

Fuchsia x hybrida
Fuchsia, Lady's-eardrops

The showy, simple flowers and thin green or variegated leaves of fuchsia form beautiful shrubs. Sepals are petal-like structures that enclose flower buds. Normally they are green; however, fuchsias have colored sepals that flare open to reveal pendant petals. The petals can be the same color as the sepals or a different hue. Colors range from white through pink, red, lavender, violet, and purple, in countless combinations. There are thousands of fuchsia strains, in a great variety of shapes and sizes. Many make excellent hanging plants or do well in window boxes.

Fuchsias thrive only in cool summer environments. Success largely depends on finding the proper spot, so choose your location carefully. During the summer, it's a good idea to plant or move them outdoors. Feed frequently and always keep the soil moist. Plants in hanging baskets dry out quickly, so check them frequently.
Light: Keep in about 4 hours of direct sun in winter. Provide curtain-filtered sunlight in summer, from a south or west window.
Water: Keep very moist at all times, but do not allow to stand in water.
Humidity: Average indoor humidity levels.
Temperatures: 50°F to 55°F at night, 60°F to 65°F during the day.
Fertilization: Fertilize only during late spring and summer months.
Propagation: Take cuttings from stems or shoots before they have hardened or matured.
Grooming: Prune in early spring. Pinch back stem tips of young or regrowing plants to improve form. Do not destroy flower buds.
Repotting: Repot each year.
Problems: Summer heat may cause plant to die back. If soil is too wet or too dry, leaves will drop. Susceptible to whiteflies.

Gardenia jasminoides
Gardenia, Cape jasmine

Discovered in China in the 1700s, there are about 200 species of this flower. The heady aroma of these creamy, spiraling blossoms is sure to please everyone. *G. jasminoides* has large, glossy, dark green

Gardenia jasminoides

leaves, and produces an abundance of flowers. It is the type most often grown indoors. Some varieties bloom in the summer, and others bloom throughout the year. Oil extracted from the flower is used in perfumes and tea. They make excellent cut flowers.

Formerly, these plants were very popular additions to the greenhouse, and rightly so. Gardenias kept indoors must have high humidity and cool nights as well as plenty of sunlight. The plant will not set buds if night temperatures exceed 65°F.
Light: Keep in about 4 hours of direct sun in winter. In summer, provide curtain-filtered sunlight from a south or west window.
Water: Keep very moist at all times, but do not allow to stand in water.
Humidity: Requires moist air. Use a humidifier for best results.
Temperatures: 50°F to 55°F at night, 65°F to 70°F during the day.
Fertilization: Use an acid-balanced fertilizer and add trace elements once in spring.
Propagation: Take cuttings from stems or shoots that have recently matured.
Grooming: Prune in early spring. Pinch back stem tips of young or regrowing plants to improve form. Do not destroy flower buds.
Repotting: Infrequent repotting is best.
Problems: Bud drop results from plant stress. If soil is too wet or too dry, leaves will drop. This plant will not bloom if light is too low.

Gazania

Gazania species
Gazania, Treasure flower

Gazanias produce large flowers on tall stems. They come in yellow, orange, red, or white. The plant needs lots of light to flower. Flowers usually close at night and on cloudy days. Leaves grow in a clump or rosette at the base of the flower stalks. Repot fairly frequently to keep the plant growing and blooming regularly. In the winter, take care to keep it warm and in plenty of light for continued blooming.

Light: Four hours or more of direct sunlight from a south window.

Water: Water thoroughly, but allow to dry out between waterings.

Humidity: Average indoor humidity levels.

Temperatures: 55°F to 60°F at night, 70°F to 75°F during the day.

Fertilization: Fertilize all year, but more heavily in summer.

Propagation: Start new plants by dividing an older specimen. Start from seeds. Begin in a small pot and transplant as needed.

Grooming: Pick off yellowed leaves.

Repotting: Transplant seedlings several times as plants grow. Repot each year.

Problems: Will not bloom if light is too low. Susceptible to spider mites, especially if plant is too dry.

Gelsemium sempervirens
Carolina jasmine

Carolina jasmine is a large vine that needs to be in a hanging basket, staked in a pot, or trained onto a small trellis. Expect vines to get 3 or 4 feet long. Their yellow flowers appear in winter and early spring. They are quite fragrant. Because it is a winter-flowering plant, take care to provide good light and sufficient warmth. Warm the water you use for irrigation to room temperature.

Light: Provide at least 4 hours of curtain-filtered sunlight from a bright south, east, or west window.

Water: Keep evenly moist. Water thoroughly and discard drainage.

Humidity: Requires moist air. Use a humidifier for best results.

Temperatures: 50°F to 55°F at night, 65°F to 70°F during the day.

Fertilization: Fertilize only when plant is growing actively or flowering.

Propagation: Take cuttings from stems or shoots that have recently matured. New plants can be started with air layering.

Grooming: Prune after flowering.

Repotting: Infrequent repotting is best.

Problems: Will not bloom if light is too low.

Gesneriads

African violets, the gesneriads most familiar to indoor gardeners, have been much improved in recent years. Many other gesneriads, such as nematanthys, gloxinias, and streptocarpus, are available in florist shops, garden centers, and supermarkets.

The variety of forms and colorings of the more than 120 genera and 2,000 species of plants in this family is truly outstanding. Gesneriads are classified according to rooting type and growth habit. African violets and episcias are two of the best known of the fibrous-rooted genera. Tuberous-rooted gesneriads include florists' gloxinias. Achimenes is an example of those gesneriads that form scaly rhizomes laterally, underground. Most genera hybridize and cross within species easily, which leads to the

Achimenes 'Menuette'

development of many varied cultivars. Many dwarf cultivars are now being developed, furthering both their usefulness and popularity. Most gesneriads are easy to propagate, where plant patents permit. They serve well as children's plant projects or as gifts for plant-collecting friends.

Gesneriads are usually grown for their blossoms. Many, such as episcias and columneas, have equally attractive foliage. Some get quite large and are useful specimens to dominate arrangements in hanging baskets, or as pedestal plants. Many indoor gardeners grow gesneriads in one place and put them temporarily in other areas when needed for decoration. Maintaining symmetry in their rosettes of foliage is the key to a gesneriad specimen. Grow them on an evenly lit light bench for best results.

Since gesneriads have such variety, the following plant descriptions have differing care guides. In general, gesneriads adapt well to indoor culture. Most bloom for long periods, given good light. Many adapt to lighted indoor gardens, plant shelves, or terrariums. They need warmth, even moisture, light fertilization, and no direct sun. The tuberous-rooted gesneriads and some of the rhizomatous kinds require a rest period after flowering, during which water and fertilizer should be lessened or completely withheld for a few weeks.

Achimenes
*Rainbow flower, Magic flower,
Nut orchid, Widow's tear*

Many cultivars of achimenes offer a variety of flower colors, from light blue to deep red and yellow. They are often found in florist shops. Like their African violet relatives, they need warmth to grow well and ample light to blossom. Achimenes are bushy plants that are often trained into hanging baskets. The foliage of many cultivars is attractive by itself, especially if the branches are properly pinched and trained when the plants are young.

Light: Provide at least 4 hours of curtain-filtered sunlight from a bright south, east, or west window.
Water: Keep evenly moist. Water thoroughly and discard drainage.
Humidity: Requires moist air. Use a humidifier for best results.
Temperatures: 65°F to 70°F at night, 75°F to 80°F during the day.
Fertilization: Fertilize 3 times a year: spring, midsummer, and early fall.
Propagation: Start new plants by dividing an older specimen. Seeds can be planted in spring.
Grooming: Pinch back stem tips of young or regrowing plants to improve form. Do not destroy flower buds.
Repotting: Let plant die back after flowering; remove rhizomes and repot. Store the rhizomes at 60°F, packed in dry peat moss or vermiculite. Keep recently potted plants warm and only moderately moist.
Problems: Will not bloom if light is too low. If soil is too wet or too dry, leaves will drop. Dry soil or high soluble salts may damage roots, causing plant to die back.

Aeschynanthus species
Basket vine, Lipstick plant

This gesneriad has thick reddish foliage, abundantly produced on trailing stems. It is best in a hanging basket. The tubelike flowers are borne at various points along the stems. In good light, basket vines can be covered with hundreds of blooms. Many cultivars are called lipstick plant because the buds resemble a tube of lipstick.

Aeschynanthus

These plants require night warmth and good winter light. They can be purchased from florists. Small plants will take some time to train and grow before they fill a large basket.
Light: Provide at least 4 hours of curtain-filtered sunlight from a south, east, or west window.
Water: Keep evenly moist. Water thoroughly and discard drainage.
Humidity: Average indoor humidity levels.
Temperatures: 65°F to 70°F at night, 75°F to 80°F during the day.
Fertilization: Fertilize lightly each month from January through September.
Propagation: Take cuttings from stems or shoots before they have hardened or matured.
Grooming: Prune after flowering. Start new plants and replace older specimens when they get weak.
Repotting: Infrequent repotting is best.
Problems: Will not bloom if light is too low. Dry soil or high soluble salts may damage roots, causing plant to die back. Watch for mealybugs.

Alloplectus species
Goldfish plant

These creeping vines are often used in hanging baskets. They have thin, hairy reddish branches that bear leaves rimmed with short petioles. Flowers occur at different points on the leaf axils. They are orange-red and have the shape of a tropical fish. Most bloom in the summer and must receive a dormancy period after flowering. When resting, they are very sensitive to overwatering and excessive soluble salts.
Light: Provide at least 4 hours of curtain-filtered sunlight from a bright south, east, or west window.
Water: Keep very moist during growth and flowering. Allow to dry between waterings at other times.
Humidity: Average indoor humidity levels.
Temperatures: 65°F to 70°F at night, 75°F to 80°F during the day.
Fertilization: Fertilize only when plant is growing actively or flowering.
Propagation: Take cuttings from stems or shoots before they have hardened or matured.
Grooming: Prune after flowering.
Repotting: Repot infrequently.

Columnea 'California Gold'

Problems: Will not bloom if light is too low. If soil is too wet or too dry, leaves will drop. Subject to crown rot if planted deeply, watered over the crown, or watered late in the day.

Chirita species
Chirita

Chirita is a gesneriad related to gloxinias and African violets. *C. lavandulaceae* is large, often growing to 2 feet or more, with leaves 8 inches long and 4 inches wide. The plant will flower best in late summer. However, if light is sufficient, it will have purple and white blossoms throughout the year. *C. sinensis* is smaller and rosetted, more suited to light benches or window boxes. Both plants need warmth and plenty of humidity.
Light: Keep in about 4 hours of direct sun in winter. Provide curtain-filtered sunlight in summer, from a south or west window.
Water: Keep very moist at all times, but do not allow to stand in water.
Humidity: Requires moist air. Use a humidifier for best results.
Temperatures: 65°F to 70°F at night, 75°F to 80°F during the day.
Fertilization: Fertilize all year, but more heavily in summer.
Propagation: Take stem cuttings at any time.
Grooming: Pinch back stem tips of young or regrowing plants to improve form. Do not destroy flower buds. Discard after flowering. Give these plants plenty of room.
Repotting: Discard after flowering.
Problems: Dry soil or high soluble salts may damage roots, causing plant to die back. Will not bloom in low light.

Columnea species
Columnea

There are 150 different species of this member of the gesneriad family. They come from Central and South America and the West Indies; their natural habitat is the damp tropical forest. They make wonderful container plants, and because they are semiupright or trailing plants, they look especially nice in hanging baskets. The brightly colored tubular flowers come in orange, scarlet, and yellow and bloom all through the winter. Flowers range in size from ½ to 4 inches, depending on the variety. Leaves vary from button size to 3 inches in length. *C. banksii*, which has waxy leaves, is one of the easiest to grow. *C. gloriosa* has hairy leaves and red flowers.
    These aren't the easiest plants to grow, but keeping the air moist will help them stay healthy and blooming. Water carefully during the winter, and keep them away from heat sources.
Light: Provide at least 4 hours of curtain-filtered sunlight from a bright south, east, or west window.
Water: Keep very moist during growth and flowering. Allow to dry between waterings at other times.
Humidity: Requires moist air. Use a humidifier for best results.
Temperatures: 55°F to 60°F at night, 70°F to 75°F during the day.
Fertilization: Fertilize only during late spring and summer months.
Propagation: Take cuttings from stems or shoots that have recently matured.
Grooming: Prune after flowering or fruiting. Pinch back new stem tips to improve form. Do not destroy flower buds.
Repotting: Infrequent repotting is best.
Problems: Subject to crown rot if planted deeply, watered over the crown, or watered late in the day. Will not bloom if light is too low.

Episcia species
Episcia

Episcias are available in many cultivars, each with distinctive foliage texture and variegated coloring. Many gardeners value them for their foliage alone. In the summer, episcias produce small flowers

Columnea

in reds, oranges, or whites. Their stems trail, and they are generally used in hanging baskets or as ground covers in well-lit terrariums. Keep them in a damp environment; to induce branching, pinch back their stems after flowering.
Light: Place in a bright, indirectly lit south, east, or west window.
Water: Keep very moist during growth and flowering. Allow to dry between waterings at other times.
Humidity: Requires moist air. Use a humidifier for best results.
Temperatures: 65°F to 70°F at night, 75°F to 80°F during the day.
Fertilization: Fertilize only during late spring and summer months.
Propagation: Remove new plantlets or rooted side shoots as they form. Runners can be layered to root and form plantlets.
Grooming: Prune after flowering or fruiting. Pinch back new stem tips to improve form. Do not destroy flower buds.
Repotting: Repot in winter or early spring, as needed.
Problems: If plant is in a draft or dry air, leaves will scorch. Poor drainage, too frequent watering, or standing in water will cause root rot.

Episcia cupreata

Above: *Kohleria 'Flirt'*
Below: *Nematanthus 'Black Gold'*

Gloxinera hybrids
Gloxinera

Gloxineras were developed by crossing the popular gloxinia with another gesneriad. There is a lot of variation from one cultivar to another in these herbaceous plants. Most flower in late spring and summer, with clusters of red or lavender blossoms borne on stalks above the foliage. Many miniature gloxineras are suited for well-lit terrariums. Keep gloxineras moist and warm when flowering, and allow them to rest afterward. If you wish, you can remove tubers from the soil, store them in a bag with some damp peat in a cool spot, and replant when they sprout.
Light: Provide at least 4 hours of curtain-filtered sunlight from a bright south, east, or west window.
Water: Keep evenly moist. Water thoroughly and discard drainage.
Humidity: Requires moist air. Use a humidifier for best results.
Temperatures: 65°F to 70°F at night, 75°F to 80°F during the day.
Fertilization: Fertilize only when plant is growing actively or flowering.
Propagation: Start new plants from the small bulblets that develop beside the parent bulb.
Grooming: Prune after flowering or fruiting.
Repotting: Repot in winter or early spring, as needed.
Problems: Will not bloom if light is too low. Leaves will scorch if plant is in a draft or dry air.

Kohleria species
Kohleria

Kohlerias are gesneriads with the typically herbaceous stems and soft, hairy foliage of many members of this large family. They are easy to grow, but tend to get leggy when subjected to warm summer nights. They are most often used in hanging baskets. Winter-flowering cultivars are common, but such plants must be given lots of light. Kohlerias need a rest after flowering. They can be cut back during this period.
Light: Provide at least 4 hours of curtain-filtered sunlight from a bright south, east, or west window.
Water: Keep very moist during growth and flowering. Allow to dry between waterings at other times.
Humidity: Requires moist air. Use a humidifier for best results.
Temperatures: 50°F to 55°F at night, 60°F to 65°F during the day.
Fertilization: Fertilize only when plant is growing actively or flowering.
Propagation: Take cuttings from stems or shoots before they have hardened or matured.
Grooming: Prune after flowering or fruiting.
Repotting: Repot after the flowering and dormancy periods.
Problems: Plants will get spindly if exposed to low light and too much warmth.

Nematanthus
Goldfish plant

Like the other plant also called goldfish plant (alloplectus), this gesneriad produces flowers along its trailing stems. The primary flowering period is late summer and fall. The flowers are structured so that they resemble a goldfish, complete with tiny "mouths." The foliage is small and produced closely along the stems, which can reach lengths of 2 feet or more. Keep the plant in a hanging basket, out of drafts and dry air.
Light: Provide at least 4 hours of curtain-filtered sunlight from a bright south, east, or west window.
Water: Keep evenly moist. Water thoroughly and discard drainage.
Humidity: Average indoor humidity levels.
Temperatures: 55°F to 60°F at night, 70°F to 75°F during the day.

Miniature Saintpaulias

Saintpaulia 'Rhapsodie Sabrina'

Fertilization: Fertilize only when plant is growing actively or flowering.
Propagation: Take stem cuttings at any time.
Grooming: Prune in early spring. Pinch back stem tips of young or regrowing plants to improve form. Do not destroy flower buds.
Repotting: Infrequent repotting is best. Repot in winter or early spring as needed.
Problems: Will not bloom if light is too low. Dry soil or high soluble salts may damage roots, causing plant to die back. Susceptible to spider mites, especially if plant is too dry.

Saintpaulia species
African violet

Originally collected in Africa in the late 19th century, these plants are first in any list of favorite flowering plants. No other plant equals the African violet in ability to thrive and bloom indoors for months on end.

Rosettes of velvety leaves on short stems surround clusters of flowers in white or shades of pink, red, violet, purple, or blue. Its compact size makes it perfect for windowsills, small tabletop arrangements, and hanging displays.

There are thousands of named African violets from which to choose. For beginners, it's best to start with varieties that have plain green leaves rather than fancier types, which are not as easy to grow. Consult local experts or plant catalogs to determine your favorite varieties.

Despite their reputation for being temperamental, African violets generally are not difficult to grow. The fact that millions of indoor gardeners grow and collect them attests to their beauty and ease of flowering. Plenty of bright indirect light is the key to constant bloom. Supplement with artificial light if the plant stops blooming, especially in the winter when it receives less than 12 hours of good light a day. Evenly moist soil, warm temperatures, high humidity, and monthly feedings are the other important factors for growth. The plants will flower best with only one crown. Use additional crown growth for rooting new plants.

Miniature African violet varieties have recently been receiving attention. Potted in 2½-inch pots, they grow only 8 inches wide and are real space savers that make wonderful additions to indoor landscapes, terrariums, or miniature greenhouses. Semiminiatures have somewhat smaller leaves and crowns than standards, but their flowers are almost as large. Some of the best miniatures are 'Midget Midnight', 'Tiny Fantasy', 'Baghdad', and 'Silver Bells'. Outstanding semiminiatures include 'Dora Baker', 'Sweet Pixie', and 'Little Dogwood'. Many trailing miniatures and semiminiatures are available. These do well in hanging baskets. Group 2 or 3 in one basket.

In addition to following the care techniques for standard African violets (given below), here are some valuable tips for these newer types. The soil must be kept moist. This is especially important but it can be difficult, because there isn't much soil in the pot and it dries out quickly. Potting several plants together in a larger pot may make your care routine a lot easier by increasing the humidity, moisture, and amount of soil and nutrients available to the plants; however, avoid crowding the plants.

Light: Bright light. Direct sun in winter is fine, but summer sun may be too strong. During winter, supplement with artificial light so that the plant receives at least 14 hours of light a day.
Water: Keep evenly moist. Use only room-temperature water. Avoid wetting foliage; cold water will spot the leaves. Leach soil occasionally.
Humidity: Provide moist air by surrounding base of plant with moist peat moss or by placing on humidifying tray.
Temperatures: Average 72°F to 75°F days; 60°F to 65°F nights. Keep plants away from cold windows. Sudden changes in temperature are harmful.
Fertilization: Fertilize all year, but more heavily in summer.
Propagation: In spring, take leaf cuttings or sow seeds.
Grooming: Remove all dead leaves and flowers promptly (stems included). Shape by removing side shoots.
Repotting: Plant does best when slightly pot-bound. Use pot about half the width of the plant's spread. Plant rooted leaf cuttings in 2½-inch pots.
Problems: Mushy, brown blooms and buds indicate botrytis blight. Pick off diseased parts. Provide good air circulation, avoid high humidity, and use fertilizer with less nitrogen.

Yellow rings on leaf surface are caused by cold water touching foliage. Streaked, misshapen leaves with irregular yellow spots are caused by a virus. There is no cure, so discard plants.

Saintpaulia 'Gypsy Red'

If a healthy plant suddenly wilts, it has crown rot, which results from an erratic watering routine. Do not allow the soil to dry out completely and then soak it. Maintain a constant level of soil moisture. Severe temperature changes may cause crown rot, and plant should be discarded.

Lack of flowering is probably caused by inadequate light. Supplement daylight with artificial light. Very dry air or very cold air may contribute to this. Repotting and moving the plant to a new location can inhibit flowering for a long time.

Yellowing leaves result from dry air, too much sun, incorrect watering, or improper fertilization. Follow fertilizer directions closely. Brown, brittle leaves develop from soil that is deficient in nutrients. Repot if soil is old; otherwise, fertilize regularly.

Slow growth and leaves curled downward indicate that the temperature is too low. Soft foliage and few flowers can be caused by temperatures that are too high. Brown-edged leaves and small flowers result from low humidity. Place plants in humidifying trays.

Sinningia speciosa
Gloxinia

These velvety-leaved Brazilian plants are members of the gesneriad family. Encircled by large, stalkless leaves, bell-shaped flowers with ruffled edges are borne in a cluster atop long stems. Some miniatures—both hybrids and species—have 1½-inch leaves and inch-long flowers that bloom all year.

To grow well and last for many years, gloxinias need humidity, full sun in the winter, and shade in the summer. Keep the soil moist but not too wet, and be sure to use tepid water. After blooming ceases and leaf growth reaches a standstill, gradually withhold water until

stems and leaves die back; put the plant in a cool, dark place for 2 to 4 months while the tuber rests. Water sparingly until new growth appears, then repot into fresh soil, move into light and warmth, and provide moisture. While they are growing, feed gloxinias every 2 weeks.

Light: Place in a bright, indirectly lit south, east, or west window.
Water: Keep evenly moist. Water thoroughly and discard drainage. After flowering, gradually withhold water and allow plant to rest.
Humidity: Average indoor humidity levels.
Temperatures: 55°F to 60°F at night, 70°F to 75°F during the day.
Fertilization: Fertilize only when plant is growing actively or flowering.
Propagation: Start from seeds. Begin in a small pot and transplant as needed. Leaf cuttings are another option.
Grooming: Pick off yellowed leaves.
Repotting: Repot after dormancy period, when growth resumes.
Problems: Subject to crown rot if planted deeply, watered over the crown, or watered late in the day. Plant will not bloom if light is too low.

Sinningia verticillata, S. cardinalis, S. leucotricha
Double-decker plant, Cardinal flower, Brazilian Edelweiss

These plants—cousins of the popular gloxinia—were called *Rechsteineria* until recently. They are taller than gloxinias and have tubular red flowers about 2 inches long. Given enough light, they will bloom during the winter holidays and on into spring and summer. Like most gesneriads, they should be kept warm and only lightly fertilized. Discard these plants or take a top cutting when they get leggy and cease to bloom.

Light: Keep in about 4 hours of direct sun in winter. Provide curtain-filtered sunlight in summer, from a south or west window.
Water: Let plant approach dryness before watering, but water thoroughly and discard drainage.
Humidity: Requires moist air. Use a humidifier for best results.
Temperatures: 65°F to 70°F at night, 75°F to 80°F during the day.
Fertilization: Fertilize only during

Above: *Sinningia speciosa*
Below: *Sinningia cardinalis*

late spring and summer months.
Propagation: Start from seeds. Begin in a small pot and transplant as needed. Cuttings can be taken in spring.
Grooming: Start new plants and replace older specimens when they get weak. Prune after flowering.
Repotting: Transplant seedlings several times as plants grow.
Problems: Subject to crown rot if planted deeply, watered over the crown, or watered late in the day. Will not bloom if light is too low. Dry soil or high soluble salts may damage roots, causing plant to die back.

Streptocarpus

Smithiantha species
Temple bells

This gesneriad produces an attractive spike of bell-shaped flowers from fall through winter, depending on the cultivar. The flowers are about 2 inches long and come in red, orange, yellow, and white. The semiwoody stems bear large, velvety leaves. Like their cousins the gloxinias, temple bells need warmth and constant moisture to bloom well. They require less light than many other gesneriads, however. Some cultivars are large plants and will need more room. After blooming, allow the plants to go dormant, remove the rhizomes, and divide and store them until it is time for repotting in the late summer.

Light: Place in a bright, indirectly lit south, east, or west window.

Water: Keep very moist during growth and flowering. Allow to dry between waterings at other times.

Humidity: Requires moist air. Use a humidifier for best results.

Temperatures: 65°F to 70°F at night, 75°F to 80°F during the day.

Fertilization: Fertilize only when plant is growing actively or flowering.

Propagation: Divide rhizomes. Seeds are also available, but can be more difficult to use.

Grooming: Remove old leaves as plant goes dormant. Cut flower stalks if you wish. Give these plants plenty of room.

Repotting: Repot each year in late summer.

Problems: Leaves will scorch if plant is in draft or dry air. Subject to crown rot if planted deeply, watered over the crown, or watered late in the day.

Streptocarpus species
Cape primrose

Commonly known as the Cape primrose because it is native to the southern tip of Africa, this plant is a relative of the African violet and gloxinia, and can be grown under similar conditions.

Stemless, narrow leaves up to 8 inches long grow beneath large trumpetlike flowers supported by stems similar to those in the primrose plant. Many colorful varieties in white, pink, red, violet, or blue are available. *S. saxorum* has small leaves and lavender flowers. The 'Weismoor' hybrids reach 6 to 8 inches and bear 1½- to 2-inch flowers for 2 months. 'Nymph' hybrids grow 10 to 12 inches high, with 1- to 2-inch flowers that bloom from spring to fall.

Although Cape primrose can be a temperamental, erratic bloomer for many indoor gardeners, it will flourish with correct treatment. This gesneriad needs a cooler environment than do African violets, with a temperature drop at night. Raise it in shallow pots that provide good drainage, and where the air is humid. Feed regularly and water freely during the flowering season.

Light: Provide at least 4 hours of curtain-filtered sunlight from a bright south, east, or west window.

Water: Keep very moist during growth and flowering. Allow to dry between waterings at other times.

Humidity: Requires moist air. Use a humidifier for best results.

Temperatures: 65°F to 70°F at night, 75°F to 80°F during the day.

Fertilization: Fertilize only when plant is growing actively or flowering.

Propagation: Sow seeds in a small pot and transplant as needed. Leaf cuttings can be made with some cultivars.

Grooming: Pick off yellowed leaves. Cut flower stalks if you wish.

Streptocarpus

Repotting: Repot when new growth starts after dormancy.

Problems: Will not bloom if light is too low. If plant is in a draft or dry air, leaves will scorch. Susceptible to spider mites, especially if plant is too dry.

Gibasis species
Tahitian bridal veil

This hanging-basket plant has small pointed leaves borne oppositely along trailing, semiwoody stems. The leaves are green above, with purple undersurfaces. If given enough light, the plant will bear a profusion of tiny, delicate white flowers on thin stalks above the foliage. This is where the name "bridal veil" comes from. The plant is very sensitive to dry air and dry soil. Pinch back growing stems frequently to maintain the proper form. Replace the plant when it gets leggy.

Light: At least moderate light levels, but no direct sunlight. Place in curtain-filtered sunlight to promote blooming.

Water: Keep very moist at all times, but do not allow to stand in water.

Humidity: Requires moist air. Use a humidifier for best results.

Temperatures: 55°F to 60°F at night, 70°F to 75°F during the day.

Fertilization: Fertilize all year, but more heavily in summer.

Propagation: Take stem cuttings.

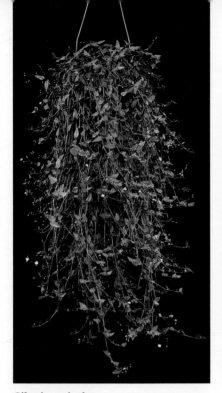

Gibasis geniculata

Gloriosa

Grooming: Start new plants and replace older specimens when they get weak. Pinch back stem tips of young or regrowing plants to improve form. Do not destroy flower buds.
Repotting: Repot in winter or early spring, as needed.
Problems: Will not bloom if light is too low. Dry soil or high soluble salts may damage roots, causing plant to die back.

Gloriosa species
Glory lily, Climbing lily

Gloriosa is a vining plant that has a most intricate, lilylike flower that grows to 4 inches across. The plant climbs vigorously and must be trained on a trellis. It will cling to the trellis with tendrils or "hooks" at the ends of its leaves. Glory lilies must be given moderate dormancy periods between growth cycles. The normal blooming period is midsummer through fall. However, it is possible, by varying the watering of the plant, to alter the resting-growing cycle and promote winter flowering. The plant needs a well-lit location with good night warmth for winter flowering.
Light: Keep in about 4 hours of direct sun in winter. Provide curtain-filtered sunlight in summer, from a south or west window.
Water: Keep very moist during growth and flowering. Allow to dry between waterings at other times.
Humidity: Average indoor levels.
Temperatures: 55°F to 60°F at night, 70°F to 75°F during the day.

Fertilization: Fertilize only when plant is growing actively or flowering.
Propagation: Start new plants from the small bulblets that develop beside the parent bulb.
Grooming: Prune after flowering.
Repotting: Repot in winter or early spring, as needed.
Problems: Will not bloom if light is too low.

Haemanthus
Blood lily

This bulbous lily is fairly easy to grow and will provide a splendid bloom to reward your efforts. The pink to red flowers are borne in a ball-like cluster at the end of a stem that is 12 to 24 inches tall. Flowering generally occurs in the early summer. The plant is large and needs room. The leaves are few but can be 6 inches wide and a foot long.
Light: Provide at least 4 hours of curtain-filtered sunlight from a bright south, east, or west window.
Water: Keep very moist during growth and flowering. Allow to dry between waterings at other times.
Humidity: Requires moist air. Use a humidifier for best results.
Temperatures: 50°F to 55°F at night, 65°F to 70°F during the day.
Fertilization: Fertilize only when plant is growing actively or flowering.
Propagation: Start new plants from the small bulblets that develop beside the parent bulb.
Grooming: Remove old leaves as plant goes dormant. Give these plants plenty of room.

Heliotropium

Repotting: Infrequent repotting is best, as pot-bound plants bloom more profusely. Plant with the tip of the bulb out of the soil.
Problems: Dry soil or high soluble salts may damage roots, causing plant to die back.

Heliotropium hybrids
Heliotrope

Heliotropes are semiwoody shrubs that can be grown as bushy plants (12 inches tall) or as single stems (3 to 4 feet tall). They are popular because of their extremely fragrant flowers. But they will bloom only if given plenty of light.

Hippeastrum

Hibiscus rosa-sinensis

There are many hybrids available with purple, blue, or white flowers. The flowers are small and are borne in clusters 3 to 4 inches wide.

Light: Four hours or more of direct sunlight from a south window. Does best in a greenhouse setting.
Water: Keep evenly moist. Water thoroughly and discard drainage.
Humidity: Requires moist air. Use a humidifier for best results.
Temperatures: 50°F to 55°F at night, 60°F to 65°F during the day.
Fertilization: Fertilize all year, but more heavily in summer.
Propagation: Take stem cuttings at any time. Seeds are available, but can be more difficult to use.
Grooming: Prune after flowering.
Repotting: Transplant seedlings several times as plants grow. Repot in winter or early spring, as needed.
Problems: Will not bloom if light is too low. If soil is too wet or too dry, leaves will drop.

Helxine soleiroli
See *Soleirolia soleirolli*

Hibiscus species
Hibiscus

This woody shrub is popular in outdoor landscapes in warm regions. If given plenty of light and kept pruned to about 3 feet, it is attractive and easy to grow

indoors. The plants have large blooms, available in pink, red, yellow, orange, or white. There are several flower forms available—singles or doubles, for instance. Individual hibiscus flowers are short-lived, but the plant blooms throughout the year.

Light: Four hours or more of direct sunlight from a south window.
Water: Keep evenly moist. Water thoroughly and discard drainage.
Humidity: Requires moist air. Use a humidifier for best results.
Temperatures: 55°F to 60°F at night, 70°F to 75°F during the day.
Fertilization: Fertilize all year, but more heavily in summer.
Propagation: Take cuttings from stems or shoots before they have hardened or matured.
Grooming: Keep to desired height and shape with light pruning or clipping at any time. Give these plants plenty of room.
Repotting: Repot in winter or early spring, as needed.
Problems: Susceptible to spider mites, especially if too dry. If plant is in a draft or dry air, leaves will scorch. Will not bloom in low light.

Hippeastrum species
Amaryllis, Barbados lily

The strap-shaped leaves of this lilylike flower emerge after the plant blooms. Its 1- to 2-foot stems have flower clusters that are 8 to 10 inches wide. They come in a wide array of colors: 'Apple Blossom' is bluish pink, 'Beautiful Lady' is salmon-orange, 'Fire Dance' is bright red, and 'Scarlet Admiral' is deep scarlet. Seed-grown bulbs are sold by color in stores. Strains available through mail-order firms tend to produce more robust flowers.

The plant blooms in late winter and is moderately easy to grow; with proper care it can last for many years. Pot bulbs in October. When flower spike appears, place in well-lit, cool (60°F) location. As buds grow and eventually flower, keep

Hoya

moist and fertilize monthly. After flowering, the foliage will die back; allow the plant to dry out and become dormant.

Light: Place in a bright, indirectly lit south, east, or west window.
Water: Keep very moist during growth and flowering. Allow to dry between waterings at other times.
Humidity: Average indoor humidity levels.
Temperatures: 50°F to 55°F at night, 65°F to 70°F during the day.
Fertilization: Fertilize only when plant is growing actively or flowering.
Propagation: Start new plants from the small bulblets that develop beside the parent bulb.
Grooming: Pick off yellowed leaves.
Repotting: Repot each year.
Problems: Subject to crown rot if planted deeply, watered over the crown, or watered late in the day.

Hoya species
Wax plant

Hoyas are vining plants with thickened leaves produced on self-branching vines. If given enough light, hoyas will produce clusters of extremely fragrant, waxy-looking flowers. Depending on the cultivar, hoyas will bloom in the summer or fall. The flowers form on spurs, so be careful not to prune off these leafless vine extensions. Train the plants on a trellis or use them in a hanging basket. The vines will get quite long, but you can double them back to give a denser appearance to the plant. Many forms have variegated or variously colored leaves.

Light: Place in a bright, indirectly lit south, east, or west window.

Water: Keep very moist during growth and flowering. Allow to dry between waterings at other times.

Humidity: Average indoor humidity levels.

Temperatures: 50°F to 55°F at night, 60°F to 65°F during the day.

Fertilization: Fertilize only when plant is growing actively or flowering.

Propagation: Take stem cuttings at any time.

Grooming: Keep to desired height and shape with light pruning or clipping at any time.

Repotting: Infrequent repotting is best. New plants need to grow in a medium to large pot until almost root-bound before they will bloom.

Problems: Will not bloom if light is too low.

Hyacinthus orientalis
Hyacinth

Hyacinths are usually purchased from florists for indoor blooms in late winter. Their fragrant blossoms come in red, blue, and white. During flowering they can be placed almost anywhere indoors, but need bright light to flourish. To force your own flowers, buy mature bulbs in October, pot them, and allow them to root in a cool, dark spot for 8 weeks. They should bloom in 2 or 3 weeks after being brought indoors. Tend the plant until it dies back, then plant it in your garden.

Light: Provide at least 4 hours of curtain-filtered sunlight from a bright south, east, or west window, after flowering has ceased.

Water: Keep very moist during growth and flowering. Allow to dry between waterings at other times.

Humidity: Average indoor humidity levels.

Temperatures: 50°F to 55°F at night, 60°F to 65°F during the day.

Hyacinthus orientalis

Fertilization: Do not fertilize when plant is blooming. Fertilize lightly at other times.

Propagation: Start new plants from the small bulblets that develop beside the parent bulb.

Grooming: Remove old leaves as plant goes dormant. Cut flower stalks if you wish.

Repotting: Place bulb into the garden after it goes dormant.

Problems: Poor drainage, too frequent watering, or standing in water will cause root rot.

Hydrangea macrophylla
Hydrangea

These plants with large flowers can be purchased in bloom during the spring or summer. The clusters 8 to 10 inches in diameter are composed of ½- to 1-inch flowers. Shiny oval leaves 2 to 6 inches long set off the cluster. Flowers are pink, red, white, blue, or mauve. Blue flowers will turn pink in neutral or alkaline soil. Aluminum sulfate or iron sulfate added to the soil will produce blue flowers; application of lime or wood ashes will neutralize the soil pH and produce pink to red flowers.

The plant is easy to care for while flowering but will not usually bloom in the home the following season. For blooms to last 6 weeks, two conditions must be met. Place the plant in a cool location and never allow the soil to dry. Daily watering may be necessary during flowering. If your tap water is very hard, to be sure to leach the soil frequently; use rainwater whenever possible. In mild climates you can plant it outdoors for summer blooms.

Light: Provide at least 4 hours of

Hydrangea macrophylla

curtain-filtered sunlight from a bright south, east, or west window.

Water: Keep very moist, but do not allow to stand in water.

Humidity: Average indoor humidity levels.

Temperatures: 50°F to 55°F at night, 65°F to 70°F during the day.

Fertilization: Fertilize only when plant is growing actively or flowering.

Propagation: Take cuttings from stems or shoots that have recently matured.

Grooming: Prune after flowering. Discard or plant outdoors after flowering.

Repotting: Not usually done.

Problems: Dry soil or high soluble salts may damage roots, causing plant to die back. If plant is in a draft or dry air, leaves will scorch.

Impatiens species
Impatiens, Balsam, Patient Lucy, Busy Lizzie

Growing impatiens is an easy way to bring natural color indoors all year. They're excellent decorations for a sunny table, window box, or windowsill.

I. balsaminii (common balsam) is an annual that will easily bloom for months in summer and winter, then die. Taller varieties of this species are

Above: *Impatiens hybrid*
Below: *Impatiens wallerana*

usually grown in the garden. Although you may be tempted to bring them indoors, their large size and lanky shape become more apparent and distracting once they are transferred indoors. Dwarf varieties are far more attractive. Another species, *I. wallerana* (busy Lizzie), an everblooming perennial, is also easy to raise indoors. These are also known as *I. holstii* and *I. sultanii;* they grow up to 15 inches high. All of these species have flowers 1 to 2 inches across in a wide array of colors—pink, red, orange, purple, white, and variegated. 'Tangerine' features a richly colored flower and handsome leaves.

Regular care will reward you with a constantly blossoming plant. Place it in a sunny spot, keep soil moist, and feed regularly. Slightly pot-bound plants will bloom more profusely. Pinch back leggy branches to control shape and encourage blossoms. If you bring impatiens in

from the garden in fall, be sure it is free of pests, particularly whiteflies and spider mites.
Light: Provide at least 4 hours of curtain-filtered sunlight from a bright south, east, or west window.
Water: Keep evenly moist. Water thoroughly and discard drainage.
Humidity: Average indoor humidity levels.
Temperatures: 50°F to 55°F at night, 60°F to 65°F during the day.
Fertilization: Fertilize all year, but more heavily in summer.
Propagation: Start from seeds. Begin in a small pot and transplant as needed.
Grooming: Discard after flowering.
Repotting: Transplant seedlings several times as plants grow.
Problems: Susceptible to spider mites, especially if plant is too dry. If soil is too wet or too dry, leaves will drop. Will not bloom if light is too low.

Ipomoea species
Morning glory

This common garden plant is enjoyed by many indoor gardeners who have well-lighted sites and room to grow this vigorous vine. Many beautiful cultivars are now available in red, blue, purple, and white. The plant will flower all year. Good fertilization will help ensure more foliage and larger blossoms. Be sure to leach-irrigate, however, to avoid soluble-salt damage to the roots. If you plan to put morning glories into the garden when they become straggly, remember that they are vigorous plants that may reseed and come up each year. They could become a weed problem.
Light: Four hours or more of direct sunlight from a south window. Does best in a greenhouse setting.
Water: Let plant approach dryness before watering, but water thoroughly and discard drainage.

Above: *Impatiens 'Orange Crush'*
Below: *Ipomoea*

Humidity: Average indoor humidity levels.
Temperatures: 65°F to 70°F at night, 75°F to 80°F during the day.
Fertilization: Fertilize all year, but more heavily in summer.
Propagation: Start from seeds. Begin in a small pot and transplant as needed.
Grooming: Discard after flowering. Start new plants and replace older specimens when they get weak.
Repotting: Generally not needed.
Problems: Will get spindly and weak if light is too low.

Ixora species
Flame-of-the-woods, Jungle geranium

Ixoras are compact shrubby plants that will bloom over an extended period beginning in the summer. The stems bear large clusters of medium-sized flowers in red, yellow, orange, or white. The flower cluster may tend to pull the stem downward, so you may wish to stake them during flowering. These

Ixora duffii

plants need lots of light and warmth to do well year after year.

Light: Four hours or more of direct sunlight from a south window. Does best in a greenhouse setting.

Water: Keep evenly moist. Water thoroughly and discard drainage.

Humidity: Requires moist air. Use a humidifier for best results.

Temperatures: 55°F to 60°F at night, 70°F to 75°F during the day.

Fertilization: Fertilize all year, but more heavily in summer.

Propagation: Take cuttings from stems or shoots before they have hardened or matured.

Grooming: Prune after flowering.

Repotting: Repot in winter or early spring, as needed.

Problems: Will not bloom if light is too low. Will get spindly and weak if light is too low.

Justicia brandegeana (Beloperone guttata)
Shrimp plant

The floral structures of the shrimp plant are 3 to 4 inches long and hang downward. The tiny flowers are borne between scalelike bracts. The entire structure resembles a shrimp. Cultivars are available in yellow, salmon, or red. The plants are woody shrubs that can get quite large. Indoors, keep them pruned to about 2 feet.

Light: Keep in about 4 hours of direct sun in winter. Provide curtain-filtered sunlight in summer, from a south or west window.

Water: Let plant approach dryness before watering, but water thoroughly and discard drainage.

Humidity: Average indoor humidity levels.

Temperatures: 50°F to 55°F at night, 65°F to 70°F during the day.

Fertilization: Fertilize all year, but more heavily in summer.

Propagation: Take stem cuttings at any time.

Grooming: Prune in early spring. Pinch back stem tips of young or re-

growing plants to improve form. Do not destroy flower buds.

Repotting: Repot at any time.

Problems: Will get spindly and weak if light is too low.

Justicia carnea
King's-crown, Brazilian plume

King's-crown is a large plant that bears rose-colored flowers in groups on spikes that appear above the foliage. It blooms in late summer. The leaves are 4 to 8 inches long, oval, and borne all along 2- to 3-foot stems. Keep the plants warm at all times; reduce fertilization after flowering.

Light: Keep in about 4 hours of direct sun in winter. Provide curtain-filtered sunlight in summer, from a south or west window.

Water: Keep evenly moist. Water thoroughly and discard drainage.

Humidity: Requires moist air. Use a humidifier for best results.

Temperatures: 55°F to 60°F at night, 70°F to 75°F during the day.

Fertilization: Fertilize all year, but more heavily in summer.

Propagation: Take cuttings from stems or shoots before they have hardened or matured.

Grooming: Prune after flowering.

Repotting: Repot in winter or early spring, as needed.

Problems: Will not bloom if light is too low. Will get spindly and weak if light is too low.

Lachenalia species
Cape cowslips, Leopard lilies

Cape cowslips are bulb plants that are becoming increasingly popular. They are easy to force into bloom. Their striking multicolored yellow and red flowers add color and cheer to any household in winter. Most cultivars that bloom in late winter are planted in the fall. The leaves are large and sometimes have purple spots, adding interest to the plant. As with any other bulb, give the plant a dormancy period after the foliage has died back.

Above: *Justicia brandegeana*
Below: *Justicia carnea*

Lantana montevidensis

Lachenalia aloides

Light: Four hours or more of direct sunlight from a south window.
Water: Keep very moist during growth and flowering. Allow to dry between waterings at other times.
Humidity: Average indoor humidity levels.
Temperatures: 40°F to 45°F at night, 60°F to 65°F during the day.
Fertilization: Fertilize only when plant is growing actively or flowering.
Propagation: Start new plants from the small bulblets that develop beside the parent bulb.
Grooming: Remove old leaves as plant goes dormant.
Repotting: Infrequent repotting is best.
Problems: Will not bloom if light is too low. Poor drainage, too frequent watering, or standing in water will cause root rot.

Lantana species
Lantana

Lantanas are widely available as annual container plants for porches or patio gardens. They are small woody shrubs that bear clusters of fragrant blossoms in red, yellow, white, and various bicolors. The foliage also has a distinctive but not unpleasant aroma when crushed or bruised. Indoors, lantanas still bloom best in early summer, but will bloom a bit throughout the year if given lots of light. The plants tend to get leggy or spindly if not clipped frequently. Lantanas are often used in hanging baskets. Some cultivars are quite trailing in habit. If you are a devoted and patient gardener, you can train and prune lantanas into the shape of a tree. It would be best to do this in a greenhouse.
Light: Four hours or more of direct sunlight from a south window. Does best in a greenhouse setting.
Water: Let plant approach dryness before watering, but water throughly and discard drainage.
Humidity: Requires moist air. Use a humidifier for best results.
Temperatures: 50°F to 55°F at night, 65°F to 70°F during the day.
Fertilization: Fertilize all year, but more heavily in summer
Propagation: Take stem cuttings at any time.
Grooming: Prune just before the heavy blossoming period. Do not cut off flower buds. Keep to desired height and shape with light pruning or clipping at any time.
Repotting: Repot in winter or early spring, as needed.
Problems: Will not bloom if light is too low. If plant is in a draft or dry air, leaves will scorch. Will get spindly and weak if light is too low. Whiteflies can be quite a nuisance on this plant.

Lavendula dentata

Lavandula species
Lavenders

These plants are popular indoors because their foliage is highly aromatic when broken or bruised. Many cultivars are used in cooking and in sachets or perfumes. Some bear small purple flowers in the winter. Lavenders are large plants that will get spindly even under the best indoor gardening conditions, so keep new plants growing to replace older specimens.

Lavandula stoechas

Light: Provide at least 4 hours of curtain-filtered sunlight from a bright south, east, or west window.
Water: Keep evenly moist. Water thoroughly and discard drainage.
Humidity: Average indoor humidity levels.
Temperatures: 50°F to 55°F at night, 60°F to 65°F during the day.
Fertilization: Fertilize all year, but more heavily in summer.
Propagation: Take cuttings from stems or shoots before they have hardened or matured.
Grooming: Keep to desired height and shape with light pruning or clipping at any time. Start new plants and replace your older specimens when they get weak.
Repotting: Not usually done.
Problems: If plant is in a draft or dry air, leaves will scorch. Will get spindly and weak if light is too low.

Lilium longiflorum
Easter lily

Easter lilies are one of the most popular flowering potted plants sold in the United States. They are occasionally used as cut flowers. Blooming plants will last longer if they are kept cool, out of drafts, and constantly moist. Remove the pollen-bearing yellow anthers just as the flower opens, to prolong its life. After flowering, care for the plant until the foliage yellows, placing it in a bright window and fertilizing it lightly. Most gardeners then plant the bulb outdoors in the garden, where it will flower every summer. You might get another

Lilium longiflorum maximum

Easter flowering if you leave the plant in its pot and move it oudoors, protect it from early freezes, and bring it indoors in late November. Force its flowering with high light and warmth.
Light: Will survive in low (reading level) light. After flowering, place in a bright, indirectly lit south, east, or west window.
Water: Keep evenly moist. Water thoroughly and discard drainage.
Humidity: Average indoor humidity levels.
Temperatures: 50°F to 55°F at night, 60°F to 65°F during the day.
Fertilization: Do not fertilize when in flower. Fertilize lightly at other times.
Propagation: Bulb scales will develop into bulbs after several years. Secondary bulbs can be removed from the parent bulb.
Grooming: Cut flower stalks if you wish.
Repotting: Plant outdoors after foliage dies back.
Problems: Poor drainage, too frequent watering, or standing in water will cause root rot.

Liriope species
Lily-turf

Liriope is used commonly in the South as an outdoor ground cover for lightly shaded areas. It is a grasslike plant with leaves about a foot long. The variegated cultivar is best for indoor gardeners. The plants look best in a mass, so do not repot often. Liriopes will bloom in the spring, with a purple flower. The leaf tips will turn brown if soil gets too dry or the plant is in a draft or dry air. Clip off the brown tips as they occur.
Light: Place in a bright, indirectly lit south, east, or west window.
Water: Keep evenly moist. Water thoroughly and discard drainage.
Humidity: Requires moist air. Use a

Lobularia maritima

humidifier for best results.
Temperatures: 50°F to 55°F at night, 65°F to 70°F during the day.
Fertilization: Fertilize 3 times a year: spring, midsummer, and early fall.
Propagation: Start new plants by dividing an older specimen.
Grooming: Pick off yellowed leaves. Trim off brown leaf tips as necessary.
Repotting: Infrequent repotting is best.
Problems: Will not bloom if light is too low. If plant is in a draft or dry air, leaves will scorch. Dry soil or high soluble salts may damage roots, causing plant to die back.

Lobularia maritima
Double sweet alyssum

Sweet alyssum is usually grown as an annual outdoor bedding plant. It is popular with indoor gardeners because of its small size and tiny fragrant white flowers. The plant must be kept warm and be in a brightly lit location such as a window box or greenhouse. If not, it will get leggy and weak. It will flower approximately 6 months after the seedling stage. Most gardeners discard the plants when they get straggly and flowering lessens.
Light: Four hours or more of direct sunlight from a south window. Does best in a greenhouse setting.
Water: Keep evenly moist. Water thoroughly and discard drainage.
Humidity: Requires moist air. Use a humidifier for best results.

Malpighia coccigera

Temperatures: 55°F to 60°F at night, 70°F to 75°F during the day.
Fertilization: Fertilize all year, but more heavily in summer.
Propagation: Start from seeds. Begin in a small pot and transplant as needed. Take stem cuttings at any time.
Grooming: Start new plants and replace older specimens when they get weak.
Repotting: Transplant seedlings several times as plants grow.
Problems: Susceptible to spider mites, especially if plant is too dry. If plant is in a draft or dry air, leaves will scorch. Soil dryness or high soluble salts may damage roots, causing plant to die back.

Malpighia coccigera
Holly malpighia, Miniature holly

Malpighias are suitable for indoor gardens because they can also bloom as small plants. In addition, they grow slowly and seldom get more than a foot tall. Their leaves are spiny and similar to those of outdoor holly. The summer flowers are small and pink and are followed by red fruits. Keep malpighias pruned into a shrub form.

Light: Provide at least 4 hours of curtain-filtered sunlight from a bright south, east, or west window.
Water: Let plant approach dryness before watering, but water thoroughly and discard drainage.
Humidity: Average indoor humidity levels.
Temperatures: 50°F to 55°F at night, 65°F to 70°F during the day.
Fertilization: Fertilize 3 times a year: spring, midsummer, and early fall.
Propagation: Take cuttings from stems or shoots that have recently matured. Seeds are available, but can be more difficult to use.
Grooming: Prune after flowering or fruiting.
Repotting: Infrequent repotting is best.
Problems: Will not bloom if light is too low. Dry soil or high soluble salts may damage roots, causing plant to die back.

Malvaviscus arboreus penduliflorus
Turk's-cap, Scotch purse

Turk's-cap is a bushy shrub that will get to be 2 feet high. The plant will bloom at various times of the year if given enough light. The large flowers are red, drooping, and never completely open. Keep the plant warm and constantly moist. Prune it frequently to maintain its shape and size.

Light: Four hours or more of direct sunlight from a south window.
Water: Keep evenly moist. Water thoroughly and discard drainage.
Humidity: Requires moist air. Use a humidifier for best results.
Temperatures: 55°F to 60°F at night, 70°F to 75°F during the day.
Fertilization: Fertilize all year, but more heavily in summer.
Propagation: Take cuttings from stems or shoots that have recently matured.
Grooming: Keep to desired height and shape with light pruning or clipping at any time. Prune in early spring.
Repotting: Repot in winter or early spring, as needed.
Problems: If plant is in a draft or dry air, leaves will scorch. Leaves will drop if soil is too wet or too dry.

Manettia cordifolia glabra
Firecracker vine

This plant has stems that tend to vine or trail, so it is usually started or trained onto a small trellis. It is a bit too leggy for use in a hanging basket. If given good light, it will blossom throughout the year. The flowers are tubular, red, and tipped with yellow. They resemble a lighted firecracker.

Light: Provide at least 4 hours of curtain-filtered sunlight from a bright south, east, or west window.
Water: Keep evenly moist. Water thoroughly and discard drainage.
Humidity: Average indoor levels.
Temperatures: 50°F to 55°F at night, 65°F to 70°F during the day.
Fertilization: Fertilize all year, but more heavily in summer.
Propagation: Take stem cuttings at any time.
Grooming: Keep to desired height and shape with light pruning or clipping at any time.
Repotting: Repot in winter or early spring, as needed.
Problems: Will get spindly and weak if light is too low.

Muscari species
Grape hyacinth

These small bulb plants are popular because they are easy to force into bloom. Their small size makes them ideal windowsill or desk plants. The tiny blue or white flowers are borne on 6-inch stalks. They are fragrant and last for quite a while in midwinter or early spring. The leaves are narrow and grass-like, and will arch outward from the bulb tip. Force them as you do other common bulbs. Purchase mature bulbs in October, pot and keep cool until January, then bring in for flowering. Tend the plant until the foliage dies back and then plant it in the garden.

Light: Place in a bright, indirectly lit south, east, or west window.
Water: Keep evenly moist. Water thoroughly and discard drainage.
Humidity: Average indoor humidity levels.
Temperatures: 40°F to 45°F at night, 60°F to 65°F during the day.
Fertilization: Do not fertilize when the plant is in flower. Fertilize lightly at other times.

Propagation: Start new plants from the small bulblets that develop beside the parent bulb.
Grooming: Pick off yellowed leaves.
Repotting: Transplant outdoors in spring.
Problems: No significant problems.

Narcissus hybrids
Daffodils, Narcissus

There are two types of narcissus bulbs used indoors for forcing. The plants that produce a single trumpet-shaped flower on a 12-inch stalk are called daffodils. Those that produce a group of smaller flowers on a single stem are called Tazetta varieties. Many cultivars in either group are suitable for indoor gardeners. Buy mature bulbs in the fall and put them in peat moss, pebbles, or sand so that half of the bulb is out of the water or planting medium. Keep them at 35°F to 40°F for several weeks until they sprout about 4 inches of growth. Then bring them indoors for flowering. Keep them cool during this time and do not fertilize. Discard the plant after flowering, or if it is hardy, place it outdoors in a flower bed. Allow the leaves to die back naturally.
Light: Will survive in low (reading level) light. After flowering, place in a bright window until foliage dies back.
Water: Keep very moist while flowering.
Humidity: Average indoor humidity levels.
Temperatures: 40°F to 45°F at night, 60°F to 65°F during the day.
Fertilization: Do not fertilize when in flower. Fertilize lightly at other times.
Propagation: Buy mature bulbs or take a large division from the bulb of a garden plant.
Grooming: Discard or plant outdoors after flowering.
Repotting: Not necessary.
Problems: No special problems.

Neomarica gracilis
Apostle plant, Walking iris

The flattened, elongated leaves and general shape of the flower give the apostle plant a resemblance to the iris. The

Narcissus poeticus

plants are large, with blue and white flowers borne together on stalks. Each stalk usually has one flower open at a time. It will last only for a day or two, but then another opens. It is a winter bloomer, so usually needs some direct winter sunlight. New plants will form at the tops of the flower stems and can be rooted to start another blooming specimen.
Light: Keep in about 4 hours of direct sun in winter. Provide curtain-filtered sunlight in summer, from a south or west window.
Water: Keep evenly moist. Water thoroughly and discard drainage.
Humidity: Average indoor humidity levels.
Temperatures: 50°F to 55°F at night, 65°F to 70°F during the day.
Fertilization: Fertilize all year, but more heavily in summer.
Propagation: Remove new plantlets or rooted side shoots as they form.
Grooming: Cut flower stalks if you wish.
Repotting: Infrequent repotting is best. Larger, pot-bound plants will bloom more abundantly.
Problems: Will not bloom if light is too low.

Nicotiana alata
Flowering tobacco

Many cultivars of dwarf nicotianas are available in flower shops and garden centers for use as outdoor annual bedding plants. They will do well indoors with lots of light. Various cultivars are available with unusual, although subtle, flower shades such as yellow-green,

Nicotiana alata

wine red, chartreuse, or chocolate brown. The flowers are borne in clusters on stalks about a foot high. Remove flowers, mature seeds, or seed capsules as desired.
Light: Four hours or more of direct sunlight from a south window.
Water: Keep evenly moist. Water thoroughly and discard drainage.
Humidity: Average indoor humidity levels.
Temperatures: 50°F to 55°F at night, 65°F to 70°F during the day.
Fertilization: Fertilize only when plant is growing actively or flowering.
Propagation: Start from seeds. Begin in a small pot and transplant after flowering.
Grooming: Remove spent blooms and yellowed leaves. Prune back after flowering.
Repotting: Not usually necessary.
Problems: Dry soil or high soluble salts may cause dieback.

Above: *Orchid: Cattleya*
Below: *Orchid: Cymbidium*

Orchids

Growing these exquisite, colorful flowers is regarded by most people as the supreme gardening achievement. But in fact some species of orchids grow quite well indoors and require less routine care than other houseplants. In addition, improved breeding techniques have significantly increased the availability and lowered the cost of many species. Placed on a windowsill in your living room, an orchid is sure to be the center of attention. It's always wise to purchase mature blooming plants. Described below are some of the best houseplant orchids.

Aerides species

Aerides is a summer-flowering epiphyte of moderate size. Given full sun, this orchid blooms profusely, with fragrant flowers in red, pink, or white on long stalks that arch outward from the plant. *A. odoratum* is particularly fragrant and very popular with indoor orchid growers.

Angraecum species
Comet orchid

Many angraecums are small plants well suited to indoor gardens. *A. distichum* bears tiny, fragrant flowers along arching stems in the fall. Other species flower in the winter. The plants need brightness and even moisture, but are tolerant of cool night temperatures and normal household humidity.

Brassia species
Spider orchid

Brassias bear flowers with long, narrow sepals that give rise to their common name. The plants are fairly large, with 15-inch flower spikes and leaves that grow to 10 inches long. They generally bloom in the fall or winter if given sunlight.

Cattleya

Cattleya, the large classical orchid most often seen in corsages, is good for beginners to try. The vigorous plants produce gorgeous blooms when they receive

Above: *Orchid: Dendrobium*
Below: *Orchid: Epidendrum*

plenty of sun and average daytime temperatures.

Cymbidium species

The miniature cymbidiums are especially well suited for many indoor gardens. Even with miniatures, the narrow, arching foliage must be given room. Give the plants cool nights to promote flowering, which usually occurs in late summer or fall. There are many hybrids available in a wide variety of colors. The flowers are long-lasting, even in arrangements.

Dendrobiums

Dendrobiums are mostly epiphytic orchids, with both evergreen and deciduous types available. Large flowers bloom in clusters or in a row along the stem. They last between a week and several months, depending on the species, and need plenty of sun, as do most orchids.

Orchid: Ludisia discolor

Epidendrum species
Buttonhole orchids, Clamshell orchids

Epidendrums are a large family of orchids, some growing as canes and others as pseudobulbs. Many species are small and suitable for warm window boxes in winter sun. Some species may bloom continuously under suitable conditions.

Laeliocattleya hybrids
Laeliocattleya orchid

These orchids are hybrids between *L. cattleya* and *L. laelia.* They bloom at various times with long-lasting 3- to 4-inch flowers. The available colors are yellow, orange, and pink. Many of the new cultivars are compact and quite suitable for indoor gardens. These plants, like most other orchids, do best in stable climatic conditions, free of dry air and drafts.

Ludisia discolor
Jewel orchid

The jewel orchid is one of several orchids grown as much for its exceptional foliage as it is for its bloom. This plant grows in regular potting soil because it is a terrestrial orchid. It may reach a height of 8 inches or so on somewhat trailing stems. Its leaves are a velvety purplish green, with a prominent networking of red and white veins. If given good indirect light, jewel orchids will bloom in winter. Small white or pinkish flowers grow on long spikes.

Odontoglossum species

Ondontoglossums need moist air and stable growing conditions. They are best suited for greenhouses where they can get direct winter sun and filtered light in the summer. There are many species and hybrids available, most bearing large flowers that are fragrant and long-lasting. Many bloom twice a year.

Oncydium
Dancing lady orchid

Oncydium is a large group of epiphytic orchids. They produce stalks of yellow flowers speckled with brown. Flower size depends on the species.

Paphiopedilum
Lady slipper orchid

Paphiopedilum will produce fragrant blooms throughout the year if given plenty of moisture and full sun.

Phalaenopsis
Moth orchid

Phalaenopsis unfurls sprays of 2- to 3-inch flowers in a range of colors. The plant can grow to a height of 30 inches. These shade-loving plants are easy to grow at temperatures of 75°F in the day and 60°F at night.

Rodriguezia species

Most of the orchids in this genus are miniatures, less than a foot tall. The plants bloom abundantly with large

Above: *Orchid: Odontoglossum*
Center: *Orchid: Oncydium*
Below: *Orchid: Paphiopedilum*

clusters of small, fragrant flowers, usually white or pinkish. Keep these plants moist and in damp air.

Sophrolaeliocattleya hybrids
Sophrolaeliocattleya orchid

As the name implies, these orchids were derived by hybridizing species of sophronitis, laelia, and cattleya orchids. Many cultivars are available, most with purple or red flowers. The plants are well suited for indoor culture because

Ornithogalum

Above: *Orchid: Phalaenopsis*
Below: *Orchid: Vanda cristata*

they are relatively compact but have large flowers. The flowers may appear throughout the year, sometimes more than once a year. Keep the environment stable and high in relative humidity, with curtain-filtered sunlight.

Vanda species

Vanda orchids are available as miniature hybrids, suited to many indoor gardens. Sunlight from a southern window is best for these plants in the winter. As with most other orchids, keep these epiphytic plants evenly moist, out of drafts, and in stable damp air.

Care of Orchids

Light: Ample light—at least 10 to 15 hours a day. Protect from direct sun. Supplement with artificial light, especially in winter.
Water: Watering is of utmost importance. The needs of each species will vary. In general, keep soil moist and always use tepid water.
Humidity: A lot of moisture in the air is essential. Place orchids on humidifying trays. Good air circulation is a must.
Temperatures: Normal daytime temperatures of 70°F to 75°F are fine. A night temperature 15° lower is good, but it should not dip below 56°F.

Fertilization: Fertilize lightly throughout the year, more heavily in summer.
Propagation: Divide plant. Stake new plants.
Grooming: Pick off yellowed leaves.
Repotting: Allow roots to extend beyond pot as long as plant continues to grow well. When growth is inhibited, repot.
Problems: Limp leaves or flowers are caused mainly by insufficient light, but can also be due to improper watering (usually overwatering). Yellowing leaves can be expected if leaves are old or plant is deciduous; otherwise, it results from overwatering or sunburn. Brown spots are due to too much sun or leaf spot disease.

Ornithogalum species
Chincherinchee, Star-of-Bethehem, False sea onion

This bulbous plant produces fragrant white flowers in a cluster on a long stalk. They will last several weeks with good care. It is easy to grow, but does need ample winter light if you intend to keep it from year to year. As with any other bulb, give it a dormancy period after the foliage dies back. These are large plants, with leaves up to 2 feet long and flower stalks often 2 or 3 feet high.

Light: Keep in about 4 hours of direct sun in winter. Provide curtain-filtered sunlight in summer, from a south or west window.
Water: Let plant approach dryness before watering, but water thoroughly and discard drainage.
Humidity: Average indoor humidity levels.
Temperatures: 50°F to 55°F at night, 65°F to 70°F during the day.

Oxalis variabilis 'Grand Duchess'

Passiflora

Fertilization: Fertilize only when plant is growing actively or flowering.
Propagation: Start new plants from the small bulblets that develop beside the parent bulb.
Grooming: Remove old leaves as plant goes dormant.
Repotting: Repot in early fall. Place bulb barely into the soil.
Problems: Will not bloom if light is too low.

Osmanthus fragrans
Holly osmanthus, Sweet olive

The flowers of osmanthus are hard to see because they are very small and greenish white. However, they are extremely fragrant, with an orange blossom scent. If given enough light, plants will bloom all year. Prune the plant into a shrub; it will grow to 3 feet in time.
Light: Four hours or more of direct sunlight from a south window. Does best in a greenhouse setting.
Water: Keep evenly moist. Water thoroughly and discard drainage.
Humidity: Requires moist air. Use a humidifier for best results.
Temperatures: 50°F to 55°F at night, 65°F to 70°F during the day.
Fertilization: Fertilize all year, but more heavily in summer.
Propagation: Take cuttings from stems or shoots that have recently matured.
Grooming: Prune in early spring.
Repotting: Repot in winter or early spring, as needed.
Problems: No blooms in low light.

Oxalis species
Oxalis

Oxalis are small bulb plants that rarely grow above 6 or 8 inches. Since they produce relatively large flowers (1- to 2-inches) all winter long, they make popular windowsill plants. Various cultivars are available in pink, white, or red. The foliage looks like clover, sometimes with a reddish hue. Prune them a bit to improve their form. Cut off the flower stalks to prevent messy petal and seed pod fall. The bulbs require a rest in the summer; the plants will die back as summer approaches.
Light: Four hours or more of direct sunlight from a south window.
Water: Keep very moist during growth and flowering. Allow to dry between waterings at other times.
Humidity: Average indoor humidity levels.
Temperatures: 50°F to 55°F at night, 65°F to 70°F during the day.
Fertilization: Fertilize only when plant is growing actively or flowering.
Propagation: Start new plants from the small bulblets that develop beside the parent bulb.
Grooming: Keep to desired height and shape with light pruning or clipping at any time. Cut flower stalks if you wish.
Repotting: Repot each year.
Problems: Susceptible to spider mites, especially if plant is too dry. If plant is in a draft or dry air, leaves will scorch. Will get spindly and weak if light is too low.

Passiflora species
Passionflower

Passionflowers are large, rapidly growing vines that cling with long tendrils to supports. The large flowers (4 to 6 inches wide) are complex in their construction and quite beautiful. Because of its size, growth habit, and light, this plant does best in a greenhouse or solarium. It should not require much care, except light pruning to keep it in control. The plant does need a dormancy period in late fall or early winter.
Light: Four hours or more of direct sunlight from a south window. Does best in a greenhouse setting.
Water: Keep very moist during growth and flowering. Allow to dry between waterings at other times.
Humidity: Requires moist air. Use a humidifier for best results.
Temperatures: 55°F to 60°F at night, 70°F to 75°F during the day.
Fertilization: Fertilize only when plant is growing actively or flowering.
Propagation: Take stem cuttings at any time. Seeds are available, but can be more difficult to use.
Grooming: Prune just before the heavy blossoming period. Do not cut off flower buds.
Repotting: Infrequent repotting is best.
Problems: No blooms in low light.

Pelargonium hortorum

Petunia grandiflora 'Burgundy'

Above: *Pelargonium peltatum 'Galilee'*
Below: *Pentas lanceolata*

Pelargonium species
Florists' geraniums

These natives of South Africa are versatile and appealing, available in thousands of species and named varieties. Some are grown outdoors, and others can be easily moved indoors from outside. They can add distinction to an indoor decor all year.

Common geraniums are hybrids of *P. hortorum,* and often have a darker green or blackish ring in each leaf. Varieties are available in red, salmon, apricot, tangerine, pink, and white. They will bloom all year, but they bloom best in January and February. Many get quite large and need plenty of room.

Fancy-leaf geraniums, *P. domesticum,* have varicolored leaves, often in bronzes, scarlets, and yellows. Many indoor gardeners particularly enjoy those with foliage scented like roses, apples, or lemons.

Never venturing above 8 inches, dwarf geraniums have the delicate proportion and shape perfect for tables and windowsills, but they are not as popular as others because they require cooler temperatures. Ivy geraniums, varieties of *P. peltatum,* bear leathery leaves with a shape similar to English ivy, and sport many clusters of showy flowers, often veined with a darker shade of the overall color. These are excellent in hanging baskets near windows.

Geraniums are easy to care for in the proper environment. A sunny windowsill where it is cool (never rising above 75°F) and dry is ideal. Fertilize once a week, and water when the soil is dry to the touch. For bushiness and strong flowering, pinch back plants in autumn and always remove dead blossoms promptly.
Light: Four hours or more of direct sunlight from a south window.
Water: Let plant approach dryness before watering, but water thoroughly and discard drainage.
Humidity: Average indoor humidity levels.
Temperatures: 55°F to 60°F at night, 70°F to 75°F during the day.

Fertilization: Fertilize all year, but more heavily in summer.
Propagation: Take stem cuttings at any time. Seeds are also available for many cultivars.
Grooming: Prune after flowering. Pinch back stem tips of young or regrowing plants to improve form. Do not destroy flower buds.
Repotting: Repot in winter or early spring, as needed. Transplant seedlings several times as the plants grow.
Problems: Will not bloom if light is too low. Will get spindly and weak if light is too low.

Pentas lanceolata
Egyptian star cluster

Pentas will bloom all year if given plenty of light. The small flowers of red, purple, pink, or white are borne in clusters at the ends of branches. Train the plant into a bushy form approximately 12 to 16 inches tall, but be careful not to cut off developing flower clusters. Stake the plant if flowers pull shoots over.
Light: Four hours or more of direct sunlight from a south window.
Water: Keep evenly moist. Water thoroughly and discard drainage.
Humidity: Average indoor humidity levels.
Temperatures: 50°F to 55°F at night, 65°F to 70°F during the day.
Fertilization: Fertilize all year, but more heavily in summer.
Propagation: Take stem cuttings at any time of the year.

Plumbago auriculata

Grooming: Keep to desired height and shape with light pruning or clipping at any time.
Repotting: Repot in winter or early spring, as needed.
Problems: If plant is in a draft or dry air, leaves will scorch.

Petunia hybrids
Petunia

Petunias can be started from seed sown in midsummer, or garden plants can be cut back, repotted, and brought indoors in early fall. They will bloom all winter if given plenty of light and cool nights. The fragrant flowers are available in many colors, including white, red, blue, yellow, and bicolors. The stems of petunias tend to trail and get leggy without frequent pinching back. Do not remove too many flower buds, however. You may wish to place petunias in a hanging basket. Discard when they get spindly and stop blooming.
Light: Four hours of direct sun in winter.
Water: Let plant approach dryness before watering, but water thoroughly and discard drainage.
Humidity: Average indoor humidity levels.
Temperatures: 50°F to 55°F at night, 65°F to 70°F during the day.
Fertilization: Fertilize only when plant is growing actively or flowering.
Propagation: Start from seeds. Begin in a small pot and transplant as needed.
Grooming: Pinch back stem tips of young or regrowing plants to improve form. Do not destroy flower buds. Discard after flowering.

Repotting: Garden plants must be repotted into a well-drained mix for indoor use.
Problems: Will not bloom if light is too low. Poor drainage, too frequent watering, or standing in water will cause root rot.

Plumbago indica
Plumbago, Leadwort

These large-leaved semiwoody plants tend to trail and are best in a hanging basket or staked in a pot. They produce clusters of red flowers that resemble those of sweet William. They grow slowly indoors and must be given ample light and warmth. For these reasons, they are best suited for greenhouses or solariums.
Light: Four hours or more of direct sunlight from a south window. Does best in a greenhouse setting.
Water: Keep evenly moist. Water thoroughly and discard drainage.
Humidity: Requires moist air. Use a humidifier for best results.
Temperatures: 65°F to 70°F at night, 75°F to 80°F during the day.
Fertilization: Fertilize all year, but more heavily in summer.
Propagation: Take stem cuttings at any time. Seeds are available, but can be more difficult to use.
Grooming: Keep to desired height and shape with light pruning or clipping at any time.
Repotting: Repot in winter or early spring, as needed.
Problems: Will not bloom if light is too low. Will get spindly and weak if light is too low.

Primula species
Fairy primrose

Fairy primroses produce magnificent clusters of large flowers on stalks above a rosette of light green leaves. Cultivars are available in red, yellow, blue, white, and bicolors. It takes a lot of light and moist air with very cool nights to get these plants to flower properly in the winter. They are usually purchased already in bloom. They can be started and grown in home greenhouses, provided they are kept moist. Any stress will

Primula malacoides

make them susceptible to spider mite infestation.

Three species especially suited to indoors are *P. malacoides, P. obconica,* and *P. sinensis.* The largest is *P. malacoides,* commonly called the fairy primrose. Starlike scented flowers are borne in tiers on tall stalks. *P. obconica* (German primrose) reaches a foot in height and blooms in white, lilac, crimson, and salmon. *P. sinensis* (Chinese primrose) is the primula usually carried by florists. This small plant features delicate, ruffled flowers in a wide range of colors, pink being the most common. All these primroses need similar care.

A well-lit, cool area such as a sun porch is ideal. If the plant is located near a warm, sunny window, pack coarse sphagnum moss up to the rim of the pot to help keep the soil and the roots cool. Pinch off blossoms as they fade, and feed once a week with a dilute concentration of liquid fertilizer.
Light: Place in a bright, indirectly lit south, east, or west window while in flower. Does best in a greenhouse setting prior to flowering.
Water: Keep evenly moist. Water thoroughly and discard drainage.
Humidity: Requires moist air. Use a humidifier for best results.
Temperatures: 40°F to 45°F at night, 60°F to 65°F during the day.

Rhododendron

Punica granatum nana

Fertilization: Do not fertilize when in flower. Fertilize lightly at other times.
Propagation: Start from seeds. Begin in a small pot and transplant as needed.
Grooming: Pick off yellowed leaves.
Repotting: Repot in winter or early spring, as needed.
Problems: Susceptible to spider mites, especially if plant is too dry. If in a draft or dry air, leaves will scorch. Dry soil or high soluble salts will damage roots, causing plant to die back.

Punica granatum nana
Dwarf pomegranate

This dwarf form of the well-known tropical fruit tree will do well in a greenhouse or solarium. The plant has small, myrtlelike leaves. It produces showy red flowers, mainly in the early summer. The 2-inch fruit is edible and will mature on the plant if kept warm and moist. The fruits may tend to pull the branches over and may require staking. Prune the plant frequently to produce a woody shrub.

Light: Four hours or more of direct sunlight from a south window. Does best in a greenhouse setting.
Water: Keep evenly moist. Water thoroughly and discard drainage.
Humidity: Requires moist air. Use a humidifier for best results.
Temperatures: 55°F to 60°F at night, 70°F to 75°F during the day.
Fertilization: Fertilize only when plant is growing actively or flowering.
Propagation: Take cuttings from stems or shoots before they have hardened or matured.
Grooming: Keep to desired height and shape with light pruning or clipping at any time.
Repotting: Infrequent repotting is best. Repot in winter or early spring, as needed.
Problems: Will not bloom if light is too low.

Rhododendron species
Azalea, Rhododendron

Many cultivars of azaleas and a few rhododendrons are available as blooming house plants. The blooms are long lasting. After flowering, many can be indoor foliage plants. Some can be placed in the garden after flowering. Most azaleas sold in this way are not hardy enough for northern gardens, however. It is difficult to get them to flower indoors in subsequent years. They need greenhouse conditions to set flower buds in the fall and must have several weeks of cool dormancy.
Light: May be placed anywhere when in bloom. Afterwards, provide at least 4 hours of curtain-filtered sunlight from a bright south, east, or west window.
Water: Keep evenly moist. Water thoroughly and discard drainage.

Humidity: Requires moist air. Use a humidifier for best results.
Temperatures: 55°F to 60°F at night, 70°F to 75°F during the day.
Fertilization: Fertilize only when plant is growing actively or flowering. Use an acid-balanced fertilizer, and add trace elements once in spring.
Propagation: Take cuttings from stems or shoots before they have hardened or matured.
Grooming: Prune after flowering.
Repotting: Infrequent repotting is best.
Problems: If plant is in a draft or dry air, leaves will scorch. Susceptible to spider mites, especially if plant is too dry.

Rosa hybrids
Miniature roses

Although usually thought of as exquisite additions to outdoor gardens, miniature roses can also grace your home. Delicate 1- to 1½-inch blooms are available in a spectrum of colors. Grown as small bushes, climbers, or standards, they make an appealing indoor display. Their limited popularity stems from the difficulty gardeners have had in making them flourish indoors. However, new hybrids have eliminated many problems. 'Beauty Secret', 'Janna', 'Green Ice', and 'Toy Clown' are a few good choices.

In order to grow the miniatures successfully, give them the same care they would receive outdoors. First, place them in a spot with abundant light and cool, well-circulated air. High humidity is a must, so place a humidifying tray beneath the pots. Allow the soil to dry slightly between thorough waterings.

Rosmarinus officinalis

Rosa hybrid

Apply a high-nitrogen fertilizer every 2 weeks. Rinse the leaves regularly with water, remove yellowing leaves, and clip off the old blossoms at once. When pests such as aphids or mites invade, treat them immediately. After the last blossoms of summer have faded, prune back your plant severely.
Light: Keep in about 4 hours of direct sun in winter. Provide curtain-filtered sunlight in summer, from a south or west window.
Water: Keep evenly moist. Water thoroughly and discard drainage.
Humidity: Average indoor humidity levels.
Temperatures: 50°F to 55°F at night, 60°F to 65°F during the day.
Fertilization: Fertilize all year, but more heavily in summer.
Propagation: Take stem cuttings at any time.
Grooming: Keep to desired height and shape with light pruning or clipping at any time.
Repotting: Repot at any time.
Problems: Susceptible to spider mites, especially if plant is too dry. Will not bloom if light is too low. If soil is too wet or too dry, leaves will drop.

Rosmarinus officinalis
Rosemary

Rosemary is fun to grow indoors because its leaves can be used as an herb in cooking. It is a small plant suited for windowsill growing. The aromatic foliage is narrow (2 inches long) and is produced on trailing stems. Tiny fra-

grant blue flowers will sometimes appear on the plant in late winter if it is getting enough light. Keep the plant cut back to avoid spindly, leggy growth.
Light: Four hours or more of direct sunlight from a south window.
Water: Let plant approach dryness before watering, but water thoroughly and discard drainage.
Humidity: Average indoor humidity levels.
Temperatures: 50°F to 55°F at night, 65°F to 70°F during the day.
Fertilization: Fertilize 3 times a year: spring, midsummer, and early fall.
Propagation: Start from seeds. Begin in a small pot and transplant as needed. Take cuttings from stems or shoots that have recently matured.
Grooming: Start new plants and replace older specimens when they get weak. Prune after flowering.
Repotting: Repot in winter or early spring, as needed.
Problems: Will get spindly and weak if light is too low.

Russelia equisetiformis
Coral plant, Fountain plant

These hanging-basket plants have arching branches with tiny needlelike or scalelike leaves. The red flowers are borne on the ends of the branches, giving a cascading appearance. The plant is large, sometimes growing to 3 or more feet across. It must have lots of light to continue blooming and to maintain a thick, vigorous branching habit.
Light: Four hours or more of direct sunlight from a south window. Does best in a greenhouse setting.
Water: Let plant approach dryness before watering, but water thoroughly and discard drainage.

Scilla peruviana

Humidity: Requires moist air. Use a humidifier for best results.
Temperatures: 50°F to 55°F at night, 65°F to 70°F during the day.
Fertilization: Fertilize all year, but more heavily in summer.
Propagation: Take cuttings from stems or shoots before they have hardened or matured.
Grooming: Start new plants and replace older specimens when they get weak. Give these plants plenty of room.
Repotting: Transplant eventually to an 8-inch basket.
Problems: Poor drainage, too frequent watering, or standing in water will cause root rot. Will not bloom if light is too low.

Scilla species
Squills

Squill bulbs are commonly used outdoors for early spring flowers. The bell-like blue flowers are produced on stalks a few inches high. The moderate size of most squills makes them especially suited for winter flowering on a windowsill in the home. Pot several mature bulbs together in the pot in October and place in a cool (not freezing) spot until January. After the foliage declines, you can place them in the garden.
Light: Provide at least 4 hours of curtain-filtered sunlight from a bright south, east, or west window.
Water: Keep very moist during growth and flowering. Allow to dry between waterings at other times.
Humidity: Average indoor levels.

Senecio x hybridus

Temperatures: 40°F to 45°F at night, 60°F to 65°F during the day.
Fertilization: Do not fertilize indoors.
Propagation: Start new plants from the small bulblets that develop beside the parent bulb.
Grooming: Cut flower stalks if you wish. Remove old leaves as plant goes dormant. Plant outdoors after it goes dormant.
Repotting: Not necessary.
Problems: None serious.

Scindapsis aureus
See *Epipremnum aureum*

Senecio confusus
Mexican flame vine

Mexican flame vine is a cousin of the more popular cineraria that is often sold in flower shops. This vine will grow to 4 feet in a short time, so train it onto a small trellis or keep it pruned back and use it in a hanging basket. The Mexican flame vine produces orange, daisylike flowers, mainly in late winter. For this reason, it is best kept in a warm greenhouse during winter.
Light: Keep in about 4 hours of direct sun in winter. Provide curtain-filtered sunlight in summer, from a south or west window.
Water: Keep evenly moist. Water thoroughly and discard drainage.
Humidity: Average indoor levels.
Temperatures: 50°F to 55°F at night, 65°F to 70°F during the day.
Fertilization: Fertilize all year, but more heavily in summer.

Propagation: Take stem cuttings.
Grooming: Prune after flowering or fruiting. Start new plants and replace older specimens when they get weak. Keep to desired height and shape with light pruning or clipping at any time.
Repotting: Cut back and repot when flowering stops.
Problems: Will not bloom if light is too low. Mexican flame vine will get spindly and weak if light is too low.

Senecio x hybridus
Cineraria

Cinerarias are popular winter-blooming plants that many florists stock regularly. They are easy to grow from seed and produce a large cluster of flowers in colors from pink to dark blue. Some of the hybrid seedlings have dark foliage with a purplish cast when viewed from below. It is interesting to start with a seed mixture and see what different forms and flower colors you will get. Keep the plants cool when blossoming. Give them plenty of light prior to flowering so they will not get too leggy.
Light: Provide at least 4 hours of curtain-filtered sunlight from a bright south, east, or west window.
Water: Keep evenly moist. Water thoroughly and discard drainage.
Humidity: Average indoor levels.
Temperatures: 40°F to 45°F at night, 60°F to 65°F during the day, or cooler during flowering.
Fertilization: Do not fertilize when in flower. Fertilize lightly at other times.
Propagation: Start from seeds. Begin in a small pot and transplant as needed.
Grooming: Discard after flowering.
Repotting: Transplant seedlings several times as plants grow.
Problems: Subject to infestations of whiteflies, aphids, and spider mites. Powdery mildew is sometimes present.

Senecio mikanioides
German ivy, Parlor ivy, Wax ivy, Natal ivy

German ivy has bright green leaves with a shape similar to English ivy's. This herbaceous, trailing plant is a member of the daisy family. In early spring, clusters of small, yellow daisylike flowers may appear on plants that get lots of light. German ivy is a fast

grower. Its growing tips need frequent pinching to obtain a branched plant. It is best suited for hanging baskets.
Light: Place in a bright, indirectly lit south, east, or west window.
Water: Keep evenly moist. Water thoroughly and discard drainage.
Humidity: Requires moist air. Use a humidifier for best results.
Temperatures: 50°F to 55°F at night, 60°F to 65°F during the day.
Fertilization: Fertilize only during late spring and summer months.
Propagation: Take stem cuttings at any time.
Grooming: Keep to desired height and shape with light pruning or clipping at any time.
Repotting: Repot in winter or early spring, as needed.
Problems: If plant is in a draft or dry air, leaves will scorch. Dry soil or high soluble salts may damage roots, causing plant to die back.

Solanum pseudocapsicum
Jerusalem cherry, Christmas cherry

Jerusalem cherries are related to tomatoes, but the fruit is not edible. They need lots of light to bloom and set fruit properly. Many gardeners grow them outdoors and bring them in from September through the holidays. If given enough light, they will bear blossoms, green (immature) fruit, and orange or red (mature) fruit, all at the same time. If you bring them in from outdoors, be sure they are free of pests such as spider mites and aphids. Pinch back the shoots on younger plants to keep their size to approximately a foot.
Light: Four hours or more of direct sunlight from a south window. Does best in a greenhouse setting.
Water: Keep evenly moist. Water thoroughly and discard drainage.
Humidity: Requires moist air. Use a humidifier for best results.
Temperatures: 50°F to 55°F at night, 60°F to 65°F during the day.
Fertilization: Fertilize only when plant is growing actively or flowering.
Propagation: Start from seeds. Begin in a small pot and transplant as needed.
Grooming: Prune after flowering or fruiting. Pinch back stem tips of young or regrowing plants to improve form. Do not destroy flower buds. Discard when plant gets too leggy.

Repotting: Repot in winter or early spring, as needed.
Problems: Foliage has an odor that some find objectionable. Susceptible to spider mites and aphids.

Spathiphyllum species
Peace lily, Spathe flower

The distinctive flower of this plant evokes an understanding of its common name, the peace lily. The spathe is a pure white bract that encloses true flowers. Sometimes more than 4 inches wide and 6 inches long, it unfurls to form a softly curved backdrop for the central column of these tiny, closely set flowers. The fragrant blossom clearly resembles its relative, anthurium. Spoon-shaped leaves on long stalks surround the flower and mirror its shape.

When not in flower, spathiphyllum makes a very attractive foliage plant, especially in a shady location. Choose the plants by size: *S. 'Clevelandii'* (white anthurium) grows to a height of 2 feet. *S. floribundum* (snowflower) has leaves less than a foot tall. The largest, *S. 'Mauna Loa'*, reaches 3 feet. They bloom in spring and sometimes in autumn. After a few days the white spathe will turn pale green.

This is one of the easiest large flowering plants to grow, especially under limited light conditions. A few hours of bright indirect light daily, normal to warm house temperatures, and regular watering and feeding is all that is needed to bring this plant to bloom. Cold drafts will harm the plant. Wash leaves occasionally to protect the plant from scales and mites.
Light: Survives in low (reading level) light.
Water: Keep very moist during growth and flowering; at other times, allow to dry between waterings.
Humidity: Average indoor humidity levels.
Temperatures: 55°F to 60°F at night, 70°F to 75°F during the day.
Fertilization: Fertilize only when plant is growing actively or flowering.
Propagation: Start new plants by dividing old specimen.
Grooming: Pick off yellowed leaves.
Repotting: Repot infrequently.
Problems: Poor drainage, too fre-

Spathiphyllum 'Mauna Loa'

quent watering, or standing in water will cause root rot. Will not bloom if light is too low.

Sprekelia formosissima
Aztec lily, Jacobean lily, St. James lily

Aztec lilies are popular bulbs for spring indoor forcing. They will last for several years in the pot if given ample light after blooming and allowed to rest in the fall. The leaves are not particularly attractive, but must be maintained to build the bulb for its next flowering. The leaves of this medium-sized plant are about 18 inches long. Keep it warm and well fertilized while growing.
Light: Four hours or more of direct sunlight from a south window.
Water: Keep moist when growing. Keep dry when dormant, but water occasionally.
Humidity: Average indoor humidity levels.
Temperatures: 60°F to 65°F at night and 70°F to 75°F during the day in the growing season (February through September); much cooler during fall and early winter.
Fertilization: Fertilize only when plant is growing actively or flowering.
Propagation: Start new plants from the small bulblets that develop beside the parent bulb.
Grooming: Cut flower stalks if you wish. Remove old leaves as plant goes dormant.
Repotting: Repot every 3 or 4 years. Plant so that top of the bulb is out of the soil.
Problems: None serious.

Stephanotis floribunda
Stephanotis

Stephanotis is a vining plant that can get quite large. It has thick leathery leaves similar to those of waxplants. The flowers, which usually appear in June, are traditionally used in wedding

Stephanotis floribunda

bouquets. They are white and extremely fragrant. If given enough light, they will bloom most of the year. Allow the plant to rest during winter.
Light: Four hours or more of direct sunlight from a south window. Does best in a greenhouse setting.
Water: Keep very moist during growth and flowering. Allow to dry between waterings at other times.
Humidity: Average indoor levels.
Temperatures: 55°F to 60°F at night, 70°F to 75°F during the day.
Fertilization: Fertilize only when plant is growing actively or flowering.
Propagation: Take stem cuttings at any time.
Grooming: Pinch back stem tips of young or regrowing plants to improve form. Do not destroy flower bud. Prune after flowering.
Repotting: Infrequent repotting is best. New plants need to grow in a medium to large pot until almost rootbound before they will bloom.
Problems: Will not bloom if light is too low.

Strelitzia
Bird-of-paradise

Bird-of-paradise flowers are famous throughout the world for their beauty and form. The large flowers are borne in clusters on a long stalk. Many say this resembles the head of a tropical bird. This is a very large plant that will bloom only when mature. It is best suited for a greenhouse. *S. reginae humilis* is a dwarf type that is more suitable for indoor culture, provided it is given plenty of light.

Strelitzia

Light: Does best in a greenhouse setting.
Water: Water thoroughly, but allow to dry between waterings.
Humidity: Average indoor levels.
Temperatures: 50°F to 55°F at night, 65°F to 70°F during the day.
Fertilization: Fertilize 3 times a year: spring, midsummer, and early fall.
Propagation: Start new plants by dividing an older specimen.
Grooming: Give these plants plenty of room.
Repotting: New plants need to grow in a medium to large pot until almost root-bound before they will bloom.
Problems: No serious problems.

Streptosolen jamesonii
Streptosolen

This winter-flowering plant produces clusters of bright orange flowers about 1 inch across. Although streptosolen is a woody shrub, it tends to get leggy, so

Streptosolen jamesonii

train it onto a small trellis or use it in a hanging basket. Many gardeners prune it into a treelike shape, with weeping or semitrailing growth at the top. Even in this form, it will need a trellis. Pruning regrowing stems will help maintain form but may limit blossoming.
Light: Keep in about 4 hours of direct sun in winter. Provide curtain-filtered sunlight in summer, from a south or west window.
Water: Keep evenly moist. Water thoroughly and discard drainage.
Humidity: Average indoor levels.
Temperatures: 50°F to 55°F at night, 60°F to 65°F during the day.
Fertilization: Fertilize all year, but more heavily in summer.
Propagation: Take stem cuttings at any time.
Grooming: Prune in early spring. Pinch back stem tips of young or re-growing plants to improve form. Do not destroy flower buds.
Repotting: Infrequent repotting is best. New plants will have to grow in a medium to large pot until almost root-bound before they will bloom.
Problems: Will get spindly and weak if light is too low. If soil is too wet or too dry, leaves will drop.

Tabernaemontana divaricata (Ervatamia coronaria)
Butterfly gardenia, Crape jasmine, Adam's-apple, Nero's-crown

This large shrub produces clusters of fragrant flowers that are about 2 inches across. Most of the flowers appear in the summer, but good light will prolong the

Tabernaemontana divaricata

blooming period. *E. coronaria plena* is a cultivar with double-petaled flowers. The plants will grow to about 2 feet and should be pruned into a proper shape. Several years of good care should produce a specimen plant. Always water thoroughly to prevent a buildup of soluble salts, which will cause the plant to decline.
Light: Four hours or more of direct sunlight from a south window. Does best in a greenhouse setting.
Water: Keep very moist at all times, but do not allow to stand in water.
Humidity: Average indoor levels.
Temperatures: 65°F to 70°F at night, 75°F to 80°F during the day.
Fertilization: Fertilize all year, but more heavily in summer.
Propagation: Take cuttings from stems or shoots before they have hardened or matured.
Grooming: Prune in early spring.
Repotting: Infrequent repotting is best.
Problems: Will not bloom if light is too low. Dry soil or high soluble salts may damage roots, causing plant to die back.

Tetranema roseum
Mexican foxglove

Mexican foxglove bears groups of tiny pink blossoms on 8-inch stalks, all year long. The dark green leaves of this small plant are formed in a rosette on a short stem. To keep it blooming, give it warmth, even moisture, and plenty of winter light. Keep Mexican foxgloves out of cold drafts.
Light: Keep in about 4 hours of direct sun in winter. Provide curtain-filtered sunlight in summer, from a south or west window.

Thunbergia alata

Water: Keep evenly moist. Water thoroughly and discard drainage.
Humidity: Average indoor humidity levels.
Temperatures: 55°F to 60°F at night, 70°F to 75°F during the day.
Fertilization: Fertilize all year, but more heavily in summer.
Propagation: Start new plants by dividing an older specimen. Seeds are available, but can be more difficult to use.
Grooming: Pick off yellowed leaves. Cut flower stalks if you wish.
Repotting: Repot at any time.
Problems: If plant is in a draft or dry air, leaves will scorch.

Thunbergia alata
Black-eyed Susan vine, Clock vine

This popular spring florists' plant is generally used in a hanging basket for a patio garden. It can also be trained onto a small trellis. Its yellow flowers with black centers resemble the pasture-weed common in northern states. In the South, thunbergia grows as a perennial vine. Indoor gardeners can keep it from year to year, but it needs lots of light to flower properly. The plants may get weak and spindly after a few years, even with the best care.
Light: Four hours or more of direct sunlight from a south window. Does best in a greenhouse setting.
Water: Keep evenly moist. Water thoroughly and discard drainage.
Humidity: Average indoor humidity levels.
Temperatures: 55°F to 60°F at night, 70°F to 75°F during the day.
Fertilization: Fertilize only when plant is growing actively or flowering.
Propagation: Start from seeds. Begin in a small pot and transplant as needed.

Trachelospermum jasminoides

Sow in early to midsummer for fall and winter flowers.
Grooming: Cut back straggly vines at their bases. Trim lightly at other times.
Repotting: Cut back and repot when flowering stops.
Problems: Will not bloom if light is too low.

Trachelospermum jasminoides
Star jasmine

Star jasmine is a woody, vining plant that bears clusters of fragrant white flowers in the spring and summer. The leaves of most are shiny green, but a variegated form, *T. jasminoides variegatum,* is available. Star jasmines do not vine vigorously and can be maintained in a shrublike form on a stake or trellis, with frequent pinching back of the stem tips. Keep the plant cool and dry in the winter.
Light: Keep in about 4 hours of direct sun in winter. Provide curtain-filtered sunlight in summer, from a south or west window.
Water: Let plant approach dryness before watering, but water thoroughly and discard drainage.
Humidity: Average indoor humidity levels.
Temperatures: 50°F to 55°F at night, 60°F to 65°F during the day.
Fertilization: Fertilize 3 times a year: spring, midsummer, and early fall.
Propagation: Take stem cuttings in fall or winter.

Tropaeolum majus

Grooming: Prune after flowering. Pinch back new stem tips to improve form. Do not destroy flower buds.
Repotting: Repot in winter or early spring, as needed.
Problems: Will not bloom if light is too low. Poor drainage, too frequent watering, or standing in water will cause root rot.

Tropaeolum majus
Common nasturtium

Nasturtiums are usually thought of as easy-to-grow summer annuals. Many indoor gardeners use them as winter-flowering plants. They should be used in hanging baskets. Some bushy varieties are available, but even these tend to get leggy and spindly indoors. The large, mildly fragrant flowers come in red, yellow, orange, or brown, depending on the cultivar. The plants need lots of light for winter flowering and will tolerate a cool spot. A window box is good for them.
Light: Keep in about 4 hours of direct sun in winter. Provide curtain-filtered sunlight in summer, from a south or west window.
Water: Keep evenly moist. Water thoroughly and discard drainage.
Humidity: Average indoor humidity levels.
Temperatures: 40°F to 45°F at night, 60°F to 65°F during the day.
Fertilization: Fertilize all year, but more heavily in summer.

Tropaeolum 'Bird Gold'

Propagation: Start from seeds. Begin in a small pot and transplant as needed. Sow in late summer for winter flowering.
Grooming: Start new plants and replace older specimans when they get weak. Discard after flowering.
Repotting: Not usually needed.
Problems: Will not bloom if light is too low.

Tulbaghia fragrans
Fragrant tulbaghia, Society garlic, Violet tulbaghia

Although tulbaghias are bulbs, they will bloom repeatedly throughout the year if given lots of light, water, and fertilizer. The flowers are borne in clusters on 15- inch-tall stalks. They are usually lavender and mildly fragrant. Do not bruise or break the leaves. Broken leaves smell like garlic, which may be an odor you do not want in your indoor garden. The bulbs of tulbaghias multiply rapidly and require frequent division.
Light: Give the plant 4 hours or more of direct sunlight from a south window.
Water: Keep evenly moist. Water thoroughly and discard drainage.
Humidity: Average indoor levels.
Temperatures: 40°F to 45°F at night, 60°F to 65°F during the day.
Fertilization: Fertilize all year, but more heavily in summer.

Propagation: Start new plants by dividing an older specimen.
Grooming: Pick off yellowed leaves.
Repotting: Repot each year.
Problems: Leaves smell of garlic when bruised or broken. Will not bloom if light is too low.

Tulipa species
Tulips

There are hundreds of tulips. Most are suitable for indoor forcing, though the smaller varieties may be best. Tulips can be purchased already in bud from many florists. To force your own, purchase several mature bulbs in October, put them together in one pot, and place them in a cool spot until January or February. Be sure to pot the bulbs with the flat side outward to get better foliage orientation. Many devoted indoor gardeners use an old refrigerator for this purpose. After the foliage has died back, most tulips can be placed in the garden. The bulbs of some varieties will divide readily, but others are difficult to propagate in this manner.
Light: Place anywhere during flowering. Before and after flowerings, provide at least 4 hours of curtain-filtered sunlight from a bright south, east, or west window.
Water: Keep very moist during growth and flowering. Allow to dry between waterings at other times.
Humidity: Average indoor levels.

Tulipa

Temperatures: 50°F to 55°F at night, 60°F to 65°F during the day.
Fertilization: Lightly fertilize after flowering.
Propagation: Start new plants from the small bulblets that develop beside the parent bulb.
Grooming: Cut flower stalks if you wish. Remove old leaves as plant goes dormant.
Repotting: Repot each year.
Problems: Subject to crown rot if planted deeply, watered over the crown, or watered late in the day.

Valotta species
Scarborough lily

This bulb produces up to 10 bright red flowers in a cluster on a 2-foot-high stalk. It usually flowers in late fall or winter. The leaves are narrow and about a foot long. After they have died back, give the plant a rest until summer. Repot it gently each summer without greatly disturbing the existing roots in the center of the rootball.
Light: Four hours or more of direct sunlight from a south window.
Water: Keep very moist during growth and flowering. Allow to dry between waterings at other times.
Humidity: Average indoor levels.
Temperatures: 50°F to 55°F at night, 60°F to 65°F during the day.
Fertilization: Do not fertilize when flowering. Fertilize lightly at other times.
Propagation: Start new plants from the small bulblets that develop beside the parent bulb.

Grooming: Cut flower stalks if you wish. Remove old leaves as plant goes dormant.
Repotting: Repot each year.
Problems: Subject to crown rot if planted deeply, watered over the crown, or watered late in the day.

Veltheimia species
Veltheimia, Forest lily

Veltheimias are large winter-flowering bulbs. The flowers, up to 10 in a cluster, are borne on a stalk that may be 2 feet high. They are light purple, tubular, and about an inch long. The glossy green leaves are 12 inches long and arch outward from the base of the flower stalk. Give the plants a rest in the summer.
Light: Provide at least 4 hours of curtain-filtered sunlight from a bright south, east, or west window, during flowering. After flowering, give plant 4 hours or more of direct sunlight from a south window.
Water: Keep very moist during growth and flowering. Allow to dry between waterings at other times.
Humidity: Average indoor humidity levels.
Temperatures: 50°F to 55°F at night, 60°F to 65°F during the day.
Fertilization: Fertilize only when plant is growing actively or flowering.
Propagation: Start new plants from the small bulblets that develop beside the parent bulb.
Grooming: Pick off yellowed leaves. Cut flower stalks if you wish.
Repotting: Infrequent repotting is best. Bulb can be repotted when growth starts in the fall.
Problems: None serious.

Zantedeschia aethiopica
Calla lily

A creamy white spathe, 5 to 10 inches in length, curves around a fragrant yellow spike to form this elegant perennial. Surrounded by wide, lance-shaped, glossy leaves, the trumpetlike flowers appear atop yard-long stems in winter and spring.

Varieties come in different sizes. 'Childsiana' produces many flowers and grows to 12 inches. 'Minor' spurts to a height of 18 inches, with flowers 4 inches long. 'Godfreyana' is somewhat smaller than other calla lily species, and bears many flowers. Other sizes and colors are available, but they are not usually grown indoors.

These imposing plants are a joy to grow as long as all their needs can be adequately met. Plenty of growing space, light, and moist soil and air produce strong growth and abundant blossoms. Place on a humidifying tray and feed your plant weekly with a mild houseplant fertilizer. The plant rests during the summer. Reduce water so leaves will yellow and die. Cut off dead growth and in autumn repot the rhizomes to a depth of an inch. Keep cool and barely moist throughout the blooming season.
Light: Keep in 4 hours of direct sun in winter. Provide curtain-filtered sun in summer, from a south or west window.
Water: Keep very moist during growth and flowering. Allow to dry between waterings at other times.
Humidity: Requires moist air. Use a humidifier for best results.
Temperatures: 50°F to 55°F at night, 65°F to 70°F during the day.
Fertilization: Fertilize only when plant is growing actively or flowering.
Propagation: Start new plants by dividing an older specimen.
Grooming: Pick off yellowed leaves. Cut flower stalks if you wish.
Repotting: Repot the rhizome in the fall, after the rest period.
Problems: If plant is in a draft or dry air, leaves will scorch.

Zephyranthes species
Zephyr lily

Many species and hybrids of zephyr lilies are available. Most are of moderate size and are easy to grow. They bloom at various times, sometimes more than once a year. Flowers can be pink, yellow, orange, or white, and are borne singly on a stalk, like a daffodils. The foliage is grasslike and about a foot long. Give the plants a rest period of 2 months after foliage has died back. Keep in a sunny, cool spot for flowering.

Zantedeschia aethiopica

Light: Four hours or more of direct sunlight from a south window.
Water: Keep very moist during growth and flowering. Allow to dry between waterings at other times.
Humidity: Average indoor humidity levels.
Temperatures: 40°F to 45°F at night, 60°F to 65°F during the day.
Fertilization: Fertilize only when plant is growing actively or flowering.
Propagation: Start new plants from the bulblets that develop beside the parent bulb.
Grooming: Cut flower stalks if you wish. Remove old leaves as plant goes dormant.
Repotting: Repot each year.
Problems: Poor drainage, too frequent watering, or standing in water will cause root rot.

Foliage Houseplants

A brief look at this section reveals the wide range of plants considered noteworthy for their foliage. These attributes range from color, variegation, and texture to size and arrangement of leaves on stems and branches. Even though striking and colorful foliage is important, a plant's size, shape, and form are the major criteria for its selection as an architectural accent or part of an indoor garden. It is the mixing of these characteristics—size, shape, form, and foliage—that gives an indoor garden its special charm. The ability to determine the relative importance of these characteristics enables interior plant designers to create striking indoor settings.

Many foliage plants produce flowers from time to time, but in general the flowers of these plants are less significant for design purposes than are their other characteristics. In some cases a plant may produce flowers only under precise cultural conditions, limiting its usefulness as a flowering specimen.

When selecting foliage plants, refer to "Designing with Houseplants" (pages 9 to 59) for design ideas. Use the cultural information given here for plant care.

Above: *Araucaria heterophylla*
Below: *Aglaonema modestum*

Acorus gramineus **'Variegatus'**

Acorus gramineus
Flagplant (miniature), Japanese sweet flag

Flagplants are often grown outdoors in southern climates, but two cultivars are suited for indoor gardening: a dwarf variety that has green leaves and a taller variegated form. Their leaves look like stiff, thick blades of grass. The plants are easy to grow in a variety of indoor settings. They do best in bright light, moist soil, and high humidity. In locations with only moderate light, keep them drier and fertilize less. Flagplants do well in cool spots if not overwatered.
Light: Provide at least moderate light but no direct sunlight.
Water: Keep evenly moist. Water thoroughly and discard drainage.
Humidity: Provide moist air. Use a humidifier for best results.
Temperatures: 40°F to 45°F at night, 60°F to 65°F during the day.
Fertilization: Fertilize 3 times a year: spring, midsummer, and early fall.
Propagation: Start new plants by dividing an older specimen.

Grooming: Pick off yellowed leaves.
Repotting: Repot at any time.
Problems: Leaves will scorch if plant is in a draft or dry air. Dry soil or high soluble salts may damage roots, causing plant to die back.

Aglaonema modestum
Chinese evergreen

The Chinese evergreen, which can grow to 2 feet, is a favorite indoors because it tolerates a wide range of conditions, including poor light and dry air. Its oblong, lance-shaped leaves are 6 to 9 inches long and 2 to 3 inches wide. The waxy, deep green leaves are marked with silver bars between pale lateral veins. Creamy, waxy flowers shaped like calla lilies bloom in late summer and early fall. Tight clusters of 1-inch-long yellowish red berries follow

the flowers. Place the plant in a moderately lit spot, and keep the soil evenly moist. Feed every 3 weeks with a mild fertilizer solution. The Chinese evergreen prefers a humid environment, so place it on a humidifying tray if the air is particularly dry. Growth slows during the winter.

Light: Will survive in low (reading level) light. Never place in direct sunlight.

Water: Keep evenly moist (somewhat drier in winter). Water thoroughly and discard drainage.

Humidity: Average indoor humidity levels.

Temperatures: 55°F to 60°F at night, 70°F to 75°F during the day.

Fertilization: Fertilize all year, more heavily in summer.

Propagation: Take root divisions or stem cuttings in spring and summer. Seeds are available, but can be more difficult to use.

Grooming: Remove yellowed leaves.

Repotting: Repot at any time. Blossoms best when pot-bound.

Problems: Leaf edges will turn brown if soluble salts are too high or if plant is in a draft or dry air.

Araucaria heterophylla
Norfolk Island pine

Norfolk Island pine is popular for indoor use because of its formal treelike appearance. These plants grow slowly indoors, so you may prefer to purchase a mature specimen. A related plant, *A. bidwillii* (monkey puzzle tree), has a less formal shape, sharp needles in two rows along its stem, and also grows indoors. Norfolk Island pine resembles a fir tree and can be decorated at Christmastime.

Light: Provide at least moderate light but no direct sunlight.

Water: Keep evenly moist. Water thoroughly and discard drainage.

Humidity: Average indoor humidity levels.

Temperatures: 50°F to 55°F at night, 65°F to 70°F during the day.

Fertilization: Fertilize 3 times a year: spring, midsummer, and early fall.

Propagation: Take a cutting from the tip of an old, damaged, or unwanted plant. Seeds are available, but can be more difficult to use.

Grooming: Pick off yellowed leaves.

Repotting: Infrequent repotting is best.

Problems: Leaves will scorch if plant is in a draft or dry air. Poor drainage, too frequent watering, or standing in water will cause root rot. Leaves will drop if soil is too wet or too dry.

Asparagus species
Asparagus fern

The two most popular asparagus plants are *A. sprengeri,* which has arching 18- to 24-inch stems covered with thousands of 1-inch-long flat needles, and *A. plumosa,* a trailing vine with 12- to 18-inch stems covered with dark green ⅛-inch needles. Both look best in hanging baskets.

These plants have been favorites for generations because they are so easy to care for. Unlike true ferns, they tolerate a wide range of temperatures and light, do not require a humid atmosphere, and can be easily propagated. To keep the plants bushy, pinch back their long stems.

Light: Provide bright indirect or curtain-filtered sunlight.

Water: Water thoroughly, but allow to dry between waterings.

Humidity: Average indoor humidity levels.

Temperatures: 60°F to 65°F at night, 68°F to 72°F during the day.

Fertilization: Fertilize 3 times a year: spring, midsummer, and early fall.

Propagation: Divide thick roots of old plants in any season.

Grooming: When plant gets leggy, cut stems to soil level. Fresh new stems will soon grow.

Repotting: Repot any time plant becomes overcrowded.

Problems: Leaves will turn yellow and drop if plant is suddenly moved to a location with low light.

Above: *Asparagus sprengeri*
Below: *Aspidistra elatior*

Aspidistra elatior
Cast-iron plant

This tough plant was one of the most popular houseplants of the Victorian era. It can survive extreme heat and low light which would be deadly to most other plants. Its leaves are oblong, shiny, dark green, and leathery, growing 15 to 30 inches long and 3 to 4 inches wide. They intermingle above a clump of 6-inch-long stems. In spring, dark purple, bell-shaped flowers are borne singly at the soil surface.

This slow-growing, long-lasting plant responds well to proper attention, but it can survive poor treatment for a long time. Place out of direct sun, in average warmth, and water regularly from spring to fall. Reduce water and keep the plant cool during the winter when it rests. Although it can withstand most abuse, this plant cannot endure soggy soil or frequent repotting.

Light: Will survive in low (reading level) light.

Water: Water thoroughly, but allow to dry between waterings. In winter, keep plant dry and water infrequently.

Humidity: Dry air is generally not harmful, but keep plant out of drafts.

Temperatures: 50°F to 55°F at night, 60°F to 65°F during the day.

Fertilization: Fertilize only during late spring and summer.
Propagation: Start new plants by dividing an older specimen.
Grooming: Pick off yellowed leaves.
Repotting: Can be repotted at any time, but infrequent repotting is best.
Problems: Poor drainage, too frequent watering, or standing in water will cause root rot.

Aucuba japonica
Japanese aucuba, Gold-dust tree

Aucubas are woody shrubs used outdoors in tropical climates. The various cultivars have yellow variegation patterns or speckles on shiny green leaves when grown in bright light. Keep the plants cool at night and out of direct sun during the day. Be careful not to overfertilize. Prune and train into a bushy plant.
Light: Provide at least 4 hours of curtain-filtered sunlight from a bright south, east, or west window.
Water: Let soil get almost dry before watering, but water thoroughly and discard drainage.
Humidity: Average indoor humidity levels.
Temperatures: 40°F to 45°F at night, 60°F to 65°F during the day.
Fertilization: Fertilize 3 times a year: spring, midsummer, and early fall.
Propagation: Take root cuttings at any time.
Grooming: Prune in early spring.
Repotting: Repot in winter or early spring, as needed.
Problems: Poor drainage, too frequent watering, or standing in water will cause root rot. Dry soil or high soluble salts may damage roots, causing plant to die back.

Bamboo

Several genera of plants are known as bamboo, including *Bambusa, Phyllostachys,* and *Arundinaria. A. pygmaea* (formerly known as *Sasa pygmaea*) is tolerant of most indoor conditions. It is a dwarf, growing only to about 1 foot, but many other bamboos are large plants that grow rapidly, given enough warmth and moisture. Bamboo is often used indoors because of its columnar shape; at a window, it can frame or

Aucuba japonica 'Picturata'

partially obscure a view. In warm climates, bamboo often becomes a pest outdoors because it spreads so rapidly.
Light: Provide 4 hours or more of direct sunlight from a south window.
Water: Keep very moist at all times, but do not allow to stand in water.
Humidity: Provide moist air. Use a humidifier for best results.
Temperatures: 55°F to 60°F at night, 70°F to 75°F during the day.
Fertilization: Fertilize all year, but more heavily in summer.
Propagation: Take cuttings from rhizomes or underground stems at any time.
Grooming: Cut back and thin out older shoots at any time.
Repotting: Grow in individual pots, not in a bed. Infrequent repotting is best.
Problems: None serious.

Begonia species

There are thousands of begonia species, hybrids, and cultivars. Most in this book are popular as flowering plants, but some are more useful and attractive as foliage plants. Even these will produce small flowers on long, graceful stalks if given enough light. You can place these begonias outdoors on a shaded patio for the summer and, when blooms appear, temporarily move the plants indoors as decorative accents. In winter move them back indoors.

Cultivars of foliage begonias are usually selected for the color, shape, and variegation of the foliage. Because many have shades of red or maroon in the foliage, a plant light (bluish purple) will greatly enchance the brightness of the leaf colors. In fact, these foliage begonias generally thrive under lights.

Angel-wing begonias are cane-type begonias. Their leaves are borne vertically

Bamboo: Arundinaria pygmaea

on upright stems. Many cultivars get quite large and need a lot of room. Rex begonias are rhizomatous and have creeping stems. They can get quite large, but they generally remain close to the soil surface. The iron cross begonia is not a rex begonia, but it has a similar growth habit. For best results, keep these begonias warm and avoid crown rot by not overwatering.

Begonia coccinea
Angel-wing begonias, Cane begonias

B. coccinea is the most common and easiest to grow of the large group of canelike begonias. Cane begonias generally have erect, smooth stems somewhat like those of bamboo. Most are large plants; some grow several feet high. Although grown primarily for their decorative foliage, many will bloom intermittently throughout the year if given enough light. The leaves of the various cultivars (and species of cane begonias) are asymmetrical and quite diverse in color, size, and variegation. Angel-wing begonias get their name from the shape of their leaves. Many cane begonias have trailing stems and are used in hanging baskets.
Light: Provide bright but indirect light from a south, east, or west window.
Water: Let plant approach dryness before watering, but water thoroughly and discard drainage.
Humidity: Average indoor humidity levels.
Temperatures: 65°F to 70°F at night, 75°F to 80°F during the day.
Fertilization: Fertilize only during late spring and summer.
Propagation: Take stem cuttings at any time. Seeds are available, but can be more difficult to use.
Grooming: Keep to desired height and shape with light pruning or clipping at any time.
Repotting: Repot infrequently.

Problems: Subject to crown rot if planted deeply, watered over the crown, or watered late in the day. Leaves will drop if soil is too wet or too dry.

Begonia masoniana
Iron cross

Iron cross is one of the most popular of the rhizomatous begonias, the largest group of begonias. Species in this group have jointed rhizomes that grow along or under the soil surface. A cousin of the rex begonias, iron cross is grown for its beautiful foliage. The leaves can get quite large, so give this plant plenty of room. The leaf surface is bumpy, or *rugose,* with a dark pattern resembling a Maltese cross in the center of a yellow-green background. In ample light, most rhizomatous begonias produce many small white flowers on tall stalks above the leaves. Iron cross tolerates most indoor settings with indirect light and moderate humidity. Many of the other rhizomatous begonias need high humidity, such as that provided by a well-lighted terrarium.

Light: Provide at least moderate light but no direct sunlight.

Water: Let plant approach dryness before watering, but water thoroughly and discard drainage.

Humidity: Provide moist air. Use a humidifier for best results.

Temperatures: 65°F to 70°F at night, 75°F to 80°F during the day.

Fertilization: Fertilize only during late spring and summer.

Propagation: Take leaf or stem cuttings at any time.

Grooming: Keep to desired height and shape with light pruning or clipping at any time.

Repotting: Infrequent repotting is best.

Problems: Subject to crown rot if planted deeply, watered over the crown, or watered late in the day.

Begonia x rex-cultorum
Rex begonias

Rex begonias are a large group of plants grown primarily for their foliage. They will bloom if given good light, producing tiny flowers on long stems. The leaves of most cultivars are large and have asymmetrical blades with diverse, brilliant coloration and textures. The rex begonias are rhizomatous in habit;

their stems may grow horizontally across the soil surface. Keep them warm and take care not to overwater. Fertilize lightly.

Light: Provide bright but indirect light from a south, east, or west window.

Water: Let plant approach dryness before watering, but water thoroughly and discard drainage.

Humidity: Average indoor humidity levels.

Temperatures: 65°F to 70°F at night, 75°F to 80°F during the day.

Fertilization: Fertilize only during late spring and summer.

Propagation: Take stem or leaf cuttings at any time. Seeds are available, but can be more difficult to use.

Grooming: Keep to desired height and shape with light pruning or clipping at any time. Give it plenty of room.

Repotting: Infrequent repotting is best.

Problems: Subject to crown rot if planted deeply, watered over the crown, or watered late in the day.

Brassaia species
Schefflera, Umbrella tree

Scheffleras are often used in commercial settings because they grow fast and are relatively easy to care for. *B. actinophylla,* although sold as a small seedling, can become extremely large. Its leaves are palmately compound and may be a foot or more across, spreading out like the sections of an umbrella. The small *B. arboricola* is becoming more common because it can survive in less light and is less susceptible to spider mites.

Light: Provide bright but indirect light from a south, east, or west window.

Water: Let plant approach dryness before watering, but water thoroughly and discard drainage.

Buxus sempervirens 'Suffruticosa'

Humidity: Average indoor humidity levels.
Temperatures: 50°F to 55°F at night, 60°F to 65°F during the day.
Fertilization: Fertilize only during late spring and summer.
Propagation: Take stem cuttings at any time. Seeds are available, but can be more difficult to use.
Grooming: Give this plant plenty of room. Pick off yellowed leaves.
Repotting: Infrequent repotting is best.
Problems: Will get spindly and weak if light is too low. Leaves will drop if the soil is too wet or too dry. Spider mites can be a problem, especially if plant is too dry.

Buxus species
Boxwood

These woody shrubs are found in many outdoor gardens, and can easily be made into a formal hedge. Many are becoming popular as indoor plants. They have a dense branching habit, resulting in thick masses of tiny green leaves. They can be cut and pruned easily to almost any shape. Keep boxwoods cool at night and do not overwater or overfertilize.
Light: Provide at least 4 hours of curtain-filtered sunlight from a bright south, east, or west window.
Water: Let plant approach dryness before watering, but water thoroughly and discard drainage.

Humidity: Average indoor humidity levels.
Temperatures: 50°F to 55°F at night, 60°F to 65°F during the day.
Fertilization: Fertilize lightly once a year, in early spring.
Propagation: Take cuttings from stems or shoots that have recently matured.
Grooming: Keep to desired height and shape with light pruning or clipping at any time.
Repotting: Infrequent repotting is best.
Problems: Dry soil or high soluble salts may damage roots, causing plant to die back. Spider mites can be a problem, especially if plant is too dry.

Cacti

The large family of cacti has more than 2,000 plants, all of which are succulents. It is a popular misconception that spines are the characteristic that distinguishes cacti from other succulents. Although most cacti have spines, some do not. The distinguishing characteristic is the presence of *areoles,* the small sunken or raised spots on cactus stems from which spines, flowers, and leaves grow. A few of the most popular cacti are described below. Consult Ortho's *World of Cactus and Succulents* for a more complete guide.

Desert cacti are extremely tolerant plants, but they need a highly porous soil that drains well. Although they can grow in relatively dry soil, cacti should be watered occasionally and fed a low-nitrogen fertilizer every 2 weeks during their growing season, from early spring to midautumn. Place in a sunny window with warm daytime temperatures; the nighttime temperature should be 10° to 15° cooler.

Aporocactus flagelliformis
Rattail cactus

This cactus produces narrow, snakelike stems ½ inch wide and up to 6 feet long. Outdoors, it has aerial roots that grip onto trees. For indoor culture, place the plant in a hanging basket and occasionally remove the old, brown stems. The flowers are large and are borne all along the stems in the summer.

Above: *Cactus: Aporocactus flagelliformis*
Below: *Cactus: Astrophytum myriostigma*

Astrophytum species
Bishop's-cap, Star cactus

These cacti have thick green stems similar to the foliage of some succulents. Their globular forms vary in shape, accounting for their common names. Most are small plants, but some cultivars can grow to 3 feet. Yellow flowers appear on the top of the cactus. Many cultivars are spineless.

Cephalocereus senilis
Old man cactus

This upright cylindrical cactus can reach a height of 10 feet and a diameter of 8 to 10 inches. Its gray-green body develops soft, furry spines while still immature. Rose funnel-shaped flowers are borne atop the cactus when it is several years old. It grows slowly and is good on a windowsill when young.

Cereus species
Peruvian apple, Curiosity plant

Cultivars of this cactus have deeply ribbed, self-branching, blue-green stems. They can reach a height of 20 feet. Large flowers, borne all along the stems in the summer, open at night.

Echinocactus grusonii
Golden barrel cactus

This popular globe-shaped cactus has yellow to red spines prominently borne on its stem ribs. It grows slowly but can reach 3 feet in diameter. Pink to yellow bell-shaped flowers are borne on the top central ring in the summer. This plant is tolerant of moderately lit locations, but will not grow or flower in them.

Echinocereus species
Strawberry cactus

These cacti are generally upright, cylindrical plants that form self-branching clumps of stems. The various cultivars have differing spine arrangements and colors. Flowers, which are usually purple, appear near the tops of the stems in late spring or summer. The plant is sensitive to salts and crown rot and is not recommended for beginners.

Above Left: *Cactus: Cephalocereus senilis*
Left: *Cactus: Echinocactus grusonii*
Above: *Cactus: Cereus peruvianus*

Echinopsis species
Urchin cactus

Gray-green globular to oval stems, growing singly or in clusters, characterize this cactus. They are distinctly ribbed and have clusters of spines along the ribs. This cactus is best known for its large, long-lasting, funnel-shaped flowers, which range from white to pink and sometimes reach 8 inches in length. This small, abundantly flowering cactus makes a good windowsill specimen.

Left: *Cactus: Echinopsis*
Above: *Cactus: Echinocereus*

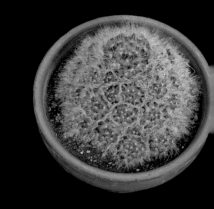

Above: *Cactus: Epiphyllum chrysocardium*
Below: *Cactus: Gymnocalycium denudatum*
Above Right: *Cactus: Hylocereus ocamponis*
Below Right: *Cactus: Lobivia allegraiana*

Epiphyllum chrysocardium
Orchid cactus

The orchid cactus is an epiphyte, as orchids are, and is grown indoors in hanging baskets. Its branches are flat and arch outward from a central crown-like area. This plant is grown primarily for its large, showy flowers, which appear anywhere on the stem in spring and early summer. Hybrids are available in reds, yellows, oranges, or white.

Gymnocalycium denudatum
Spider cactus

The globular stems of this cactus grow in clusters or singly, each stem measuring 8 to 12 inches thick, depending on the species. The spider cactus has yellowish, needle-shaped spines. The bell-shaped, white to pale rose flowers are borne near the top of the plant in spring and summer.

Hylocereus species

This plant has long, slender leaves that climb or hang. It can become quite long in time and is best used indoors in a hanging basket or trained onto a post.

All species have large white or red flowers which bloom at night. *H. undatus* (night-blooming cereus) is a commonly grown species with fragrant, white flowers. It is grown mainly for its large, fragrant white flowers, which bloom at night in spring and summer.

Lobivia species

Lobivias are small cacti often grown in clumps in a wide, flat container. They bloom more easily than many other cacti. The large yellow, red, or purple flowers appear in spring and summer and generally last a long time.

Mammillaria species
Pincushion cactus

The numerous and extremely diverse members of this genus grow in globular to cylindrical forms. Specimens can range from tiny individual heads only a few inches wide to massive clumps. Unlike other cacti, whose flowers are borne on areoles, mammillaria blooms grow from the joints of tubercles in a ring around the top of the plant. Flowering occurs from March to October.

Above: *Cactus: Mamillaria bocasana 'Inermis'*
Below: *Cactus: Notocactus eugeniae*

M. bocasana 'Inermis' (snowball cactus) has hooked yellowish spines and yellow, bell-shaped flowers. *M. prolifera* is a small globe-shaped cactus with bristly white spines and yellow flowers. It is commonly called little candles or silver cluster cactus. *M. zeilmanninana* (rose pincushion) has a solitary stem topped with purple flowers.

Notocactus species
Scarlet barrel cactus

These globe-shaped cacti grow slowly and are rarely more than a few inches high. Some species are covered with fine white spines borne in tufts on the stem. This easy-to-grow cactus will bear orange to red flowers in the winter if given enough light.

Opuntia species

Two basic growth habits—broad and flat or cylindrical—characterize this genus. Small tufts of spines create a dotted pattern over the surface of the plant. *O. microdasys* (bunny ears) has flat pads growing out of the top of larger mature pads, creating the form that gave it its name. They require very little care once they are established.

Above Left: *Cactus: Opuntia microdasys*
Below Left: *Cactus: Rhipsalis*
Above: *Cactus: Schlumbergera*

Rhipsalis species
Chain cactus

The jointed, branching, leafless stems of the chain cactus species cascade or climb in their native habitat, making them particularly suitable for hanging pots and baskets. These epiphytes have aerial roots on their flattened or cylindrical green stems. Flower shape, color, and size vary greatly within the genus.

Care of Cactus
Light: Provide at least 4 hours of curtain-filtered sunlight from a bright south, east, or west window.
Water: Water thoroughly, but allow to dry between waterings.
Humidity: Dry air is generally not harmful for these plants, but keep them out of drafts.
Temperatures: 40°F to 45°F at night, 60°F to 65°F during the day to set flower buds; 50°F to 55°F at night, 65°F to 70°F during the day at other times.

Fertilization: Fertilize lightly once a year, in early spring.
Propagation: Start new plants by dividing an older specimen. Seeds are available, but can be more difficult to use.
Grooming: None usually needed.
Repotting: Infrequent repotting is best.
Problems: Poor drainage, too frequent watering, or standing in water will cause root rot. Cacti will not bloom if light is too low.

Schlumbergera species
Christmas cactus, Easter cactus, Thanksgiving cactus

The unusual stems and timely blossoms of these commonly grown houseplants are both delightful and fascinating. Christmas cactus is an old favorite (*S. bridgesii,* also called *Zygocactus truncatus* and *Z. bridgesii*). It has striking, bright green, arched branches made up of flat, scalloped, 1½-inch-long joints. The branches droop, especially when in bloom. Its multitrumpeted, 3-inch-long, rosy red flowers appear at Christmastime. Easter cactus (*S. gaernerii,* also known as *Rhipsalidopsis gaertnerii*) is often confused with *S. bridgesii,* but it droops less and its stems and joints bear scarlet, sharp-tipped, upright or horizontal flowers. It blooms at Eastertime, and sometimes again in early fall. Cultivars in shades of pink and red are available.

Schlumbergeras are native to the tropical forests of South America, where they grow on trees. They require a rich, porous soil. Keep the soil moist but not soggy, and fertilize weekly when the plant is growing. They do well in front of a cool, bright window. During the summer you can move them outdoors into partial shade. Budding is brought on by the short days of October and November or by a cold shock. To promote flowering, place plants outdoors for a time during the fall.

S. truncatus (Thanksgiving cactus) flowers earlier in the winter. Its stem joints are longer and narrower than later-blooming schlumbergeras. The 3-inch-long flowers, borne at the ends of the stems, are shades of white and red. Place plants on the porch or patio in fall before the first frost, since flower buds will form only after the plants are exposed to short days and cool nights for a month or so. After it flowers, keep the plant drier and withhold fertilizer.

Care of Schlumbergera and Zygocactus

Light: Place in a bright but indirectly lit south, east, or west window.
Water: Keep very moist during growth and flowering. At other times, allow to dry between waterings.
Humidity: Average indoor humidity levels.
Temperatures: 40°F to 45°F at night, 60°F to 65°F during the day to set flower buds; 50°F to 55°F at night, 65°F to 70°F during the day at other times.
Fertilization: Fertilize only when plant is growing actively or flowering.
Propagation: Take cuttings from recently matured stems or shoots when plant is not in flower.
Grooming: Prune after flowering if needed.
Repotting: Infrequent repotting is best.
Problems: Dry soil or high soluble salts may damage roots, causing dieback.

Far Left: *Caladium*
Left: *Calathea louisae*
Above: *Chlorophytum comosum*
'Vittatum'

Caladium species
Caladium

The dozens of varieties of caladiums, with different leaf patterns and colors, can create a splendid display of color and are sure to rival any flowering plant. Masses of paper-thin, heart-shaped leaves 12 to 24 inches long are borne on long stalks. The exquisite foliage of this perennial dies back for a 4-month period during dormancy. *C. bicolor* is 14 inches long and 6½ inches wide, featuring wide red leaves bordered with green. *C. humboldii* is a miniature plant whose light green leaves are splotched with white.

Attention to a few basic needs will reward you with vibrant, healthy caladiums. Bright indirect light or curtain-filtered sunlight is best. Keep the pot on a humidifying tray and mist daily during the growing periods. Warmth is essential: the temperature should never drop below 70°F during the day.
Light: Provide at least 4 hours of curtain-filtered sunlight from a bright south, east, or west window.
Water: Keep evenly moist, but plant can tolerate some dryness between waterings. Allow to dry out and become dormant in the fall.
Humidity: Provide moist air. Use a humidifier for best results.

Temperatures: 55°F to 60°F at night, 70°F to 75°F during the day.
Fertilization: Fertilize 3 times a year: spring, midsummer, and early fall.
Propagation: Start new plants from the small bulblets that develop beside the parent. Pot these bulblets in late winter when the plant is dormant.
Grooming: Remove old leaves as the plant goes dormant.
Repotting: Repot each year.
Problems: Leaves will scorch if plant is in a draft or dry air. Plant will get spindly and weak if light is too low.

Calathea species
Peacock plant

Calatheas have what many consider to be the most beautifully variegated foliage of any indoor plant. Their leaves are large and have red stalks, with blades of various patterns of greens on top. Some cultivars have purples and reds on the undersides of the leaves. Calatheas will not tolerate dry air or drafts; they are often used in lighted terrariums. Give the plants plenty of room, since they can grow 2 feet high with leaves 8 inches across.
Light: Will survive in low (reading level) light.
Water: Keep very moist at all times, but do not allow to stand in water.
Humidity: Provide moist air. Use a humidifier for best results.
Temperatures: 65°F to 70°F at night, 75°F to 80°F during the day.
Fertilization: Fertilize lightly once a year in early spring, if plant is in a dimly lit spot. Otherwise, fertilize lightly during summer.
Propagation: Start plants by dividing an older specimen.
Grooming: Pick off yellowed leaves.
Repotting: Repot at any time.
Problems: Leaves will scorch if plant is in a draft or dry air. Dry soil or high soluble salts may damage roots, causing plant to die back.

Callisia elegans
Striped inch plant

Striped inch plant is a relative of the wandering Jew, which it closely resembles, but this plant has larger, more obviously striped leaves when properly grown. The purple on most callisias is more intense and more strictly limited to the undersides of the leaves. *C. fragrans* has particularly fragrant flowers in the summer. Give the plants a moderate rest in winter, cut them back in spring, and frequently pinch back stems to maintain bushiness.
Light: Provide at least 4 hours of curtain-filtered sunlight from a bright south, east, or west window.
Water: Keep moist. Water thoroughly and discard drainage. In winter, keep plant dry and water infrequently.
Humidity: Average indoor levels.
Temperatures: 50°F to 55°F at night, 65°F to 70°F during the day.
Fertilization: Fertilize 3 times a year: spring, midsummer, and early fall.
Propagation: Take stem cuttings at any time.
Grooming: Prune in early spring. Pinch back stem tips of young or re-growing plants to improve form. Do not destroy flower buds.
Repotting: Repot in winter or early spring as needed.
Problems: Will get spindly and weak if light is too low.

Chlorophytum comosum
Spider plant

The familiar spider plant has been grown indoors since nearly 200 years ago when Goethe, German writer and philosopher, brought the plant inside because of his fascination with its habit of producing miniature plants on shoots. The spider plant can grow to be 3 feet tall. Wiry stems up to 5 feet long, bearing plantlets, spring forth among grassy green, arching leaves striped with yellow or white. This plant is perfect for a hanging basket.

The spider plant will grow in almost any location—sunny or shady, dry or damp. Water freely from spring to autumn and keep in a moderate to cool location. Feed every other week. The plantlets can be left on the stems of the mother plant for a full look, or they can be removed for propagation. The plant will produce the most plantlets when slightly pot-bound.

Light: Provide at least moderate light but no direct sunlight.

Water: Keep very moist during growth and flowering. Allow to dry between waterings at other times.

Humidity: Average indoor humidity levels.

Temperatures: 50°F to 55°F nights; 60°F to 65°F days.

Fertilization: Fertilize all year, but more heavily in summer.

Propagation: Remove new plantlets or rooted side shoots as they form.

Grooming: Give these plants plenty of room.

Repotting: Repot in winter or early spring as needed.

Problems: Brown leaf tips can be caused by high soluble salts. Dry soil or high soluble salts may damage roots, causing plant to die back.

Cissus species

These members of the grape family are trailing or vining plants that become woodier with age. They are attractive in hanging baskets or trained onto trellises. Of all the genera in the grape family, *Cissus* is the only one suitable for indoor culture, given moderate light and dry air. Several species are mentioned here. Although their culture is similar, enough differences exist to warrant individual care guides.

These plants are popular in commercial settings. They grow rapidly in greenhouses and acclimate easily to poor light and infrequent watering. With care, plants can be maintained for many months, but they will not grow unless they are given bright indirect or even full sunlight, and are kept moderately moist and well fertilized. Prune stem tips and train the vines frequently to encourage proper form.

Above: *Cissus rhombifolia*
Right: *Cissus antarctica*

Cissus antarctica
Kangaroo ivy, Kangaroo vine

Kangaroo ivy, a member of the grape family, is a vigorous indoor climber. It is usually trained onto a trellis, string, or post, and can be used in hanging baskets. The foliage is large and shiny but may be sparse along the stem if the plant is not in good light. To counter this spindly appearance, many indoor gardeners train or wrap several vines to achieve the appearance of denser foliage.

Light: Provide at least moderate light but no direct sunlight.

Water: Let plant approach dryness before watering, but water thoroughly and discard drainage.

Humidity: Average indoor levels.

Temperatures: 50°F to 55°F at night, 65°F to 70°F during the day.

Fertilization: Fertilize 3 times a year: spring, midsummer, and early fall.

Propagation: Take stem cuttings at any time.

Grooming: Keep to desired height and shape with light pruning or clipping at any time.

Repotting: Repot at any time.

Problems: Will get spindly and weak if light is too low.

Cissus discolor
Begonia treebine

Begonia treebine is a vigorous vine that will grow to 6 feet or more unless pruned. It needs more light than its cousins, kangaroo and grape ivy. The leaves resemble those of the begonia, velvety with toothed edges and red veins. In ample light, pink and white coloration will also be present.

Light: Four hours or more of direct sunlight from a south window.

Water: Keep evenly moist. Water thoroughly and discard drainage.

Humidity: Requires moist air. Use a humidifier for best results.

Temperatures: 55°F to 60°F at night, 70°F to 75°F during the day.

Fertilization: Fertilize all year, but more heavily in summer.

Propagation: Take stem cuttings at any time.

Grooming: Keep to desired height and shape with light pruning or clipping at any time.

Repotting: Repot in winter or early spring as needed.

Problems: Will get spindly and weak if light is too low.

Cissus rhombifolia
Grape ivy

Grape ivy, a member of the grape family, grows wild in the West Indies and South America. It is a vining plant best used in a hanging basket. The stems and buds are brown and have reddish-hairs, and its shiny 3-leaflet leaves are similar to poison ivy's. In recent years, this plant has become popular with indoor gardeners because it tolerates a wide range of growing conditions. It grows rapidly, even in moderate light.

Light: Will survive in low (reading level) light.
Water: Let plant approach dryness before watering, but water thoroughly and discard drainage.
Humidity: Dry air is generally not harmful for this plant, but keep it out of drafts.
Temperatures: 50°F to 55°F at night, 60°F to 65°F during the day.
Fertilization: Fertilize 3 times a year: spring, midsummer, and early fall.
Propagation: Take stem cuttings at any time.
Grooming: Keep to desired height and shape with light pruning or clipping at any time.
Repotting: Repot at any time.
Problems: The leaves will drop if soil is too wet or too dry. Dry soil or high soluble salts may damage roots, causing plant to die back. Powdery mildew occurs occasionally.

Codiaeum variegatum
Croton

The varied shapes and exotic colors of the croton's leaves make it an especially attractive indoor plant. Growing to 3 feet high, its lance-shaped, leathery leaves (up to 18 inches long) grow from a single stem or trunk. Foliage colors of the many varieties include red, pink, orange, brown, and white. Color markings vary considerably among leaves on the same plant. In addition, the plant may change color as it matures.

C. variegatum pictum (Joseph's coat) is a popular croton featuring oval, lobed leaves, somewhat resembling oak leaves. It is a narrow shrub that usually attains a height of 2 to 4 feet.

Crotons are not easy to grow unless you can satisy all their environmental needs. Lots of sunshine and a warm, draft-free location are essential. The key to success is keeping the air humid enough so the plant can cope with the sun and warm temperatures. Place it on a humidifying tray to ensure adequate moisture. Dry air or dry soil will cause the leaves to wither rapidly and die.
Light: Four hours or more of direct sunlight from a south window.
Water: Keep evenly moist. Water thoroughly and discard drainage.
Humidity: Average indoor levels.

Temperatures: 65°F to 70°F nights; 75°F to 80°F days.
Fertilization: Fertilize 3 times a year: spring, midsummer, and early fall.
Propagation: Take cuttings from stems or shoots before they have hardened or matured.
Grooming: Clean leaves and inspect for pests regularly.
Repotting: Repot in winter or early spring as needed.
Problems: The leaves will scorch if plant is in a draft or dry air. They will drop if soil is too wet or too dry.

Coffea arabica
Coffee plant

The plant that produces the coffee bean is an evergreen native to Asia and tropical Africa. Extremely popular and adaptable as a container plant, it has a thin main trunk with willowy branches of dark green oval leaves. Fragrant white flowers and bright red berries appear on the tree during the fall when it is 3 to 4 years old, making it a unique and attractive addition to any room.

The coffee plant has only a few demands. Keep the soil moist, since dryness will cause severe wilting and possibly permanent damage, and keep the plant in a warm draft-free spot.
Light: Provide at least 4 hours of curtain-filtered sunlight from a bright south, east, or west window.
Water: Keep very moist at all times, but do not allow to stand in water.
Humidity: Average indoor levels.

Left: *Codiaeum variegatum pictum*
Above: *Coffea arabica*

Temperatures: 55°F to 60°F nights; 70°F to 75°F days.
Fertilization: Fertilize only during late spring and summer months.
Propagation: Take cuttings from stems or shoots before they have hardened or matured.
Grooming: Keep to desired height and shape with light pruning or clipping at any time.
Repotting: Repot in winter or early spring as needed.
Problems: The leaves of this plant will drop if soil is too wet or too dry.

Coleus x hybridus
Coleus

So richly colored are the leaves of the coleus that many people find it a colorful, inexpensive substitute for the croton. It is a fast-growing tropical shrub whose oval, scalloped leaves taper to a point. The velvety leaves come in a multitude of colors with toothed or fringed margins, depending on the variety. Dark blue or white flowers form in the fall.

Coleus is easy to care for, provided it's in a brightly lit, warm spot. Water it regularly and fertilize monthly. Nip flowers when they appear, to encourage compact growth and branching; otherwise the plant will become leggy.
Light: Place in a bright, indirectly lit south, east, or west window.
Water: Keep evenly moist. Water thoroughly and discard drainage.
Humidity: Average indoor humidity levels.
Temperatures: 55°F to 60°F nights; 70°F to 75°F days.
Fertilization: Fertilize only when plant is growing actively or flowering.
Propagation: Take stem cuttings at any time.

Left: *Coleus x hybridus*
Above: *Cordyline terminalis 'Kiwi'*
Right: *Cyperus alternifolius*

Grooming: Prune in early spring. Pinch back stem tips of young or re-growing plants to improve form.
Repotting: Repot each year.
Problems: Some leaf drop will occur in winter. Plant will get spindly and weak if light is too low.

Cordyline terminalis
Hawaiian ti

Cordylines are large outdoor plants in their native South Sea Islands. The narrow leaves, which can be 18 inches long, are often used for hula skirts. Popular indoor cultivars will grow to about 3 feet and have foliage with pink variegations and stripes along the leaf edges. Although cordylines will tolerate low light, foliage color will not develop well under such conditions. For a more interesting look, use a fairly large section of stem for propagation so that the resulting plant will have several shoots within the pot. The foliage is sensitive to dry air and drafts.
Light: Will survive in low (reading level) light.
Water: Let plant approach dryness before watering, but water thoroughly and discard drainage.
Humidity: Requires moist air. Use a humidifier for best results.
Temperatures: 65°F to 70°F at night, 75°F to 80°F during the day.

Fertilization: Fertilize 3 times a year: spring, midsummer, and early fall.
Propagation: Take stem cuttings at any time. New plants can be started with air layering.
Grooming: Pick off yellowed leaves.
Repotting: Repot at any time.
Problems: The leaves will scorch if this plant is in a draft or dry air. Spider mites can be a problem, especially if the plant is too dry.

Cyperus species
Umbrella plant, Pygmy papyrus

These plants are members of the sedge family. *C. papyrus,* which is common in the Near East, was used historically in making the writing material known as papyrus. Cultivars are available as tiny plants, but most soon grow to 2 to 4 feet. The long green stems bear whorls of leaves, resembling an umbrella's spokes. Dwarf cultivars are sometimes more suited for indoor gardening. These plants, like all the sedges, like wet conditions. The leaves may scorch or burn in dry indoor air. Tall plants may require staking.
Light: In winter, keep in about 4 hours of direct sun. In summer, provide curtain-filtered sunlight from a south or west window.
Water: Keep very moist at all times, but do not allow to stand in water.
Humidity: Requires moist air. Use a humidifier for best results.
Temperatures: 40°F to 45°F at night, 60°F to 65°F during the day.
Fertilization: Fertilize 3 times a year: spring, midsummer, and early fall.
Propagation: Start new plants by dividing an older specimen. You can use seeds, but they are more difficult.

Grooming: Pick off yellowed leaves.
Repotting: Repot in winter or early spring as needed.
Problems: Spider mites can be a problem, especially if plant is too dry. The leaves will scorch if the plant is in a draft or dry air.

Dieffenbachia
Dieffenbachia, Dumb cane

When touched to the tongue, the sap from the canelike stems of dieffenbachia can cause temporary speechlessness and much pain, hence the name "dumb cane." This handsome evergreen features a single thick trunk when young; it unwinds into multiple trunks to create a palmlike appearance as the plant matures. Arching, oblong, pointed leaves 10 to 12 inches long spiral around the trunk. *D. maculata* 'Randolph Roehrs' has chartreuse leaves marbled with ivory, divided by a dark green central rib. Mature plants reach ceiling height. For planter and large container decorations, dieffenbachias have few equals. They do well indoors all year or outdoors in warm shade.

Dieffenbachia maculata
'Randolph Roehrs'

Indoors, place them in a moderately bright spot, such as a northern or eastern exposure, with average humidity. Allow soil to dry between thorough waterings, and feed monthly during the growing season. Remove yellowed foliage promptly, and wash leaves occasionally.

Light: Will survive in low (reading level) light.

Water: Water thoroughly, but allow to dry between waterings.

Humidity: Average indoor humidity levels.

Temperatures: 50°F to 55°F nights; 65°F to 70°F days.

Fertilization: Fertilize all year, but more heavily in summer.

Propagation: Take stem cuttings or air-layer at any time.

Grooming: Pick off yellowed leaves.

Repotting: Repot at any time.

Problems: Poor drainage, too frequent watering, or standing in water will cause root rot.

Dizygotheca elegantissima
False aralia

This is one of the most graceful plants you can bring indoors. Thin, dark green leaves with lighter veins spread into 9 fingerlike segments with saw-toothed edges. You can buy thumb-sized seedlings for a terrarium, or a mature plant large enough to sit under.

With proper care, this slow grower should cause few problems. It is, however, extremely sensitive to soil moisture and won't tolerate either soggy soil or a dry rootball. Don't move it around often; it does best when kept in the same location. Moist air is another important factor in keeping it healthy.

Light: Place in a bright, indirectly lit south, east, or west window. Older plants can endure less light.

Water: Keep evenly moist. Water thoroughly and discard drainage. In winter, keep plant dry with infrequent waterings.

Humidity: Average indoor humidity levels.

Temperatures: 55°F to 60°F nights; 70°F to 75°F days.

Fertilization: Fertilize 3 times a year: spring, midsummer, and early fall.

Propagation: This plant is difficult to propagate. Start from seeds. Begin in a small pot and transplant as necessary.

Grooming: Keep to desired height and shape with light pruning or clipping at any time.

Repotting: Infrequent repotting is best. Repot in winter or early spring as needed

Problems: The leaves of this plant will drop if soil is too wet or too dry. Spider mites can be a problem, especially if plant is too dry.

Dracaena species

Dracaenas have tall stems with tufts of narrow, swordlike leaves near the top. Most grow into large plants, often 10 feet or more in height. To counter this tendency for tall, leggy growth, stems of different heights are often planted together in the same pot. Specimens may also be produced with bent or contorted stems to achieve different heights. In addition, many indoor gardeners air-layer these palmlike plants to reduce their height. The canes that are left after the air layers are removed will usually sprout to form new leafy growth.

Many varieties of dracaenas are available. Most are used as large architectural plants indoors. Dracaenas are usually selected for their foliage and form. Some have narrow, spikelike foliage and others have wider, more arching leaves. Most of the popular cultivars are variegated in some manner. *D. fragrans* 'Massangeana' occasionally produces sprays of extremely fragrant white flowers among its large leaves. In many commercial interiors these flowers are removed because of their overpowering aroma.

If conditioned properly, dracaenas will tolerate low light and infrequent waterings; but they will grow little—if at all—under such conditions. Because their care depends somewhat on the cultivar chosen, individual care guides are given for the species described.

Above: *Dizygotheca elegantissima*
Below: *Dracaena deremensis* **'Warneckii'**

Dracaena deremensis
Warneckii dracaena, Janet Craig dracaena

These dracaenas grow as single-stemmed plants with long narrow leaves arching outward all along the stem. It is common to grow several plants of differing heights in one pot for added beauty. 'Janet Craig', the larger of the two, has dark green shiny leaves and will grow to 5 or 6 feet if given ample light. 'Warneckii' is usually smaller. It has narrower leaves with

**Above: *Dracaena deremensis*
 'Janet Craig'
Below: *Dracaena fragrans*
 'Massangeana'**

thin white stripes along the leaf edges. Both plants are quite tolerant of stressful indoor environments. Do not overwater or overfertilize plants that are growing in low light.

Light: 'Warneckii' will survive in low (reading level) light, but never place in direct sunlight. 'Janet Craig' needs moderate light or better, but no direct sunlight.

Water: Let plant approach dryness before watering, but water thoroughly and discard drainage.

Humidity: Average indoor humidity levels.

Temperatures: 55°F to 60°F at night, 70°F to 75°F during the day.

Fertilization: Fertilize all year, but more heavily in summer.

Propagation: Take stem cuttings at any time. New plants can be started with air layering.

Grooming: Pick off yellowed leaves. Trim off brown leaf tips.

Repotting: Repot at any time.

Problems: The leaves will drop if soil is too wet or too dry. Leaf tips will turn brown from excessive dryness or high soluble salts.

Dracaena fragrans 'Massangeana'
Corn plant

The leaves of this dracaena are long and narrow with yellowish striping, resembling corn leaves. It is often potted as a series of canes or stems with leaves growing only on a short stalk that has sprouted near the cut end of the parent cane. At other times, it is grown as a single stem with leaves reaching outward all along the trunk. In ample light, the corn plant may occasionally produce an extremely fragrant flower. It can tolerate many abuses, but be careful not to overwater or overfertilize a plant growing in low light.

Light: Will survive in low (reading level) light.

Water: Let plant approach dryness before watering, but water thoroughly and discard drainage.

Humidity: Average indoor humidity levels.

Temperatures: 55°F to 60°F at night, 70°F to 75°F during the day.

Fertilization: Fertilize all year, but more heavily in summer.

Propagation: Take stem cuttings at any time. New plants can be started with air layering.

Grooming: Pick off yellowed leaves. Trim off brown leaf tips.

Repotting: Repot at any time.

Problems: The leaves will drop if soil is too wet or too dry. Leaf tips will turn brown from excessive dryness or high soluble salts.

Dracaena surculosa
Gold-dust dracaena

This plant's form and the shape of its leaves make it different from other

Dracaena surculosa

dracaenas. Gold-dust dracaena is small, bushy, and shrublike. It has fairly broad leaves, somewhat like those of an elm tree. The leaves are brilliantly spotted with yellow or cream markings. It must have good light and be kept constantly moist. This slow-growing plant will rarely be more than 2 feet tall, even in ample light.

Light: Place in a bright, indirectly lit south, east, or west window.

Water: Keep evenly moist. Water thoroughly and discard drainage.

Humidity: Average indoor humidity levels.

Temperatures: 55°F to 60°F at night, 70°F to 75°F during the day.

Fertilization: Fertilize only during late spring and summer months.

Propagation: Take stem cuttings at any time.

Grooming: Keep to desired height and shape with light pruning or clipping at any time.

Repotting: Repot in winter or early spring as needed.

Problems: The leaves will scorch if plant is in a draft or dry air. They will drop if soil is too wet or too dry.

Left: *Dracaena marginata*
Above: *Dracaena reflexa*
Right: *Epipremnum aureum*

Dracaena marginata
Madagascar dragon tree, Red-margined dracaena

D. marginata has the narrowest leaves of all the commonly cultured dracaenas. Most cultivars have red striping on the edges of the leaves. The plants are normally potted as a series of stems or canes with the foliage at the top. As the plant grows, the older leaves will yellow and die back from time to time. Older canes may branch at the top as well. Avoid leaf tip burn by keeping the plant evenly moist and out of drafts.
Light: Provide at least moderate light but no direct sunlight.
Water: Keep evenly moist. Water thoroughly and discard drainage.
Humidity: Average indoor humidity levels.
Temperatures: 55°F to 60°F at night, 70°F to 75°F during the day.
Fertilization: Fertilize only during late spring and summer months.
Propagation: Take stem cuttings at any time. New plants can be started with air layering.
Grooming: Pick off yellowed leaves. Trim leaves with brown tips.
Repotting: Repot at any time.
Problems: The leaves will scorch if plant is in a draft or dry air. Watch for spider mites, especially if plant is dry.

Dracaena reflexa
Pleomele

Until recently, this dracaena was known by the botanical name *Pleomele reflexa.* It can grow into a large plant with reflexed or downward-pointing leaves closely set along canelike stems. The leaves are usually variegated, with white or cream edges. Because it is tolerant of many indoor environments, pleomele is often seen in commercial interiors. Keep it away from drafts or cold air.
Light: Provide at least moderate light but no direct sunlight.
Water: Let plant approach dryness before watering, but water thoroughly and discard drainage.
Humidity: Average indoor humidity levels.
Temperatures: 65°F to 70°F at night, 75°F to 80°F during the day.
Fertilization: Fertilize 3 times a year: spring, midsummer, and early fall.
Propagation: Take stem cuttings at any time. New plants can be started with air layering.
Grooming: Pick off yellowed leaves. Trim off browned leaf tips.
Repotting: Infrequent repotting is best.
Problems: The leaves will drop if soil is too wet or too dry.

Dracaena sanderana
Ribbon plant, Sander's dracaena

Ribbon plant will get tall in time, but it is usually sold and grown as a small plant less than a foot tall. The leathery narrow leaves have white stripes along the edges. It does well in a dish garden, terrarium, or dimly lit spot. If the plant gets too leggy or spindly, air-layer it and replant. Remember to water

and fertilize it lightly if the plant is in low light. Keep it out of drafts to avoid leaf scorch.
Light: Will survive in low (reading level) light.
Water: Let plant approach dryness before watering, but water thoroughly and discard drainage.
Humidity: Average indoor humidity levels.
Temperatures: 55°F to 60°F at night, 70°F to 75°F during the day.
Fertilization: Fertilize all year, but more heavily in summer.
Propagation: Take stem cuttings at any time. New plants can be started with air layering.
Grooming: Pick off yellowed leaves.
Repotting: Infrequent repotting is best.
Problems: The leaves will scorch if plant is in a draft or dry air.

Epipremnum aureum
Pothos, Devil's ivy

Epipremnum (also known as *Scindapsus*) is commonly used as a vining ground cover, cascading accent plant, or hanging basket in commercial interiors. Its heart-shaped, leathery leaves look somewhat like the heart-leaf philodendron's. Variegated forms are available. Pinch back stem tips occasionally to promote branching. Cut back old runners or vines when they get leggy. You can also loop old vines back up over the pot and root them near their ends.
Light: Provide at least moderate light but no direct sunlight.
Water: Keep evenly moist. Water thoroughly and discard drainage.
Humidity: Average indoor humidity levels.
Temperatures: 50°F to 55°F at night, 60°F to 65°F during the day.
Fertilization: Fertilize 3 times a year: spring, midsummer, and early fall.

Left: *Euonymus japonica 'Silver Queen'*
Above: *x Fatshedera lizei*

Propagation: Take stem cuttings at any time.
Grooming: Pick off yellowed leaves. Keep to desired height and shape with light pruning or clipping at any time.
Repotting: Repot at any time.
Problems: Poor drainage, too frequent watering, or standing in water will cause root rot. Will get spindly and weak if light is too low.

Euonymus fortunei
Winter creeper

Winter creeper is often used outdoors in northern states as a semievergreen climbing plant. Indoors, it does best in a cool location such as an entranceway. The trailing stems will climb and attach themselves to vertical surfaces, so it is best to train the plant onto a wall or post. The variegated form of this slow-growing plant is particularly popular. Indoors, it will grow to 2 feet or more.
Light: Place in a bright, indirectly lit south, east, or west window.
Water: Keep evenly moist. Water thoroughly and discard drainage.
Humidity: Average indoor humidity levels.
Temperatures: 40°F to 45°F at night, 60°F to 65°F during the day.
Fertilization: Fertilize 3 times a year: spring, midsummer, and early fall.

Propagation: Take cuttings from stems or shoots before they have hardened or matured.
Grooming: Keep to desired height and shape with light pruning or clipping at any time.
Repotting: Infrequent repotting is best.
Problems: Subject to infestations of scale or mealybug.

Euonymus japonica
Euonymus (evergreen)

Many cultivars of euonymus are used outdoors as semievergreen foundation plantings. The woody, bushy plants do well indoors if given ample light. Many cultivars have variegated foliage, about ½ inch long, produced abundantly all along the stems. Keep these plants constantly moist and do not allow them to become pot-bound. Stress may make them susceptible to spider mites.
Light: Provide at least 4 hours of curtain-filtered sunlight from a bright south, east, or west window.
Water: Keep evenly moist. Water thoroughly and discard drainage.
Humidity: Average indoor humidity levels.
Temperatures: 40°F to 45°F at night, 60°F to 65°F during the day.
Fertilization: Fertilize only during late spring and summer months.
Propagation: Take cuttings from stems or shoots before they have hardened or matured.
Grooming: Keep to desired height and shape with light pruning or clipping at any time.

Repotting: Infrequent repotting is best.
Problems: Spider mites can be a problem, especially if plant is too dry. Subject to crown rot if planted deeply, watered over the crown, or watered late in the day. The leaves will drop if soil is too wet or too dry.

x Fatshedera lizei
Tree ivy, Aralia ivy

This plant is a hybrid between English ivy and Japanese aralia. It is semierect, with a green, partially woody stem. Tree ivy usually has to be staked to keep upright. It's large leaves are sometimes 10 inches across. The variegated cultivar, *F. lizei variegata,* is particularly good for indoor culture.
Light: In winter, keep in about 4 hours of direct sun. In summer, provide curtain-filtered sunlight from a south or west window.
Water: Keep evenly moist. Water thoroughly and discard drainage.
Humidity: Requires moist air. Use a humidifier for best results.
Temperatures: 40°F to 45°F at night, 60°F to 65°F during the day.
Fertilization: Fertilize 3 times a year: spring, midsummer, and early fall.
Propagation: Take stem cuttings at any time. New plants can be started with air layering.
Grooming: Prune in early spring. Give it plenty of room.
Repotting: Repot in winter or early spring as needed.
Problems: The leaves will drop if soil is too wet or too dry.

Fatsia japonica

Fatsia japonica
Japanese aralia

This handsome evergreen foliage plant has bold, lobed leaves of shiny green, occasionally variegated with white. In frost-free climates it can be grown outdoors, but it also makes an excellent contribution to indoor gardens. The smaller plant *Fatshedera* (aralia ivy or tree ivy) is a hybrid of *Fatsia* and English ivy; it has Fatsia's leaves and the growth habit of ivy.

The fast-growing Japanese aralia is durable and tolerant of many environments. It is easily grown in a cool, well-ventilated location with bright light. Wash and mist the leaves regularly and feed every 2 weeks during the growing season, otherwise the leaves may yellow from lack of nitrogen. The plant needs to rest during winter, so move it to a cool, dry spot. Remove any flower buds that may emerge on the mature plant to prevent it from going into the reproductive cycle. If it begins to look gangly or has misshapen leaves, trim it back to its stalk. New shoots will appear soon.
Light: Place in a bright, indirectly lit south, east, or west window.
Water: Keep evenly moist. Water thoroughly and discard drainage. In winter, keep dry. Water infrequently.
Humidity: Average indoor levels.
Temperatures: 50°F to 55°F at night, 60°F to 65°F during the day.
Fertilization: Fertilize only during late spring and summer months.
Propagation: Take cuttings from recently matured stems or shoots.
Grooming: Keep to desired height and shape with light pruning or clipping at any time.
Repotting: Infrequent repotting is best. Repot in winter or early spring, as needed.
Problems: Poor drainage, too frequent watering, or standing in water will cause root rot.

Ferns

Although ferns do not produce flowers, the delicate composition of their flowing fronds instills a room with a peaceful air. Ferns are among the oldest plants on earth; only the algae and the mosses are older. They come in a multitude of shapes and sizes, from the small ribbon fern, with its ribbonlike leaves, to the larger maidenhair fern, which has fan-shaped leaflets. Several types grouped together in entryways, patios, or conservatories can create a stunning design. They also work well displayed alone, in pots or hanging baskets.

The secret of success in growing ferns lies in your ability to match as nearly as possible their natural environment. The better you can imitate the moist, cool air and light shade of a tropical forest, the better your fern will grow. Providing proper growing conditions will require regular attention to the plant's needs. Since the fern's natural habitat has only dappled light, it's best to avoid exposing your plant to the direct sunlight that strikes a windowsill. Hot dry air is a real problem for ferns. Both the air and the soil must always be kept moist. Provide humidity by placing the pot on a humidifying tray or in a larger pot of moist peat moss. Most ferns will grow well in average indoor temperatures during the day, with a drop of temperature at night.

The variety of ferns is enormous. Of the 2,000 species to choose from, the ones described below are some of the best types to grow indoors.

Adiantum species
Maidenhair fern

Maidenhair ferns are known in northern states for growing in damp, cool spots near mountain streams. Their fronds have striking black stems and leaflets that are broad but frilled. The leaflets tend to be borne horizontally and seem to be suspended in midair on a mature plant. Their main limitation indoors is that they require an extremely damp atmosphere. A lighted terrarium is best for growing maidenhair ferns. Give them plenty of room so they can mature properly.
Light: Provide at least moderate light but no direct sunlight.
Water: Keep plant very moist, but do not allow to stand in water.

*Above: **Fern: Adiantum***
*Below: **Fern: Alsophila australis***

Humidity: Requires moist air. Use a humidifier for best results. Best suited for terrarium growing.
Temperatures: 50°F to 55°F at night, 60°F to 65°F during the day.
Fertilization: Fertilize lightly once a year in early spring.
Propagation: New plants are started by dividing an older specimen.
Grooming: Prune in early spring.
Repotting: Repot in winter or early spring, as needed.
Problems: Dry soil or high soluble salts may damage roots, causing plant to die back. The leaves will scorch if plant is in a draft or dry air.

Alsophila species
Tree fern

These large tree ferns are best suited for a solarium, indoor swimming pool area, or similar indoor setting. The fronds are several feet long and have hairy stems. They generally grow from a central

crown at the end of a long trunk. Plants of this size are quite old, but can be purchased from a specialty shop. Keep the soil moist and the air humid and warm.
Light: Place in a bright, indirectly lit south, east, or west window.
Water: Keep very moist at all times, but do not allow to stand in water.
Humidity: Requires moist air. Use a humidifier for best results.
Temperatures: 65°F to 70°F at night, 75°F to 80°F during the day.
Fertilization: Fertilize lightly once a year in early spring.
Propagation: Not generally attempted but can be done from spores.
Grooming: Pick off yellowed leaves.
Repotting: Infrequent repotting is best.
Problems: The leaves will scorch if plant is in a draft or dry air.

Asplenium bulbiferum
Mother fern

The mother fern's fronds arch outward from a central growing point, like those of its cousin the bird's-nest fern, but the fronds of the mother fern are finely divided into extremely narrow leaflets. The plant forms very small plantlets on the fronds that can be used for propagation, which gives it its common name.
Light: Provide at least moderate light but no direct sunlight.
Water: Keep evenly moist. Water thoroughly and discard drainage.
Humidity: Requires moist air. Use a humidifier for best results.
Temperatures: 50°F to 55°F at night, 60°F to 65°F during the day.
Fertilization: Fertilize twice a year, in early spring and midsummer.
Propagation: Remove new plantlets or rooted side shoots as they form.
Grooming: Pick off yellowed leaves.
Repotting: Repot in winter or early spring, as needed.
Problems: The leaves will scorch if plant is in a draft or dry air.

Asplenium nidus
Bird's-nest fern, Spleenwort

Bird's-nest fern will grow into a large plant in time. The graceful, arching fronds can grow to 15 inches. They emerge from a dark, round central

Above: *Fern: Asplenium nidus*
Right: *Fern: Asplenium bulbiferum*

crown that looks like a bird's nest. The plant is relatively easy to grow indoors, but be sure to give it plenty of room. Fertilize lightly.
Light: Will survive in low (reading level) light.
Water: Let plant approach dryness before watering, but water thoroughly and discard drainage.
Humidity: Average indoor humidity levels.
Temperatures: 48°F to 45°F at night, 60°F to 65°F during the day.
Fertilization: Fertilize 3 times a year: spring, midsummer, and early fall.
Propagation: From spores brushed onto a clay pot and covered with a plastic bag to maintain dampness. Keep out of direct sunlight.
Grooming: Pick off yellowed leaves.
Repotting: Transplant when young plants are big enough to put into soil. Repot in winter or early spring, as needed.
Problems: The leaves will scorch if plant is in a draft or dry air.

Cibotium chamissoi
Hawaiian tree fern

These very large plants are suited only for spacious locations. They are magnificent plants in an indoor solarium, beside an indoor pool, or in a greenhouse. The fronds are finely divided and up to 6 feet long. The plants can be purchased with a trunk several feet high if desired. A related fern, *C. schiedei* (Mexican tree fern), usually has a "trunk" only a few inches high, if not completely beneath the soil surface.

Light: Provide at least 4 hours of curtain-filtered sunlight from a bright south, east, or west window.
Water: Keep evenly moist. Water thoroughly and discard drainage.
Humidity: Requires moist air. Use a humidifier for best results.
Temperatures: 55°F to 60°F at night, 60°F to 75°F during the day.
Fertilization: Fertilize only during late spring and summer months.
Propagation: Propagation is difficult but can be done from spores.
Grooming: Pick off yellowed leaves.
Repotting: Repot in winter or early spring, as needed.
Problems: The leaves will scorch if plant is in a draft or dry air.

Above: *Fern: Davallia mariesii*
Left: *Fern: Nephrolepis exaltata*
  'Bostoniensis'

Temperatures: 50°F to 55°F at night, 65°F to 70°F during the day.
Fertilization: Fertilize lightly once a year in early spring
Propagation: Not generally attempted but can be done from spores.
Grooming: Pick off yellowed leaves.
Repotting: Infrequent repotting is best. Repot in winter or early spring, as needed.
Problems: The leaves will scorch if plant is in a draft or dry air.

Cyrtomium falcatum
Holly fern

Of all the ferns, holly fern is perhaps most tolerant of indoor environments. It is a slow-growing plant that may grow to 2 feet in time. The fronds are divided into fairly large leaflets 3 to 5 inches long and up to 1 or 2 inches wide. Because of their glistening green color, they may resemble holly leaves.
Light: Will survive in low (reading level) light.
Water: Keep evenly moist. Water thoroughly and discard drainage.
Humidity: Requires moist air. Use a humidifier for best results.
Temperatures: 40°F to 45°F at night, 60°F to 65°F during the day.
Fertilization: Fertilize lightly once a year in early spring.
Propagation: New plants are started by dividing an older specimen.
Grooming: Pick off yellowed leaves.
Repotting: Repot in winter or early spring, as needed.
Problems: Leaves will scorch if plant is in a draft or dry air. Subject to crown rot if planted deeply, watered over the crown, or watered late in the day.

Cyathea species
Tree fern

These ferns can become huge trees outdoors in tropical environments. Indoors, they grow slowly and can be used if given enough room. Their finely divided fronds, which emerge from the end of a 3- or 4-foot-high trunk, may reach 2 feet in length. Purchase a fairly large plant so that you can enjoy its treelike nature without having to wait for 10 years. Keep the soil wet. Place plant in a humid spot protected from drafts.
Light: Place in a bright, indirectly lit south, east, or west window.
Water: Keep very moist at all times, but do not allow to stand in water.
Humidity: Requires moist air. Use a humidifier for best results.

Davallia species
Deer's-foot fern, Rabbit's-foot fern, Squirrel's-foot fern

Like the polypody fern, these ferns are noted for their furry rhizomes that creep over and down the sides of the growing container and resemble animal feet. The plants become more interesting with age, so do not repot them often. They can be used in a hanging basket to allow the "feet" to cascade or creep downward. The fronds of most of these ferns are finely divided and delicate. Fertilize lightly, keep the soil moist and the air humid, and keep in moderate light.
Light: Provide at least moderate light but no direct sunlight.
Water: Keep evenly moist. Water thoroughly and discard drainage.
Humidity: Requires moist air. Use a humidifier for best results.
Temperatures: 50°F to 55°F at night, 65°F to 70°F during the day.
Fertilization: Fertilize 3 times a year: spring, midsummer, and early fall.
Propagation: New plants are started by dividing an older speciman.
Grooming: Pick off yellowed leaves.
Repotting: Infrequent repotting is best.
Problems: The leaves will scorch if plant is in a draft or dry air.

Nephrolepis exaltata 'Bostoniensis'
Boston fern, Sword fern

Boston ferns are the most popular indoor ferns because they can tolerate a variety of indoor settings. Their arching nature makes them useful for hanging baskets. Many new cultivars are available. Some have very long fronds and others, such as 'Fluffy Ruffles', are smaller plants with more finely divided fronds. If plants begin to thin out and weaken, repot and place in better light.
Light: Provide at least moderate light but no direct sunlight.
Water: Let plant approach dryness before watering, but water thoroughly and discard drainage.
Humidity: Average indoor humidity levels.
Temperatures: 50°F to 55°F at night, 65°F to 70°F during the day.
Fertilization: Fertilize all year, but more heavily in summer.

Left: *Fern: Platycerium bifurcatum*
Above: *Fern: Polypodium aureum*
Right: *Fern: Pteris cretica*

Propagation: New plants are started by dividing an older specimen. The tips of the runners can be rooted as well.
Grooming: Pick off yellowed leaves. Keep to desired height and shape with light pruning or clipping at any time.
Repotting: Infrequent repotting is best.
Problems: Poor drainage, too frequent watering, or standing in water will cause root rot. The leaves will drop if plant is suddenly moved into low light. Will get spindly and weak if light is too low.

Platycerium bifurcatum
Staghorn fern

Staghorn ferns are epiphytes and grow on surfaces rather than in soil or potting media. They can be purchased on bark slabs, clumps of sphagnum moss, or cork boards. They will grow slowly and develop massive fronds that resemble a large animal's antlers. Hanging on a wall in a humid, brightly lit location is best. Small plantlets will eventually form at the base of the parent plant and emerge between the large, flat basal fronds. Water staghorn ferns by attaching some moisture-holding material, such as sphagnum moss, to the growing surface at the base of the plant. Take the plant down and soak it once a week in a pail or sink.
Light: Provide at least 4 hours of curtain-filtered sunlight from a bright south, east, or west window.
Water: Keep evenly moist. Water thoroughly and discard drainage.
Humidity: Requires moist air. Use a humidifier for best results.

Temperatures: 50°F to 55°F at night, 65°F to 70°F during the day.
Fertilization: Do not fertilize.
Propagation: Remove new plantlets or rooted side shoots as they form.
Grooming: Pick off yellowed leaves.
Repotting: Replace or replenish the water-holding sphagnum when needed.
Problems: The leaves will scorch if plant is in a draft or dry air.

Polypodium species
Bear's-paw fern, Hare's-foot fern, Golden polypody fern

These easy-to-grow ferns are named after their furry rhizomes that grow along the surface of the soil. The rhizomes eventually creep down over the sides of the pot and resemble animal feet. The tough fronds of this fern are divided into a few large lobes. As with most ferns, coolness, light fertilization, and infrequent repotting are best. Many indoor gardeners grow this fern on a bark slab, but they usually keep it in a terrarium where high humidity can be maintained.
Light: Provide at least 4 hours of curtain-filtered sunlight from a bright south, east, or west window.
Water: Let plant approach dryness before watering, but water thoroughly and discard drainage.
Humidity: Average indoor humidity levels.
Temperatures: 50°F to 55°F at night, 60°F to 65°F during the day.
Fertilization: Fertilize only during late spring and summer months.
Propagation: New plants are started by dividing an older specimen.
Grooming: Pick off yellowed leaves.
Repotting: Infrequent repotting is best.
Problems: Leaves will scorch if plant is in a draft or dry air; leaves will drop if plant is suddenly moved into low light.

Polystichum setiferum
English hedge fern

This fern has graceful, finely divided fronds that are an unusual dark green. It grows to about 12 inches and will tolerate moderate light if not overfertilized. The mature fronds of *P. setiferum proliferum* produce plantlets suitable for rooting.
Light: Provide at least moderate light but no direct sunlight.
Water: Let plant approach dryness before watering, but water thoroughly and discard drainage.
Humidity: Requires moist air. Use a humidifer for best results.
Temperatures: 50°F to 55°F at night, 60°F to 65°F during the day.
Fertilization: Fertilize only during late spring and summer months.
Propagation: New plants are started by dividing an older speciman.
Grooming: Pick off yellowed leaves.
Repotting: Repot in late spring, if needed.
Problems: The leaves will drop if soil is too wet or too dry. Dry soil or high soluble salts may damage roots, causing plant to die back.

Pteris species
Brake ferns, Table ferns

Table ferns are so named because they grow slowly indoors, remaining small and useful as a table centerpiece. The fronds of these plants are variously divided and variegated. Crested spider table fern has unusual fronds that end in a frilly growth of leaf tissue that looks like a crest. Despite their name, do not keep these ferns permanently on a table in dim light. They require a bit more

Left: *Ficus benjamina*
Above: *Ficus diversifolia*
Right: *Ficus elastica* 'Variegata'

light and humidity than is generally available indoors.

Light: Provide at least moderate light but no direct sunlight.

Water: Keep evenly moist. Water thoroughly and discard drainage.

Humidity: Requires moist air. Use a humidifier for best results.

Temperatures: 50°F to 55°F at night, 60°F to 65°F during the day.

Fertilization: Fertilize 3 times a year: spring, midsummer, and early fall.

Propagation: New plants are started by dividing an older specimen.

Grooming: Pick off yellowed leaves.

Repotting: Repot at any time.

Problems: The leaves will scorch if plant is in a draft or dry air.

Ficus species
Ficus, Ornamental fig tree

This large, diverse family of more than 800 tropical trees and shrubs includes not only the edible fig, *F. carica,* but a number of ornamentals perfect for container gardening. Here we discuss some indoor favorites.

Ficus will do well if it has good light, rich soil kept evenly moist, and frequent light feeding. Guard against overwatering, and protect from cold drafts, dry heat, and sudden changes in environment. If moved to a new location, the tree will often lose most of its leaves. It will need a period of adjust-

ment, but with care it will flourish again. (See "Acclimating New Plants," page 68.)

Ficus benjamina
Weeping fig

F. benjamina holds a prominent position among container plants because it is favored by so many designers. It has birchlike bark and graceful, arching branches loaded with glossy, pointed leaves. It grows from 2 to 18 feet tall.

Ficus diversifolia
Mistletoe fig

The mistletoe fig is an interesting miniature upright tree. It grows to a height of 36 inches, bearing many tiny (but inedible) figs that turn red in bright sun. Its small rounded leaves are flecked with translucent silver.

Ficus elastica
Rubber plant

F. elastica and the larger-leaved 'Decora' are old favorites commonly known as rubber plants. They have bold, deep green leaves on stems 2 to 10 feet tall. 'Variegata' has long, narrow leaves that make rippling patterns of grass green, metallic gray, and creamy yellow. When a rubber plant becomes too lanky, cut off the top and select a side branch to form a new main shoot, or air-layer.

Ficus lyrata
Fiddleleaf fig

F. lyrata (also known as *F. pandurata*) is a striking container plant. It has durable papery leaves of deep green in a fiddle shape. The plant grows 5 to 10 feet tall.

Ficus pumila
Creeping fig

F. pumila has tiny, heart-shaped leaves. This fast-growing trailer is a good plant for hanging baskets or cascading from a shelf. It is becoming quite popular in commercial interiors.

Ficus retusa mitida
Indian laurel

This plant is one of the easiest to grow indoors as an evergreen tree. It is similar to weeping fig, *F. benjamina,* but has a slightly larger leaf and is more upright in its branching habit. The plants are commonly seen in commercial interiors. Grow the plant as a single-stemmed shrub when it is small. As it grows, gradually prune it into a tree form.

Care of Ficus

Light: Place in a bright, indirectly lit south, east, or west window.

Water: Let plant approach dryness before watering, but water thoroughly and discard drainage.

Fittonia verschaffeltii var. argyroneura

Above: Ficus pumila
Below: Ficus lyrata

Humidity: Average indoor humidity levels.
Temperatures: 50°F to 55°F at night, 65°F to 70°F during the day.
Fertilization: Fertilize all year, but more heavily in summer.
Propagation: Take cuttings from stems or shoots before they have hardened or matured.
Grooming: Prune to a tree form as the plant matures. Keep to desired height and shape with light pruning or clipping at any time.
Repotting: Repot in winter or early spring, as needed. Infrequent repotting is best.
Problems: Dry soil or high soluble salts may damage roots, causing plant to die back. The leaves will drop if plant is suddenly moved into low light.

Fittonia species
Nerve plant, Mosaic plant

The intricately veined oval leaves of these plants grow semiupright and trail over the sides of their containers.

F. verschaffeltii var. *argyroneura* displays a mosaic pattern of white veins; another variety, *F. verschaffeltii* var. *pearcei,* has intense red veins on paperthin, olive green leaves. They make striking hanging plants, and small types are good for terrariums.

These plants will thrive in most households. Place them in a warm spot that receives some light from a north or east window. Let soil dry out between waterings, and use a humidifying tray to provide moisture. Feed monthly during the growing season. During the winter, move the plants to a cool spot and water lightly.
Light: Provide at least moderate light but no direct sunlight.
Water: Water thoroughly, but allow to dry between waterings.
Humidity: Requires moist air. Use a humidifier for best results.
Temperatures: 65°F to 70°F at night, 75°F to 80°F during the day.
Fertilization: Fertilize lightly once a year in early spring.
Propagation: Take cuttings from recently matured stems or shoots.

Grooming: Keep to desired height and shape with light pruning or clipping at any time.
Repotting: Repot in winter or early spring, as needed.
Problems: Subject to crown rot if planted deeply, watered over the crown, or watered late in the day. Will get spindly and weak if light is too low.

Geogenanthus undatus
Seersucker plant

These easy-to-grow plants form 2-inch leaves on short stems. The leaves have white stripes and a puckered texture similar to seersucker. The plant will remain small and grow well indoors if given warmth at night.
Light: Provide at least 4 hours of curtain-filtered sunlight from a bright south, east, or west window.
Water: Keep evenly moist. Water thoroughly and discard drainage.
Humidity: Requires moist air. Use a humidifier for best results.
Temperatures: 65°F to 70°F at night, 75°F to 80°F during the day.
Fertilization: Fertilize all year, but more heavily in summer.
Propagation: Take stem cuttings at any time.
Grooming: Pick off yellowed leaves.
Repotting: Repot at any time.
Problems: The leaves will scorch if plant is in a draft or dry air.

Grevillea robusta
Silk oak

Silk oaks are vigorously growing plants well suited for sunny, dry locations. Their leaves are deeply divided and resemble the fronds of some ferns. Small flowers appear in the spring. These plants are easy to grow from seed. Prune in early spring, but do not cut out the leader or terminal shoot.

Light: In winter, keep in about 4 hours of direct sun. In summer, provide curtain-filtered sunlight from a south or west window.

Water: Let plant approach dryness before watering, but water thoroughly and discard drainage.

Humidity: Dry air is generally not harmful for this plant, but keep it out of drafts.

Temperatures: 50°F to 55°F at night, 60°F to 65°F during the day.

Fertilization: Fertilize all year, but more heavily in summer.

Propagation: Start from seeds. Begin in small pot and transplant as needed.

Grooming: Prune in early spring. Give these plants plenty of room.

Repotting: Infrequent repotting is best.

Problems: Its leaves will drop if soil is too wet or too dry. Will get spindly and weak if light is too low.

Gynura aurantiaca
Velvet plant, Purple passion plant

This trailing plant has intensely purple leaves and stems with thick reddish hairs covering all surfaces. It is easy to grow, and, if pruned, is attractive in a hanging basket. With enough light, the plant will produce clusters of tiny flowers with white petals and yellow centers. It is best to pick these off quickly, however, because they have an unpleasant aroma and will produce a mess of dropping petals and seed pods. The plant probably won't flower if it is grown in low light.

Light: Place in a bright, indirectly lit south, east, or west window.

Water: Keep evenly moist. Water thoroughly and discard drainage.

Humidity: Average indoor humidity levels.

Temperatures: 55°F to 60°F at night, 70°F to 75°F during the day.

Above: *Gynura aurantiaca*
Right: *Hedera helix*

Fertilization: Fertilize only during late spring and summer months.

Propagation: Take stem cuttings at any time.

Grooming: Keep to desired height and shape with light pruning or clipping at any time.

Repotting: Repot at any time.

Problems: Dry soil or high soluble salts may damage roots, causing plant to die back. Subject to infestations of whiteflies or aphids.

Gynura scandens
Gynura

G. scandens is rarely grown indoors. It is a pleasing semiwoody shrub that tends to climb, so it is often trained on a trellis or staked. Like all plants in this genus, it produces flowers that are not particularly attractive and have an unpleasant scent. Keep the plant out of direct sun so that it will not flower.

Light: Place in a bright, indirectly lit south, east, or west window.

Water: Keep evenly moist. Water thoroughly and discard drainage.

Humidity: Requires moist air. Use a humidifier for best results.

Temperatures: 55°F to 60°F at night, 70°F to 75°F during the day.

Fertilization: Fertilize only during late spring and summer months.

Propagation: Take stem cuttings at any time.

Grooming: Keep to desired height and shape with light pruning or clipping at any time.

Repotting: Repot in winter or early spring, as needed.

Problems: Poor drainage, too frequent watering, or standing in water will cause root rot.

Hedera canariensis
Canary Island ivy, Algerian ivy

Canary Island ivy is a fast-growing plant with large leaves. It can be grown in a basket or trained on a trellis. The most popular cultivar has green leaves with white variegation. Keep these ivies moist and warm when growing them indoors.

Light: Provide at least 4 hours of curtain-filtered sunlight from a bright south, east, or west window.

Water: Keep evenly moist. Water thoroughly and discard drainage.

Humidity Average indoor humidity levels.

Temperatures: 65°F to 70°F at night, 75°F to 80°F during the day.

Fertilization: Fertilize all year, but more heavily in summer.

Propagation: Take stem cuttings at any time.

Grooming: Keep to desired height and shape with light pruning or clipping at any time.

Repotting: Repot at any time.

Problems: Will get spindly and weak if light is too low.

Hedera helix
English ivy

Many plants are called ivy, but the most famous is *H. helix*. Countless varieties of this trailing and climbing plant are available. 'Merlon Beauty' has small leaves in the characteristic English ivy shape. 'Itsy Bitsy' is a tiny variety. Others have the same leaf shape, but leaves are curled, waved, or crinkled. 'Curlilocks' is an example. Still others have color variegation, such as the yellow-gold and green 'California Gold'. Many ivies send out aerial roots and climb rough surfaces—a brick fireplace wall, for example. You can also use them in large planters as a ground cover. They are excellent in hanging baskets and can be trained on a trellis.

Protected from hot, dry air, English ivy will flourish as long as a few basics are followed. Place it in a cool, bright location and keep the soil and air moist. During the growing season, feed every 2 weeks. Bathe the foliage occasionally. Plants rest in both fall and winter.

Light: Place in a bright, indirectly lit south, east, or west window.

Water: Let plant approach dryness before watering, but water thoroughly and discard drainage.

Humidity: Average indoor humidity levels.

Temperatures: 40°F to 45°F at night, 60°F to 65°F during the day.

Fertilization: Fertilize 3 times a year: spring, midsummer, and early fall.

Propagation: Take stem cuttings at any time.

Grooming: Keep to desired height and shape with light pruning or clipping at any time.

Repotting: Repot at any time.

Problems: Spider mites can be a problem, especially if plant is too dry. Small leaves and too much stem indicate lack of light. Brown leaf tips result from dry air. Green leaves on variegated types result from too little light.

Hypoestes species
Hypoestes, Pink polka dot, Freckle face

This plant's common names come from the unusual pink spots on its leaves. This bushy herbaceous plant grows rapidly with good light. It will need fre-

quent pruning to keep it well branched and to a height of 12 inches.

Light: Provide at least 4 hours of curtain-filtered sunlight from a bright south, east, or west window.

Water: Let plant approach dryness before watering, but water thoroughly and discard drainage.

Humidity: Requires moist air. Use a humidifier for best results.

Temperatures: 65°F to 70°F at night, 75°F to 80°F during the day.

Fertilization: Fertilize lightly once a year in early spring.

Propagation: Take stem cuttings at any time.

Grooming: Start new plants and replace older specimens when they get weak. Keep to desired height and shape with light pruning or clipping at any time.

Repotting: Repot in winter or early spring, as needed.

Problems: Will get spindly and weak if light is too low.

Left: *Hypoestes*
Above: *Iresine herbstii*

Iresine herbstii
Beefsteak plant, Bloodleaf

The ornamental foliage of this plant is an intense, full-bodied red, as its common name, bloodleaf, suggests. *I. herbstii* has heart-shaped leaves with light red veins. *I. herbstii* 'Aureo-reticulata' produces green leaves tinted with red and lined with yellow veins. The small plants add brilliant accents to groupings of larger plants.

These plants are easy to care for but, without a good deal of light, the leaves turn pale and the plant becomes leggy rather than bushy and compact. Water regularly and keep the air humid. In the summer, revive your plants with a vacation outdoors.

Light: Four hours or more of direct sunlight from a south window.

Water: Keep evenly moist. Water thoroughly and discard drainage.

Humidity: Requires moist air. Use a humidifier for best results.

Temperatures: 55°F to 60°F at night, 70°F to 75°F during the day.

Fertilization: Fertilize all year, but more heavily in summer.

Propagation: Take cuttings from stems or shoots that have recently matured.

Grooming: Keep to desired height and shape with light pruning or clipping at any time.

Repotting: Repot in winter or early spring, as needed.

Problems: Will get spindly and weak if light is too low.

Left: *Laurus nobilis*
Above: *Ligustrum japonicum*
Right: *Ligularia tussilaginea*

Laurus nobilis
Laurel, Sweet bay

This plant is seen in ancient artwork depicting people wearing leafy crowns. The leaves of sweet bay are also used in cooking. As a houseplant it grows slowly, but eventually will become a 4-foot shrub. It prefers a well-lit, cool spot such as an entranceway. Try to buy a large plant, since it will take several years for sweet bay to develop its bushy form.
Light: Four hours or more of direct sunlight from a south window.
Water: Let plant approach dryness before watering, but water thoroughly and discard drainage.
Humidity: Average indoor levels.
Temperatures: 40°F to 45°F at night, 60°F to 65°F during the day.
Fertilization: Fertilize only during late spring and summer months.
Propagation: Take stem cuttings at any time.
Grooming: Keep to desired height and shape with light pruning or clipping at any time.
Repotting: Repot infrequently.
Problems: Poor drainage, too frequent watering, or standing in water will cause root rot. The leaves will drop if soil is too wet or too dry.

Ligularia species
Leopard plant

Leopard plant is a semiwoody plant whose large, shiny leaves resemble those of ivy. Many forms have variegated foliage. Keep the plants in a location that is cool and humid and has good light. They can become large if given

room and repotted frequently. Daisylike flowers are sometimes produced in late summer.
Light: In winter, keep in about 4 hours of direct sun. In summer, provide curtain-filtered sunlight from a south or west window.
Water: Keep evenly moist. Water thoroughly and discard drainage.
Humidity: Requires moist air. Use a humidifier for best results.
Temperatures: 40°F to 45°F at night, 60°F to 65°F during the day.
Fertilization: Fertilize 3 times a year: spring, midsummer, and early fall.
Propagation: New plants are started by dividing an older specimen.
Grooming: Pick off yellowed leaves.
Repotting: Repot in winter or early spring as needed.
Problems: The leaves will scorch if plant is in a draft or dry air.

Ligustrum japonicum
Privet (wax-leaf), Texas privet

Wax-leaf privet has been grown in southern gardens for many years. If pruned frequently and given ample light, it also does well indoors. The shiny, somewhat thick leaves are borne abundantly on woody stems. If you wish, you can allow the plant to get quite large (4 to 6 feet). Keep it in a cool location with good light for best performance.
Light: In winter, keep in about 4 hours of direct sun. In summer, provide curtain-filtered sunlight from a south or west window.

Water: Let plant approach dryness before watering, but water thoroughly and discard drainage.
Humidity: Average indoor levels.
Temperatures: 40°F to 45°F at night, 60°F to 65°F during the day.
Fertilization: Fertilize only when plant is growing actively or flowering.
Propagation: Take stem cuttings at any time.
Grooming: Prune in early spring. Keep to desired height and shape with light pruning or clipping at any time.
Repotting: Repot in winter or early spring, as needed.
Problems: The leaves drop if soil is too wet or too dry.

Maranta leuconeura
Prayer plant

The common name of this plant refers to the growth habit of *M. leuconeura* var. *kerchoveana.* In the daytime its satiny foliage lies flat, but at night the leaves turn upward, giving the appearance of praying hands. The plant reaches a height of about 8 inches. There are many other varieties; all bear spectacular foliage with colored veins and brush strokes of color on backgrounds of white to black.

M. leuconeura var. *massangeana* is a showy variety; it is sometimes called cathedral windows because its foliage resembles stained-glass color patterns.

Although the prayer plant is fairly easy to grow, some of the less common types are better left for the experienced gardener. These plants grow best in a warm, humid environment with partial shade. Direct sunlight will cause the

Left: *Maranta leuconeura erythroneura*
Above: *Mimosa pudica*
Right: *Monstera deliciosa*

leaves to fade. Surround pots with peat moss or plant them in a grouping to provide needed humidity. Keep the soil moist at all times.

Light: Provide at least moderate light but no direct sunlight.

Water: Keep very moist during growth and flowering. Allow to dry between waterings at other times.

Humidity: Requires moist air. Use a humidifier for best results.

Temperatures: 55°F to 60°F at night, 70°F to 75°F during the day.

Fertilization: Fertilize 3 times a year: spring, midsummer, and early fall.

Propagation: New plants are started by dividing an older specimen. Take stem cuttings at any time.

Grooming: Pick off yellowed leaves. Start new plants and replace older specimens when they get weak.

Repotting: Infrequent repotting is best. Repot in winter or early spring, as needed.

Problems: The leaves will scorch if plant is in a draft or dry air. Poor drainage, too frequent watering, or standing in water will cause root rot.

Mimosa pudica
Sensitive plant

This slow-growing plant is easily started from seed. When the finely divided leaflets are touched, they immediately fold up. This habit makes the plant especially popular with children. After the seedling has several leaves, pinch back the stem tip to promote branching. Prune frequently to prevent legginess. Keep the plants warm and in good light.

Light: Provide at least 4 hours of curtain-filtered sunlight from a bright south, east, or west window.

Water: Keep evenly moist. Water thoroughly and discard drainage.

Humidity: Average indoor levels.

Temperatures: 65°F to 70°F at night, 75°F to 80°F during the day.

Fertilization: Fertilize only during late spring and summer months.

Propagation: Start from seeds. Begin in a small pot and transplant as needed.

Grooming: Keep to desired height and shape with light pruning or clipping at any time. Do not prune seedlings until several leaves have formed.

Repotting: Repot at any time.

Problems: Poor drainage, too frequent watering, or standing in water will cause root rot. Will get spindly and weak if light is too low. The leaves will scorch if plant is in a draft or dry air.

Monstera deliciosa
Monstera, Split-leaf philodendron

Found in many homes, *M. deliciosa* climbs and sends out aerial roots that attach to supports or grow to the ground. Stems can reach a length of 6 feet or more; they bear large perforated and deeply cut leaves.

These plants are easy to grow as long as you provide a few essentials. Direct the aerial roots into the soil to give support to the weak stem and grow under average room conditions. Keep soil barely moist in winter. Feed every 2 weeks during the growing season.

Light: Provide at least moderate light but no direct sunlight.

Water: Water thoroughly, but allow to dry between waterings.

Humidity: Average indoor humidity levels.

Temperatures: 55°F to 60°F at night, 70°F to 75°F during the day.

Fertilization: Fertilize all year, but more heavily in summer.

Propagation: Take stem cuttings at any time. Air-layer the plant at any time.

Grooming: Wash and polish mature leaves. Guide aerial roots into soil or onto a support. Cut tops of tall plants to limit growth.

Repotting: Infrequent repotting is best.

Problems: Waterlogged soil will cause leaves to weep around edges. Leaves with brown, brittle edges result from dry air. Brown edges and yellowed leaves are a symptom of overwatering or, less frequently, underfeeding. Dropping of lower leaves is normal. Serious leaf drop results from moving the plant or an abrupt change. Young leaves often have no perforation. Low light may cause small, unperforated leaves.

Far Left: *Musa ensete*
Left: *Myrtus communis 'Compacta'*
Above: *Nandina domestica*

Musa species
Banana

The many plants in this group are large tropical trees best suited for greenhouses. Some species have attractive foliage and a semidwarf habit. Commercial container-plant growers are beginning to sell these smaller varieties to florists, but even these plants will grow large and need plenty of room. They require lots of water and light. They are also very subject to damage from cool nights. Do not expect them to flower and set fruit indoors unless they are in a greenhouse.
Light: Does best in a greenhouse setting.
Water: Keep very moist at all times, but do not allow to stand in water.
Humidity: Requires moist air. Use a humidifier for best results.
Temperatures: 65°F to 70°F at night, 75°F to 80°F during the day.
Fertilization: Fertilize all year, but more heavily in summer.
Propagation: Take root cuttings at any time.
Grooming: Do not prune or cut plants back. Give these plants plenty of room.
Repotting: Repot at any time.
Problems: The leaves will scorch if plant is in a draft or dry air.

Myrtus communis
True myrtle, Greek myrtle

True myrtle is commonly seen as a garden shrub in dry, warm climates. The dwarf cultivar is suitable for well-lighted indoor gardens. It is a woody shrub that will grow 4 feet across if given enough room. The aromatic leaves are tiny and abundantly produced all along the stems. The species has bright green leaves, but some cultivars have variegated foliage. Many gardeners prune or clip myrtles into shaped plants.
Light: In winter, keep in about 4 hours of direct sun. In summer, provide curtain-filtered sunlight from a south or west window.
Water: Let plant approach dryness before watering, but water thoroughly and discard drainage.
Humidity: Average indoor levels.
Temperatures: 40°F to 45°F at night, 60°F to 65°F during the day.
Fertilization: Fertilize only during late spring and summer months.
Propagation: Take cuttings from stems or shoots that have recently matured.
Grooming: Keep to desired height and shape with light pruning or clipping at any time.
Repotting: Repot in winter or early spring, as needed.
Problems: Spider mites can be a problem, especially if plant is too dry. Dry soil or high soluble salts may damage roots, causing plant to die back. The leaves will scorch if plant is in a draft or dry air.

Nandina domestica
Heavenly bamboo

Nandina is a summer-flowering shrub that needs plenty of sun. Since it can grow to 8 feet, it is best suited for a greenhouse or solarium. The small white flowers are borne in a drooping panicle, sometimes as long as a foot. If given enough light, nandina will bear ¼-inch red berries well into the fall. Keep the plant constantly wet and out of cold drafts.

Light: Four hours or more of direct sunlight from a south window. Does best in a greenhouse setting.
Water: Keep very moist at all times, but do not allow to stand in water.
Humidity: Requires moist air. Use a humidifier for best results.
Temperatures: 55°F to 60°F at night, 70°F to 75°F during the day.
Fertilization: Fertilize only when plant is growing actively or flowering.
Propagation: Start from seeds. Begin in a small pot and transplant as needed.
Grooming: Prune after flowering or fruiting.
Repotting: Cut back and repot when flowering stops. New plants need to grow in a medium to large pot until almost root-bound before they will bloom or set fruit.
Problems: If plant is in a draft or dry air, leaves will scorch.

Nicodemia species
Indoor oak

This woody plant has small, shiny leaves shaped like those of a California live oak. With proper pruning, the plant will make an attractive indoor shrub about 1½ feet tall. Nicodemia grows slowly in the summer and needs a moderate dormant period during the winter. While it is resting, keep it warm, do not add fertilizer, and allow it to dry out between waterings.
Light: Provide at least 4 hours of curtain-filtered sunlight from a bright south, east, or west window.
Water: Let plant approach dryness before watering, but water thoroughly and discard drainage.
Humidity: Average indoor levels.
Temperatures: 65°F to 70°F at night, 75°F to 80°F during the day.
Fertilization: Fertilize only when plant is growing actively or flowering.

Propagation: Take cuttings from stems or shoots before they have hardened or matured.
Grooming: Keep to desired height and shape with light pruning or clipping at any time. Prune in early spring.
Repotting: Repot in winter or early spring, as needed.
Problems: Dry soil or high soluble salts may damage roots, causing plant to die back.

Olea europaea

Olea europaea
Olive

Olives are orchard trees, useful for their fruits as well as their oil. If pruned properly, they make attractive indoor garden plants. The long narrow leaves are green on top and a bit silvery beneath. If the light is ample the plant will blossom, but it will probably not set fruit because pollination indoors is usually unsuccessful. The white flowers are tiny and fragrant. Some gardeners prune olives into a single-stemmed

tree over the years. However, they are best pruned as a shrub and kept 2 or 3 feet high.
Light: Place in a bright, indirectly lit south, east, or west window.
Water: Water thoroughly, but allow to dry between waterings.
Humidity: Dry air is generally not harmful for this plant, but keep it out of drafts.
Temperatures: 40°F to 45°F at night, 60°F to 65°F during the day.
Fertilization: Fertilize in spring and again in early fall.
Propagation: Take stem cuttings at any time.
Grooming: Prune in early spring. Keep to desired height and shape with light pruning or clipping at any time.
Repotting: Infrequent repotting is best. Repot in winter or early spring as needed.
Problems: If soil is too wet or too dry, leaves will drop.

Palms

Palms are consistently popular as houseplants. Their graceful fans and rich green color can give even the coldest northern home a tropical air. The family is large and varied, but only a few plants are grown indoors. Although they are among the most expensive plants, palms are well worth the investment. These very tolerant plants adapt well to the limited light and controlled temperatures of indoors. You can save money by purchasing small young plants that will slowly grow into large trees. Some types will flourish for decades.

Most palms are easy to care for and have uniform growing requirements. During the spring and summer growing season, water plants heavily and feed them once a month. Reduce water and stop feeding them in winter. Protect them from dry air and direct sunlight, especially if you move your palm outdoors. Do not prune palm trees unless an old branch dies naturally. Unlike most plants, the life support systems of palms are located directly in the tip of the stalk. Pinching back this tip or cutting off the newest frond below its point of attachment to the trunk will eliminate all new growth.

Above: *Palm: Caryota mitis*
Below: *Palm: Chamaedorea elegans*

Caryota mitis
Fishtail palm

This large palm has a thick trunk and many spreading branches, each laden with fans of dark green leaves. The ribbed texture of the leaves and their wedged shape evoke the plant's common name. This palm is often used in commercial interiors because it grows relatively slowly and is easy to care for.

Chamaedorea elegans
Parlor palm

This palm (also known as *Neanthe bella*) has handsome light green fronds. If given enough light, it will bear bunches of yellow fruit near the base of the trunk. It is a small palm, growing to a height of 6 feet, so it is suitable for entryways or living rooms. Many of the newer cultivars are very popular in commercial interiors.

Left: *Palm: Chamaerops humilis*
Above: *Palm: Chrysalidocarpus lutescens*
Right: *Palm: Cycas revoluta*

Chamaerops humilis
European fan palm

Stiff, severely cut leaves form fans about 1 foot wide atop 4-foot stems when this palm reaches maturity. The fans grow to varying heights and at different angles, rising from a rough, black trunk. This palm is a striking plant for any room.

Chrysalidocarpus lutescens
Areca palm, Butterfly palm

This medium-sized, slow-growing palm has a cluster of thin, canelike stems with arching fronds and strap-shaped, shiny green leaflets.

Cycas species
Cycas fern palm, Sago palm

The foliage of this large palm resembles that of a fern. Fossils of this plant have been found in some of the oldest geologic formations on earth. Its trunk is very short and round, and is usually no more than 3 or 4 inches tall. The leaves arch outward for 2 or 3 feet. These palms grow slowly but do need a lot of room.

Howea forsterana
Kentia palm

Outdoors, this popular palm grows to be a very large tree, but indoors it will rarely exceed 7 or 8 feet. Feather-shaped leaves arch outward from sturdy branches to create a full appearance. Outside in bright light the leaves will scorch easily, so take care to place this plant in the shade.

Livistona species
Chinese fan palms

The Chinese fan palms are large plants with deeply lobed, fanlike leaves up to 2 feet across. The plants will eventually grow to 10 feet if given enough room and a large enough container. They will tolerate bright, indirect light. Keep the soil very moist, but not soggy, and keep the plants warm at night.

Phoenix roebelenii
Pygmy date palm

This date palm is a dwarf palm, growing to a height of only 4 feet. A delicate plant, its arching narrow-leaved fronds branch to form a symmetrical shape. Like the other palms, it requires a minimum of attention.

Rhapis excelsa
Large lady palm

Also called *R. aspera,* this large palm features 6- to 12-inch-wide fans composed of 4 to 10 thick, shiny leaves. The leaves grow at the ends of thin, arching stems along a brown, hairy main trunk.

Howea forsterana

Above: **Palm: Phoenix roebelenii**
Below: **Palm: Rhapsis**

Care of Palms

Light: Provide at least moderate light but no direct sunlight.
Water: Let plant approach dryness before watering, but water thoroughly and discard drainage.
Humidity: Average indoor humidity levels.
Temperatures: 50°F to 55°F at night, 60°F to 65°F during the day.
Fertilization: Fertilize all year, but more heavily in summer.
Propagation: Start from seeds. Begin in a small pot and transplant as needed. This is usually done only by professionals.
Grooming: Pick off yellowed leaves. Wash leaves from time to time.
Repotting: Infrequent repotting is best.
Problems: Poor drainage, too frequent watering, or standing in water will cause root rot. Spider mites can be a problem, especially if plant is too dry.

Pandanus veitchii

Pandanus species
Screw pine

This plant is commonly referred to as screw pine because its cornlike, prickly-edged leaves spiral upward, corkscrew fashion, in a compact rosette. It is a tough but graceful plant. Some varieties have white vertical stripes; others have burgundy edges. Aerial roots grow downward, searching for moist soil.

This is an almost foolproof, pest-free specimen to add to your indoor collection. Place it on a humidifying tray in a warm location. Water frequently from spring to fall, keeping the soil moist. In winter, let the soil dry between waterings. Be careful with this plant; its prickly leaves can injure you and plants that are close to it.
Light: In winter, keep in about 4 hours of direct sun. In summer, provide curtain-filtered sunlight from a south or west window.
Water: Keep very moist during growth and flowering. Allow to dry between waterings at other times.
Humidity: Requires moist air. Use a humidifier for best results.
Temperatures: 55°F to 60°F at night, 70°F to 75°F during the day.
Fertilization: Fertilize only during late spring and summer months.
Propagation: Remove new plantlets or rooted side shoots as they form.

Grooming: Wash foliage from time to time. Train aerial roots into the soil.
Repotting: Repot in winter or early spring, as needed.
Problems: Dry soil or high soluble salts may damage roots, causing plant to die back.

Pedilanthus tithymaloides
Devil's backbone

Devil's backbone has woody but green stems that zigzag from side to side, giving the plant its common name. The plant will grow 3 feet tall and branch unpredictably. Its attractive foliage has white, green, and pink variegations. The plant's milky sap will irritate skin and damage eyes, so pruning or clipping must be done carefully. It grows slowly indoors and will probably not flower.
Light: Provide at least 4 hours of curtain-filtered sunlight from a bright south, east, or west window.
Water: Let plant approach dryness before watering, but water thoroughly and discard drainage.
Humidity: Average indoor humidity levels.
Temperatures: 55°F to 60°F at night, 70°F to 75°F during the day.
Fertilization: Fertilize 3 times a year: spring, midsummer, and early fall.

Grooming: Keep to desired height and shape with light pruning or clipping at any time.
Repotting: Infrequent repotting is best.
Problems: Dry soil or high soluble salts may damage roots, causing plant to die back. The leaves will drop if soil is too wet or too dry.

Left: *Pellionia pulchra*
Above: *Peperomia*

Pellionia species
Pellionia

These woody, trailing plants are best for small hanging baskets. They are also occasionally used as ground covers in terrariums or bed plantings because the stems will root wherever they contact the soil. The small leaves of most pellionias are borne closely along the stems. Many variegated cultivars are available. Keep pellionias warm and out of drafts.
Light: Place in a bright, indirectly lit south, east, or west window.
Water: Keep evenly moist. Water thoroughly and discard drainage.
Humidity: Requires moist air. Use a humidifier for best results.
Temperatures: 55°F to 60°F at night, 70°F to 75°F during the day.

Fertilization: Fertilize only during late spring and summer months.
Propagation: Take stem cuttings at any time.
Grooming: Keep to desired height and shape with light pruning or clipping at any time.
Repotting: Repot in winter or early spring, as needed.
Problems: The leaves will scorch if plant is in a draft or dry air. They will drop if soil is too wet or too dry.

Peperomia species
Peperomia

Many popular cultivars of peperomias are available for indoor gardens. These bushy herbaceous plants are suitable for small gardening spots that have bright light and warmth. The thick leaves of most peperomias are variously colored and variegated; many have bright red petioles. Specimens that have deeply ridged or wrinkled leaves are particularly popular. In the spring, some cultivars produce long, taillike blooms that are creamy white and have no petals.
Light: Place in a bright, indirectly lit south, east, or west window.
Water: Provide moist air. Use a humidifier for best results.
Temperatures: 55°F to 60°F at night, 70°F to 75°F during the day.

Fertilization: Fertilize 3 times a year: spring, midsummer, and early fall.
Propagation: New plants are started by dividing an older specimen. Stem or leaf cuttings may be taken.
Grooming: Pick off yellowed leaves.
Problems: Subject to crown rot if planted deeply, watered over the crown, or watered late in the day. Will get spindly and weak if light is too low.

Persea americana
Avocado

Avocados are popular classroom plants because the seeds germinate so easily if partially submerged in water. They make attractive pot plants after several years of pinching back to encourage branching. Give them plenty of light so they do not get spindly. The plant may require staking. It will not flower or set fruit indoors.
Light: Four hours or more of direct sunlight from a south window.
Water: Keep evenly moist. Water thoroughly and discard drainage.
Humidity: Requires moist air. Use a humidifier for best results.
Temperatures: 55°F to 60°F at night, 70°F to 75°F during the day.
Fertilization: Fertilize all year, but more heavily in summer.
Propagation: Put pit of the fruit halfway into water, at any time. Place in a pot with soil when well rooted.

Grooming: Pinch back stem tips routinely to encourage branching. Will have to be staked to keep it standing upright.

Repotting: Repot at any time. Pot so that half of the pit is above the soil.

Problems: The leaves will scorch if plant is in a draft or dry air.

Philodendrons

No other group of plants is so widely used indoors. The great variety of sizes and growth habits (vines, shrubs, and trees), as well as uniquely shaped glossy leaves, give the indoor gardener many choices for almost any situation. And you don't have to worry about providing perfect growing conditions. Originally from South American tropical forests, philodendrons are strong, tolerant plants that don't need a lot of sunshine.

The 200 species are classified according to their growth habit as either climbers or nonclimbers. The climbing species are the ones most commonly grown in the home. The name is a bit of a misnomer, though, since none of them climb very well. They must be tied to supports as they grow. Aerial roots should be tied to the stem or directed to the ground.

The nonclimbing philodendrons can become large plants 6 to 8 feet tall. Their leaves, of varying shapes, extend from self-supporting trunks. These plants are ideal for offices or for large rooms with high ceilings.

A few basic techniques will keep your philodendron healthy and thriving. It will do best in bright light, but it doesn't need direct sunlight. Water regularly to keep the soil moist, and wash the leaves about once a month. An undersized pot, low temperatures, or poor drainage will cause leaves to yellow and drop. However, it is natural for the climbing types to drop their lower leaves as they grow.

Philodendron bipinnatifidum
Twice-cut philodendron,
Fiddle-leaf philodendron

The deeply cut, star-shaped leaves of this plant are very large. It is a nonclimbing type, so it needs no support.

Above: *Philodendron hastatum*
Below: *Philodendron 'Red Emerald'*
Right: *Philodendron oxycardium*

Philodendron gloriosum

This very full-looking climber is covered with velvety, heart-shaped leaves that are dappled with red and cream.

Philodendron hastatum
Spade-leaf philodendron

This philodendron is a lush evergreen climbing vine with aerial roots. Deeply veined, bright green leaves take the shape of giant spearheads, 8 to 12 inches long. Older plants will produce perfumed tubular blossoms similar in appearance to calla lilies.

Philodendron oxycardium
Heart-leaf philodendron

This vigorous climber with many long, glossy, deep green leaves is the most popular philodendron grown in the United States. It is also known as *Philodendron cordatum.* Train it on a column, frame a window with it, or hang it from a beamed ceiling. This plant does fine in the shade.

Philodendron pertusum
See *Monstera deliciosa.*

Philodendron 'Red Emerald'

This climbing philodendron has red stems topped with bright green, yellow-veined, spear-shaped leaves.

Pilea cadierei

Philodendron selloum

Philodendron selloum
Lacy tree philodendron

This nonclimbing, cut-leaf philoden-dron is often used to decorate offices. As the plant ages, the cuts deepen and cause the leaves to ruffle.

Care of Philodendrons

Light: Provide at least moderate light but no direct sunlight.
Water: Keep evenly moist. Water thoroughly and discard drainage.
Humidity: Average indoor humidity levels.
Temperatures: 50°F to 55°F at night, 60°F to 65°F during the day.
Fertilization: Fertilize all year, but more heavily in summer.
Propagation: Take stem cuttings at any time. Air-layer climbing types.
Grooming: Keep to desired height and shape with light pruning or clip-ping at any time. Place aerial roots in soil. Clean the leaves from time to time.

Repotting: Repot in winter or early spring, as needed.
Problems: It is natural for most philodendrons to drop lower leaves.

Pilea species

There are more than 200 species in this widely varied genus. Most of the ones that are suitable for indoor gardening are moderately sized herbaceous plants. They grow about a foot tall and have variegated leaves with depressed veins, giving them a quilted appearance. The dark green coloration of the leaves of many species is tinged with red, silver, or copper. Others are harmless but bear a resemblance to their wild cousins, the stinging nettles. Still others have a creeping or trailing habit that makes them particularly useful in hanging baskets. Some species produce inconspic-uous flowers in the summer.

The plants described here are all suf-ficiently different in their culture to require individualized care guides. Keep them reasonably warm and evenly moist. Pinch back the fleshy stems of-ten to maintain their size and form. Many require a rest during the fall and early winter. Be careful not to over-water or overfertilize during this time. With age, these plants tend to become spindly and unattractive. Many indoor gardeners easily grow new plants each spring from cuttings. For a fuller plant-ing, place several rooted cuttings in one basket or pot.

Pilea cadierei
Aluminum plant, Watermelon plant

Aluminum plant is popular for indoor use. It is often sold as a small plant, but it can become large if given good light and warmth. The foliage is attractively variegated, appearing to have been brushed with aluminum paint. There is a dwarf form, *P. cadieri minima,* which has smaller leaves with pink petioles. Keep the stems of this plant pinched back to encourage branching and main-tain the proper form.
Light: Place in a bright, indirectly lit south, east, or west window.
Water: Let plant approach dryness before watering, but water thoroughly and discard drainage.
Humidity: Average indoor levels.

Temperatures: 55°F to 60°F at night, 70°F to 75°F during the day.
Fertilization: Fertilize 3 times a year: spring, midsummer, and early fall.
Propagation: Take stem cuttings at any time.
Grooming: Start new plants and re-place older specimens when they get weak. Keep to desired height and shape with light pruning or clipping at any time.
Repotting: Repot at any time.
Problems: Poor drainage, too fre-quent watering, or standing in water will cause root rot.

Pilea involucrata
Panamiga, Pan-American friendship plant

Several species are known as panamigas. They are all small plants that are suit-able for indoor gardens. The plants are herbaceous, with semifleshy stems that need to be pinched back frequently to encourage branching. The Pan-Ameri-can friendship plant has textured, hairy leaves that are a dark copper color when viewed from above, and are reddish underneath. Other panamigas have sil-very variegated leaves. One species, *P. repens,* has leaves so darkly colored it is called the black-leaved panamiga. Keep panamigas warm, out of drafts, and constantly moist.
Light: Place in a bright, indirectly lit south, east, or west window.
Water: Keep evenly moist. Water thoroughly and discard drainage.
Humidity: Requires moist air. Use a humidifier for best results.
Temperatures: 60°F to 65°F at night, above 70°F during the day.
Fertilization: Fertilize all year, but more heavily in summer.
Propagation: Take stem cuttings.

Grooming: Keep to desired height and shape with light pruning or clipping at any time.
Repotting: Repot at any time.
Problems: Dry soil or high soluble salts may damage roots, causing plant to die back. The leaves will scorch if plant is in a draft or dry air.

Pilea nummulariifolia
Creeping Charlie

Creeping Charlie is a popular herbaceous vine often used in hanging baskets or on a pedestal. It looks best if several rooted cuttings are grown in one container. You can keep adding new rooted cuttings to the pot to counter any spindliness that may occur as these fast-growing plants get older. If placed too near a window, cold drafts will cause it to weaken and decline.
Light: Place in a bright, indirectly lit south, east, or west window.
Water: Keep evenly moist. Water thoroughly and discard drainage.
Humidity: Requires moist air. Use a humidifier for best results.
Temperatures: 65°F to 70°F at night, 75°F to 80°F during the day.
Fertilization: Fertilize 3 times a year: spring, midsummer, and early fall.
Propagation: Take stem cuttings at any time.
Grooming: Start new plants and replace older specimens when they get weak. Keep to desired height and shape with light pruning or clipping at any time.
Repotting: Repot each year in the late spring.
Problems: Poor drainage, too frequent watering, or standing in water will cause root rot. Plant is very sensitive to chilling from cold drafts or cold irrigation water. Will get spindly and weak in low light.

Pittosporum tobira
Pittosporum (Japanese)

Japanese pittosporums are widely used in commercial interiors because they are tolerant of moderate light and many diverse indoor environments. They are woody shrubs that eventually get quite large. Their glossy leaves somewhat resemble those of a rhododendron. One cultivar has variegated foliage. In ample light, the plant may bloom in the

spring; its flowers have a fragrance similar to that of orange blossoms.
Light: Place in a bright, indirectly lit south, east, or west window.
Water: Let plant approach dryness before watering, but water thoroughly and discard drainage.
Humidity: Average indoor humidity levels.
Temperatures: 40°F to 45°F at night, 60°F to 65°F during the day.
Fertilization: Fertilize 3 times a year: spring, midsummer, and early fall.
Propagation: Take cuttings from stems or shoots that have recently matured. New plants can be started with air layering.
Grooming: Keep to desired height and shape with light pruning or clipping at any time.

*Left: **Pittosporum tobira***
*Above: **Plectranthus***

Repotting: Infrequent repotting is best. Repot in winter or early spring, as needed.
Problems: Will not bloom if light is too low. Scale and mealybugs can be present.

Plectranthus species
Swedish ivy

P. australis has waxy, leathery, bright green leaves and a trailing habit. Although commonly known as Swedish ivy, it is neither from Sweden nor an ivy. The name comes from its popularity in Scandinavia as a hanging and trailing plant. Spikes of white flowers appear occasionally to complement the foliage. Variegated varieties such as *P. coleoides, P. oertendahlii,* and *P. purpuratus* have shadings of silver, purple, and gray-greens and bear pink or lavender blossoms.

This beautiful trailing plant is fairly tolerant and requires a minimum of care. Place it in bright light, and water regularly.
Light: Place in a bright, indirectly lit south, east, or west window.
Water: Keep evenly moist. Water thoroughly and discard drainage.
Humidity: Average indoor levels.

Temperatures: 55°F to 60°F at night, 70°F to 75°F during the day.
Fertilization: Fertilize all year, but more heavily in summer.
Propagation: Take cuttings from stems or shoots that have recently matured.
Grooming: Pinch back stem tips of young or regrowing plants to improve form. Do not destroy flower buds. Start new plants and replace older specimens when they get weak.
Repotting: Repot at any time.
Problems: Poor drainage, too frequent watering, or standing in water will cause root rot. Dry soil or high soluble salts may damage roots, causing plant to die back.

Podocarpus macrophyllus
Podocarpus, Japanese yew

A more pleasing compact shrub than *P. macrophyllus* var. *maki* is hard to find. A group of branches supports spirals of thin, yellow-green leaves, each 3 inches long. As the branches lengthen, they gradually arch downward, becoming less upright. Some species of podocarpus can grow to 10 feet.

In the right environment the slow-growing podocarpus will thrive for many years. It's a tolerant plant that grows best in cool temperatures and bright filtered light. During the winter, place this plant in an unheated sunporch or other cool room. Too much heat will harm the plant. Control the size of your plant by pinching back the tips; this will encourage branching and enhance the bush shape.
Light: Place in a bright, indirectly lit south, east, or west window.
Water: Let plant approach dryness before watering, but water thoroughly and discard drainage.
Humidity: Average indoor humidity levels.
Temperatures: 50°F to 55°F at night, 60°F to 65°F during the day.
Fertilization: Fertilize only during the late spring and summer months.
Propagation: Take cuttings from stems or shoots that have recently matured.
Grooming: Keep to desired height and shape with light pruning or clipping at any time.
Repotting: Repot in winter or early spring, as needed.

Above: *Podocarpus macrophyllus*
Above Right: *Polyscias fruticosa 'Elegans'*
Below Right: *Rhoeo spathacea*

Problems: The leaves will scorch if plant is in a draft or dry air. Poor drainage, too frequent watering, or standing in water will cause root rot.

Polyscias species
Aralias

Aralias are woody shrubs frequently grown indoors for their lacy, often variegated foliage. Balfour aralia is a popular cultivar that has a more solid variegated foliage. The leaves of some cultivars are aromatic when crushed or bruised. The plants will grow into large bushy shrubs and are popular large plants in commercial interiors. Give them plenty of room, and prune frequently to achieve good form.
Light: Provide at least moderate light but no direct sunlight.
Water: Let plant approach dryness before watering, but water thoroughly and discard drainage.
Humidity: Requires moist air. Use a humidifier for best results.
Temperatures: 55°F to 60°F at night, 70°F to 75°F during the day.
Fertilization: Fertilize 3 times a year: spring, midsummer, and early fall.
Propagation: Take stem cuttings.

Grooming: Keep to desired height and shape with light pruning or clipping at any time.
Repotting: Repot in winter or early spring, as needed.
Problems: Will get spindly and weak if light is too low. Poor drainage, too frequent watering, or standing in water will cause root rot. Mites, scale, and mealybugs can be present.

Rhoeo species
Moses in the cradle, Boat lily, Oyster plant

The common names of these plants come from the odd way the plant bears flowers. Small white blooms appear within cupped bracts at the base of the terminal leaves on the shoots. The foliage of rhoeo is striking: it is green on top and deep purple or maroon when viewed from beneath. Variegated cultivars are especially noteworthy. The plant grows in canelike stems that trail as they get older, so older plants are generally grown in hanging baskets. Fertilize lightly, and flush occasionally to keep older leaves from dropping.

Light: Place in a bright, indirectly lit south, east, or west window.

Water: Keep evenly moist. Water thoroughly and discard drainage.

Humidity: Average indoor humidity levels.

Temperatures: 55°F to 60°F at night, 70°F to 75°F during the day.

Fertilization: Fertilize only during late spring and summer months.

Propagation: New plants are started by dividing an older specimen.

Grooming: Keep to desired height and shape with light pruning or clipping at any time.

Repotting: Infrequent repotting is best. Repot at any time.

Problems: The leaves will drop if soil is too wet or too dry. Dry soil or high soluble salts may damage roots, causing plant to die back.

Ruellia species
Velvet plant (trailing)

These winter-flowering plants will grow to 24 inches, usually in a trailing or drooping manner. For this reason they are generally staked or used in hanging baskets. Give them plenty of light, keep them out of cold drafts, and keep them constantly moist to get satisfactory winter flowering. After they flower, allow the plants to become semidormant with less frequent waterings. Replace them when they get leggy.

Light: In winter, keep in about 4 hours of direct sun. In summer, provide curtain-filtered sunlight from a south or west window.

Water: Keep very moist during growth and flowering. Allow to dry between waterings at other times.

Humidity: Requires moist air. Use a humidifier for best results.

Temperatures: 55°F to 60°F at night, 70°F to 75°F during the day.

Fertilization: Fertilize only when plant is growing actively or flowering.

Propagation: Take cuttings from stems or shoots before they have hardened or matured.

Above: *Ruellia*
Below: *Salvia officinalis*
Right: *Sansevieria trifasciata*

Grooming: Start new plants and replace older specimens when they get weak. Keep to desired height and shape with light pruning or clipping at any time.

Repotting: Repot in winter or early spring, as needed.

Problems: Will get spindly and weak if light is too low. The leaves will scorch if plant is in a draft or dry air.

Salvia officinalis
Common sage

Sage can be grown indoors if it is kept in a cool but sunny location. An east- or west-facing window box would be ideal. The leaves are known for their usefulness in cooking and in medicinal teas. The plant is a semiwoody shrub and needs frequent clipping to maintain a convenient size and pleasing form. Most of the cultivars have small leaves, but *S. elegans* (pineapple-scented sage) has large foliage.

Light: In winter, keep in about 4 hours of direct sun. In summer, provide curtain-filtered sunlight in front of a south or west window.

Water: Keep evenly moist. Water thoroughly and discard drainage.

Humidity: Requires moist air. Use a humidifier for best results.

Temperatures: 40°F to 45°F at night, 60°F to 65°F during the day.

Fertilization: Fertilize all year, but more heavily in summer.

Propagation: Take stem cuttings at any time. Sage can also be started from seeds sown in spring.

Grooming: Prune in early spring. Keep to desired height and shape with light pruning or clipping at any time.

Repotting: Repot in winter or early spring, as needed.

Problems: Will get spindly and weak if light is too low.

Sansevieria species
Sansevieria, Snake plant, Mother-in-law's tongue

One of the hardiest of all indoor plants is *S. trifasciata.* Erect, dark green, lance-shaped leaves emerge from a central rosette. Golden yellow stripes along the margins and horizontal bands of grayish green create a striking pattern similar to the coloring of an exotic snake. *S. cylindrica* has round leaves with pointed tips. Mature plants produce fragrant pink and white blooms in spring.

Given proper care, sansevieria can be a showy accent for any indoor decor. Place it in a brightly lit, warm location and water regularly when the soil becomes dry. Overwatering will cause root rot. Fertilize every 2 or 3 months.

Light: Place in a bright, indirectly lit south, east, or west window.

Water: Water thoroughly, but allow to dry between waterings.

Humidity: Dry air is generally not harmful for this plant, but keep it out of drafts.

Temperatures: 55°F to 60°F at night, 70°F to 75°F during the day.

Fertilization: Fertilize 3 times a year: spring, midsummer, and early fall.

Propagation: New plants are started by dividing an older specimen. Remove new plantlets or rooted side shoots as they form.

Grooming: Pick off yellowed leaves.

Repotting: Infrequent repotting is best.

Problems: Poor drainage, too frequent watering, or standing in water will cause root rot.

Saxifraga stolonifera
Strawberry geranium, Strawberry begonia

These plants are neither geraniums nor begonias; their names come from the shape and colors of their foliage. Several cultivars of these easy-to-grow plants are available. They are best suited for ground covers or hanging baskets. They will divide quickly in the pot, sending out runners that form plantlets much as strawberries do. In the summer, small white flowers appear on long stalks above the foliage. Many gardeners use these plants as patio plants during the summer. Make sure they are pest-free before bringing them back indoors.

Light: Place in a bright, indirectly lit south, east, or west window.

Water: Let plant approach dryness before watering, but water thoroughly and discard drainage.

Above: *Saxifraga stolonifera*
Right: *Schizocentron elegans*

Humidity: Average indoor humidity levels.

Temperatures: 50°F to 55°F at night, 60°F to 65°F during the day.

Fertilization: Fertilize only during late spring and summer months.

Propagation: New plants are started by dividing an older specimen. Remove new plantlets or rooted side shoots as they form.

Grooming: Cut flower stalks if you wish.

Repotting: Repot each year. Cut back and repot when flowering stops.

Problems: Will get spindly and weak if light is too low. Dry soil or high soluble salts may damage roots, causing plant to die back. The leaves will scorch if plant is in a draft or dry air.

Schizocentron elegans
Spanish shawl

Spanish shawl is a woody trailing plant that is best used in a hanging basket. In the summer, the plant will be covered with 1-inch rose or purple flowers. Pinch back stem tips frequently to keep the plant well branched and in good form.

Light: Provide at least 4 hours of curtain-filtered sunlight from a bright south, east, or west window.

Water: Keep evenly moist. Water thoroughly and discard drainage.

Humidity: Average indoor humidity levels.

Temperatures: 50°F to 55°F at night, 60°F to 65°F during the day.

Fertilization: Fertilize only during late spring and summer months.

Propagation: Take stem cuttings at any time. Seeds are available, but can be more difficult to use.

Grooming: Prune back after flowering. Pinch back stem tips of young or regrowing plants to improve form. Do not destroy flower buds.

Repotting: Cut back and repot when flowering stops.

Problems: Will get spindly and weak if light is too low.

Setcreasea purpura
Purple heart

These plants are so named because of the deep purple of their leaves and stems. The leaves are narrow and about 6 inches long. Because the stems tend to trail as they grow, the plant looks best in a small hanging basket.

Light: Place in a bright, indirectly lit south, east, or west window.

Water: Let plant approach dryness before watering, but water thoroughly and discard drainage.

Humidity: Average indoor humidity levels.

Temperatures: 55°F to 60°F at night, 70°F to 75°F during the day.

Fertilization: Fertilize 3 times a year: spring, midsummer, and early fall.

Propagation: Take stem cuttings at any time.

Grooming: Prune in early spring.

Repotting: Repot in winter or early spring, as needed.

Problems: Will get spindly and weak if light is too low.

Soleirolia soleirolii

Succulent: Adromischus mammilaris

Soleirolia soleirolii
Baby's tears

Baby's tears, often sold as *Helxine soleirolii,* is a compact creeper that has tiny, delicate rounded leaves on thin, trailing stems. It grows into a dense mat and makes a good terrarium ground cover. It thrives in high humidity.
Light: Place in a bright, indirectly lit south, east, or west window.
Water: Keep evenly moist. Water thoroughly and discard drainage.
Humidity: Requires moist air. Use a humidifier for best results.
Temperatures: 50°F to 55°F at night, 60°F to 65°F during the day.
Fertilization: Fertilize all year, but more heavily in summer.
Propagation: New plants are started by dividing an older specimen.
Grooming: Keep to desired height and shape with light pruning or clipping at any time.
Repotting: Repot at any time.
Problems: Dry soil or high soluble salts may damage roots, causing plant to die back.

Sonerila species
Sonerila

These small plants have fleshy stems. Their foliage is silver on top and reddish on the underside. The plants are very sensitive to dry air and are best suited to a terrarium or other humid location. If given ample light, sonerilas occasionally produce clusters of small lavender flowers.
Light: Place in a bright, indirectly lit south, east, or west window.
Water: Keep evenly moist. Water thoroughly and discard drainage.
Humidity: Average indoor humidity levels.
Temperatures: 55°F to 60°F at night, 70°F to 75°F during the day.
Fertilization: Fertilize only during late spring and summer months.
Propagation: Take stem cuttings at any time.
Grooming: Pinch back stem tips of young or regrowing plants to improve form. Do not destroy flower buds.
Repotting: Repot in winter or early spring, as needed.
Problems: The leaves will scorch if plant is in a draft or dry air. Poor drainage, too frequent watering, or standing in water will cause root rot.

Succulents

A succulent stores water in its stems or leaves. These plants have mastered the art of water conservation. By reducing their leaf surface in order to cut down on water loss from transpiration, and by storing water in their stems or leaves, succulents can control both the amount of water they need and the amount they use.

Succulents are generally easy to care for and are a good starting point for beginning gardeners. Despite the many different types of succulent plants, they basically require the same care. To grow well they need a porous, well-draining soil, lots of sunshine, good air circulation, and plenty of water. During the winter they must go dormant in a cool, dry environment. This rest time is essential if you want your plants to bloom the following season. In summer, revitalize the plants by moving them outdoors.

Here we describe some succulents excellent for indoor culture. For a more complete guide, see Ortho's *World of Cactus and Succulents.*

Adromischus species
Adromischus, Pretty pebbles, Sea shells, Plover eggs, Leopard's spots, Crinkle-leaf

The many cultivars of adromischus are stout-stemmed succulents that grow in clumps and look best in a shallow, broad container. Many have egg-shaped leaves with speckles or spots, giving rise to their unusual common names. Some species have crinkled leaves. The plants will grow in indirect light but develop better leaf color in bright light. Like most succulents, they can be allowed to dry out between waterings if they are not overfertilized. Many indoor gardeners use them in bonsai plantings.

Above Left: *Succulent: Agave victoriae-reginae*
Below Left: *Succulent: Aloe barbadensis*
Above: *Succulent: Beaucarnea recurvata*
Right: *Succulent: Ceropegia woodii*

Water: Water thoroughly, but allow to dry between waterings.
Humidity: Dry air is generally not harmful for this plant, but keep it out of drafts.
Temperatures: 50°F to 55°F at night, 65°F to 70°F during the day.
Fertilization: Fertilize 3 times a year: spring, midsummer, and early fall.
Propagation: New plants are started by dividing an older specimen.
Grooming: None needed.
Repotting: Infrequent repotting is best.
Problems: Subject to infestations of mealybug. Poor drainage, too frequent watering, or standing in water will cause root rot.

Aloe species
Aloe

There is great diversity among the plants in this genus. *A. aristata* (torch plant, lace aloe) is a dwarf species that has stemless rosettes edged with soft white spines or teeth. In winter it bears orange-red flowers. *A. barbadensis* (also known as *A. vera*) is commonly called medicine plant or burn aloe, since it is most widely known for the healing properties of its sap. Many people use the liquid from a broken leaf to treat minor burns. It is a stemless plant with green leaves and yellow flowers. *A. variegata* (tiger aloe) has white-spotted green leaves in triangular rosettes. Pink to dull red flower clusters appear intermittently throughout the year.

Agave species
Century plant

Agaves are large plants with thick pointed leaves. Several of the smaller types, such as *A. picta* (painted century plant), are suitable for indoor gardening. Agaves grow very slowly but need good light. Keep them drier in winter to give them a moderate dormancy period. Repot very infrequently. After several years, a plant becomes mature, and may produce a tall flower spike. Contrary to popular belief, agaves do not die after flowering.
Light: Place in a bright, indirectly lit south, east, or west window.

Beaucarnea recurvata
Elephant-foot tree, Ponytail palm

The common names of *B. recurvata* come from its somewhat unusual appearance. Its trunk resembles that of a palm, and mature specimens have a greatly swollen base that resembles an elephant's foot. It has a cluster of long, narrow leaves that arch outward from the top. Although the plant can grow to more than 30 feet, it is usually limited to 6 or 8 feet when grown indoors. This succulent stores water in its trunk, so it can go without water or much other care for long periods. Because it grows so slowly, purchase a large specimen for the indoor garden.

Ceropegia species
Rosary vine, Hearts entangled

This vining plant produces long purple runners with tiny heart-shaped leaves. The leaves, borne in pairs at regular intervals along the vine, are patterned with silver on top and purple beneath. Tiny tubers that form at the leaf joints as the plant matures can be removed and rooted to start new plants.

Crassula argentea
Jade plant

This compact, treelike succulent has stout, branching limbs with oblong, fleshy leaves 1 to 2 inches long. In direct sun, the smooth, dark green leaves become tinged with red. This popular plant ranges in height from 1 to 5 feet. Repot infrequently, but prune it occasionally to maintain shape and size.

BARRY COOPER

Above Left: *Crassula argentea*
Below Left: *Echeveria elegans*
Above: *Faucaria*
Above Right: *Haworthia*
Below Right: *Kalanchoe*

Echeveria species
Echeveria, Hen and chicks

All echeverias have in common a rosette form. Their greatly varied leaf color ranges from pale green through deep purple. Many are luminous pink. *E. elegans* (pearl echeveria) forms a tight rosette of small, whitish green leaves. Rose-colored flowers tipped with yellow are borne on pink stems in spring or summer. Echeverias are ideal for dish gardens. 'Morning Light' is a hybrid that has rosettes of luminous pink foliage.

Echeverias generally do well with more water, more fertilizer, and richer soil than most succulents. Exposure to light has a direct effect on the intensity of foliage color. If stems become leggy, the plant can be cut down and rerooted.

Faucaria species
Tiger's jaws

This popular short-stemmed succulent takes its common name from triangular leaves with small teeth along their margins. The leaves are often spotted and grow in small, low clumps, ranging in color from bluish green to olive green. *F. tigrina* has gray-green skin with white dots. *F. tuberculosa* has dark green leaves with small white bumps on the upper side. In summer, both produce yellow to white flowers that resemble dandelion blossoms. This plant is a good choice for beginners.

Gasteria species
Pencil-leaf

The leaves of these plants form rosettes, spiraling one on top of another. Their thickened leaves are usually dark green with variously colored dark or light spots. In summer, reddish orange flowers appear on a long stalk that may dip or arch. These plants will tolerate a bit less light than many other succulents.

Haworthia species

There is wide variation in this group of plants, but all are excellent indoors. Although they will grow in moderate light, bright indirect light will improve their foliage color and texture. The leaves of most species are thick and form rosettes on stemless plants. Depending on the species, they may flower at any time during the year. The flowers are small and borne in clusters on long stems. After flowering, the plants may go dormant and will need repotting.

Kalanchoe species

These popular succulents are grown for both their flowers and foliage. The leaves of *K. beharensis* (felt plant) are covered with brown hairs that give them a feltlike appearance. The large triangular leaves have curving, rippling edges. Pink flowers appear in the spring. *K. blossfeldiana* (flaming Katy) produces brilliant heads of scarlet flowers on thin stems 15 inches high. Shiny green oval leaves are tinged with red. *K. tomentosa* (panda plant) grows to 15 inches. Plump leaves covered with silvery hairs branch from a central stem. Pointed leaves are tipped with rusty brown bumps. This species rarely flowers indoors.

Above: *Lithops*
Above Right: *Sedum morganianum*
Above Far Right: *Senecio rowleyanus*
Below Right: *Stapelia pulvinata*

Lithops
Living stones

Often called living stones because it looks like small rocks, this plant grows in stemless clumps of paired leaves approximately 1 to 2 inches in diameter. In November, yellow to white flowers resembling dandelion blossoms emerge.

Mesembryanthemum species
Ice plant, Baby toes, Desert rose

These low-growing succulents come in many forms, usually with spreading prostrate stems. They produce daisylike flowers in many colors, generally in the summer. Ice plants are commonly used in the Southwest for ground covers, on sloping ground subject to erosion. *M. rhopalophyllum* (baby toes) and *M. densum* are often grown indoors in well-lighted locations. Baby toes is particularly noteworthy because it blooms in winter. Grow these plants in sandy potting soil and do not water too often.

Sedum morganianum
Donkey's tail, Burro's tail

This sedum is a trailing, slow-growing succulent. Light gray to blue-green leaves are ½ to 1 inch long, oval, and plump. The 3- to 4-foot-long trailing stems, covered with clusters of these leaves, create a braided or ropelike effect. This plant is ideal for hanging containers. Locate it where it won't be disturbed, because it is very easy to break off the leaflets. Also, don't be alarmed by the powdery bluish dust covering the leaves; it's called *bloom.*

Senecio rowleyanus
String-of-beads

The string-of-beads has hanging stems that bear ½-inch spherical leaves. These unusual leaves look like light green beads with pointed tips and have a single translucent band across them. Small, fragrant white flowers appear in winter.

Stapelia species
Hairy toad plant

These plants have leafless brownish stems that are about 1 inch in diameter and can grow to 2 feet long. The large star-shaped flowers are generally yellow or red with maroon spotting. They are borne along the stems in late summer and fall. The flowers sometimes have a very unpleasant scent, like decaying meat. Although it does serve to attract pollinating flies to the flowers, the odor is undesirable for most indoor gardens unless the plants are placed away from people. The plants are sensitive to crown rot and mealybugs if the soil is kept too wet or too dry.

Care of Succulents

Light: Place in a bright, indirectly lit south, east, or west window.

Water: Water thoroughly when the soil a half-inch below the surface is dry. Discard drainage.

Humidity: Dry air does not generally harm these plants.

Temperatures: 50°F to 55°F at night, 65°F to 70°F during the day.

Fertilization: Fertilize lightly. For slow-growing succulents, fertilize once a year in early spring. For others, fertilize in spring, midsummer, and early fall.

Propagation: Cuttings and offsets root easily. Dry the offset or cutting for a few days until a callus forms on the cut, then plant in appropriate soil mix and keep barely moist.

Grooming: Cut off flower stalks as the blooms age.

Repotting: Repot only every 3 or 4 years, when essential. Use a shallow pot rather than a deep one.

Problems: Root rot can result from soggy soil caused by poor drainage or excessive watering. Stem and leaf rot may be caused by cool, damp air. Leaves wilt and discolor from too much water, especially in winter. Brown dry spots are caused by underwatering.

Syngonium podophyllum

Syngonium podophyllum
Arrowhead vine

This plant closely resembles its relatives, the climbing philodendrons, in both appearance and care. An unusual feature is the change that occurs in the leaf shape as the plant ages. Young leaves are 3 inches long, arrow-shaped, and borne at the ends of erect stalks. They are dark green and have bold silvery white variegation. With age, the leaves become lobed and the stems begin to climb. Eventually each leaf fans out into several leaflets. Older leaves may have as many as 11 leaflets and turn solid green. All stages of leaf development occur together on mature plants.

Arrowhead vines do best in a warm, moist environment protected from direct sunlight. Older climbing stems require support; a moss stick works well. To retain the juvenile leaf form and variegation, prune the climbing stems and aerial roots as they appear.

Light: Place in a bright, indirectly lit south, east, or west window.
Water: Keep very moist during growth and flowering. Allow to dry between waterings at other times.
Humidity: Requires moist air. Use a humidifier for best results.
Temperatures: 55°F to 60°F at night, 70°F to 75°F during the day.
Fertilization: Fertilize 3 times a year: spring, midsummer, and early fall.
Propagation: Take cuttings from stems or shoots that have recently matured.
Grooming: Keep to desired height and shape with light pruning or clipping at any time.

Repotting: Repot in winter or early spring, as needed.
Problems: Poor drainage, too frequent watering, or standing in water will cause root rot.

Tetrapanax papyriferus
Rice-paper plant

The pith or center spongy tissue of this plant's stem is used to make rice paper. It grows to be a very large plant, with fan-shaped leaves more than a foot across. The plant will eventually send up suckers from its base, giving it a fuller appearance. Rice-paper plant needs a lot of room.

Light: Place in a bright, indirectly lit south, east, or west window.
Water: Let plant approach dryness before watering, but water thoroughly and discard drainage.
Humidity: Requires moist air. Use a humidifier for best results.
Temperatures: 50°F to 55°F at night, 65°F to 70°F during the day.
Fertilization: Fertilize all year, but more heavily in summer.
Propagation: Start from seeds. Begin in a small pot and transplant as needed. Remove new plantlets or rooted side shoots as they form.
Grooming: Pick off yellowed leaves. Give these plants plenty of room.
Repotting: Transplant seedlings several times as plants grow.
Problems: The leaves will drop if soil is too wet or too dry.

Tolmiea menziesii
Piggyback plant

Piggyback plants are popular with indoor gardeners because of the way the plant produces new plantlets at the juncture of the leaf blade and petiole. Under proper conditions, the trailing stems will quickly produce a large plant suitable for a hanging basket or on a pedestal. A variegated form is available. These plants must be kept cool at night, and constantly moist. They need only light fertilization and will not tolerate drafts or dry air.

Light: Place in a bright, indirectly lit south, east, or west window.

Tolmiea menziesii

Water: Keep evenly moist. Water thoroughly and discard drainage.
Humidity: Requires moist air. Use a humidifier for best results.
Temperatures: 40°F to 45°F at night, 60°F to 65°F during the day.
Fertilization: Fertilize only during late spring and summer months.
Propagation: Remove new plantlets as they form.
Grooming: Keep to the desired height and shape with light pruning or clipping at any time.
Repotting: Repot each year.
Problems: The leaves will scorch if plant is in a draft or dry air. Dry soil or high soluble salts may damage roots, causing plant to die back, and making it subject to infestations of spider mites.

Yucca pendula glauca

Tradescantia species
Wandering Jew, Inch plant, Spiderwort

Both tradescantias and zebrinas are called wandering Jew, since they are almost identical. Leaves are borne alternately along thick, trailing stems. Tradescantias tend to have lighter, less purplish coloration. Many variegated cultivars are available in about 20 species. In low light, some of the variegated forms will occasionally produce a branch with solid green leaves. Remove this branch because it will outgrow the others and take over the plant. It is best to keep the long vines or stems pruned so the plant does not become too spindly and weak. Tradescantias are used as ground cover, in hanging baskets, or as trailing plants on shelves or windowsills.

Light: Provide at least moderate light but no direct sunlight.
Water: Let plant approach dryness before watering, but water thoroughly and discard drainage.
Humidity: Average indoor humidity levels.
Temperatures: 50°F to 55°F at night, 65°F to 70°F during the day.

Fertilization: Fertilize all year but more heavily in summer.
Propagation: Take stem cuttings at any time.
Grooming: Keep to desired height and shape with light pruning or clipping at any time.
Repotting: Repot at any time.
Problems: Will get spindly and weak if light is too low. Dry soil or high soluble salts may damage roots, causing plant to die back.

Yucca species
Yucca

Yuccas are commonly grown outdoors as accent or specimen ornamentals. Because they are large and tolerate adverse conditions, yuccas are frequently used in commercial interiors. The thick, swordlike leaves have sharp tips that can puncture the skin. Older plants have a canelike trunk with whorls of foliage at the end. Side shoots form occasionally. Recently rooted cane plants taken from sections of large stock plants will produce a floor-sized specimen in little time.

Light: Will tolerate light levels from moderate to direct sun.
Water: Water thoroughly, but allow to dry between waterings.
Humidity: Average indoor humidity levels.
Temperatures: 50°F to 55°F at night, 60°F to 65°F during the day.
Fertilization: Fertilize 3 times a year: spring, midsummer, and early fall.
Propagation: Remove new plantlets or rooted side shots as they form. Seeds are available, but can be more difficult to use. Cane cuttings can be rooted as well.
Grooming: Pick off yellowed leaves.
Repotting: Infrequent repotting is best.
Problems: Leaf tips will turn brown from a buildup of soluble salts.

Zebrina pendula
Wandering Jew (purple)

Zebrinas, which are similar to tradescantias, are available in several cultivars that have variegated leaves in white, purple, and pink. The semiwoody plant has trailing stems and is best suited for a hanging basket or as a ground cover.

Zebrina

Zebrinas grow a bit faster than tradescantias, but otherwise they are practically identical. Pinch back the stem tips frequently to prevent legginess or a spindly appearance.

Light: Provide at least moderate light but no direct sunlight.
Water: Keep evenly moist. Water thoroughly and discard drainage.
Humidity: Average indoor humidity levels.
Temperatures: 50°F to 55°F at night, 60°F to 65°F during the day.
Fertilization: Fertilize all year, but more heavily in summer.
Propagation: Take stem cuttings at any time.
Grooming: Keep to desired height and shape with light pruning or clipping at any time.
Repotting: Repot at any time.
Problems: Will get spindly and weak if light is too low. Dry soil or high soluble salts may damage roots, causing plant to die back.

Index of common names

If a plant's common and Latin names are the same, it will not be on this list. For more detailed information, see the Index at the back of the book.

A

Adam's-apple: *Tabernaemontana*
Adromischus: Succulents, *Adromischus*
Aerides: Orchids, *Aerides*
African violet: Gesneriads, *Saintpaulia*
Agave: Succulents, *Agave*
Algerian ivy: *Hedera*
Aloe: Succulents, *Aloe*
Alpine strawberry: *Fragaria*
Aluminum plant: *Pilea*
Amaryllis: *Hippeastrum*
Amazon lily: *Eucharis*
Angel-wing begonia: *Begonia*
Angraecum: Orchids, *Angraecum*
Aporocactus: Cacti, *Aporocactus*
Apostle plant: *Neomarica*
Arabian violet: *Exacum*
Aralia: *Polyscias*
Aralia ivy: x *Fatshedera*
Areca palm: Palms, *Chrysalidocarpus*
Arrowhead vine: *Syngonium*
Astrophytum: Cacti, *Astrophytum*
Avocado: *Persea americana*
Azalea: *Rhododendron*
Aztec lily: *Sprekelia*

B

Baby toes: Succulents,
    Mesembryanthemum
Baby's tears: *Soleirolia*
Balfour aralia: *Polyscias*
Balsam: *Impatiens*
Banana: *Musa*
Barbados lily: *Hippeastrum*
Basket vine: Gesneriads, *Aeschynanthus*
Bear's-paw fern: Ferns, *Polypodium*
Beefsteak plant: *Acalypha or Iresine*
Begonia treebine: *Cissus*
Bellflower: *Campanula*
Bengal lily: *Crinum*
Bird's nest bromeliad: Bromeliads,
    Nidularium
Bird's-nest fern: Ferns, *Asplenium*
Bird-of-paradise: *Strelitzia*
Bishop's-cap: Cacti, *Astrophytum*
Black-eyed Susan vine: *Thunbergia*
Black-leafed panamiga: *Pilea*
Bleeding heart: *Clerodendrum*
Blood lily: *Haemanthus*
Bloodleaf: *Iresine*
Blue African lily: *Agapanthus*
Blue daisy: *Felicia*
Blue marguerite: *Felicia*
Blue sage: *Eranthemum*
Blue torch: Bromeliads, *Tillandsia*
Blushing bromeliad: Bromeliads,
    Neoregelia

Boat lily: *Rhoeo*
Boston daisy: *Chrysanthemum*
Boston fern: Ferns, *Nephrolepis*
Botanical-wonder: x *Fatshedera*
Boxwood: *Buxus*
Brake ferns: Ferns, *Pteris*
Brassia: Orchids, *Brassia*
Brazilian edelweiss: Gesneriads, *Sinningia*
Brazilian plume: *Justicia*
Bunny ears: Cacti, *Opuntia*
Burn aloe: Succulents, *Aloe*
Burro's tail: Succulents, *Sedum*
Busy Lizzie: *Impatiens*
Butterfly gardenia: *Tabernaemontana*
Butterfly palm: Palms, *Chrysalidocarpus*
Buttonhole orchid: Orchids, *Epidendrum*

C

Calla lily: *Zantedeschia*
Canary Island ivy: *Hedera*
Cane begonia: *Begonia*
Cape cowslips: *Lachenalia*
Cape jasmine: *Gardenia*
Cape primrose: Gesneriads, *Streptocarpus*
Cardinal flower: Gesneriads, *Sinningia*
Carolina jasmine: *Gelsemium*
Cast-iron plant: *Aspidistra*
Catopsis: Bromeliads, *Catopsis*
Cattleya: Orchids, *Cattleya*
Century plant: Succulents, *Agave*
Cephalocereus: Cacti, *Cephalocereus*
Cereus: Cacti, *Cereus or Hylocereus*
Chain cactus: Cacti, *Rhipsalis*
Chenille plant: *Acalypha*
Chincherinchee: *Ornithogalum*
Chinese evergreen: *Aglaonema*
Chinese fan palms: Palms, *Livistona*
Chinese primrose: *Primula*
Chirita: Gesneriads, *Chirita*
Chives: *Allium*
Christmas begonia: *Begonia*
Christmas cactus: Cacti, *Schlumbergera*
Christmas cherry: *Solanum*
Cigar plant: *Cuphea*
Cineraria: *Senecio*
Clamshell orchid: Orchids, *Epidendrum*
Climbing lily: *Gloriosa*
Clock vine: *Thunbergia*
Coffee plant: *Coffea*
Columnea: Gesneriads, *Columnea*
Comet orchid: Orchids, *Angraecum*
Copper leaf: *Acalypha*
Coral plant: *Russelia*
Coralberry: *Ardisia* or Bromeliads,
    Aechmea
Corn plant: *Dracaena*

Crape jasmine: *Tabernaemontana*
Creeping Charlie: *Pilea*
Creeping fig: *Ficus*
Crested spider table fern: Ferns, *Pteris*
Crinkle-leaf: Succulents, *Adromischus*
Croton: *Codiaeum*
Crown of thorns: *Euphorbia*
Curiosity plant: Cacti, *Cereus*
Cycas fern palm: Palms, *Cycas*
Cymbidium: Orchids, *Cymbidium*

D

Daffodils: *Narcissus* hybrids
Dancing lady orchid: Orchids, *Oncydium*
Deer's-foot fern: Ferns, *Davallia*
Dendrobium: Orchids, *Dendrobium*
Desert rose: Succulents,
    Mesembryanthemum
Devil's backbone: *Pedilanthus*
Devil's ivy: *Epipremnum*
Donkey's tail: Succulents, *Sedum*
Double sweet alyssum: *Lobularia*
Double-decker plant: Gesneriads,
    Sinningia
Dumb cane: *Dieffenbachia*
Dwarf pomegranate: *Punica*
Dyckia: Bromeliads, *Dyckia*

E

Earth stars: Bromeliads, *Cryptanthus*
Easter cactus: Cacti, *Schlumbergera*
Easter lily: *Lilium*
Echeveria: Succulents, *Echeveria*
Echinocactus: Cacti, *Echinocactus*
Echinocereus: Cacti, *Echinocereus*
Egyptian star cluster: *Pentas*
Elephant-foot tree: Succulents, *Beaucarnea*
English hedge fern: Ferns, *Polystichum*
English ivy: *Hedera*
Epidendrum: Orchids, *Epidendrum*
Epiphyllum: Cacti, *Epiphyllum*
Epsicia: Gesneriads, *Episcia*
European fan palm: Palms, *Chamaerops*

F

Fairy primrose: *Primula*
False aralia: *Dizygotheca*
False sea onion: *Ornithogalum*
Fancy-leaf geranium: *Pelargonium*
Felt plant: Succulents, *Kalanchoe*
Fibrous-rooted begonia: *Begonia*
Fiddle-leaf philodendron: *Philodendron*
Fiddleleaf fig: *Ficus*
Firecracker flower: *Crossandra*
Firecracker vine: *Manettia*
Fishtail palm: Palms, *Caryota*
Flame-of-the-woods: *Ixora*

Solving Plant Problems

Plants, like humans, are susceptible to destructive environmental forces and to individual genetic vulnerabilities. When a plant is weakened—perhaps by loving but inconsistent care—those environmental or genetic elements can cause a variety of problems.

This chapter addresses some of the more serious conditions your plants may develop, identifying them by symptom and suggesting a cure. If you notice anything unusual (such as constant wilting) or see a change in your plants (such as spots or bugs on the leaves), consult the individual care guides in The Gallery of Houseplants. If you've followed those care requirements and still have significant or ongoing problems, check the following pages.

Some problems are easy to identify and have a universal treatment. Aphids, for example, can be found on a number of species, and the cure is a particular pesticide. These general problems are listed in the front of this chapter. Another way problems are identified is by the plant or plant family that is susceptible. Cacti are susceptible to stem rot, for instance, which is listed under the heading ''Cactus,'' not ''Stem rot.''

An ounce of prevention is worth a pound of cure, and the best and simplest way to deal with plant problems is to try to avoid them. Always be careful not to spread a disease or pest from one plant to your whole collection. Don't allow sick plants to come into contact with healthy ones, and don't touch sick plants and then go on to touch or groom healthy ones. When you first purchase plants, isolate them until you are sure that all they are bringing into your house is joy and beauty. If there is no way to cure a plant, throw it away. Also, throw away the soil it was in. It is wise to discard the pot too, unless you're sure you can sanitize it.

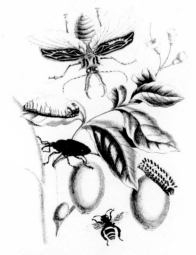

O'er folded blooms
On swirls of musk,
The beetle booms adown the
* glooms*
And bumps along the dusk.

The Beetle,
James Whitcomb Riley,
1849-1916

Aphids

Aphids on ivy (half size)

SYMPTOM: New leaves are curled, discolored, and smaller than normal. A shiny or sticky substance may coat the leaves. Tiny (⅛ inch), wingless, green, soft-bodied insects cluster on buds, young stems, and leaves. *Aphids* in small numbers do little damage, but they are extremely prolific and populations can rapidly build up to damaging numbers on houseplants. Damage results when the aphids suck sap from the leaves and stems. Aphids are unable to digest all the sugar in the plant sap and excrete the excess in a fluid called honeydew, which often drops onto leaves or surfaces below.

CURE: Spray with a pesticide containing *resmethrin.* Make sure your plant is listed on the product label. Follow label directions carefully.

Fungus gnats

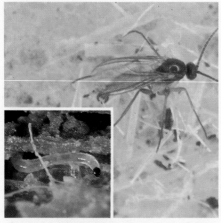

Fungus gnat and larva (10 times life size)

SYMPTOM: Small (up to ⅛ inch), slender dark insects fly around when plants are disturbed. They frequently run across the foliage and soil and may also be found on windows. Roots may be damaged and seedlings may die. *Fungus gnats* are small flies that do little damage, but they are unpleasant when present in large numbers. They lay their eggs in soil that contains organic material. After a week the eggs hatch and the larvae crawl through the upper layer of the soil. The larvae are white, ¼ inch long, and have black heads. They feed on fungi that grow on organic matter. The larvae usually do not damage plants, but when present in large numbers they may feed on the roots of some plants, killing very young seedlings. The larvae feed for about 2 weeks before maturing into adults. There can be many generations in a year.

CURE: Spray with a pesticide containing *diazinon.* Make sure your plant is listed on the product label. Follow label directions carefully. It may be necessary to repeat applications. Keep doors and windows closed to keep fungus gnats out.

Iron deficiency

Iron-deficient piggyback plant

SYMPTOM: The newest leaves turn yellow at the margins. The yellowing progresses inward, so that in the advanced stages the last tissues to lose their green color are the veins. In severe cases, the entire leaf is yellow and small. The plant may be stunted. *Iron deficiency* is a common problem for acid-loving plants, which grow best in soil with a pH between 5.5 and 6.5. The leaf yellowing is due to a deficiency of iron and other minor nutrients. Although soil is seldom deficient in iron, when the pH is 7.0 or higher the iron is chemically unavailable to some plants. Plants use iron in the formation of cholorophyll, the green pigment in the leaves. When it is lacking, the new leaves become yellow.

CURE: Apply a solution containing chelated iron. Spray the foliage and apply it to the soil in the pot to correct iron deficiency. Use acid-balanced fertilizers for feeding the plant. When planting or transplanting acid-loving plants, use an acidic soil mix that contains at least 50 percent peat moss. Use a minimum amount of lime or dolomite in the soil mix.

Low light

Leaf drop on zebra plant

SYMPTOM: Plants fail to grow well. Leaves may be lighter green and smaller than normal. Lobes and splits normal in mature leaves may not develop. Lower leaves may yellow and drop. Stems and leaf stalks may elongate and be spindly and weak. Plants grow toward a light source. Flowering plants fail to produce flowers, and plants with colorful foliage become pale. Variegated plants may lose their variegation and become green. *Insufficient light* causes a variety of problems. Plants use light as a source of energy; they grow slowly in light that is too dim for their needs. If most of the available light comes from one direction, stems and leaves bend in that direction. If the light is much too dim, plants have little energy and grow poorly. Although foliage plants generally need less light than plants grown for their flowers or fruit, plants with colorful foliage have a relatively high need for light.

CURE: Move the plant to a brighter location, such as a sunny window. To avoid sunburn on sensitive plants, close lightweight curtains when the sun shines directly on the plant. If the available light is not bright enough, provide supplemental lighting.

Mealybugs

Citrus mealybugs on coleus (twice life size)

SYMPTOM: Insects up to ¼ inch long cluster in cottony masses on the undersides of leaves, on stems, and where leaves are attached. Egg masses may also be present. A sticky substance may cover the leaves or drop onto surfaces below the plant. Leaves may be spotted or deformed. Female mealybugs may produce live young or deposit hundreds of eggs in a white fluffy mass. The young nymphs crawl over the plant and onto nearby plants. Soon after they begin to feed, they produce white filaments that cover their bodies, giving them a cottony appearance. As they mature, they become less mobile. They excrete a fluid called honeydew, which coats the leaves and may drop to surfaces below.

CURE: Spray with a pesticide containing *resmethrin.* Make sure your plant is listed on the product label. Follow label directions carefully. Continue for a while after it appears the mealybugs have been controlled. If only a few mealybugs are present, wipe them off with a damp cloth or use cotton swabs dipped in rubbing alcohol. Search for egg sacs on and around the pots and remove them. Discard severely infested plants, and do not take cuttings from them. Clean the growing area with soapy water before starting new plants.

Nitrogen deficiency

Nitrogen-deficient Swedish ivy plant

SYMPTOM: The oldest leaves, usually the lower ones, turn yellow and may drop. Yellowing starts at the leaf margins and progresses inward without producing a distinct pattern. The yellowing may progress upward until only the newest leaves remain green. Growth is slow, new leaves are small, and the whole plant may be stunted. *Nitrogen deficiency* affects plants in many ways. The nutrient nitrogen is used by plants in large amounts, including the production of chlorophyll (the green pigment in leaves and stems). When there is not enough nitrogen for the entire plant, it is taken from the older leaves for use in new growth. Nitrogen is easily leached from soil during regular watering. Of all the plant nutrients, it is the one most likely to be lacking in the soil.

CURE: Feed plants with a water-soluble fertilizer that contains more nitrogen than phosphorus or potassium (10-8-7, for example), or use fish emulsion. Add the fertilizer at regular intervals, as recommended on the label.

Poor drainage

Overwatering damage to schefflera

SYMPTOM: Plants fail to grow and may wilt. Leaves lose their glossiness and may become light green or yellow. The roots are brown and soft and do not have white tips. The soil in the bottom of the pot may be very wet and have a foul odor. Plants may die. *Poor drainage or overwatering* may be the cause. Although plants need water to live, the roots also need air. If the soil is kept too wet, the air spaces fill with water so that the roots can't get enough oxygen. Then the roots weaken and may die. Weak plants are more susceptible to root-rotting fungi, which favor wet soils. Plants with diseased roots do not absorb as much water as they did when they were healthy, so the soil remains wet. If roots are damaged or diseased, they cannot pick up water and nutrients needed for plant growth.

CURE: Discard severely wilted plants and those without white root tips. For plants that are less severely affected, do not water again until the soil is almost dry (barely moist). Prevent the problem by using a light soil with good drainage.

Salt damage

Salt damage to a spathiphyllum

SYMPTOM: The leaf margins of plants with broad leaves or the leaf tips of plants with long narrow leaves die and turn brown and brittle. This browning occurs on the older leaves first; but when the condition is severe, new leaves may also be affected. On some plants the older leaves may yellow and die. *Salt damage* is a common problem on container-grown plants. Soluble salts are picked up by the roots and accumulate in the margins and tips of the leaves, where concentrations may become high enough to kill the tissues. Salts can accumulate from water or from the use of fertilizers, or they may be present in the potting soil. Salts accumulate faster if plants are not watered thoroughly.

CURE: Leach excess salts from the soil by flushing with water at least 3 times, letting the water drain completely each time. This is most easily done if the pot is placed in a bathtub or laundry sink, or outside in the shade. Always water your plant from the top of the pot. If the plant is too large to lift, empty the saucer with a turkey baster. Never let a plant stand in the drainage water. Trim off dead stem tips with scissors. Do not overfertilize.

Scales

Brown scale on fern stalk (twice life size)

SYMPTOM: Stems and leaves or fronds are covered with white, cottony, cushionlike masses or brown crusty bumps that can be scraped off easily. Leaves or fronds turn yellow and may drop. A shiny or sticky material may cover the stems and leaves or fronds. On ferns, the bumps are sometimes mistaken for reproductive spores. The round, flat spores are found only on the undersides of fronds, spaced at regular intervals, and are difficult to pick off. *Scale insects* of several different types attack houseplants. The young, called crawlers, are small (about $\frac{1}{10}$ inch), soft-bodied, and move about on the plant and onto other plants. After a short time they insert their mouthparts into the plant so they can feed on the sap. The legs disappear, and the scales remain in the same place for the rest of their lives. Some develop a soft covering, and others are hard. Some species can't digest all the sugar in the plant sap and excrete the excess in a fluid called honeydew, which may cover the leaves or fronds and drip onto surfaces below.

CURE: Spray with a pesticide containing *resmethrin.* Make sure your plant is listed on the product label. Follow label directions carefully. It may be necessary to repeat the spraying.

Spider mites

Spider mite damage to prayer plant

SYMPTOM: Leaves are stippled, yellow, and dirty; they may dry out and drop. There may be webbing over flower buds, between leaves, or on the lower surfaces of the leaves. To determine whether a plant is infested with mites, hold a sheet of white paper beneath an affected area and tap the leaf or stem sharply. Minute green, red, or yellow specks the size of pepper grains will drop to the paper and begin to crawl around. The pests are easily seen against the white background. *Spider mites,* related to spiders, are major pests of many houseplants. They cause damage by sucking sap from the undersides of the leaves. As a result of this feeding, the green pigment (chlorophyll) disappears, causing the stippled appearance. Under warm, dry conditions, these insects multiply rapidly.

CURE: Spray with a pesticide containing *resmethrin.* Make sure your plant is listed on the product label. Follow label directions carefully. Plants need several weekly sprayings to kill the mites as they hatch. Inspect new plants thoroughly before bringing them into your home.

Sunburn

SYMPTOM: Dead tan or brown patches develop on leaves exposed to direct sunlight. Leaves may lighten or turn gray. In some cases the plant remains green but growth is stunted. *Sunburn or bleaching* occurs when a plant is exposed to more intense sunlight than it can tolerate. Some plants can tolerate full sunlight, but others will burn or bleach if exposed to any direct sun. Bleaching occurs when light and heat break down chlorophyll (green plant pigment), causing a lightening or graying of the damaged leaf tissue. On more sensitive plants, or when light and heat increase in intensity, damage is more severe and plant tissues die. Sometimes tissue inside the leaf is damaged but outer symptoms do not develop; instead, growth is stunted. Plants are more susceptible to bleaching and sunburn when they are allowed to dry out because the normal cooling effect that results when water evaporates from leaves is reduced. Plants that are grown in low light burn very easily if they are suddenly moved to a sunny location.

CURE: Move plants to a shaded spot or close curtains when the plant is exposed to direct sun. Prune off badly damaged leaves, or trim away damaged leaf areas to improve the plant's appearance. Keep plants well watered.

Sunburn on dieffenbachia

Too dry

SYMPTOM: Leaves are small; plant fails to grow well and may be stunted. Plant parts or whole plants wilt. Margins of broad leaves or tips of narrow leaves may dry and become brittle but still retain a dull green color. Bleached areas may occur between the veins. Leaf tissues may die and remain bleached or turn tan or brown. Plants may die. *Too little water* may be the cause. Plants need water in order to grow. Besides making up most of the plant tissue, water is also the medium that carries nutrients into the plant, so a plant that is frequently short of water is also short of nutrients. Water also cools the leaves as it evaporates. If a leaf has no water to evaporate, it may overheat in the sun and burn. If plants wilt and then are given water, sometimes the margins or tips of the leaves will have completely dried out and will not recover. If this occurs, the margins or tips will die and become dry and brittle but will retain a dull green color.

CURE: Water plants immediately and thoroughly. If the soil is completely dry, add a bit of wetting agent (available at garden centers) or soak the entire pot in water for a couple of hours.

Dry poinsettia

Aphelandra

Salt damage on aphelandra

SYMPTOM: Margins of older leaves die and turn brown. The brown tissues are brittle. When the condition is severe, all leaves may have dead margins. Tissue adjacent to the dead margins of older leaves may turn yellow. *Salt damage* is a common problem for container-grown plants, and aphelandra is sensitive to excess salts. Soluble salts are picked up by the roots and accumulate in the leaf margins, where concentrations may become high enough to kill the tissues. Salts can accumulate from water or from the use of fertilizers, or they may be present in the potting soil. Salts accumulate faster and do more harm if the plant is not watered thoroughly.

CURE: Leach excess salts from the soil by flushing with water at least 3 times, letting the water drain completely each time. This is most easily done if the pot is placed in a bathtub or laundry sink, or outside in the shade. Always water aphelandra from the top of the pot. If you use a saucer to catch the water, empty it after the pot has finished draining. If the plant is too large to lift, empty the saucer with a turkey baster. Never let a plant stand in the drainage water. Do not overfertilize your plants.

Aphelandra

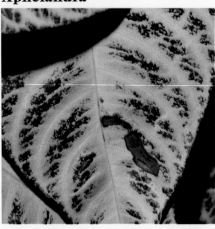

Sunburn

SYMPTOM: Leaves that are exposed to sunlight become yellow between the veins, and they may die and turn brown. The brown areas may have a silver cast. If the condition is severe, the dead areas may coalesce and large areas may be affected. Aphelandra grows best in very bright indirect light. When exposed to direct sunlight, the plant may burn. *Sunburn* causes the affected tissues to lose their green color between the veins and then die and turn brown. Plants that are allowed to dry out are more susceptible to sunburn than those that are given adequate water.

CURE: Move the plant to a location that receives bright indirect light. Or cut down the light intensity by closing the curtains when the plant is exposed to direct sun. Prune off badly damaged leaves, or trim away damaged leaf areas to improve the plant's appearance. Keep plants well watered.

Asparagus Fern

Weak stems on asparagus fern

SYMPTOM: The needlelike leaves turn pale green or yellow, beginning with the older leaves and progressing toward the tip of the stem. Yellow leaves may drop. Stems may be elongated and weak; sometimes they bend toward the light. Stems in the center of the plant may die and turn tan or brown. *Insufficient light* can cause problems for many indoor plants. Plants use light as a source of energy; they grow slowly in light that is too dim for their needs. If most of the available light comes from one direction, stems bend in that direction. If the light is much too dim, the plant has little energy and grows poorly. Although foliage plants generally need less light than plants grown for their flowers or fruit, asparagus fern has a relatively high need for light.

CURE: Move the plant to a brighter location, such as a sunny window. Asparagus fern will tolerate direct sun if it is kept well watered, but it will sunburn if it is allowed to dry out. If the available light is not bright enough, provide supplemental lighting.

Begonia

Sparse growth

SYMPTOM: Leaves fade to light green. In variegated varieties, the colors in the leaves become lighter and less intense. Stems become elongated and weak. Lower leaves may yellow and drop. Flowering varieties stop producing flowers. *Insufficient light* causes a variety of problems for flowering plants. Plants use light as a source of energy; they grow slowly in light that is too dim for their needs. If most of the available light comes from one direction, stems and leaves bend in that direction. If the light is much too dim, the plant has little energy and grows poorly. Plants grown for their brightly colored leaves or for their flowers have a relatively high need for light.

CURE: Move the plant to a brighter location, such as a lightly curtained sunny window. If the available light is not bright enough, provide supplemental lighting.

Begonia

Powdery mildew

SYMPTOM: White powdery patches appear on the leaves, stems, and flowers. Leaves may be covered with the powdery growth. This material usually appears first on older leaves and on the upper surfaces of the leaves. Tissue under the powdery growth may turn yellow or brown. Affected leaves may drop from the plant. *Powdery mildew* on begonia is caused by a fungus (*Erysiphe cichoracearum*). The powdery patches are fungus strands and spores. The windborne spores are capable of infecting leaves, stems, and flowers on the same plant or on nearby plants. The disease is favored by dim light and warm days with cool nights. Older leaves are more susceptible than new leaves. Plants in dry soil are more susceptible than plants kept evenly moist. Severe infections cause the leaves to turn yellow or brown or to drop.

CURE: Spray with a fungicide containing *dinocap, cycloheximide,* or *wettable sulfur.* Make sure begonia is listed on the product label. Follow label directions carefully. Remove infected leaves. Move plants to locations with more light. Keep plants out of cool drafts and in rooms with temperatures as even as possible.

Begonia

Whiteflies (life size)

SYMPTOM: Tiny winged insects, $\frac{1}{12}$ inch long, feed on the undersides of the leaves. The insects are covered with white waxy powder. When the plant is touched, insects flutter rapidly around it. Leaves may be mottled and yellowing. *Greenhouse whitefly* (*Trialeurodes vaporariorum*) is a common insect pest of begonia. The 4-winged adult lays eggs on the undersides of leaves. The larvae are the size of a pinhead, flat, oval, immobile, and semitransparent, with radiating white waxy filaments. They feed for about a month before changing to the winged adult form. Both larvae and adults suck sap from the leaves, but the larvae do more damage because they feed more heavily. Whiteflies cannot digest all the sugar in the sap and excrete the excess in a sugary material called honeydew, which coats the leaves and may drop from the plant.

CURE: Spray with a pesticide containing *resmethrin.* Make sure begonia is listed on the product label. Follow label directions carefully. Spray weekly as long as the problem continues. Remove heavily infested leaves.

Brassaia

Root rot

SYMPTOM: Plants fail to grow. Lower leaves may turn yellow and drop. Roots are brown, soft, and mushy and do not have white tips. When the condition is severe, all the roots are rotted and plants may wilt and die. *Root and stem rot* is caused by soil-dwelling fungi (*Pythium* species), also known as water molds, that attack the roots. Severely damaged or dead roots cannot supply the plant with moisture and nutrients. The disease usually indicates that the plant has been watered too frequently or that the soil mix does not drain well. The fungi are common in garden soils, but sterilized soil and soilless potting mixes are free of them unless introduced on a plant or dirty pot, or transferred on dirty fingers or tools. Rot spreads quickly through a root system if the soil remains wet.

CURE: If the plant is only mildly affected, let the soil dry out between waterings. If the soil mix is heavy or the container does not drain well, transplant into fast-draining soil mix in a container that drains freely. Discard severely infected plants and soil. Wash pots thoroughly and soak them in a mixture of 1 part household bleach to 9 parts water for 30 minutes. Rinse with plain water and dry thoroughly before reuse. You can also sterilize the pots.

Brassaia

Spider mite damage

SYMPTOM: Leaves are stippled, yellow, and dirty; they may dry out and drop. There may be webbing between leaves or on the lower surfaces of the leaves. To determine whether a plant is infested with mites, hold a sheet of white paper beneath an affected plant and tap the leaves sharply. Minute green, red, or yellow specks the size of pepper grains will drop to the paper and begin to crawl around. The pests are easily seen against the white background. *Spider mites,* related to spiders, are major pests of many houseplants, including schefflera. They cause damage by sucking sap from the undersides of the leaves. As a result of this feeding, the green pigment (chlorophyll) disappears, causing the stippled appearance. Under warm, dry conditions, which favor mites, they can increase to enormous numbers.

CURE: Spray with a pesticide containing *resmethrin.* Make sure schefflera is listed on the product label. Follow label directions carefully. Plants need several weekly sprayings to kill the mites as they hatch. To avoid introducing mites, inspect new plants carefully before bringing them into your home.

Cactus

Stem rot

SYMPTOM: Plants fail to grow well, and may die. Roots fail to grow, and may be dead and brown. *Overwatering* is a common problem for cacti. Most cacti are native to hot, dry areas with very sandy soils. Such soils have large spaces between the particles and little ability to retain moisture. Cacti do well in sandy soils because they need a lot of air around their roots. If deprived of air, the roots decay and the plants fail to grow, or they die.

CURE: Discard rotted plants. Repot mildly affected plants in a potting mix that is very sandy or loose, ensuring good drainage. Cacti should be watered thoroughly and then allowed to dry out before watering again, but they will die if left completely dry in containers for very long.

Chlorophytum

Dead leaf tips

SYMPTOM: Tips of leaves turn brown or tan. The damaged area spreads slowly along the leaf. Older leaves are most severely affected. The problem can be any combination of the following factors: (1) Salt accumulating in the soil from water or fertilizer is carried to the tips of leaves causing them to die. Salts accumulate most rapidly when the soil is dry. (2) If the plant is not getting enough water, the leaf tip is the first part to die. (3) Some chemicals, especially chloride and borate, are very damaging even in small amounts. They accumulate in leaf tips, killing the tissue.

CURE: Trim off dead tips with a pair of scissors. The following solutions correspond to the numbered problems listed above: (1) Place the plant in a bathtub or laundry sink and leach excess salts by flushing with water at least 3 times. Let the water drain completely each time. Always water spider plants from the top of the pot. If you use a saucer to catch the water, empty it after each watering. Never let a plant stand in the drainage water. Do not overfertilize. (2) Water the plant regularly. (3) There isn't much you can do about traces of toxic chemicals other than to use distilled or deionized water that is free of chemicals.

Chrysanthemum

Weak growth

SYMPTOM: Soon after potted plants are brought inside, their leaves turn yellow, wilt, and fall off. The plants are located in dim light. *Insufficient light* is a problem for chrysanthemums. They are outdoor plants that need full sun, but they will tolerate household conditions for a few weeks if they are kept in a bright place and are well watered. Flowering mums from a florist have been grown in bright sun and will not remain healthy in a location that does not allow them full sun for at least part of the day.

CURE: Move the plants to a brighter location. If the leaves are very yellow they will not be able to tolerate direct sun until they become accustomed to higher light levels. Put the plants in or near a lightly curtained window for a week before exposing them to full sun. It is difficult to get satisfactory flowers from a forced mum a second time the same season. As soon as possible after the blossoms die, cut the flower stalks to the ground and plant the mums in the garden. They may not bloom until the following year.

Chrysanthemum

Whiteflies (life size)

SYMPTOM: Tiny winged insects, about $\frac{1}{12}$ inch long, feed on the undersides of the leaves. The insects are covered with white waxy powder. When the plant is touched, insects flutter rapidly around it. Leaves may be mottled and yellowing. *Greenhouse whitefly (Trialeurodes vaporariorum)* is a common pest of chrysanthemums. The 4-winged adult lays eggs on the undersides of leaves. The larvae are the size of a pinhead, flat, oval, immobile, and semitransparent, with radiating white waxy filaments. They feed for about a month before changing to the adult form. Both larvae and adults suck sap from the leaves, but the larvae do more damage because they feed more heavily. Whiteflies cannot digest all the sugar in the sap and excrete the excess in a sugary material called honeydew, which coats the leaves and may drop from the plant.

CURE: Spray with a pesticide containing *resmethrin*. Make sure chrysanthemum is listed on the product label. Follow label directions carefully. Spray weekly as long as the problem continues. Remove heavily infested leaves.

Chrysanthemum

Spider mite damage

SYMPTOM: Leaves are stippled, yellow, and dirty. They may dry out and drop. There may be webbing over flower buds, between leaves, or on the lower surfaces of the leaves. To determine whether a plant is infested with mites, hold a sheet of white paper below an affected plant and tap the stems or leaves sharply. Minute green, red, or yellow specks the size of pepper grains will drop to the paper and begin to crawl around. The pests are easily seen against the white background. *Spider mites,* related to spiders, are major pests of many houseplants, including chrysanthemums. They cause damage by sucking sap from the undersides of the leaves. As a result of this feeding, the green pigment (chlorophyll) disappears, causing the stippled appearance. Under warm, dry conditions, which favor mites, they can increase to enormous numbers.

CURE: Spray with a pesticide containing *resmethrin.* Make sure chrysanthemum is listed on the product label. Follow label directions carefully. Plants need several weekly sprayings to kill the mites as they hatch. To avoid introducing mites, inspect new plants carefully before bringing them into your home.

Cissus

Salt damage

SYMPTOM: Margins of older leaves die and turn brown and brittle. In severe cases, all leaves may have dead margins. Tissues adjacent to the dead margins of older leaves may turn yellow. New leaves may be distorted. *Salt damage* is a problem for many container-grown plants, and both grape ivy and kangaroo ivy are sensitive to excess salts. Soluble salts are picked up by the roots and accumulate in the leaf margins, where concentrations may become high enough to kill the tissues. Salts can accumulate from water or the use of fertilizers, or they may be present in the potting soil. Salts accumulate more rapidly and do more harm if the plant is not watered thoroughly.

CURE: Leach excess salts from the soil by flushing with water at least 3 times, letting the water drain completely each time. This is done most easily in a bathtub or laundry sink or outside in the shade. Always water grape ivy and kangaroo ivy from the top of the pot. If you use a saucer to catch the water, empty it after the pot has finished draining. If the plant is too large to lift, use a turkey baster to remove the drainage water. Do not overfertilize.

Codiaeum

New leaves are green

SYMPTOM: New leaves are green instead of brightly colored. Stems may be thin and bend toward a light source. The lower leaves may drop. *Insufficient light* is a problem for plants with brightly colored foliage. Plants use light as a source of energy; they grow slowly in light that is too dim for their needs. If most of the available light comes from one direction, the stems and leaves bend in that direction. Although foliage plants generally need less light than plants grown for their flowers or fruit, plants with colorful foliage need fairly bright light in order to produce the pigments that color their leaves.

CURE: Move the plant to a brighter location, such as a lightly curtained east, west, or south window. If the available light is not bright enough, provide supplemental lighting. Crotons may be grown outside in the summer. When moving them from indoors to outdoors, place the plants in light shade for at least 2 days before putting them in full sun.

Coleus

SYMPTOM: Old leaves drop off. Leaves fade and look bleached. Stems are long, with large spaces between the leaves. Young stems may be weak and unable to support themselves. Young stems tend to grow toward the light source. Brown patches may appear in the faded area. *Insufficient light* is a problem for brightly colored foliage plants. Plants use light as a source of energy; they grow slowly in light that is too dim for their needs. If most of the available light comes from one direction, the stems and leaves bend in that direction. If the light is much too dim, the plant has little energy and grows poorly. Plants with brightly colored foliage have a relatively high need for light.

CURE: Move the plant to a brighter location, such as a lightly curtained sunny window. If available light is not bright enough, provide supplemental lighting.

Insufficient light

Coleus

SYMPTOM: Tiny winged insects, about 1/12 inch long, feed on the undersides of the leaves. The insects are covered with white waxy powder. When the plant is touched, insects flutter rapidly around it. Leaves may be mottled and yellowing. *Greenhouse whitefly (Trialeurodes vaporariorum)* is a common pest of coleus. The 4-winged adult lays eggs on the undersides of leaves. The larvae are the size of a pinhead, flat, oval, mobile, and semitransparent, with radiating white waxy filaments. They feed for about a month before changing to the adult form. Both larvae and adults suck sap from the leaves, but the larvae do more damage because they feed more heavily. Whiteflies cannot digest all the sugar in the sap and excrete the excess in a sugary material called honeydew, which coats the leaves and may drop from the plant.

CURE: Spray with a pesticide containing *resmethrin*. Make sure coleus is listed on the product label. Follow label directions carefully. Spray weekly as long as the problem continues. Remove heavily infested leaves.

Greenhouse whiteflies (life size)

Coleus

SYMPTOM: Oval white insects up to ¼ inch long cluster in cottony masses on leaves, stems, and in the crotches where leaves are attached. A sticky substance may cover the leaves or drop onto surfaces below the plant. Leaves may be spotted or deformed. *Mealybugs* damage plants by sucking sap, causing leaf distortion and death. Several species of this common insect feed on coleus. The adult female mealybug may produce live young or lay eggs in a white fluffy mass. The immature mealybugs, called nymphs, crawl over the plant and onto nearby plants. Soon after they begin to feed, they produce white waxy filaments that cover their bodies, giving them a cottony appearance. As they mature, they become less mobile. Mealybugs excrete a fluid called honeydew, which coats the leaves and may drop from the plant onto surfaces below.

CURE: Spray with a pesticide containing *resmethrin*. Make sure coleus is listed on the product label. Follow label directions carefully. Where practical, wipe mealybugs off the plant with a damp cloth or with cotton swabs dipped in rubbing alcohol. Inspect the pot, including the bottom, for egg masses. Carefully inspect new plants before bringing them into the house.

Mealybugs (half life size)

Cyclamen

High-temperature damage

SYMPTOM: Outer leaves turn yellow. Leaves may die and turn brown. Stems become soft. Plants stop flowering. *High temperatures* cause problems for cyclamens. Although cyclamens are cool-weather plants, they will tolerate warm days as long as they have cool nights (below 55°F). Cool temperatures initiate flower buds. Constant high temperatures inhibit flower buds, and plants stop flowering. High temperatures also keep the plant from growing well, causing leaves to lose their green color and die.

CURE: Grow cyclamen plants in a cool room with as much light as possible. If a cool room is not available, put them near a window at night. If temperatures are not below freezing, put the plants outside at night. Under alternating temperatures, they will flower for long periods. Keep plants adequately watered and fertilized.

Cyclamen

Cyclamen mite damage

SYMPTOM: Leaves become curled, wrinkled, and cupped in scattered areas. New leaves may be more severely affected, remain very small, have a bronze discoloration, and be severely misshapen. Flower buds are distorted and may drop or fail to open. *Cyclamen mite* (*Steneotarsonemus pallidus*) is a very small mite related to spiders. These mites attack a number of houseplants and can be very damaging to cyclamens. Their feeding injures the plant tissues, causing the leaves and flower buds to be malformed and stunted. They infest the new growth most heavily, but will crawl to other parts of the plant or to other plants. Cyclamen mites reproduce rapidly.

CURE: Spray plants with a pesticide containing *dicofol* at 2-week intervals until new growth is no longer affected. Discard severely infested plants. Houseplants showing cyclamen mite damage should be isolated from other plants until the mites are under control. Nearby plants should be observed closely so that they can be sprayed if symptoms appear. Avoid touching leaves of infested plants and then touching leaves of other plants.

Cyclamen

Root rot

SYMPTOM: Older leaves turn yellow and may curl up at the margins. The leaf stems and flower stems may wilt. The plant may be stunted. All the leaves may wilt, die, and turn brown. The roots are brown, dead, and soft, with no white tips. All the roots may be rotted, and the bulb may be lifted easily from the soil. *Root rot* is caused by any of several soil-dwelling fungi also known as water molds. These fungi are favored by wet soil and poor drainage. Plants weakened by other factors are more susceptible to attack by the fungi, which invade the roots and kill them, causing the plant to wilt. The fungi may invade so much of the root system that the plant dies.

CURE: If the plant is only mildly affected, let the soil dry out between waterings. If the soil mix is heavy or the container does not drain well, transplant the plant into a container that drains freely. Use a fast-draining soil mix. Discard severely infected plants and soil. Wash the pots thoroughly, and soak them in a mixture of 1 part household bleach to 9 parts water for 30 minutes. Rinse with plain water and dry thoroughly before reuse. Alternatively, you can sterilize the pots.

Dieffenbachia

Bacterial stem blight

SYMPTOM: Soft sunken areas with water-soaked margins appear on the stems. Cracks sometimes appear in the affected areas. Lower leaves may turn yellow and become severely wilted. They tend to hang on the stem even when collapsed. If the condition is severe, the stem may rot through so that the top of the plant breaks off. Brown streaks occur inside infected stems. *Bacterial stem blight* is caused by the bacterium *Erwinia chrysanthemi.* Under wet conditions, the bacteria gain entrance through wounds on the stem. Propagation pieces from infected plants may be infected. Inside the stems, the bacteria cause a soft rot of the tissue, resulting in sunken areas or complete collapse of the stem. Inner stem tissue is discolored brown. Cuttings from infected stems may produce infected plants, or they simply may not root.

CURE: There is no cure for this disease. Discard severely infected plants. If some stems are still healthy, cut them off above the diseased area and reroot them. Do not use any stems than have brown streaks.

Dieffenbachia

Sunburn

SYMPTOM: Areas between the veins near the margins of older leaves turn yellow, and then tan or light brown. Very light green or white tissues of variegated varieties turn brown between the veins. *Sunburn* occurs when a plant is exposed to more intense sunlight than it can tolerate. Dieffenbachia is adaptable to varying amounts of light, from bright to relatively dim. Leaf tissue that is deficient in green pigment (chlorophyll) is very susceptible to sunburn, so if variegated dieffenbachias are grown in very bright light, they may sunburn. Leaves on plants that dry out are also susceptible to sunburn. Older leaves are the first to be affected by sunburn when a plant dries out.

CURE: Grow variegated dieffenbachias that have white areas in filtered light. Avoid letting plants dry out. Avoid moving plants directly from very dim light to very bright light.

Dieffenbachia

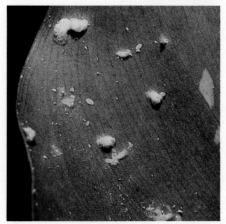

Mealybugs (half life size)

SYMPTOM: Leaves may be spotted or deformed. When the condition is severe, leaves and plants may wither and die. *Mealybugs* damage plants by sucking sap. Several species of this common insect feed on dieffenbachia. The adult female may produce live young or lay eggs in a white fluffy mass of wax. The immature mealybugs, called nymphs, crawl all over the plant and onto nearby plants. Soon after they begin to feed, they produce white waxy filaments that cover their bodies, giving them the characteristic cottony appearance. As they mature, they become less mobile. Mealybugs cannot digest all the sugar in the sap and excrete the excess in a fluid called honeydew, which coats the leaves and may drop onto surfaces below the plant.

CURE: Spray with a pesticide containing *resmethrin.* Make sure dieffenbachia is listed on the product label. Follow label directions carefully. Where practical, wipe mealybugs off the plant with a damp cloth or with cotton swabs dipped in alcohol. Inspect the pot, including the bottom, for mealybug egg masses. Wipe them off. Carefully inspect new plants before bringing them into the house.

Dizygotheca

Mealybugs (one-third life size)

SYMPTOM: Oval white insects up to ¼ inch long cluster in cottony masses on leaves, stems, and in the crotches where branches or leaves are attached. A sticky material may coat the leaves. *Mealybugs* damage plants by sucking sap. Several species of this common insect feed on false aralia. The adult female may produce live young or lay eggs in a white fluffy mass of wax. The immature mealybugs, called nymphs, crawl all over the plant and onto nearby plants. Soon after they begin to feed, they produce white waxy filaments that cover their bodies, giving them the characteristic cottony appearance. As they mature, they become less mobile. Mealybugs cannot digest all the sugar in the sap and excrete the excess in a fluid called honeydew, which coats the leaves and may drop onto surfaces below the plant.

CURE: Spray with a pesticide containing *resmethrin.* Make sure false aralia is listed on the product label. Follow label directions carefully. Where practical, wipe mealybugs off the plant with a damp cloth or with cotton swabs dipped in alcohol. Inspect the pot, including the bottom, for mealybug egg masses. Wipe them off. Carefully inspect new plants before bringing them into the house.

Dracaena

Fusarium leaf spot

SYMPTOM: Circular reddish brown spots appear on the leaves. The spots are surrounded by a yellow margin. Several spots may join to form blotches. Badly spotted leaves may turn yellow and die. *Fusarium leaf spot* is caused by a fungus (*Fusarium moniliforme*). Fungal spores are spread from plant to plant by splashing water. The spores germinate on a wet leaf surface within a matter of hours, causing a new spot. In most cases spotting is unsightly but not harmful; but if spotting is severe, the leaf may weaken and die.

CURE: Clip off badly spotted leaves. Keep the foliage dry to prevent the spread of the fungus. If spotting continues, spray the plant with a fungicide containing *chlorothalonil.*

Euphorbia

Sporadic flowering

SYMPTOM: Plants continue to produce new leaves but fail to produce flower heads. Poinsettias set flower buds in the fall, when the days are less than 12 hours long. Plants need to be kept in total darkness for at least 13 hours a day for 7 weeks to produce flower buds. If they do not have an adequate amount of darkness, the plants will continue to grow and produce new leaves but no flower heads.

CURE: Place poinsettias in a dark closet for at least 13 hours every night. To get flowers by Christmas, begin this process by September 15, and no later than October 1. Be sure the plants are not exposed to any light while they are in the closet. During the day, place plants where they will receive direct sunlight. In the summer, you can grow poinsettias outside. To prevent sunburn, place them in partial shade for at least 2 days before moving them into direct sun outdoors. If poinsettia stems are weak and long, prune them back in July or August.

Ferns

Root rot

SYMPTOM: Plants fail to grow and are stunted. Roots are soft and decayed. The outer portion of the roots slips off easily from the central portion. The top of the plant may fall over or be lifted easily out of the soil. Infected plants may die. *Root rot* is caused by soil-dwelling fungi (*Pythium* species), also known as water molds, that attack the roots of many plants. The fungi may invade only the smaller rootlets, stunting the plant; or they may invade the main root system and cause severe rotting. Fern roots are dark, so inspecting them may be difficult. Infected roots are unable to pick up enough moisture and nutrients to support the plant. Fern leaves are so stiff that they wilt only slightly. Plants in soil that is too dry or too wet are more susceptible.

CURE: If the plant is only mildly affected, let the soil dry out between waterings. If the soil mix is heavy or the container does not drain well, transplant the fern into a container that drains freely. Use a fast-draining soil mix. Discard severely infected plants and soil. Wash the pots thoroughly, and soak them in a mixture of 1 part household bleach to 9 parts water for 30 minutes. Rinse with plain water and dry well before reuse. Alternatively, sterilize the pots.

Ferns

SYMPTOM: Leaves turn yellow and eventually die. Fronds may die from the tips down. The center parts of the plant are more severely affected than are the outer portions. *Low humidity* can cause problems for ferns. Most ferns need higher humidity than homes usually provide. The ferns used as houseplants are adapted to forest floors and creeksides, where the air is usually moist. Air is particularly dry near heater vents or radiators. The problem is more severe if the soil is allowed to dry out.

CURE: Move the fern to a more humid location, such as a well-lit bathroom. Misting does not help relieve stress on the fern. The mist only dampens the fronds for a few minutes at a time. Placing the plant on a humidifying tray raises the humidity around the plant only if the damp air is not allowed to escape. If there is free movement of air around the plant, the practice is of little value. A portable humidifier will raise the humidity in the immediate vicinity while it is operating. Plant ferns in a fast-draining potting mix that contains a high proportion of organic material, such as peat moss or ground bark. Never allow the potting mix to dry out.

Dieback caused by low humidity

Ferns

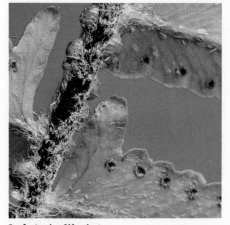

SYMPTOM: Stems and fronds are covered with white, cottony, cushionlike masses or brown crusty bumps that can be scraped off easily. Fronds turn yellow and may drop. A shiny or sticky material may cover fronds and stems. The bumps are sometimes mistaken for reproductive spores produced by the fern. The round, flat spores are found only on the undersides of fronds, spaced at regular intervals, and are difficult to pick or scrape off. *Scale insects* of several different types attack ferns. The young, called crawlers, are small (about $\frac{1}{10}$ inch), soft-bodied, and move about on the plant and onto other plants. After a short time, they attach themselves to the plant so they can feed on the sap. Their legs usually disappear, and the scales remain in the same place for the rest of their lives. Some develop a soft covering, and others develop a hard covering. Some species of scales excrete honeydew, which may cover the fronds or drip onto surfaces below.

CURE: Spray with a pesticide containing *resmethrin.* Make sure your fern is listed on the product label. Follow label directions carefully. Spraying is more effective against the crawlers than against adults. It may be necessary to repeat applications until there is no longer any evidence of the scales.

Scale (twice life size)

Ficus

Leaf yellowing on rubber plant

SYMPTOM: Older leaves begin to yellow at the margins. This condition progresses inward until the whole leaf is yellow. Yellow leaves usually drop from the plant. Sometimes only a few leaves are left on a plant. New leaves are small and may be light green. *Insufficient light* causes a variety of problems for houseplants. Plants use light as a source of energy; they grow slowly in light that is too dim for their needs. If the light is much too dim, the plant has little energy and grows poorly. Although foliage plants generally need less light than plants grown for their flowers or fruit, ficus has a relatively high need for light.

CURE: Move the plant to a brighter location. Ficus will tolerate direct sun if kept well watered but will sunburn if allowed to dry out while in direct sunlight. If available light is not bright enough, provide supplemental lighting.

Hedera

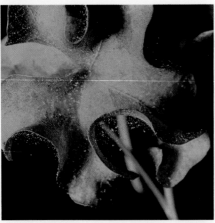

Spider mites (twice life size) and webs

SYMPTOM: Leaves are stippled, yellow, and dirty; they may dry out and drop. There may be webbing between leaves or on the lower surfaces of the leaves. To determine whether a plant is infested with mites, hold a sheet of white paper beneath an affected plant and tap the leaves sharply. Minute green, red, or yellow specks the size of pepper grains will drop to the paper and begin to crawl around. The pests are easily seen against the white background. *Spider mites,* related to spiders, are major pests of many houseplants, including ivy. They cause damage by sucking sap from the undersides of the leaves. As a result of this feeding, the green pigment (chlorophyll) disappears, causing the stippled appearance. Under warm, dry conditions, they can increase to enormous numbers.

CURE: Spray with a pesticide containing *resmethrin.* Make sure ivy is listed on the product label. Follow label directions carefully. Plants need several weekly sprayings to kill the mites as they hatch. To avoid introducing mites, inspect new plants carefully before bringing them into your house.

Hedera

Brown soft scale (twice life size)

SYMPTOM: Stems and leaves are covered with white, cottony, cushionlike masses or brown crusty bumps or clusters of somewhat flattened, reddish, gray, or brown scaly bumps. Leaves turn yellow and may drop. A shiny or sticky material may cover leaves and stems. *Scale insects* of several different types attack ivy. Scales hatch from eggs. The young, called crawlers, are small (about 1/10 inch), soft-bodied, and move about on the plant and onto other plants. After a short time, they insert their mouthparts into the plant so they can feed on the sap. Their legs usually disappear, and the scales remain in the same place for the rest of their lives. Some develop a soft covering, and others develop a hard covering. Some species of scales are unable to digest all the sugar in the plant sap and excrete the excess in a fluid called honeydew, which may cover the leaves or drip onto surfaces below.

CURE: Spray infested plants with a pesticide containing *resmethrin.* Make sure ivy is listed on the product label. Follow label directions carefully. Spraying is more effective against the crawlers than against the adults. Repeated applications may be necessary.

Hedera

SYMPTOM: Pale green to yellow blotches appear between the leaf veins. These blotches may become bleached white or tan as the tissue between the veins dies. Whole sections between veins may be affected. Spots may merge, affecting larger areas. *Sunburn* occurs when a plant is exposed to more intense sunlight than it can tolerate. Excessive sunlight causes the green pigment (chlorophyll) to disappear in ivy leaves. This happens most easily if the plant is allowed to dry out. Once the tissues have lost their chlorophyll, the sunlight kills the tissues between the veins. The underlying color of different ivy species determines the color of the dead tissues. Plants moved from indoors to direct sunlight outdoors will sunburn very severely.

CURE: Keep ivy plants well watered so they do not dry out, particularly if they are in direct sunlight. If you are moving plants from inside to outside, place them in the shade for several days before putting them in direct sunlight.

Sunburn

Maranta

SYMPTOM: Margins of older leaves die and turn brown and brittle. In severe cases, all leaves may have dead margins. Tissues adjacent to the dead margins of older leaves may turn yellow. *Salt damage* can be a problem for container-grown plants, and prayer plant is very sensitive to excess salts. Soluble salts are picked up by the roots and accumulate in the leaf margins, where concentrations may become high enough to kill the tissues. Salts can accumulate from water or the use of fertilizers; or they may be present in the potting soil. Salts accumulate faster and do more harm if the plant is not watered thoroughly.

CURE: Leach excess salts from the soil by flushing with water at least 3 times, letting the water drain completely each time. This is most easily done if the pot is placed in a bathtub or laundry sink or outside in the shade. Always water prayer plant from the top of the pot. If you use a saucer to catch the water, empty it after the pot has finished draining. If the plant is too large to lift, empty the saucer with a turkey baster. Never let a plant stand in the drainage water.

Salt damage

Monstera

SYMPTOM: New leaves do not grow as large as older leaves. New leaves are darker green, and have fewer or no splits in them. The stem is elongated, with more space between the new leaves. The leaves turn toward the light. Older leaves may turn yellow. *Insufficient light* keeps split-leaf philodendrons from forming the large split leaves for which they are known. Without enough light, the new leaves will be smaller and darker green with no splits, so that the plant can use all the available light to manufacture food.

CURE: Give split-leaf philodendrons enough light so that normal splitting of the leaves occurs. If leaves do not split, move the plant to a brighter area. Although they will tolerate somewhat lower levels of light, split-leaf philodendrons grow best in a curtained south, east, or west window.

Failure to split

Orchids

Failure to bloom

SYMPTOM: Plants do not bloom. The leaves are a deep green. *Insufficient light* causes problems for orchids. Plants use light as a source of energy; they will not bloom unless they have enough light. Although orchids are adapted to blooming in shaded locations, they still need relatively bright light.

CURE: Move the plants to a brighter location, but do not put them in direct sun. If the light is too bright, the leaves will turn yellow and burn. A lightly curtained window that receives more than 4 hours of sun a day is an ideal location for orchids. If necessary, provide supplemental lighting.

Palms

Scale (life size)

SYMPTOM: Stems and fronds are covered with white, cottony, cushionlike masses or brown crusty bumps. The bumps can be scraped or picked off easily. Fronds turn yellow and may drop. A shiny or sticky material may cover fronds and stems. *Scale insects* of several different types attack palms. Scales hatch from eggs. The young, called crawlers, are small (about 1/10 inch), soft-bodied, and move about on the plant and onto other plants. After a short time, they insert their mouthparts into the plant so they can feed on the sap. Their legs usually disappear, and the scales remain in the same place for the rest of their lives. Some develop a soft covering, and others develop a hard covering. Some species of scales are unable to digest all the sugar in the plant sap and excrete the excess in a fluid called honeydew, which may cover the fronds or drip onto surfaces below.

CURE: Spray with a pesticide containing *resmethrin*. Make sure palms are listed on the product label. Follow label directions carefully. Spraying is more effective against the crawlers than against the adults. It may be necessary to repeat applications until you no longer see evidence of the scales.

Palms

Spider mites (half life size), webs, and damage

SYMPTOM: Fronds or leaflets are stippled, yellow, and dirty; they may dry out and drop. There may be webbing between leaflets or on the lower surfaces of the leaflets. To determine whether a palm is infested with mites, hold a sheet of white paper beneath the plant and tap the fronds sharply. Minute green, red, or yellow specks the size of pepper grains will drop to the paper and begin to crawl around. The pests are easily seen against the white background. *Spider mites,* related to spiders, are major pests of many houseplants, including palms. They cause damage by sucking sap from the undersides of the leaflets. As a result of this feeding, the green pigment (chlorophyll) disappears, causing the stippled appearance. Under warm, dry conditions mites can multiply rapidly.

CURE: Spray with a pesticide containing *resmethrin*. Make sure palms are listed on the product label. Follow label directions carefully. Plants may need several weekly sprayings to kill the mites as they hatch. To avoid introducing mites, inspect new plants carefully before bringing them into your home.

Palms

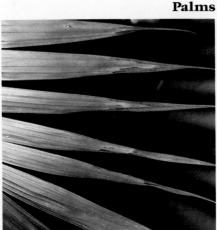

Salt damage

SYMPTOM: Margins of the older leaves die and turn brown, beginning at the base of the fronds and progressing outward. In severe cases, all fronds may have dead margins. Tissues adjacent to the dead margins of older fronds may turn yellow. *Salt damage* is a common problem for container-grown plants, and palms are sensitive to excess salts. Soluble salts are picked up by the roots and accumulate in the leaf margins, where concentrations may become high enough to kill the tissues. Salts can accumulate from water or the use of fertilizers, or they may be present in the potting soil. Salts accumulate more rapidly and do more harm if the plant is not watered thoroughly.

CURE: Leach excess salts from the soil by flushing with water at least 3 times, letting the water drain completely each time. This is done most easily if the pot is placed in a bathtub or laundry sink or outside in the shade. Always water palms from the top of the pot. If you use a saucer to catch the water, empty it after the pot has finished draining. If the plant is too large to lift, empty the saucer with a turkey baster. Do not overfertilize. If practical, trim the damaged leaf tips to a point with scissors.

Pelargonium

SYMPTOM: Lower leaves turn yellow and may drop. New leaves are pale green. Plants fail to produce flower buds. Stems become elongated and lean toward the light. *Insufficient light* causes a variety of problems for pelargoniums. Plants use light as a source of energy; they grow slowly in light that is too dim for their needs. If most of the available light comes from one direction, the stems and leaves bend in that direction. If the light is much too dim, the plant has little energy and grows poorly. Plants grown for their flowers, such as geranium and pelargonium, have a relatively high need for light.

CURE: Move the plant to a brighter location. Geranium and pelargonium need direct sun. But if they are allowed to become dry while in direct sunlight, they will sunburn. If the available light is not bright enough, provide supplemental lighting. Geranium and pelargonium can be grown outside in full sun. When moving them from inside to outside, put them in a semishady area for several days before moving them to direct sunlight. This will prevent sunburn.

Spindly growth

Plectranthus

Nitrogen deficiency

SYMPTOM: The oldest leaves, usually the ones nearest the bottom of the plant, turn yellow and may drop. Yellowing starts at the leaf margins and progresses inward without producing a distinct pattern. The yellowing may progress upward until only the newest leaves remain green. Growth is slow, new leaves are small, and the whole plant may be stunted. *Nitrogen deficiency* affects plants in many ways. Nitrogen is a nutrient that is used by plants in large amounts, especially for foliage and chlorophyll production. When there is not enough nitrogen for the entire plant, it is taken from the older leaves for use in new growth. Nitrogen is easily leached from the soil during regular watering. Of all the plant nutrients, it is the one most likely to be lacking in the soil.

CURE: Apply a water-soluble fertilizer that contains more nitrogen than phosphorus or potassium (10-8-7, for example), or use fish emulsion. Add the fertilizer at regular intervals, as recommended on the label.

Saintpaulia

Failure to flower

SYMPTOM: Although the plant seems healthy, it does not bloom. *Insufficient light* can prevent blooming. Violets, like other flowering plants, won't bloom unless they are properly fed and watered. But if the plant is a good green color and is growing well but not blooming, it is probably not receiving enough light. Plants use light as a source of energy; they will not bloom unless they can afford the energy to do so. African violets will bloom at lower levels of light than most other plants, but they do require a fairly bright location to bloom well.

CURE: Move the plant to a brighter location. The ideal light level for African violets is as bright as possible without being direct sun. If the light is coming through a window that is exposed to the sun, the window should be curtained so that the sunlight is not quite bright enough to make shadows. If the light is too bright, the leaves will lose their bright green color and become pale, with an orange or yellow cast. If the light is both bright and hot, the leaves will burn. If you don't have a location that is bright enough, give the plants supplemental light. Place fluorescent fixtures as close as possible to the top of the plants.

Saintpaulia

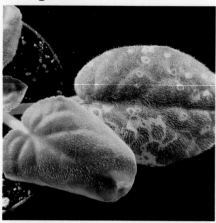

Water spots

SYMPTOM: White to light yellow blotches in various patterns, including circles, occur on the older leaves. Small islands of green may be separated by the discolored areas. Brown spots sometimes appear in the colored areas. *Water spots* are a common problem for African violets. Members of this plant family are very sensitive to rapid temperature changes. Water spots occur most commonly when cold water is splashed on the leaves while the plant is being watered. If this happens in light, the chlorophyll (green pigment) is destroyed. In African violets, all the chlorophyll in the leaves is found in a single layer of cells near the upper surface. If the chlorophyll in that layer is broken down, the green color disappears and the color of the underlying leaf tissue is exposed.

CURE: Avoid getting cold water on African violet leaves when watering. Or use tepid water, which will not cause spotting if it touches the leaves. Spotted leaves will not recover. Pick them off if they are unsightly.

Saintpaulia

Mealybugs (twice life size)

SYMPTOM: Oval white insects up to ¼ inch long cluster in cottony masses on the stems and leaves. They tend to congregate in the crotches where the leaves or branches are attached. Leaves may be spotted, deformed, and withered. Infested leaves may be shiny and sticky. Severely infested plants may die. *Mealybugs* damage plants by sucking sap. Several species of this common insect feed on African violets. The adult female may produce live young or lay eggs in a white, fluffy mass. The immature mealybugs, called nymphs, crawl over the plant and onto nearby plants. Soon after they begin to feed, they produce white waxy filaments that cover their bodies, giving them a cottony appearance. As they mature, they become less mobile. Mealybugs excrete a fluid called honeydew, which coats the leaves and may drop onto surfaces below the plant.

CURE: Spray with a pesticide containing *resmethrin.* Make sure African violets are listed on the product label. Follow label directions carefully. Where practical, wipe mealybugs off the plant with a damp cloth or with cotton swabs dipped in alcohol. Inspect the pot, including the bottom, for mealybug egg masses. Wipe them off. Carefully inspect new plants before bringing them into the house.

Tolmiea

Spider mite damage

SYMPTOM: Leaves are stippled, yellow, and dirty; they may dry out and drop. There may be webbing between the leaves or on the lower surfaces of the leaves. To determine whether a plant is infested with mites, hold a sheet of white paper beneath it and tap the leaves sharply. Minute green, red, or yellow specks the size of pepper grains will drop to the paper and begin to crawl around. The pests are easily seen against the white background. *Spider mites*, related to spiders, are major pests of many houseplants, including piggyback plants. They cause damage by sucking sap from the undersides of the leaves. As a result of this feeding, the green pigment (chlorophyll) disappears, causing the stippled appearance. Under warm, dry conditions, which favor mites, they can increase to enormous numbers.

CURE: Spray with a pesticide containing *resmethrin.* Make sure piggyback plant is listed on the product label. Follow label directions carefully. Plants may need several weekly sprayings to kill the mites as they hatch. To avoid introducing mites, inspect new plants carefully before bringing them into your home.

Tolmiea

Salt damage

SYMPTOM: Margins of older leaves die and turn brown and brittle. In severe cases, all leaves may have dead margins. Tissues adjacent to the dead margins of older leaves may turn yellow. *Salt damage* is a common problem for container-grown plants, and piggyback is sensitive to excess salts. Soluble salts are picked up by the roots and accumulate in the leaf margins, where concentrations may become high enough to kill the tissues. Salts can accumulate from water or the use of fertilizers, or they may be present in the potting soil. Salts accumulate more rapidly and do more harm if the plant is not watered thoroughly.

CURE: Leach excess salts from the soil by flushing with water at least 3 times, letting the water drain completely each time. This is most easily done in a bathtub or laundry sink or outside in the shade. Always water piggyback from the top of the pot. If you use a saucer to catch the water, empty it after the plant has finished draining. If the plant is too large to lift, empty the saucer with a turkey baster. Never let the plant stand in drainage water. Do not overfertilize.

Tradescantia

Dieback

SYMPTOM: Tips of older leaves turn yellow, then die and turn brown. This condition occurs more frequently on long stems than on short stems. The longer the stem, the more tip burn is found. *Dieback* looks like salt damage, but it often occurs on plants that have been leached regularly. Its cause is unknown. As the stems of wandering Jew grow long, the plant does not support the old leaves and they turn yellow and die, starting at the tips.

CURE: Remove dead leaves as they appear. Keep pinching the tips of the stems so they do not become too long. This will force new buds to grow farther back on the stems. New leaves will not show this problem. Plants may occasionally need to be cut back severely so that only several inches are left on each stem. After cutting back, reduce water and fertilizer until the plant is actively growing again.

INDEX

NOTE: Page numbers in **bold** refer to the Gallery of Houseplants. Page numbers in *italic* refer to illustrations.